CHARLES WARREN

ROYAL ENGINEER IN THE AGE OF EMPIRE

CHARLES WARREN

ROYAL ENGINEER IN THE AGE OF EMPIRE

KEVIN SHILLINGTON

PROTEA BOOK HOUSE
Pretoria
2021

Charles Warren: Royal Engineer in the Age of Empire
Kevin Shillington

First edition published in 2020 by Brown Dog Books and
The Self-Publishing Partnership

Second edition published in 2021 by Protea Book House
PO Box 35110, Menlo Park, 0102
1067 Burnett Street, Hatfield, Pretoria
8 Minni Street, Clydesdale, Pretoria
info@proteaboekhuis.co.za
www.proteaboekhuis.com

COVER DESIGN: Hanli Deysel
INTERNAL DESIGN: Tim Jollands
FRONT COVER IMAGE: C.N. Robinson, *Celebrities of the Army*
(Vandyk ABO Trust), Private Collection,
Nicol Stassen (image of Charles Warren) and
Bonfils, "Route de la Station à Jerusalem",
Private Collection, Nicol Stassen (image of Jerusalem).
PRINTED BY TANDYM PRINT, CAPE TOWN

ISBN: 978-1-4853-1281-9

© Original text: Kevin Shillington 2020 and 2021
© Published edition: Protea Book House 2021

Contents

List of Maps

Preface

At the time of writing, 'empire', and statues of imperialists, have been very much in the news. The issue has been given focus in Britain by the country's widespread failure to recognise the reality of empire, upon which so much of the country's wealth and claim to 'world power' status was built. That reality was at the expense of colonised peoples, and that is where the concept of 'benevolent empire' falls down.

My choice of biographical subject is therefore very apt, for the background to the life of Charles Warren is the British empire during the period of its maximum expansion through the second half of the 19th century. At times, as a Royal Engineer, Charles Warren was a key player in that expansion. The art of surveying and map-making was a central ingredient in the expanding empire of the Victorian era. This placed Royal Engineers, the élite corps of the Victorian Army by virtue of their training, in a powerful and prestigious position in terms of career opportunities, not solely in military affairs. And Charles Warren, a gifted mathematician with a scientific mind, was a Royal Engineer *par excellence*.

He was born into empire and accepted it as a fact of life. Through his childhood, his father fought as an infantry officer in India and the First Opium War against China. And through his adult career, Charles Warren tried to find a moral imperative within the imperial project. From today's perspective, that may appear a contradiction in terms. But the reality of empire, however one judges it, is never as clear and simple as may appear at first glance, and the ambiguities of empire are well revealed through the life of Charles Warren.

He had a strong sense of duty, instilled in him from an early age by his father, and he accepted whatever task was presented to him. This ranged from pioneering archaeology under the Old City of Jerusalem, to hunting for lost British spies in the desert of the Exodus, even Metropolitan Police Commissioner at the time of the 'Jack the Ripper' murders. But it was in Southern Africa where he most directly faced the contradictions inherent in an expansive British empire. And it was here, over the basic concepts of empire – benevolent or rapacious – that Warren, a man with a strong religious moral code, first clashed with Cecil Rhodes. Through their clash of moral perceptions, Warren won some victories, but so too, ultimately more powerfully, did Cecil Rhodes.

* * *

There has to date been only one full biography of Charles Warren, written by his grandson Watkin Williams. Published in 1941, fourteen years after Warren's death, it was based largely upon his private papers.[1] It is a rare book now, seldom read, and those papers upon which it was based were subsequently destroyed. There has, however, been some compensation for the present biographer in that Williams quoted extensively from those papers and Warren himself compiled two books on his work in Jerusalem and in South Africa, both of which drew heavily upon his contemporaneous letters and journals.[2] The researcher, of course, must treat these sources with a certain level of caution; for they are themselves a *selection* from the originals and one is left with the intriguing thought of what might have been left out.

To make up for that lack of unpublished private papers, I have researched extensively in libraries and archives and visited all the major places of his long and active life, from Ireland of his early childhood, Sandhurst and the Royal Military Academy of his training, the home of the Royal Engineers in Chatham and his various postings around the world, from Gibraltar where he started his career, to Jerusalem where his name first came to wide public attention, to Southern Africa where on several occasions he played an important role in the nature of the imperial presence there. I have visited Singapore; indeed, the only place that featured prominently in his career that I have not visited is the Sinai desert. At the time of my research it was considered too dangerous on account of current conflict, although no more dangerous, one must admit, than when Warren was there in 1882.

Historians have tended to cast Warren either as 'the Metropolitan Police Commissioner who failed to catch Jack the Ripper' or 'the General who lost the Battle of Spion Kop', one of the greatest British military disasters of the Anglo-Boer War. He has thus been a much neglected figure. As I have found in researching and writing this biography, it is an important and fascinating story, with many contemporary resonances.

It has been a long haul bringing the book to fruition, and over the years

[1] Williams, Watkin W., *The Life of General Sir Charles Warren* (Blackwell, Oxford, 1941).
[2] Charles Warren, *Underground Jerusalem* (Bentley and Son, London, 1876); and Sir Charles Warren, *On the Veldt in the Seventies* (Isbister, London, 1902).

Warren has often had to be placed on the back burner as other, commissioned work has taken over. But it has been a project that I have always been pleased to return to. One of its greatest rewards has been tracking down some of his descendants, swapping stories of family traditions and memories and comparing them with my own discoveries. It is to his descendants and to all those who have helped me over the years that I dedicate this book.

Kevin Shillington
Dorset, England
June 2020

KEVIN SHILLINGTON, an independent historian and biographer, is a graduate of Trinity College Dublin who holds a PhD from SOAS, University of London. His recent books include *History of Africa* (4th edition 2019) and *Patrick van Rensburg: Rebel, Visionary and Radical Educationist* (2020).

CHAPTER 1

Background and Early Life

In March 1838 Major Charles Warren (Senior) and his young family boarded ship at Madras. It was the first stage of the long journey home to England for three years' well-earned leave. Steam-powered ships were in their infancy, and the Warrens would have travelled under sail, probably calling at numerous ports along the way before heading up the Red Sea for the Gulf of Suez. The weeks of inactivity aboard ship would have provided the 40-year-old major with an unaccustomed amount of time to spend with his wife and young children, as well as to reflect on the past eight years in the service of the East India Company.

He had first arrived in India in October 1830 as a Captain of the 55th Regiment of Foot. He came with his wife of six months, Mary Anne Hughes, who early the following year gave birth to a son. They named their first-born John. It was a name common to every generation of Warrens. Charles had a brother John, Rector of a parish in Cambridgeshire, and their father was Very Revd John Warren, Dean of Bangor Cathedral in North Wales. Over the next six years in India Mary Warren gave birth to three daughters, Margaret, Mary and Charlotte.[3]

A year after their arrival in Madras, the Warren family had moved with the regiment to Bellary in the Karnataka district of south-western India; and over the following years Captain Warren and the 55th distinguished themselves in, among other things, action against the Rajah of Coorg in the southern region of Karnataka.[4] During this action Captain Warren was severely wounded in the leg while leading a charge through thick jungle. A fellow officer recalled seeing the captain give up his litter to two private soldiers whom he considered more severely wounded than himself. The wounded Warren was lucky to make it back to the rearguard, faint from loss of blood.[5] He was later to regale his younger sons with stories of heroic deeds in this and other wars, though

---

[3] Williams, *The Life*, p 2.
[4] Noakes, George, *A Historical Account of the Services of the 34th and 55th Regiments* (Thurnam & Sons, Carlisle, 1875), pp 74–77.
[5] Williams, *The Life*, p 3.

with characteristic modesty about his own courage. In 1834 Captain Warren purchased a promotion to the rank of Major[6] and two years later the regiment was moved to Secunderabad. It was from here that the Warrens departed for home leave in 1838.[7]

It was a long and difficult journey through the summer heat of the Red Sea and overland from Suez to the Mediterranean. They finally reached their destination, the home of the major's elder brother, Revd John Warren, Rector of Graveley in south Cambridgeshire, three and a half months after leaving India. Three-year-old Mary had fallen ill during the journey and a few weeks after their arrival in Graveley, she died. With her Uncle John officiating at the funeral, she was laid to rest close to the chancery wall of Graveley's medieval church of St Botolph. Shortly after this sad event, the Warren brothers heard the news of the death of their father, Dean Warren of Bangor.[8] With no rapid transport of the sort taken for granted today, the two brothers were unable to attend their father's funeral.

Major Warren, who had been born and brought up in the Deanery of Bangor Cathedral, felt drawn back to the city of his childhood, and before the year was out he had moved his family to Bangor where they leased a house called 'Fairview'. The house itself has not survived, but 'Fairview Road', half a mile north-east of the Cathedral, indicates where it would have stood, and assuming no houses between it and the sea, Fairview House would have had an excellent view of the northern approach to the Menai Strait and the Great Orme's Head Lighthouse in the distance. Having lost both a daughter and a father so soon after returning from India, it would have been a peaceful place for Major Warren and his young family to rest and grieve.

And it was here, eighteen months later, on 7 February 1840, that Charles, the subject of this biography, was born. Named after his father, he was baptised, like his father, in Bangor Cathedral. As the grandson of the late Dean of the Cathedral, the service might well have been conducted by the Rt. Rev. Christopher Bethell, Bishop of Bangor (1830–59). The Bethell family was connected to the Warren's by marriage. Indeed, some 24 years later, the young Charles, known in the family as Charlie, was to strengthen that connection through his own marriage.

In June 1841, when he was just sixteen months old and his mother was pregnant again, by four months, Major Warren was recalled to the regiment.

---

[6] *Hart's Annual Army List*, 1866, p 379.
[7] Noakes, *Historical Account*, p 77.
[8] Williams, *The Life*, p 3.

This time he did not take his family with him, but sailed for Madras leaving his wife and four children at Fairview. That November Mary gave birth to a third son, William, known as 'Billie'. It is thought that Billie was not as robust, mentally or physically, as Charlie, who was the elder by 21 months, and from the very beginning Charlie took a protective interest in his younger brother's well-being, particularly as from this time their mother's health began to suffer.[9]

Meanwhile, their father had sailed into a war zone. The 'First Opium War' had broken out between Britain and China the previous year. For many years the East India Company had been financing its extensive tea imports from China by flooding the Chinese market with opium, the product of poppies grown in India. In 1839 the Chinese government, concerned at the mounting level of opium addiction in China, confiscated 20,000 chests of opium from British warehouses in Guangzhou (Canton). In a foretaste of 21st-century 'trade wars', the British Foreign Secretary, Lord Palmerston, famous for his 'gunboat diplomacy', sent a large army, aboard fifteen troopships, accompanied by four steam-powered gunboats, to enforce British trading interests. During 1841 the fleet gathered at Hong Kong, a small island off the estuary leading to Guangzhou, and by the end of the year Major Warren had joined them there in charge of a strong draft of new recruits of the 55th.[10]

Having subdued Guangzhou and raided and garrisoned several coastal trading cities northwards from Hong Kong, the British task force proceeded up the Yangtze Kiang towards the imperial city of Nanjing (Nanking). On 20 July 1842 they dropped anchor, 60 kilometres short of their destination, opposite the walled city of Zhenjiang (Tching-Kiang-Foo), famous for its defence against seaborne pirates. The city was defended by 2600 'Manchu Tartars', the élite corps of the Manchu dynasty, as well as 3400 regular Chinese troops.[11]

Colonel Schoedde of the 55th was assigned the local rank of Major-General in charge of the 2nd Brigade. This left the field command of the 55th in the hands of Major Warren, promoted to Brevet Lt.-Colonel.[12] Once again, he was noted for his conspicuous bravery in leading his men up the scaling ladders and into hand-to-hand bayonet fighting with the Tartars.[13] In due

[9] *Ibid.*, p 4.
[10] Noakes, *Historical Account*, pp 77–84.
[11] *Ibid.*, p 87.
[12] *Hart's Army List*, 1866, p 379.
[13] Noakes, *Historical Account*, p 89.

course Lt.-Colonel Warren was to relate to his two younger sons a sanitised version of this battle as if it were little more than an exciting adventure.

Unnerved by the vigour of the British assault on its cities, the Chinese emperor sued for peace. By the Treaty of Nanjing of August 1842 the Chinese agreed to pay a large indemnity, effectively paying for the war against them. In addition, they were obliged to cede Hong Kong to the British Government and grant British merchants free trading rights in five Chinese coastal cities.

The 55th had suffered heavy losses in the war and they regrouped at Hong Kong, a much reduced force. They were stationed there for a further two years under the charge of Lt.-Colonel Warren, his promotion by then confirmed. Ordered to return to England in 1844, the regiment reached Portsmouth in September of that year and was stationed initially at Chichester, near the south coast.[14]

* * *

Colonel Warren gave up the lease on Fairview and brought his family to join him in Chichester. His children had grown considerably during his three-year absence. The eldest, John, was thirteen, of an age to go to boarding school, while Margaret and Charlotte were eleven and seven, respectively. Charlie was four and a half and Billie, whom his father now saw for the first time, was nearly three.

Charlie was a strong, fearless and adventurous child: something possibly inherited from his father, and even as a small child he liked nothing better than a physical test of his own courage. The incident of the swan probably dates from this period. It was one of those stories of childhood antics that are handed down in many families: laughed at in retrospect, but high drama at the time. The family story as related by his grandson is that the children were visiting a neighbour whose garden bordered a stream when the adults were startled by a commotion on the lawn. On looking out, they were horrified to see four-year-old Charlie firmly grasping an adult swan by the neck 'and running with all his might just ahead of the struggling, angry bird'.[15] It is not recorded how he was rescued from this predicament, but Charlie, unperturbed, explained triumphantly: he had been advised that the best way to avoid the powerful wingstrokes of an attacking swan was to grasp the bird firmly by the neck. He had put it to the test and proudly declared the advice to be correct!

---

[14] *Ibid.*, p 93.
[15] Williams, *The Life*, p 4.

The following April, 1845, the regiment was transferred to Winchester where the Warrens took a house two doors away from an officer of the King's Own Scottish Borderers named Terry. Charlie, then five, became friendly with their seven-year-old son Fred. Despite the two years' difference in age and the fact that the Warrens were only in Winchester for six months, the two boys developed what was to become a lifelong friendship.

That September their father, now confirmed as full Colonel, was ordered with his regiment to Devonport in South Devon for twelve months' 'very severe' training in preparation for a spell of duty in Ireland.[16] He appears to have felt that Devonport was not a suitable posting for his young family and he made alternative arrangements. John was by this time boarding at Bridgnorth Grammar School in Shropshire, and Margaret was probably also at boarding school. It was decided that their mother, whose health was not good, should take the three younger children to France for the winter to stay with an uncle in Paris. She was familiar with the French capital as she and her husband had been married in the British Embassy there fifteen years previously. Thus, in October 1845 Mary Warren set off for Paris with Charlotte, aged seven, Charlie, five and a half, and Billie, aged four.[17] She probably took a servant with her to help with the children.

For Charlie, leaving Winchester meant parting from his new best friend, Fred Terry. The two boys did not know if they would ever meet again and so, in memory of their friendship, Fred planted a rose tree in the garden and called it 'Charlie Warren'.[18]

Any sad partings from father and friends, however, would soon have been forgotten through the excitement of the journey to Paris by ship. What better way to see the great French capital for the first time than by steamboat up the Seine? And as they came round the long bend of the river, into the heart of the city, they would have seen, ahead and to the left, the newly constructed Arc de Triomphe gleaming in the autumn sunlight. The famous future landmarks of the Tour Eiffel and the Basilica of the Sacré-Cœur were not yet even an architect's dream and the great medieval Cathedral of Notre-Dame, sitting on its island in the middle of the Seine, still defined the centre of the city.

The children settled into their uncle's apartment and what should have been a time of happiness and adventure soon turned into one of great anxiety as it became clear that their mother was seriously ill. She was confined to

16 Noakes, *Historical Account*, p 95.
17 Williams, *The Life*, p 8.
18 *Ibid.*, p 5.

bed, and over Christmas and New Year her condition worsened to the extent that the children were no longer allowed to visit her. The memory of sitting anxiously on the landing outside his mother's bedroom remained with Charlie for the rest of his life. And then the worst happened: on 10 January 1846 Mary Warren died.[19]

It was a heavy blow. The children had lost the security and the certainty at the heart of their lives. In those days international travel was neither quick nor easy, and there is no suggestion that their father got leave to come to Paris; indeed, she may have been in her grave by the time he heard the news. Nor has it been recorded what happened over the ensuing months. The children appear to have stayed in Paris, at least until the spring when they returned to England to the care of their Uncle John Warren at Graveley Rectory in south Cambridgeshire.

But tragedy was not yet finished with the Warren family as, on 4 May, a few weeks after returning to England, Charlie's nearest remaining sister, Charlotte, died: cause of death unknown.[20] Charlie was six at the time, and Charlotte had been nine. In his youngest years, before Billie grew up, she had been Charlie's closest playmate and companion. The loss of both mother and sister in such a short space of time would have been hard enough to bear, but Charlie took upon himself, even more so than normally, responsibility for providing emotional support for Billie.

Fortunately, at this point Mary Chamberlain came into their lives. She was a local Graveley woman whom their father employed to look after the children. She was to become nurse, governess and mother figure to all four of them, but especially to the youngest two.

* * *

By the autumn of 1846, the 55th was ready to embark for Ireland. With his older two children, John and Margaret, safe in their boarding schools, Colonel Warren took his two younger sons and Mary Chamberlain with him. They sailed into the estuary of the River Lee and disembarked at Cove ('Queenstown', 'Cobh'), newly linked by railway to Cork city further upstream.[21] The regiment was initially garrisoned in Cork; but in November

---

[19] *Idem.*

[20] *Ibid.*, pp 5–6.

[21] Cove, established as a port town in 1750, was renamed Queenstown in 1850 in honour of a visit the previous year by Queen Victoria. It was renamed Cobh (the Gaelic spelling of the original Cove) following Irish independence in 1922.

they moved to a large Army camp at Buttevant, north of Cork, while they waited for a new barracks to be built in Limerick. They moved into the new barracks in January 1847.

It was a difficult time to be in Ireland. The 18th-century Penal Laws had been rescinded by the Catholic Emancipation Act of 1829, passed by the Westminster parliament; but the Catholic peasant majority of Ireland, who rented small plots of land for their subsistence, remained at the mercy of absentee landlords and their agents who were ruthless in their collection of rents and eviction for indebtedness. Rural protest, always a feature of 19th-century Ireland, was widespread, and small, secret bands of rural poor, known as 'Ribbonmen', enforced their own form of justice – threats, sabotage and assault – against those whom they identified as their oppressors. The state responded with coercive legislation aimed at suppressing the Ribbonmen and generally quelling Irish rural protest. And it was largely in defence of law and order, especially the protection of the lives and property of the landed class, that the 55th and other British regiments were stationed in rural Ireland.

The situation had been compounded in September 1845 when a fungus known as 'potato blight' decimated the potato crop. The potato was the peasants' staple food. A small plot of land could grow enough for a family's needs. It was a reasonably healthy diet; but overreliance on a single source of food, born of necessity, was inherently dangerous, and the potato was a fickle crop. In a good year, the potato would feed a family, while casual labour or the raising of a pig would bring in enough cash to pay the rent; but now suddenly the main source of food was gone, and landlords were evicting for non-payment of rent.

When the 55th arrived in the autumn of 1846, the potato harvest had just failed for the second successive year and famine was in the land. By 1847, when the famine was at its peak, thousands were dying every week in the workhouses and cottages of Ireland. Within five years of 1845 Ireland lost a quarter of its eight million population, half of those dead from starvation and disease; the rest fled the country in mass migration, across the Irish Sea to Liverpool and Glasgow, and across the Atlantic to North America. The worst-hit regions were County Mayo in the north-west and the south-western counties of Tipperary, Clare and Limerick. And it was in the city of Limerick that the 55th was stationed.

Charlie and Billie Warren were certainly aware that all was not well in the countryside around them. In his old age Charlie was to recall that the house where they were living had been threatened by 'rebels', probably Ribbonmen.

BOY AND GIRL AT CAHERA.

A famished boy and girl search for edible potatoes in a field in West Cork in February 1847. From a sketch by James Mahony for the Illustrated London News, *20 February 1847.*

He also recalled seeing rebels shot in the Limerick barrack square.[22] This, however, may have been a false memory, for the rebellion of that period did not happen until July 1848, by which time the Warrens and the 55th were in Dublin.[23] Even then, the only ones shot were those who died in the small amount of fighting that took place in Eastern Tipperary. The normal penalty for murder was death by hanging, not firing squad. For other serious offences, convicted felons, including the leaders of the 1848 rebellion, were transported, mostly to Australia.[24]

For Charlie, the period in Ireland was best remembered for the amount of time spent in the company of his father. Mary Chamberlain supervised much of the boys' education during the daytime when their father was busy with the

[22] *Ibid.*, pp 8–9.
[23] Noakes, *Historical Account*, p 95.
[24] Thomas Keneally, *The Great Shame* (BCA, London, 1998), pp 144–205.

regiment; but Colonel Warren was actively involved in his sons' upbringing. His input to their education was based upon four things: imparting the beliefs and principles of Christianity, which guided his own moral code, encouraging them to read, entertaining them with stories of his military adventures, and allowing them a good deal of personal freedom to explore the world around them. The Colonel's own personal interests would have provided further stimulation and inspiration. He had an unusual ability with mathematics, being able to do intricate calculations in his head and alter or correct the figures at will. He was a keen chess player, being able to play two games at once, blindfold, which would have excited his young sons. He also had a good understanding of the principles of science and was keen on solving astronomical problems. The latter certainly had an influence on Charlie in later life.[25]

Charles Warren senior's first concern was to impart to his sons his own deep Christian beliefs, and he used the Bible as his textbook, with a particular focus on the Psalms. His own favourite, which became one of Charlie's, and must have been a comfort to him through many a perilous situation in the heat of war, was Psalm 91:

> … I will say of the Lord, He is my refuge and my fortress: my God; in Him will I trust.
>
> … He shall cover thee with feathers, and under his wings shalt thou trust: his truth shall be thy shield and buckler.[26]

Charlie learned to refer to his own favourite, Psalm 15, as the 'gentleman's psalm', for it described the conduct of a true gentleman, or, as King David would have it, 'a worthy citizen of Zion':

> Lord, who shall abide in thy tabernacle? Who shall dwell in thy holy hill?
>
> He that walketh uprightly, and worketh righteousness, and speaketh the truth in his heart.
>
> He that backbiteth not with his tongue, nor doeth evil to his neighbour, nor taketh up a reproach against his neighbour.

Despite his young age, death was a harsh reality for Charlie and he would have taken strength from his favourite hymn, 'Glory to Thee, my God, this night', which contains the verses:

[25] Williams, *The Life*, p 27.
[26] The Biblical quotations are taken from the *King James Holy Bible*, the version that would have belonged to the Warren family.

Teach me to live, that I may dread
The grave as little as my bed;
Teach me to die, that so I may
Rise glorious at the awful day.

O may my soul on Thee repose,
And may sweet sleep mine eyelids close,
Sleep that shall me more vigorous make
To serve my God when I awake.[27]

Psalms and hymns such as these would have not only helped the young boy to come to terms with the loss of his mother and sister, but also provided him with the guiding principles for his life to come. It should not be supposed from this that Charlie was a sombre lad. He was an active, fun-loving boy, full of humour: something that was to serve him well in some awkward moments in later life.

Mary Chamberlain believed in the use of rhyme in education and Charlie loved this form of learning. In his old age he was to recall with fond humour:

They used to teach me:
    'Seven Days in a week,
    A bird's nose is called a beak.'
And I never forgot it![28]

Throughout his life Charlie retained an enthusiasm for rhyme as the best way to remember facts – always provided it did not distort their accuracy. His father, too, believed in the power of poetry. He gave his sons a copy of Aikin's *British Poets* and set them to learn a number of poems by heart. At this age they were mostly rhythmic and amusing fables from which lessons could be learned.

Charlie set to the task with gusto and while still only seven he could recite from memory numerous poems, some of them quite long. Among those he remembered in old age were John Gay's *Sweet William's Farewell to Black-eyed Susan* (perhaps imagining his brother Billie in the title role), *The Goat Without a Beard* (with the lesson that pride will make a fool of one), and *The Hare and Many Friends* (which showed that to make a friend of everyone leaves one with

---

[27] Hymn 23, *Hymns Ancient and Modern* (edition of 1889, reset, William Clowes and Sons, London, 1924), p 18.
[28] Williams, *The Life*, p 10.

no real friends at all).[29] But Charlie's favourite poem was Alexander Pope's *The Town Mouse and the Country Mouse.* He loved the cheek, the humour, the rhythm and the rhyme. In later life, when about to start a meal with his children or grandchildren, he would quote the invitation of the Town Mouse to the Country Mouse: 'Pray dip your whiskers and your tail in!'[30] And in the final couplet of the poem he found the words that fitted his own love of the simple, independent, outdoor life:

> Give me again my hollow tree,
> A crust of bread and liberty!

Other books that the young Charlie was given to read included *Eyes and No Eyes* by Arabella Buckley[31] and *The Arabian Nights' Entertainments.* The former, a set of six small books designed to teach children about the natural world around them, was written in such a way as to encourage outdoor exploration. The topics ranged from the wildlife of wood and field, to pond life, birds, insects and the identification of trees by flower, seed and leaf. Besides promoting a love of nature, the level of technical detail in word and illustration may have sown the seed of that love of scientific and mathematical precision that was to become the adult Charles Warren's *forte.* He also developed a habit of recording his outdoor observations.

From the *Arabian Nights,* he read and reread his favourite stories and was later to remark that in them he found 'a far greater reverence for God's Holy Name than was ever accorded in our every day speech then prevalent in England'.[32] It should be stressed that his would have been a carefully expurgated edition of the *Arabian Nights.* Richard Burton's unexpurgated translation, *A Thousand Nights and One Night,* which shocked the prudish of Victorian Britain, was not published until 1885. The stories the young Warren read impressed upon him a belief in 'an ever-present Providence'. His biographer grandson speculated that 'Perhaps, too, [they] put him in sympathy with the mind of the Arab … when he was in service [in Sinai] in 1882, [for] he seemed remarkably well at home with the Sheikhs and their followers whom

---

[29] Aikin, Dr., *Select Works of the British Poets with biographical and critical prefaces* (first published, Longman Hurst, London, 1820), pp 297–300.
[30] Williams, *The Life,* p 10.
[31] Arabella B. Buckley (Mrs Fisher), *Eyes and No Eyes, with numerous illustrations* (Cassell, London, no date).
[32] Williams, *The Life,* p 12, from a speech to a gathering of Scouts in Weston-super-Mare, October 1925.

he had known in imagination since his childhood in Ireland'.[33]

But life was not all serious education and learning poetry. One can imagine that two small boys would have been eager to hear stories of their father's heroic adventures in foreign lands and Charles Warren senior was happy to entertain his young sons with sanitised versions of some of his wartime experiences. The Coorg War has already been referred to,[34] but his account of the battle of 'Tching-Kiang-Foo' (Zhenjiang) against the Manchu Tartars was a favourite in Charlie's memory. As his father told it, after scaling the ladders and mounting the wall of the city, Major Warren found himself in hand-to-hand combat with three Tartars who were blocking the way through a narrow corner bastion. After despatching two of them, Warren and the third Tartar were at death blows when an almighty explosion blew him out of one door and the Tartar out of the other![35] The regimental history records a more mundane version, in which one of the men of the 55th bayoneted the third Tartar as the major lay at his mercy. The explosion did indeed happen, but shortly afterwards.[36] The father's version, however, made for a far better story.

Stories such as these probably contributed to Charlie's interest in his father's military life. The Colonel would occasionally take his son into the officers' mess, but Charlie loved to just follow his father around watching him at work, such as teaching the officers the use of the sextant. He would also watch the regiment drilling in the barrack square, fascinated by the precision of the intricate movements of the ranks, especially their marching 'inside out', as he used to call it. And he would go into the carpenter's shop where the master-carpenter instructed him in the use of his tools.

In the winter of 1846/47, when the regiment was still at Buttevant, his elder brother John, home on holiday from Bridgnorth, took Charlie into a nearby field and showed him how to use a pistol. Here Charlie had his first lesson in firearm safety with the rhyming couplet: 'Never, never point a gun/ Even in fun, at anyone'. In later life it was something he stressed with his own students and recruits. That winter holiday the two brothers enjoyed plenty of shooting practice, mainly at birds.[37]

In September 1847, the Irish potato harvest failed for the third successive year. Death and the lethargy of starvation and disease were everywhere

---

[33] *Ibid.*, p 9.
[34] See above, p 1.
[35] Williams, *The Life*, pp 4–5.
[36] Noakes, *Historical Account*, p 89.
[37] Williams, *The Life*, pp 7–9.

apparent and food riots were a regular occurrence in Cork and Tipperary. The 55th was ordered to Templemore in Eastern Tipperary. They marched the 40 miles from Limerick as that part of the new rail system had not yet been built.[38] The Warren boys and Mary Chamberlain probably travelled by coach.

That open rebellion did not erupt at this stage was probably more to do with the people's physical weakness and lack of effective leadership than any lack of hostility to the authorities.

Talk of rebellion, however, was brewing in Dublin. Daniel O'Connell, the 'Liberator', was dead and a new generation of 'Young Irelanders' had taken over the nationalist leadership.[39] Young Ireland was a 'loose alliance of writers, orators and activists', who through their radical newspaper, *The Nation*, advocated open defiance of the British authorities amid calls for rebellion and independence.[40] Then in February 1848 the barricades went up in Paris. Within three days the French monarchy was overthrown and a republic was declared. The effect in Ireland was electrifying. Young Ireland leaders rushed to Paris, only to find the new French regime too precarious to offer them any support. The British, nevertheless, took the threat seriously and the Lord-Lieutenant, the Earl of Clarendon, stationed 12,000 troops in Dublin to man the principal buildings of the city, including Trinity College, and to forestall any barricades going up in the Irish capital.[41]

It was this that brought the 55th from Templemore to Dublin Castle, the official headquarters of the Lord-Lieutenant, in March 1848.[42] This time the Warrens and the regiment travelled by steam train, the new railway line to Dublin having recently been completed. For Charlie and Billie, and indeed for their father and all of the 55th, it would have been their first journey by this new form of transport.

On arrival in Dublin the Colonel took a house in Ship Street, just outside one of the main entrances to the castle. Here Charlie and Billie had the added excitement of exploring the castle itself. Somehow Charlie acquired the key to a door that gave access to passages and private rooms. He was so excited with his discovery that he offered to show his father around the castle. After their

---

[38] Noakes, *Historical Account*, p 95.
[39] O'Connell, the man who had pushed Catholic Emancipation through the Westminster parliament, had gone to Southern Europe to recover from ill health and died in Genoa, Italy, on 15 May 1847, aged 71.
[40] Keneally, *The Great Shame*, p 100.
[41] *Ibid.*, pp 147–9.
[42] Noakes, *Historical Account*, p 95.

A contemporary artist's impression of an aerial view of Dublin, with the square of Dublin Castle left of centre and Trinity College to the right.
ILLUSTRATED LONDON NEWS, 9 MAY 1846.

tour, his father, though amused at his son's audacity, felt obliged to confiscate the key, which put paid to that little adventure. But this did not put Charlie off. Besides watching the soldiers drilling, he befriended the castle gardener and spent many happy hours with Billie exploring the grounds, often late into the evening and early in the morning.[43] The two boys were so absorbed in their own lives that they would have been unaware that a small, abortive rebellion occurred on the Tipperary border in late-July.

The idyllic life of home education and exploration was bound to come to an end, and in August 1848 Charlie accompanied his brother John across the Irish Sea to Bridgnorth Grammar School in Shropshire. The school normally only took boys from the age of ten or eleven, but the headmaster, Dr Thomas Rowley, accepted Charlie at eight and a half, perhaps because John had been at the school for a number of years and now, in his final year, was head boy. The headmaster and his wife lived in the school's boarding house, and in that

[43] Williams, *The Life*, pp 10–11.

first year Mrs Rowley kept a close eye on her youngest charge, putting him in the same bedroom as his elder brother.[44]

Bridgnorth Grammar was one of those new breeds of boys' private school that followed the principles developed by Dr Arnold at Rugby, that of trusting the boys to be responsible for their own discipline, supervised by the seniors and only *overseen* by the masters.[45]

Dr Rowley was both benevolent and inspiring as headmaster, at least in the memory of the old boys. When speaking at Bridgnorth as first President of the Old Bridgnorthians' Association, on the eve of the First World War, [the then General Sir] Charles Warren referred to Dr Rowley as 'one of the great men of the last century, [whose] wonderful personality still pervades and influences those around us now … he put everybody upon his honour to obey both the laws of God and of man. He said that if they were gentlemen they would carry them out, and that system went very far to make the Bridgnorth boy the great character he has always been.'[46] What particularly enthused the young Charlie Warren was Dr Rowley's habit of 'making fun and amusement out of the merest trifles', for instance, getting the boys to translate all the nursery rhymes they knew into Latin.[47] It was an amusement that was to remain with Charles Warren all his life.

When Charlie first arrived at Bridgnorth, it was a small school of only 80 boys and, although he was by far the youngest, he settled in well. Already an avid reader, he enjoyed his lessons; and there was plenty of physical sport, which appealed to his active nature. On his first holiday home from school for the Christmas of 1848, he would have entertained Billie with tales of his exciting life at school, so much so that by the time it came to the Easter holiday, his father decided that Billie, clearly missing Charlie, must join his brothers at Bridgnorth for the summer term of 1849. Colonel Warren must have been confident that Charlie would keep a close eye on his younger brother and 'show him the ropes'.

Head boy John would only be at the school for one more term. He was due to leave that summer and it was presumed that he would go to Oxford; but he preferred his father's career and in September 1849 he joined the Army.

---

[44] *Ibid.*, p 11.

[45] J. F. A. Mason, 'Thomas Rowley: Energy and Pre-eminence 1821–1850', in Maureen Jones, ed, *Bridgnorth Grammar & Endowed Schools: Five hundred years of change, 1503–2003* (BGS 500th Anniversary Group, Bridgnorth, 2003), pp 8–16.

[46] Quoted in Williams, *The Life*, pp 11–12.

[47] *Ibid.*, pp 13–14.

Williams does not mention any military college, so it is probable that his father bought him a commission; and in January 1850 2nd Lieutenant John Warren sailed with his regiment for Gibraltar.[48]

By then the Warren boys were spending most of their school holidays in England, sometimes with their Uncle John at Graveley Rectory, where they made the most of the freedom of the surrounding countryside. On other occasions they stayed with Colonel Warren's younger brother, Revd William Warren, Rector of Wroot on the Lincolnshire border, and his wife Anne Bethell.

In February 1851 Colonel Warren led the service companies of the 55th to an assignment in Gibraltar where his eldest son, Lt John Warren, was already serving.[49] After Colonel Warren's arrival, John was able to transfer into his father's regiment. The eldest daughter Margaret, then aged about eighteen and about whom we know little else, accompanied her father to Gibraltar where she met and married a young Lieutenant, John Henry St John, of the 92nd (Gordon Highlanders) Regiment of Foot.[50] Meanwhile, Charlie and Billie were left in England under the care of their Uncle John Warren at Graveley, and would not see their father again for a number of years.

* * *

In December 1850 Dr Rowley retired after 30 years of leading Bridgnorth Grammar,[51] and the Warren boys were transferred to Wem Grammar, another private school of good repute in Shropshire.

The washing and sleeping conditions at Wem were much more basic than at Bridgnorth, but Charlie reckoned that they toughened him up for 'roughing it in strange countries' in later life.[52] As a newcomer Charlie found himself bullied for a while at Wem, but was fortunate in that he had the self-confidence to stand up for himself and defy his tormentors. In retrospect, he came to believe that this was an important lesson in mental and physical courage. In his opinion men would suffer many knocks through their lives and it was important to gain experience of these as a youngster rather than be

[48] *Ibid.*, p 12.
[49] Noakes, *Historical Account*, p 95.
[50] Williams, *The Life*, p 22, *fn*. Margaret Warren's birth in India and marriage in Gibraltar are the only occasions she is mentioned in Williams' account. The 92nd arrived in Gibraltar in 1853 and was transferred to India in 1858, at which point the family appear to have lost touch with Margaret.
[51] J. F. A. Mason, 'More Struggles, 1851–1907', in Jones, ed., *Bridgnorth Grammar*, p 17.
[52] Williams, *The Life*, p 21.

confronted unprepared in later life. At least, that is the lesson that he preached to the boys of Wem Grammar School when asked in his old age to speak at their Speech Day in December 1925. Looking back on his life, he told his audience that he was grateful for the 'knocks' that he received at school for they gave him the courage to stand up and do what was right. As he was to teach many who came under his guidance – face your fear and you will find courage!

Not that Charlie was ever short of tests for his courage. While at Bridgnorth he had developed the practice of jumping off high places to see if he could land safely. To jump off a six-foot wall was nothing to Charlie. He made a sort of air bag or parachute out of an old sofa cover and used it to jump off much greater heights. 'When I came to Wem at the age of ten,' he recalled, 'I was rather expert at it'. By then he could jump off a twelve-foot wall and land lightly. In retrospect, he believed that it was this early 'parachuting' that sparked his later interest in military balloons and airships.[53]

During the summer holiday of 1852, Revd John Warren, Rector of Graveley, died while on a visit to Bangor Cathedral, where he was Chancellor. With their father abroad in Gibraltar, Charlie and Billie had probably regarded Graveley Rectory as the nearest place they had to 'home'. That was now lost to them, but the family rallied round and their Uncle Revd William Warren and his wife Anne, who had no children of their own, took them in and provided them at Wroot Rectory with the security of a second 'home from home'.

Another death, of a prominent figure that September, was to prompt Charlie into thinking about his future adult life.

[53] *Ibid.*, pp 17–21.

CHAPTER 2

To Be a Soldier

The death of Arthur Wellesley, 1st Duke of Wellington, on 14 September 1852 marked the passing of an era. The victor of the Peninsular War and of Waterloo had gone on to become Prime Minister (twice) and for 25 years, Commander-in-Chief of the Armed Forces of the United Kingdom. He was the most famous man in England. Queen Victoria wrote to her uncle, the King of the Belgians, lamenting the loss of 'the GREATEST MAN this country has ever produced'.[54] Victorian hyperbole, perhaps, but sentiments widely shared in this mid-Victorian age. The nearest equivalent in more recent times was the death of Sir Winston Churchill in 1965.

As the news spread along the highways and new railway lines of Britain, cathedrals and parish churches tolled muffled bells, while newspapers published black-margined editions, mostly extolling the Duke's martial exploits. The *Illustrated London News*, the world's first mass-market illustrated weekly 'news magazine', went so far as to produce two successive 16-page supplements.[55] There had not been a war in Europe for nearly 40 years and military enthusiasm in the country at large was high, as people, prompted by the media, recalled past military glories. All too soon they would have the opportunity to put their enthusiasm for war to the test, as trouble was brewing in Eastern Europe. In the meantime, the Duke's state funeral in November drew one and a half million people to line the streets of the capital in silent tribute. It was posted by *The Times* as the largest-ever gathering for a single event in the country's history.[56]

125 miles (200 km) north-west of London, Charlie and Billie Warren eagerly lapped up the voluminous newspaper accounts of the famous Duke's career, not least because their father had, as a young sixteen-year-old subaltern of the 30th Regiment of Foot, served in 1815 under the Duke of Wellington

---

[54] A.C. Benson and Viscount Esher (eds.), *The Letters of Queen Victoria, 1837–61*, Vol. II (John Murray, London, 1908), p 394, her emphasis.
[55] *Illustrated London News (ILN)*, 18 and 29 September 1852.
[56] *The Times*, 19 November 1852. See also *ILN*, 20 November 1852.

during his occupation of Paris after the Battle of Waterloo.[57] Their father transferred to the 55th Regiment for the rest of his military career after the 2nd Battalion 30th Foot was disbanded in 1817.[58]

It was about the time of the Duke's funeral that Charlie, apparently inspired by these events, wrote to his father in Gibraltar, telling him of his desire to join the Army.[59]

Colonel Warren would have known that his second son had the academic ability to win a commission by examination rather than have one bought for him, as had been done for the eldest son John. Clearly his money would be better spent sending Charlie to the Royal Military College (RMC) Sandhurst. A purchased commission would cost £450, while for a regimental field officer like himself, the College would charge Colonel Warren £150 for the three years, and that included full board and lodging for nine months of each year.[60] The RMC was prepared to accept cadets from the age of thirteen,[61] but Colonel Warren clearly felt that Charlie should wait until he was a little older and he delayed his approval for a year, by which time Billie had decided that he, too, wanted to join his brother in the Army. At the end of 1853 their father arranged to transfer both of them from Wem Grammar to Cheltenham College, a school founded in 1841 by two Cheltenham residents for the purpose of 'educating the sons of gentlemen'.[62] It was also designed to prepare candidates for entry into one of the military training institutions.

In January 1854 Charlie Warren, one month short of his fourteenth birthday, and Billie, aged twelve years and two months, entered Cheltenham College, boarding together in Clark House, and began their studies in the military side of the college.[63] Here they were introduced to natural science through a new publication, *The Chemistry of Modern Science* by the renowned agricultural chemist of Durham University, James Finlay Weir Johnston.[64] It

[57] Williams, *The Life*, p 2.
[58] http://www.nam.ac.uk/research/famous-units/30th-cambridgeshire-regiment-foot, accessed November 2014.
[59] Williams, *The Life*, p 23.
[60] *A List of the Royal Military College Sandhurst: Corrected to 1 May 1855* (Parker and Co, London, 1855), p 24.
[61] *Ibid.*, p 26.
[62] http://www.cheltenhamcollege.org/history-and-archives, accessed November 2014.
[63] Private communication, Mrs D. A. Leighton, Cheltenham College Archivist, 11 November 2014.
[64] J. F. W. Johnston, *The Chemistry of Modern Life*, 2 Vols (D. Appleton & Co, New York, 1853–54).

is not clear how Billie coped with science: he was not as academically gifted as his elder brother; but Charlie appears to have absorbed it all enthusiastically.[65]

In order to prepare candidates for the Sandhurst entry examination, Cheltenham College placed particular emphasis upon all branches of mathematics, besides French and English composition. The masters soon discovered that the elder of the two Warren boys had a particular flair for mathematics, especially Euclid's geometry, an important requirement for military training, and after only two terms Charlie passed the Sandhurst entry examination. He left Cheltenham in June 1854, and in doing so he left behind his younger brother Billie.[66] It was to be a further eighteen months before Billie had passed the entrance exam and was old enough to follow his brother to Sandhurst, by which time Charlie was already in the process of moving on.

It was an exciting time to be preparing for entry into military service for the British public's appetite for war was at that moment being rewarded by its army's involvement in the Crimean War.[67] This conflict, the first of its kind to be independently reported by war correspondents, is best known in British history for Florence Nightingale and the 'Charge of the Light Brigade', the latter being a tale of incompetence and bravery in equal proportions.

The war involved nothing so crude as commercial advantage. Rather, it was a product of grand alliances, imperial ambition, strategic interests and international prestige. Ostensibly, it was about who had the right to protect Christians within the Turkish Ottoman Empire. The problem stemmed from the age-old schism between the Eastern Orthodox (or Greek) Church, championed by the Czar of Russia, and the Western Roman (or Latin) Church, championed by the King of France. So far as the places of Christian pilgrimage in the Holy Land were concerned, it came down to who held which keys to the doors of the Church of the Nativity in Bethlehem and the Church of the Holy Sepulchre in Jerusalem. Both Russia and France held contradictory *firmins* from the Ottoman sultan, the 'Sublime Porte', in Constantinople. A *firmin* was an Ottoman agreement or letter of permission, and its often vague and contradictory nature was something with which Charles Warren, as a lieutenant of the Royal Engineers in Jerusalem in the 1860s, was to become all too familiar.

---

[65] Williams, *The Life*, p 12.
[66] Williams (*The Life*, p 23) believed that Charlie was only at Cheltenham for one term, but the College records show it to have been two terms (information from Mrs D. A. Leighton, Cheltenham College Archivist).
[67] For a good narrative account of the war, see Trevor Royle, *Crimea: The Great Crimean War 1854–1856* (Little, Brown & Co, London, 1999).

In a foretaste of 21st-century 'Middle Eastern' wars, the reality behind the religious posturing was that the Russian Czar, Nicholas I, hoped to capitalise on a declining Turkish Empire and seize enough territory to give his Black Sea fleet access to the Mediterranean. Britain, on the other hand, sought to aid and strengthen Turkey so as to forestall just such an eventuality: a Russian fleet in the Mediterranean might endanger Britain's overland route through Egypt to the Red Sea and thus to India. Meanwhile, Napoleon III, who had overthrown the short-lived French Republic in 1851, was seeking international recognition of his assumed title of 'Emperor'. Besides, conscious of the humiliation that the Russians had inflicted on his uncle Napoleon Bonaparte in 1812, he wanted to be prominent in any conflict with Russia.

The Russian Empire had already expanded in the late-18th century to include Ukraine and the Crimean Peninsula, and in July 1853 Russian troops invaded two nominal territories of the Ottoman Empire, Moldavia and Wallachia (present-day Moldova and Romania). The British and French governments responded by sending their fleets to anchor in the Dardanelles, the eastern gateway to the Mediterranean, and from that point on, Britain and France were inevitably drawn into the war, although they did not formally declare until the following March.

In May 1854 Colonel Charles Warren senior and his eldest son, Lieutenant John Warren, sailed with the 55th Regiment from Gibraltar to the theatre of war where they formed part of First Brigade of the Second Division. This was to become known as the 'fighting division', following their prominent role in the Battle of Alma.[68] Lt.-Colonel Warren was promoted to full Colonel, and through June and July the combined armies of Britain and France assembled at Varna on the Bulgarian Black Sea coast, in preparation for a seaborne landing on Crimea.

* * *

Meanwhile, back in England, on 11 July 1854 Charles Warren junior, aged fourteen years and five months, was 'received into the Junior Department' of RMC Sandhurst.[69] In doing so, he left behind his childhood and entered adult life.

Sandhurst was run along military lines. Indeed, in conformity with a Royal Warrant dating back to 1808, 'all gentleman cadets at the Royal

---

[68] Noakes, *Historical Account*, pp 96–7.
[69] Sandhurst Archive, RMC, WO 99/21, Box 26, *Report of the Collegiate Board*; and RMC, WO 151, Vol I, *Gentleman Cadet Register*, A24, Warren, Charles.

Military College [were] subject to the Articles of War'.[70] All of the senior administrative positions of the College, as well as several of the more important teaching posts, were held by experienced regimental officers.[71] The general conduct and discipline of the cadets was maintained by experienced, 'respectable and intelligent' sergeants, drawn from all branches of military service. They were particularly vigilant to prevent 'fagging': that practice common in English public schools whereby senior boys enforced a form of servitude on their juniors. According to the *Complete Guide*, it was the 'zeal, vigilance and rectitude' of the sergeants that accounted for the 'excellent discipline and general good conduct of the cadets, as compared with most public schools, without having recourse to the flogging system'.[72] It was the 'grown-up' sort of discipline that Warren would have appreciated. Tobacco and alcohol were forbidden and swearing and lying were severely punished as being 'un-gentlemanly'. Those who transgressed were put on guard duty out of study time.

In military terms cadets were 'Privates', although within each Company some with proven 'good conduct' could be promoted to 'Lance Corporal' or 'Corporal'.[73] These would have some authority and certain privileges. During the short periods of free time, mostly Sundays and summer evenings, cadets were allowed to venture beyond the walls of the College, but were strictly banned from the nearby Blackwater village, apparently because of the potential moral corruption of its numerous public houses.

The academic year consisted of two long terms: eighteen weeks from July to November, followed by an eight-week break, and then a twenty-week term from January to May. The hours of study were long: seven hours a day, Monday to Saturday. All study was done in the halls, under the instruction or direct supervision of the masters. There were in addition practical classes, especially Fortification, taking place in the model room, where the cadets' military drawings were placed on display, or in the grounds for practical work. There were sappers (NCOs from the Royal Engineers) to teach sapping (trenching) and mining, and there was a Riding School, headed by a captain from a Hounslow cavalry regiment.

---

[70] *List, RMC, 1855*, p 27.
[71] The following description of the College is based upon the *Complete Guide*. Although published five years before Warren's entry, it is assumed for the purposes of this biography that the basic running of the College had not changed significantly in the interim.
[72] *Complete Guide*, p 24.
[73] *List, RMC, 1855*, 'Roll of the Gentleman Cadets', p 14.

The principal subjects of study were divided into units, and cadets had to pass a public oral examination in each unit before progressing to the next one. To gain recommendation for commission, cadets had to pass a minimum of six units, including Mathematics (the first six books of Euclid for two units), Fortification, Military Drawing and French. Other optional subjects included History, Geography, the Classics and German.

On 12 July, the day after his entry to the College, Cadet A24 Warren passed his first unit in Military Drawing, an indication that the skills of precision drawing – essential to a successful military surveyor – were something with which he was already familiar. And at the end of that month he passed his first unit in Mathematics, the first three books of Euclid. By the end of his first term he had passed three more Mathematical units, completing the required six books of Euclid, and been awarded 'One Decoration of Merit'.[74] Warren was good, but he was not unique: there were several other cadets in his year who were at least as good as him.

* * *

The Crimean War was the first major conflict attended by newspaper correspondents, and their regular reports, relayed by the Army's telegraph system, provided the British public with up-to-date news on the progress of the war. These regular bulletins from the Crimean front line in the autumn of 1854 would have added an extra puissance of excitement to the lives of the military cadets, many of whom, like Warren, had family or friends serving in Crimea. The first major battle of the land war occurred on 20 September as the Allied armies reached the River Alma in their southward advance down the Crimean Peninsula to the naval port of Sevastopol. Faced with a strong Russian position on the south bank of the river, the Second Division was given the task of forcing a crossing in the centre. In due course Colonel Warren led the badly battered 55th across the river to capture one of the Russian gun emplacements.[75] Colonel Warren's brave 'exercion' [sic] received the praise of the Divisional Commander and in due course he received mention in Lord Raglan's despatch to London.[76]

Back in England, Cadet Charles Warren had just finished his first term at Sandhurst when news came through that both his father and his brother

<hr/>

[74] RMC Sandhurst Archive, WO 151, Gentleman Cadet Register, Vol I (1806–1864), A24, Warren, Charles.

[75] Noakes, *Historical Account*, p 101.

[76] UKNA, WO 1/369, Raglan, Balaklava, 28 September 1854.

had been wounded at the Battle of Inkerman, fought on 5 November 1854. The Colonel had been promoted to lead the First Battalion, and on the night before the battle he had gathered the 55th together and read to them the 91st Psalm, the soldier's Psalm, reassuring them that those who trusted in God would receive His protection.[77] Once again, Warren's leadership of his men in the battle the following day was 'commended highly' in Lord Raglan's despatches;[78] but he was 'severely' wounded and was shipped out to the hospital at Scutari, where Florence Nightingale had just arrived to try and sort out the appalling conditions and the notoriously high mortality rate.

His son John, who had been given a field promotion to Captain, had received a bayonet wound in the leg, inflicted by one of his own men in the confusion of battle. He bound his leg and continued the fight, and because his wound at the time was considered 'slight', it was not attended to immediately. This was several months before the arrival of Mary Seacole who set up her 'British Hotel' to tend to the needs of the wounded on the front line;[79] and Captain John Warren had to lie unattended in a roofless building for two nights, exposed to cold and rain, before being transferred to Scutari. By this time, he had developed septicaemia and was beyond saving. Before the year was out, he was dead. Ironically, his 'severely wounded' father recovered. He was sent home on sick leave, and in February 1855, he was awarded a CB (Companion of the Bath).[80]

* * *

In the spring term of 1855 his son, Sandhurst Cadet Warren, was promoted to B Company and made a Lance Corporal.[81] During that term he passed two further units, in Defensive Fortification and in French, which meant that within ten months of his arrival at the RMC, he had passed his six units, all of them in the required subjects.[82] He would have appreciated the presence in England at the time of his father, with whom he could discuss his future. He was still only just fifteen, but it appears that he had already made up his mind: he wanted to become a Royal Engineer.

[77] Williams, *The Life*, p 23.
[78] WO 1/369, Raglan, Before Sevastopol, 8 and 11 November 1854.
[79] Jane Robinson, *Mary Seacole: The Charismatic Black Nurse Who Became a Heroine of the Crimea* (Robinson, London, 2006), pp 113–15.
[80] Williams, *The Life*, pp 23–4; and *Hart's Army Lists*, 1856.
[81] *List, RMC, 1855*, 'Roll of the Gentleman Cadets', p 14.
[82] RMC, WO 151, Register, Vol I, A24, Warren.

The Royal Engineers, together with the Royal Artillery, were known as the 'Scientific Corps'. Entry into their officer corps could not be purchased: it had to be won by examination, following specialist training at the Royal Military Academy (RMA) at Woolwich. In March 1855, Charles Warren was nominated for entry into the Academy. In August he heard that his application to Woolwich had been approved, subject to a medical examination which took place that month. The Medical Examiner, however, appears to have identified some problem. In the Woolwich Register an intriguing note appears next to Warren's name:

> Mr Warren's Admission to the Academy was deferred for 6 months by the recommendation of the Medical Board, see letter dated 14/8/55.[83]

The letter referred to does not appear to have survived, so one is left to speculate on the possible reason for his deferral. There was no recorded sign of illness or physical weakness. He was a tall, robust youth: the Sandhurst Register recording his height on entry to the College the previous year as 5 feet 7 inches (1.70m), a good 5 inches (0.13m) taller than the average height of his fellow fourteen-year-olds.[84] It seems probable that the Medical Examiner had identified his short-sightedness, for when he entered the RMA at Woolwich the following year he was wearing a monocle in his right eye. As Williams was to observe:

> From this time onwards it would be impossible to imagine Charles Warren without his eyeglass: he depended very much on it and used to say that if the standard of eyesight for officers had been as high in his early days as it later became, he would have been excluded from the army for his shortness of sight.[85]

During the deferment he stayed on at Sandhurst and gained two further units, in Military Drawing in September, and Offensive Fortification in November.[86] These two subjects were fundamental to his life as a Royal Engineer. They involved a large amount of practical plan drawing, besides four actual

---

[83] RMA Woolwich Archive (at Sandhurst), WO149, Register, Vol 6 (1855–1888), 2298, Warren, Charles.
[84] RMC Sandhurst, WO 151, Vol I, A24 Warren. There is no record of his eventual adult height. In photographs he is either standing alone, or seated when with others, but he was certainly not small and probably ended up above average height for the period.
[85] Williams, *The Life*, p 25.
[86] RMC, WO 151, Vol I, A24 Warren.

surveys on the ground. The fortification classes entailed 'permanent and field fortification, theoretical and practical, including sapping and mining, pontooning and field entrenchments on the field'.[87] A description of the examination of June that year recorded that 'the Cadets had to demonstrate the construction of temporary bridges, trenches, gabions, fascines … and the dismantling and formation of a pontoon bridge across the lake'[88] – all essential work when Warren, as a senior officer, was commanding troops in South Africa.

Meanwhile, his father had returned to the Crimea with the temporary rank of Brigadier-General in July 1855 to find the battle for Sevastopol at its height. The city was not captured and peace finally concluded until the following March. The 55th did not leave the Crimea and return to Gibraltar until the end of May 1856. By this time his youngest son Billie had commenced his first term at RMC Sandhurst, while his elder son Cadet Charles Warren had moved on to the Royal Military Academy (RMA) at Woolwich.[89]

The founding purpose of the Academy was to produce 'good officers of Artillery and perfect Engineers'.[90] It was housed in the same grounds as the Woolwich Arsenal Barracks, the home until 1856 of both the Royal Engineers and the Royal Artillery. It was known colloquially as 'The Shop', because its original building was a former workshop of the Royal Arsenal. It is believed that it is from this nickname that the expression 'talking shop' derives, meaning 'to talk about things that nobody else understands'.[91] In 1855 the Royal Engineers moved from Woolwich Barracks to their current home at Chatham in Kent, on the River Medway, just above its confluence with the Thames Estuary.[92]

In some ways the Woolwich Academy was very similar to Sandhurst. It was run on military lines: the cadets slept in small dormitories and the hours of study were long; but at Woolwich there was additional time allocated to drill, including horse, sword, field gun and small-arms drill. There was no more history, geography or Latin; but in addition to all branches of mathematics, military drawing, surveying, map drawing and fortification, there were classes

---

[87] *Report from the Select Committee on Sandhurst Royal Military College*, submitted to the House of Commons, 18 June 1855, p v.

[88] *United Service Magazine*, No. 319, June 1855, p 25.

[89] RMA Archive, WO 149, Register, Vol. 6 (1855–1888), Warren, Charles.

[90] http://www.army.mod.uk/documents/general/history_of_rmas.pdf (accessed, 3 July 2014).

[91] http://www.royalengineers.ca/RMA.html (accessed, 3 July 2014).

[92] F. G. Guggisberg, *The Shop: The Story of the Royal Military Academy* (Cassell, London, 1900), p 87.

in astronomy and free-hand drawing as well as theoretical and practical classes in artillery. The latter took place in a newly constructed battery at the back of 'The Shop'. At that time there were still open fields around Woolwich and mortar practice was carried out from a position to the west of the barracks while sapping and mining were practised in the fields of Nightingale Vale, just to the east of the present South Circular Road. So far as study and training was concerned, there was no distinction drawn between engineering and artillery: all cadets were trained equally in both disciplines. This was an advantage that Warren was to appreciate in his professional life, as the two branches of the 'scientific corps' were often closely intertwined.

When Warren arrived at the Academy in 1856 the Governor was General Lewis RE, a 'Waterloo man', who was relaxed about bullying and was not a harsh disciplinarian. The following year Lewis was replaced by Colonel E. N. Wilford RA who had a very different attitude to discipline. The cadets were to be deprived of all things he considered to be luxuries: rugs, carpets, tablecloths and armchairs. These were removed from the cadets' rooms. This would not have bothered Warren, who was never one for luxury. He preferred the simple life, and had been well-prepared for 'roughing it' by his boarding school experience at Wem. Perhaps more seriously for the cadets' personal comfort, however, there was to be no more tea in their rooms! According to a contemporary, there was not even tea for breakfast:

> … for breakfast we had coffee (ugh!) and brown bread and butter, commonly known as 'oilstone'.

Although the breakfast menu was in due course improved by the addition of bacon and sausages, 'we needed it, for we were hard-worked then'.[93]

Progression through the classes at the RMA normally took three years, although this had been shortened by six months due to the pressure for more officers caused by the Crimean War. Warren progressed rapidly at the Academy. Despite his delayed start in the first term of 1856, by the end of the year he had moved up through two of the four classes.

He spent the six weeks of that winter holiday on leave in Malta where his father, with the temporary rank of Major-General, was stationed in charge of a brigade.[94] What Williams does not reveal is that, despite being in charge of a Brigade, his father was on half pay, presumably the product of post-war

---

[93] Quoted in Guggisberg, *The Shop*, pp 91–92.
[94] Williams, *The Life*, p 26.

retrenchment. Perhaps he was expected to retire on a Colonel's pension. But Warren senior could not afford to retire. He remained on half pay for two years, until October 1858, when his full promotion to Major-General was finally confirmed.[95] He was to remain in Malta until 1862.

Meanwhile, his elder surviving son, Charles, as a student of military engineering, would have found the medieval and early modern fortifications of Malta of particular interest, and he probably spent much of his leave studying them. In February 1857 he returned to the Academy to join the third class. At the end of that term in June he passed his probationary exam, his half-yearly report stating: 'Mr Warren greatly distinguished himself in Mathematics and is deserving of all praise'.[96]

By August 1857, a mere sixteen months after joining the Academy, Warren had moved up into the first-class and was in a position to go for his finals. He passed his final theoretical examination on 26 September and his final practical on 22 December.[97] The following day Governor Wilford wrote to the War Office recommending the 29 candidates considered suitable for commission. Listed according to merit, Warren was third on the list. The top fourteen were recommended for the Royal Engineers, while the others were offered the Royal Artillery.[98] Warren's commission into the Royal Engineers was officially dated from that day, which meant he started getting paid as a 2nd Lieutenant, RE, from 23 December 1857. The War Office confirmed his commission on 8 January 1858, one month before his eighteenth birthday.[99]

[95] *Hart's Army Lists*, 1856–58.
[96] Quoted in Williams, *The Life*, p 26.
[97] RMA, WO 149, Register, Vol 6, 2298, Warren, Charles.
[98] RMA, WO 150/43, Governor's Confidential Letter Book, 1856–1861, Wilford to War Office, 23 December 1857.
[99] RMA, WO 150/43, In-letters to Governor, No. 47, 8 January 1858.

CHAPTER 3

Where Duty and Glory Lead [100]

On 2 February 1858, five days before his eighteenth birthday, 2nd Lieutenant Charles Warren took a train from Charing Cross to Chatham in Kent. Wearing his newly tailored uniform of scarlet, single-breasted tunic and dark blue trousers with red stripe, he climbed Brompton Hill, overlooking the Chatham Royal Navy Dockyards on the Medway, and, for the first time, entered the Brompton Barracks of the Royal Engineers. The large building that housed the officers' mess faced the majestic Memorial Arch. Down one side of the spacious Barrack Square stood the officers' accommodation block, and opposite, those for the NCOs and men, known as 'sappers' and 'miners'. There were halls of instruction and plenty of parkland for practical classes and exercises. There was also a large Model Room which contained standing models of famous fortifications, as well as models made by current trainees.

The Corps of Royal Engineers normally expected newly commissioned officers to undergo two years of practical training at Chatham before being sent out on their various postings. The main focus was on trigonometrical surveying, and the standard handbook for the course was that by Lieutenant Edward Frome RE.[101] He had been instructor of surveying to the Royal Engineers in the 1830s.

As well as all the basic technical information about how to conduct a trigonometrical survey, Frome provided tips on how to maintain accuracy when working under difficult conditions in the field. There was a chapter on practical astronomy and how to measure astral latitude and longitude. Warren was to maintain a keen interest in astronomy throughout his adult life. Frome's handbook, along with a compass, protractor, sextant, field telescope, small aneroid barometer and sketching portfolio, was to become part of Warren's standard equipment. In due course he not only met Frome, who, as we shall see, was then a colonel and became for a few years his commanding officer

---

[100] '*Quo fas et Gloria ducunt*', the motto of the Royal Engineers.
[101] E. C. Frome, *Outline of the Method of Conducting a Trigonometrical Survey, for the Formation of Geographical and Topographical Maps and Plans* (Lockwood and Co, London, 1840).

and personal friend, but also worked with him on revising the handbook for its fourth edition.

After Warren had been in training at Chatham for just eight months, his supervisor, Lt.-Colonel Ross, directed Warren and three other trainees to report with their exercises for inspection by the Deputy Adjutant General. Their conduct judged 'favourable' and their training officially approved, the three others were sent to Portsmouth, while Warren was reserved at Chatham to await a special posting.[102] He was notified just before Christmas: he was bound for Gibraltar.

For the previous two years the Warren boys had spent their Christmas and New Year leave with their father in Malta; but there was no time for them to go that far this year as Charlie had to report back to Chatham on 30 December. The two brothers probably spent Christmas with their uncle and aunt at Wroot. Charlie would have been filled with the anticipation of finally getting out into the field and practising his chosen profession as a Royal Engineer. Billie's thoughts, however, probably dwelled on his impending parting from his beloved elder brother. This was to be their last time together, perhaps for many years. Neither would have imagined that it would be six and a half years before they met again.

Billie finally completed his training at Sandhurst in June 1860, but not well enough to pass up into the Academy at Woolwich and his father purchased him a commission in the 60th Rifles.[103] Following the outbreak of the American Civil War in 1861, he was posted to Canada.

Meanwhile, after their final Christmas together, 2nd Lieutenant Charles Warren reported back to barracks in Chatham where he and the 102 men of the 3rd Company, Royal Engineers, under the command of Captain Sedley, underwent formal inspection prior to their departure for Gibraltar.[104] On Monday 3 January 1859 the Company travelled by train to Portsmouth Harbour where they embarked on HM troopship *Himalaya*, one of a new class of steamship driven by screw propeller.[105] Loading the ship took a further two days and they left Portsmouth on 5 January with a total of about 400

---

[102] *UKNA*, WO 25/3945, Lt Col. Ross to Colonel Gordon CB, RE Establishment, Chatham, 2 October 1858.

[103] Sandhurst Archives, WO 151, Vol I for the RMC Register: Warren, William, admitted 15 January 1856.

[104] *The Times*, 1 January 1859.

[105] The early steamships had been driven by paddles, mounted either on the side or at the rear of the ship. From the late-1850s, however, propulsion by propeller or 'screw' was found to be much more efficient and generally faster.

2nd Lieutenant Charles Warren RE.
WARREN FAMILY COLLECTION

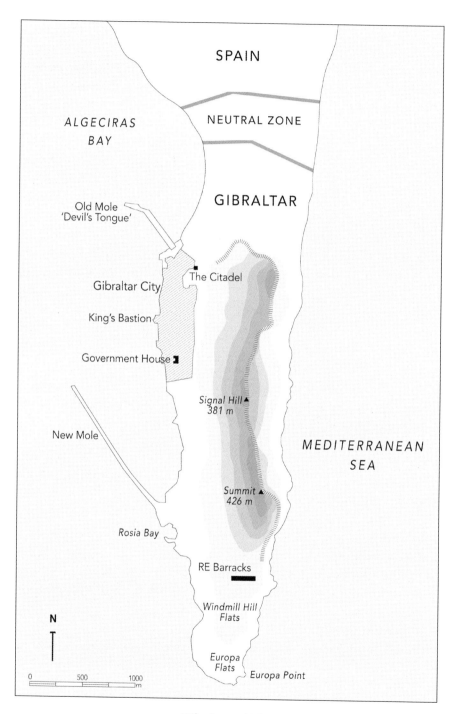

SPAIN

NEUTRAL ZONE

ALGECIRAS
BAY

GIBRALTAR

Old Mole
'Devil's Tongue'

The Citadel

Gibraltar City

King's Bastion

Government House

Signal Hill
381 m

New Mole

MEDITERRANEAN
SEA

Summit
426 m

Rosia Bay

RE Barracks

N

Windmill Hill
Flats

0   500   1000
m

Europa
Flats
Europa Point

Gibraltar, c.1860.

officers and men, some bound for Gibraltar, others for Malta.[106] There was a strong west wind blowing and it took the ship two days to reach her first port of call, Queenstown (Cobh), in Cork. For Warren it would have brought back memories of his previous arrival in Ireland when he was an adventurous child of seven. Now, at the age of eighteen, he was setting out on his first real adult adventure.

The *Himalaya* spent a day in Queenstown taking on more troops before departing for Gibraltar, which they reached in four days, long after sunset. The ship dropped anchor in the darkness and lay offshore for the night. It was not until dawn the following morning that Warren caught his first sight of the land that was to be his home for the next six and a half years.

One can imagine that he would have been on deck at first light to find the *Himalaya* anchored in a large bay. Behind him to the west and to the north lay Spain; but rising up in front on the eastern seaboard was the 'Rock'. That famous limestone landmark, virtually barren of vegetation from overgrazing by goats, dominated the peninsula of Gibraltar, pointing south towards Africa clearly visible on the southern horizon, and north to the mainland of Spain. Approximately 400 metres in height, the western face of the Rock would have been in morning shadow, but Warren could have made out the city nestled near its northern end. Most clearly visible from the sea was the bright limestone of the recently strengthened curtain wall that lined the waterfront. At its centre stood the King's Bastion, a classic late-18th-century fortress that had fended off attacks from the French and Spanish fleets during the Great Siege of 1779–83.[107] Warren would have learned of the King's Bastion and its success in the siege while in training at Woolwich, as well as at Chatham, where a model of it was on display.

At the north end of the city the Old Mole, known as 'the Devil's Tongue' from the fire of its guns during the siege, jutted out into the bay, while beyond and above it the great Rock ended in a north-facing cliff. This stood above the flat, sandy isthmus that connected British Gibraltar to the Spanish mainland, across which now stretches Gibraltar's international airport. From the sea it could be seen that the city itself was contained within two walls. The northern wall stretched up from the Old Mole to the medieval 'Moorish' citadel that stood out nearly halfway up the mountain, while a southern wall seemed to

---

[106] *Gibraltar Chronicle*, 13 January 1859. The *Chronicle*, a daily newspaper produced by the military establishment, regularly reported the comings and goings of troopships.
[107] F. A. Darren & Clive Finlayson, *The Fortifications of Gibraltar 1068–1945* (Osprey, Oxford, 2006), pp 25–9.

stretch all the way to the top.[108] The great ridge of the Rock itself reached its highest peak at the southern end, from where it fell away steeply to two plateaux, Windmill Hill Flats and Europa Flats, before reaching the sea at Europa Point.

The whole territory was only five kilometres from end to end and just over a kilometre wide, and over the years that followed Warren was to get to know 'every inch' of it, from sea wall to mountain peak, as he fulfilled his commission to make a comprehensive trigonometrical survey of Gibraltar. But that was yet to come. In the meantime he had more immediate duties to attend to.

Soon after sunrise the *Himalaya* entered Gibraltar Harbour and disembarked its passengers at the New Mole, the long southern breakwater that protected military shipping from westerly winds.[109] Commercial shipping had to lie at anchor in the bay. The Governor of Gibraltar was also Commander-in-Chief of the Garrison, and Captain Sedley and Lieutenant Warren would have reported immediately to Government House and to Colonel Savage, Commander of the Royal Engineers (CRE) in Gibraltar. Warren probably then saw to the offloading of his company's baggage before marching the 102 sappers up the steep climb through the town of Rosia and south along Europa Pass to their barracks on Windmill Hill Flats overlooking Europa Point. Hitherto, the Royal Engineer Corps in Gibraltar had contained just two companies. The arrival of a third company brought the total corps up to 280. The officer corps now consisted of one colonel, one lieutenant colonel, three captains and five lieutenants, of whom Warren was the most junior.[110]

Warren would have spent his first few weeks settling in, looking after his platoon and getting to know the various projects that the engineers were working on. At the end of January Colonel Savage left on promotion and was replaced by Colonel B. S. Stehelin. Stehelin was a commanding officer who appreciated initiative in his men, and Lieutenant Warren did not disappoint him.

Gibraltar was essentially a garrison, described by one contemporary civilian visitor as a 'military hothouse'.[111] It had been captured by the British in 1704, during the War of the Spanish Succession, and was subsequently ceded to

---

[108] See W. H. Bartlett, *Gleanings on The Overland Route* (Nelson and Sons, London, 1868), pp 128 and 162 for a description of the Rock from the sea in the 1860s.
[109] *Gibraltar Chronicle*, 13 January 1859.
[110] *UKNA*, WO 17/1845, Monthly Return of the General and Staff Officers serving in Gibraltar for 1859.
[111] Bartlett, *Gleanings*, pp 165–6.

Britain 'in perpetuity' by the Treaty of Utrecht of 1713.[112] Through the 18th century Spain had made several unsuccessful attempts to wrest it back, most famously during the Great Siege. But Britain held it then and continued to do so right through the Napoleonic Wars, during which Gibraltar was an important refitting and victualling base.[113] Indeed, following Nelson's victory over the combined French and Spanish fleets off Cape Trafalgar in 1805, the flagship *Victory* had been towed into Rosia Bay for repairs before returning to England with the embalmed body of her admiral.

Contrary to what many who had not visited the territory imagined, the importance of Gibraltar to Britain was not primarily to control the shipping that passed through the Straits. The Spanish batteries at Tarifa dominated the narrowest part and the distance from Gibraltar to Morocco was too great for effective control from Gibraltar. But positioned as it was near the western entrance to the Mediterranean, Gibraltar provided Britain with a major naval base and a valuable garrison from which, together with Malta (ceded to Britain in 1814), the British could protect their interests in the Mediterranean and in particular the route to India through Egypt. This role increased during the course of the 19th century, especially from 1859 when French engineers began the construction of the Suez Canal.

Thus Warren arrived on the Rock at a key moment in the evolution of 'fortress Gibraltar'. Following the Crimean War, the late-1850s had seen the Great Powers of Europe initiating moves to expand and consolidate their territories. International tension, combined with mid-century technical innovation, especially in steam power, stimulated what was in effect an 'arms race'. In 1855 the Newcastle shipbuilder Sir William Armstrong had designed and produced the first wrought-iron, rifled, breech-loading field gun, and from 1858 various models of Armstrong guns were widely adopted throughout the British Empire and beyond; although from the 1860s and for a further two decades most large guns reverted to muzzle loading as the breech-loading mechanism was not yet perfected.[114]

Meanwhile, the French had embarked on 'an aggressive shipbuilding programme'.[115] In 1858 the French engineer and architect Dupuy de Lôme

[112] G. Hills, *Rock of Contention: A History of Gibraltar* (Robert Hale, London, 1974).
[113] Ernle Bradford, *Gibraltar: The History of a Fortress* (Grenada, London, 1971), pp 139–40.
[114] Tony Hill, *Guns and Gunners at Shoeburyness: The Experimental Establishment and Garrison* (Baron Books, Buckingham, 1999), p 49. Warren was to be involved in experimental artillery practices at Shoeburyness in the early 1870s.
[115] http://www.hmswarrior.org/history, accessed 2 December 1814.

laid the keel for the first iron-clad warship, *La Gloire*. Whereas the French built their ships on a wooden frame, the British responded with the world's first iron-hulled warship, HMS *Warrior*.[116] Launched in 1861 and in service the following year, when she visited Gibraltar, for a while the *Warrior* was the largest, fastest and best-armed warship in the world. The adoption of iron-hulled shipping that could move quickly in and out of range meant that land-based sea batteries had to be much better protected and armed with much more powerful guns.

At the same time the prospect of war with France had arisen once again. An assassination attempt on Napoleon III by a British-based Italian revolutionary in January 1858 heightened tension between the two traditional enemies. The Emperor survived the bomb blasts, but eight bystanders were killed and 150 wounded. The French blamed the British Government's relaxed asylum policy for the terrorist outrage, and for a few months war was a distinct possibility. This awoke some within the British establishment to the weakness of their southern coastal defences; although the realisation came amid post-Crimean War retrenchment and Parliament was reluctant to take on extra military costs.

In February 1859 Sir John Fox Burgoyne RE, Inspector-General of Fortifications, reported that Southern England's fortifications were no match for the new rifled cannon.[117] In the immediate aftermath of Burgoyne's report, a special two-man commission was sent to Gibraltar to determine what immediate action could be taken to strengthen the colony's defences without recourse to any additional grant from parliament. This brought Colonel J. H. Lefroy RA and Lt Colonel H. C. Owen RE to Gibraltar in March 1859, shortly after Warren's arrival.[118]

The two colonels made a brief survey of the Rock's defences before Lefroy conducted an experiment at Europa Point, observed by Colonel Stehelin and officers of the Royal Engineers, which would have included Lieutenant Warren. Lefroy ordered that a 68-pound (30kg) rifled gun loaded with 14 pounds (6.3kg) of powder should be fired from a distance of 175 metres at one of Europa's defensive walls, 1.6 metres thick. The first shot penetrated the outer limestone facing, the second enlarged the hole, and the third demolished the wall.

---

[116] Ian V. Hogg, *Coast Defences of England and Wales 1856–1956* (David & Charles, London, 1974). HMS *Warrior* has been restored and is on display in Portsmouth Harbour. See: http://www.hmswarrior.org/history.
[117] *UKNA*, WO 33/7, Confidential Print 018, 7 February 1859.
[118] Lefroy was to become a member of the Royal Commission. He was also appointed Secretary of a reorganised Ordnance Select Committee.

The view today from the King's Bastion, across the bay to the Spanish city of Algeciras. KEVIN SHILLINGTON

It was probably more of a demonstration than an experiment, for Lefroy and Owen must have been aware of the gun's capabilities; but it enabled them to recommend that the coastal parapets along Gibraltar's eastern seaboard and at Europa Point should be at least 3 metres thick and 2.5 metres in height.[119] They called for all 24- and 32-pound guns to be replaced by a higher calibre and for the sea batteries to be prepared to receive these armaments, with extra cover provided against enfilade and reverse fire. In the opinion of the commissioners, 'until this is done, we do not consider the Fortress safe from attack from the sea'. They stressed that the Royal Engineers should start immediately on this 'work of the most national importance'.[120]

Warren was allocated Europa Point, for which he prepared plans and estimates that would bring the Europa Bastions up to these requirements. He worked with a small platoon of sappers and had the use of convicts for

[119] *UKNA, WO 33/7, Memorandum on the Present and Proposed Garrisons of the Mediterranean*, Lefroy and Owen, 14 April 1859, pp 20–21, 37, 72.
[120] *Ibid.*, pp 71–73. See also, Royal Artillery Institute, Fortress Archives, Woolwich, MD 1143/36, typescript by Major Denis Rollo, ' The British Fortifications, Batteries & Barracks of Gibraltar", pp 11–12.

*Europa Point and Lighthouse, with Africa on the distant horizon. Warren's
Europa Bastion was in this area, though no evidence of it survives today.*
KEVIN SHILLINGTON

the heavy labour of construction. He was fortunate in that for much of his
early professional career he was to be given a series of tasks and left to his own
initiative to get on with it, usually with the aid of a few NCOs. This was the
first such occasion and he proved well up to the challenge. Despite his youth,
he seemed to have a natural way with the men and respected their abilities.
Physically working with them, he led by example, inspiring dedication and
teamwork.

Warren's first task was to design and build splinter-proof parapets for the
new guns. In doing so he realised that four men were required to work each
gun and that they had precious little space on the transverse platform in which
to load, swivel and run out the gun. Furthermore, the old-fashioned 'truck
lever' required three men to operate, during which they were exposed to the
dangers of enfilading fire. To solve this problem, Warren designed and drew
up plans for a 'side lever' that could be operated by one man from either side
under the cover of the traverse. Colonel Stehelin submitted the plan to Army
Headquarters in London, together with a dismantled specimen side lever that
Warren himself had made.

Initially, Warren's truck lever invention was rejected, the reason being revealed several years later in a minute of the Ordnance Select Committee. Apparently the model that Warren had sent in 1860 had been reassembled incorrectly, with the lever handles pointing in the wrong direction. This was clearly why it had been rejected as unworkable. It was not until years later, while he was still in Gibraltar, that Warren saw a copy of the report on his design and realised the error. He wrote immediately to Horse Guards explaining the apparent error and enclosing a working drawing of his proposed fitment for forwarding to the Committee. This time his design was successfully referred to the Superintendent of the Royal Carriage Department, from where it was brought into the Service and used for many years.[121]

* * *

Towards the end of his first year on the Rock, Warren made a decision that was to have a significant impact on his future life and career, not only in Gibraltar, but also wherever he was subsequently stationed. He accepted an invitation to become a Freemason.

Freemasonry had been practised in Gibraltar since the 18th century, with a mixture of local lodges and itinerant military lodges that came and went with their regiments. Warren's father was a Mason and almost certainly practised the Craft during his time on the Rock in the early 1850s. Warren senior had left Gibraltar for the Crimea only five years before his son arrived, and it is likely that some brother Masons who had known his father invited Charles Warren junior to join the fraternity of Freemasonry. The minimum age for admission was normally 21, but exceptions could be made, as for instance for a 'Lewis', one whose father was a Mason. And so on 30 December 1859, when he was still not yet twenty, Charles Warren became an initiate of the Royal Lodge of Friendship, Lodge 278. He was a keen student and within three weeks he was formally 'passed' from Entered Apprentice to Fellow Craft and 'raised' to the rank of Master Mason.[122]

Throughout his life Warren appears to have been guided by the simple maxim: 'If it's worth doing at all, it's worth doing well'. He certainly applied this to his Freemasonry. He appreciated its basic moral principles of honour and duty as well as its fraternity, and in particular the egalitarianism of its

---

[121] *UKNA*, WO 33/15, 2066, Minute 15,602, 26/5/65. 'Fitment to facilitate the running out of sliding carriages on traversing platforms. Proposed by Lieut. Warren, R.E.'

[122] Colin Macdonald, *WARREN! The Bond of Brotherhood* (C. N. Macdonald, Singapore, 2007), p 7.

structure. No matter what a brother's situation or status in daily life, within the lodge all were equal. In principle there were no bars to a man of humble origin attaining high office in Freemasonry, always provided that he was sufficiently dedicated to the Craft. This was certainly the case for the colonial lodges of the mid-19th century, although some of the more prestigious lodges in England were not so egalitarian, and some of the Caribbean lodges made strenuous efforts to exclude black men. For many initiates, Freemasonry was a means of social climbing. The fraternal bond of Freemasonry enabled an enthusiastic young man like Warren to develop personal relationships with people who otherwise would have been outside his normal social circle. A case in point was his friendship with Sir James Cochrane, Chief Justice of Gibraltar (1841–77), who was a Freemason. According to Williams, Warren became a frequent guest at the table of the Cochrane family.[123]

Freemasonry, however, was not just an open door into high social circles. A prominent Mason whom Warren much admired was Francis George Irwin, a sapper sergeant in the Royal Engineers. Twelve years older than Warren, Irwin was initiated into the Gibraltar Lodge in 1857 and became the driving force behind the revival of the defunct Inhabitants Lodge in 1858. The following year he was installed as its 'Worshipful Master'. Irwin researched Masonic history and its ancient rituals. Some of his interests were somewhat esoteric and on the fringe of mainstream Freemasonry, but he lectured periodically on the subjects of his research.

One of his lectures concerned the mythical origins of Freemasonry. Irwin followed many of his contemporaries in locating its origins in the brotherhood of stonemasons who had constructed the Biblical Temple of Solomon on Mount Moriah, in what is today the Old City of Jerusalem. He referred to King Solomon as 'our Grand Master'. The lecture was delivered a few weeks before Warren's arrival on the Rock, but printed copies were widely disseminated among the brethren. Once Warren joined the brotherhood of Freemasons, it would have been one of the things that he read as he set about immersing himself in everything Masonic. It is not too far-fetched to imagine that Irwin's reference to 'the still visible foundations of King's Solomon's Temple' may have awoken in Warren's mind a desire to someday explore the Holy Land.[124] He may well have discussed the Temple and its origins with Irwin himself. The two men did not belong to the same lodge: by the time Warren joined Inhabitant's

---

123 Williams, *The Life*, p 34.
124 Macdonald, *WARREN!*, p 204. Macdonald has reproduced the whole of Irwin's lecture in an Appendix, pp 197–205.

The banner of the Royal Lodge of Friendship, No. 278.
KEVIN SHILLINGTON, WITH PERMISSION FROM THE
GIBRALTAR MASONIC INSTITUTE

Lodge in January 1861, Irwin had left Gibraltar. Nor did they work together on the same engineering projects; but according to Robert Freke Gould, a fellow subaltern and former Master of Inhabitants Lodge who knew both men in Gibraltar, Warren had 'great respect for Irwin, both as a Freemason and as a soldier'.[125] The respect appears to have been mutual.

Other lodges that Warren joined in 1861 were the Royal Calpean Chapter and the Gibraltar Mark Lodge. His main loyalty, however, remained to the Friendship Lodge, and in December 1862 he was installed as its Worshipful Master, unusually, without ever having been its Warden. This would normally have been considered a rapid rise, although not that unusual in a place like Gibraltar where many of the brethren were transient soldiers. What was unusual was his age: he was still only 22, and yet among the officers of the Lodge during his year as Master were four other Royal Engineers, all

---

[125] Williams, *The Life*, p 11.

older than Warren and senior to him in Freemasonry membership, as well as in military rank.[126] He was clearly widely respected within the Masonic community of Gibraltar and during 1863 he was received into the prestigious Calpe Preceptory of Knights Templar.[127] At the end of his year as Master of Friendship Lodge, he was succeeded in the normal way by his Senior Warden, Brian Melville, a fellow lieutenant of Royal Engineers. Melville left on home leave in March 1864 and Warren, as a Past Master, acted for him. At the end of that year Warren was awarded his second Master's Jewel for service as acting Master, despite himself being absent on leave for three months of that year.[128]

* * *

Early in 1860 Colonel Stehelin gave Warren the task of preparing the first full trigonometrical ordnance survey of Gibraltar. It was *the* plum job for any young RE lieutenant on the Rock where variety and challenge of work were limited. The survey was a project of the highest importance, and yet Stehelin gave it to his most junior lieutenant, who had been under his command for little more than a year. Clearly Stehelin was impressed by the dedication, precision and initiative that Warren brought to his work. Was Stehelin a Freemason, and therefore favoured Warren? A search through available lodge records has not yet revealed his name; but there were many military lodges and it is possible that Stehelin was a Mason. But then so, too, were several other RE lieutenants, all senior to Warren, and yet Warren was the one that Stehelin chose.

From Warren's point of view it was a wonderful opportunity. At last he could put into practice all the Euclid's geometry and trigonometry that he had learned and loved since his schooldays at Cheltenham and before. And with it went the knowledge that his survey would form part of the work of the great Ordnance Survey Department based in Southampton.

The British Ordnance Survey, that producer of maps so beloved by modern hikers and cyclists, was founded in the 18th century to produce accurate maps for the Army, initially in Scotland to assist the 'pacification' of the Highlands following the Jacobite Rising of 1745–6. It was then extended to Ireland,

[126] Freemasons' Hall, Gibraltar, Lodge of Friendship, Attendance Book, 1862–64. I am indebted to Bro Keith Sheriff for granting me access to the attendance book, and making copies of these entries for me.
[127] Macdonald, *WARREN!*, pp 7–8.
[128] Lodge of Friendship, Attendance Book, 1862–64. See also Keith Sheriff, *The Rough Ashlar: The History of English Freemasonry in Gibraltar 1727–2002* (private pub., n.d.).

where the Army was always active, before focussing on the south coast of England, under threat of French invasion from the 1790s. During the first half of the 19th century it was to map the whole of the rest of the United Kingdom. Many eminent Royal Engineers led the project over the years, inventing and developing new methods and equipment along the way. It was the stuff that made reputations and careers. The trigonometric triangulation of Britain was finally completed in the early 1850s by Lieutenant Alexander Ross Clarke RE. His account of the observations and calculations, which contained detailed descriptions of the instruments used, was published in 1858.[129] It would almost certainly have been seen by Warren at Chatham, before his departure for Gibraltar. And it would have been clear to Warren that, in taking on the Gibraltar survey, he was following in the footsteps of Clarke and his renowned predecessors.

It took Warren the best part of four years to complete the Gibraltar survey, although he was not working on it to the exclusion of all else. During this time he honed his skills as a surveyor. He recognised that those who came after him would need to know they could rely upon the accuracy of his work. He clearly took great pride in the precision of his measurements and drawings, as anyone who has seen this or his subsequent work can attest. His survey, to a scale of 1:600 (50 feet to the inch), produced four long tracing sheets which were submitted to Southampton and now reside in the National Archives in Kew, West London.[130]

Subsequently, after Warren had left Gibraltar, two models of the 'Rock', based on his survey, were built out of plaster of Paris on a wooden frame. Completed in 1867, one was painted in natural colours by Captain R. A. Branfill of the 68th Regiment. It was sent to the Rotunda Museum in Woolwich where it remained until 1928 when it was sold back to the Gibraltar Government. It was cut into several sections before being safely packed for transfer back to Gibraltar by sea. Here it was reassembled and displayed for a couple of years at the Waterport, by the Old Mole, where disembarking visitors were charged to view it. This was not a financial success and in 1930 it was transferred to the newly opened Gibraltar Museum where a special upstairs gallery had to be extended out over the street to take in the full length of the model. And there it remains, a unique record of Warren's Gibraltar, as it was in the 1860s,

[129] A. R. Clarke, *Account of the Observations and Calculations of the Principal Triangulation of Great Britain and Ireland* (Eyre & Spottiswoode, London, 1858).
[130] *UKNA*, WO 78/2439.

The eastern face of the Rock. In his spare time Warren would climb this surface and chip off any footholds that might aid an assaulting enemy to clamber up Gibraltar's 'blind side'.
KEVIN SHILLINGTON

complete with houses, streets and bastions.[131]

Parallel to the survey work, Warren took on a number of other tasks. For instance, from the beginning of 1861 he was put in charge of the meteorological observations at the Royal Engineers' Observatory at Europa Point. His observations, together with his report on the current and recent weather, were vital for shipping in a place like Gibraltar and they were published regularly on the front page of the *Gibraltar Chronicle*.

And it was here at the Gibraltar Observatory that Warren first worked with Corporal Henry Birtles: a reliable and dedicated sapper, as fearless as Warren himself. Warren taught Birtles all he knew about astronomy, and the corporal managed to transfer to Warren's survey team. They developed a good working relationship and established a strong professional and personal respect for each other that was to pay off in the future when Warren chose Birtles as his senior NCO to accompany him to Jerusalem in 1867.

While conducting his survey of the steep, eastern side of the Rock, Warren noticed that on close examination the eastern face was not as sheer as might appear from below. There were a large number of crevices and potential footholds that, in his opinion, might enable an assaulting enemy to clamber up, on Gibraltar's blind side, so to speak, and attack the western garrison from above. He pointed this out to Colonel Stehelin and was put to work to rectify it. Thus, from 1861, whenever he needed a break from the survey work, Warren would climb the eastern face, unsupported, and chip away at any footholds that might aid an enemy.[132] At times he lowered himself down from the top by rope and used explosives to dislodge large rocks. It was a dangerous operation, but Warren took challenges like this in his stride. It may have reminded him of the excitement he got from jumping off great heights while at school.

* * *

In October 1861 the *Himalaya* docked at the South Mole and disembarked a new company of Royal Engineers to replace one that was returning to England. To Warren's delight the lieutenant of the new company was William Salmond, a former student colleague from RMA Woolwich who had been commissioned a few months ahead of himself. The two young men became close friends during their years on the Rock.

A few months after Salmond's arrival, Warren introduced him to

---

[131] S. G. Benady and T. J. Finlayson, 'Models of the Rock', *Gibraltar Heritage Journal*, 1994, Vol 2 (2nd edition 2006), pp 55–9.
[132] Williams, *The Life*, p 31.

Freemasonry. He was initiated into the Friendship Lodge in January 1862 and passed and raised to Master Mason within a month, an indication of the regularity of Lodge meetings.[133] On the engineering side, Salmond was put in charge of erecting barrack buildings at Catalan Bay, on the narrow strip of land between the eastern face of the Rock and the sea. Henceforth Warren had to be careful when blasting away at footholds that he did not drop any boulders on Salmond, his men or the new barracks.[134]

Ever since his schooldays Warren had taken any opportunity to test his courage and his physicality, and he saw a good challenge in his work on the Rock. He proposed to his friends Salmond and two other subalterns, Montgomery and Gamble, that they climb the eastern face of the Rock, unaided, from sea level to its highest point, for it was something that would not be possible once he had chipped away all the footholds. Warren was very much the leader in his group of friends, and when he suggested something, they followed. That challenge completed, Warren and his friends 'often climbed [the Rock] in many places'.[135] Clearly, he never made the eastern face 'unclimbable'.

Warren probably knew the Rock better than anyone in Gibraltar at the time and he was determined to explore every crevice of it. He was particularly interested in the numerous caves to be found on both sides of the Rock, and he explored just about all of them. This was not uncommon among young military officers in Gibraltar where there were few interesting off-duty pursuits, and senior officers encouraged it accordingly.

The largest cave, St Michael's, had been explored by several officers in the 1840s and reports from them had been recorded in the Royal Engineers' office in Chatham, along with a plan of the whole cavern, completed by Lieutenant Goodall RE in 1858. Warren had probably seen these, as he would have been keen to find out all there was to be known about Gibraltar before his departure. The entrance to St Michael's Cave is 300 metres above sea level, 100 metres below the summit on the western side. The entrance opens into a huge, cathedral-like cavern, full of stalactites and stalagmites. Today its dramatic beauty is displayed by electric light of varying colours, but Warren would have explored it by candlelight. Beyond the main cavern, he found numerous passageways that led steeply down to other caverns. According to his own report, he went to the bottom of St Michael's 'more than twenty

[133] Lodge of Friendship, Attendance Book, 1862–64. See also Sheriff, *The Rough Ashlar*.
[134] Williams, *The Life*, p 31.
[135] *Ibid.*, pp 32–3.

The galleries of Gibraltar's siege tunnels followed the natural seams in the rock. It may have been from scenes such as this that Warren developed his fascination for geology. KEVIN SHILLINGTON

times' and broke into new caverns 'with crowbars and jumpers'.[136]

Although neither he nor Williams mentions it, he must have visited the siege tunnels for which Gibraltar was so famous. These were man-made horizontal galleries cut high up through the inside of the north face of the Rock. They were constructed during the Great Siege by the 'Corps of Artificers', the ancestor to the Royal Engineers.[137] As an engineer himself, Warren would have appreciated the way the galleries made use of the natural geology to

---

[136] Charles Warren, 'Notes on the Caves of Gibraltar', *Quarterly Journal of the Geological Society*, 1865, Vol 21, p 371.

[137] The Corps of Artificers had been founded at Gibraltar in 1772: see '*Memorandum* by Captain Conolly RE', Appendix D in Francis B. Head, *The Royal Engineers* (Murray, London, 1869), pp 380–84.

follow seams in the rock. At regular intervals, holes were cut through to the outside so that cannons could be pointed down onto the 'neutral ground' that separated Gibraltar from Spain. To this day they can be seen from the direction of the airport, which runs across that neutral ground, as a line of black holes high up on the white rock of the north face. These and the caverns that Warren explored stimulated his interest in geology, and he made copious notes on his observations in and around Gibraltar. Salmond observed that he was an inveterate writer of notes, always carrying a large notebook, the leaves of which he covered in tiny writing.[138]

It should be remembered that in the year Warren arrived on the Rock, Charles Darwin published his theory of evolution by natural selection, *On the Origin of Species*, and the Oxford Debate the following year gave evolutionary theory enormous publicity.[139] The general concept of evolution had been around for some time. It was widely debated in scientific circles from the 1820s, with reference to the geology of the earth. By then it was realised that the earth must be many millions of years old, rather than the 6000 years promoted by a literal reading of the Biblical story of Creation. The concept of geological evolution was encapsulated in Sir Charles Lyell's three-volume work, *Principles of Geology*, published in 1830–33.[140] It explained in particular the principle of stratigraphy, the laying down of layers of rock, the oldest of which must necessarily be at the bottom. It was a concept that appealed to Charles Warren's scientific mind. He may well have read Lyell's work before he came to Gibraltar, but in any case there was a copy in the Garrison Library where Warren was a regular reader. And he was able to see an example of Lyell's stratigraphy in Gibraltar's eastern face, where 'the strata of the rock … [was] usually covered over by a very recent formation'.[141]

∗ ∗ ∗

Apart from rock climbing and cavern exploring, whenever he could get a few days or a week or so of local leave, Warren would go off on long walking trips into Spain, usually accompanied by Salmond or some other fellow officer.

---

[138] Williams, *The Life*, p 77. The keeping of a diary like this was a habit that Warren retained throughout his working life. Unfortunately his notebooks have not survived.
[139] For more on the 'Great Debate', see: http://www.oum.ox.ac.uk/learning/pdfs/debate.pdf.
[140] Charles Lyell, *Principles of Geology: Being an Attempt to Explain the Former Changes of the Earth's Surface, by Reference to Causes Now in Operation*, 3 vols (John Murray, London, 1830–33).
[141] Warren, 'Notes on the Caves of Gibraltar', p 371.

Gibraltar and Southern Spain.

There seemed to be no barrier to British officers passing to and fro across the 'neutral ground', in the same way that Spanish civilians commuted daily from La Línea into Gibraltar for work, as they do today. Within half a day's walk of the colony was the town of San Roque and the nearby corkwoods, in whose pleasant glades officers and their ladies were accustomed to picnic. But Warren was for longer walks, up into the Ronda Mountains to the dramatic clifftop Moorish city of Ronda, or around the bay to Algeciras and the villages beyond. He would think nothing of covering 60 kilometres in a day.

Warren never travelled with servant or guide, but relied on a compass and local maps that he sketched for himself on his travels, adding to them on every trip. He was not fussy about accommodation and stayed overnight in whatever local *venta* or *posada* he could find. A two-day walk could take him to Spain's southernmost point at Tarifa where at least once he boarded a ship across the Straits to Tangier. On one occasion in 1861 he went as far as the Canary Islands. Alternatively, from Algeciras he could take a train to Granada. On a few occasions, when leave was of a week or more, he and a friend took ship to Cádiz on Southern Spain's Atlantic Coast from where they could travel by train to Seville or Córdoba which they would explore on foot.

In this way he got the exercise he enjoyed and at the same time satisfied his irrepressible curiosity. He learned to appreciate other countries and cultures, and picked up some rudimentary Spanish. Besides, it was a relief to get away from the unhealthy atmosphere that often characterised Gibraltar.[142] The 'Levanter', that easterly wind that blows through the Western Mediterranean, particularly plagues Gibraltar. At times it brings an oppressive moist air that can hang as a foggy cloud for long periods over the Rock and its city. Warren's brother John had written to a friend in 1850: 'Don't envy me this climate, as there is neither luck nor grace in it, and since I have made its acquaintance I have not felt properly healthy.'[143] Reason enough for his younger brother Charles to get away into the Spanish mountains as often as he could.

Towards the end of July 1862, after three and a half years on the Rock, Warren departed on his first home leave. He was to be away for a total of four months, during which time he met someone who was to have an important impact on the rest of his life.

---

[142] *Ibid.*, pp 34–36.
[143] Quoted in Williams, *The Life*, p 34.

CHAPTER 4

From Gibraltar to Jerusalem

Lieutenant Warren arrived in Portsmouth in the first week of August 1862 to be met by his father, who was himself on long leave having just completed a six-year assignment in Malta. Warren senior had recently been appointed Honorary Regimental Colonel of the 96th Foot, a position that he would take up, in Belfast, the following February.[144] For the moment, he was able to spend time with his son, whom he had not seen since he was first commissioned four and a half years previously. According to Williams, Warren went 'on a round of visits with his father at Wroot and Guildford and at various places in Scotland'.[145] What Williams does not reveal, perhaps because of his grandfather's reticence, was that it was while on this leave that Charles Warren junior began courting the young lady who would in due course become his wife.

They probably met at Wroot, the home of his uncle and aunt, Revd William and Anne Warren, who had acted as surrogate parents to Charlie and Billie during their boarding school holidays. The young lady in question, Fanny Margaretta Haydon, was a niece to Anne Warren (née Bethell).

Anne Warren's father, Revd George Bethell, Fellow of Eton College and Rector of Worplesdon, Surrey, had one son and seven daughters. Anne was the eldest, and one of her sisters, Fanny, had married Samuel Haydon, Esquire, banker and Mayor of Guildford in Surrey.[146] They had two children, a son and a daughter. The daughter, Fanny Margaretta Haydon, was born 2 May 1840, just three months after Charles Warren. She was christened by her grandfather, Revd George Bethell, at Worplesdon on 2 July. Young Fanny Margaretta and Charles were, in effect, first cousins by marriage, Revd William Warren being Charles's uncle and his wife Anne being aunt to Fanny.

As such, both families would have regarded this as a very suitable match. Not only was there the family connection, and the fact that they were both

---

[144] See the *Army Lists* for 1862–63.
[145] Williams, *The Life*, p 33.
[146] *UKNA*, PROB 11/2250.353. Here, the Will of Revd George Bethell lays out the relationship.

from good High Anglican families, but also there was an additional advantage from the Warren point of view: the banker Samuel Haydon was a wealthy man. Fanny would almost certainly bring a considerable dowry to the marriage, an important consideration for a young Army officer from a financially modest background who would need more than his Army salary to maintain the social expectations of an advancing military career.

Charles and Fanny may well have met previously, during the school holidays of the early 1850s. But whether the first meeting was then, or now at Wroot, their interest in each other would have been the reason for Charles' and his father's visit to Guildford that summer. Of course, it is possible that they did not meet at Wroot, had possibly never met before, and the visit to Guildford was part of a family plan to bring the two of them together. However it came about, there was clearly a meeting of minds and the young lieutenant was smitten.

Williams, who made no mention of this, records Warren's home leave as lasting just six weeks, whereas the *Return of General and Staff Officers serving in Gibraltar* reveals that in September 1862 Warren applied for an extension of leave by a further two months, to 2 December. This may have been so that he could spend more time getting to know Fanny. But the extension coincided with one applied for by William Salmond, who had come home on leave in September.[147] It seems likely that the two friends met up in England and the extension of leave by both of them was so they could spend time together, probably walking and climbing in Scotland.

On 2 December 1862 Lieutenants Warren and Salmond reported back for duty in Gibraltar to find that, while they had been away, the Royal Engineers commander, Colonel Stehelin, had been succeeded by Colonel Edward Charles Frome, author of the handbook on surveying that had been Warren's daily guide since his days at RMA Woolwich. Warren could not have asked for a better commanding officer if he had had the choice, for through that handbook Frome had, vicariously, been his mentor of surveying. Furthermore, Frome was a Freemason, which no doubt aided Warren's becoming a close family friend.

Warren's Masonic brethren were clearly pleased to welcome him back, for later that month they elected him Worshipful Master of the Friendship Lodge. Warren had clearly made a strong and favourable impression among Gibraltar's Masonic brethren over the previous two years, for not only had he

---

[147] WO 17/1848.

Fanny Margaretta Haydon.
WARREN FAMILY COLLECTION

not previously served as Senior Warden, the usual route to preferment, but also to be elected Master of a Masonic lodge at the age of only 22 was indeed an unusual and significant honour. And the importance of personal friendship within the Masonic fraternity was illustrated by Warren's first decision as Master. The position of Junior Warden in the Friendship Lodge being vacant, he appointed William Salmond to the post.[148]

Any high spirits that Warren may have felt that December, however, would have been somewhat dampened by a particularly bad bout of stomach cramp. Gastric problems were common in Gibraltar on account of the poor state of the fresh water and drainage systems on the Rock, something that was only finally sorted out towards the end of Warren's time there.[149] As it was, he suffered persistently through the winter of 1863 and grew frustrated that he should have every outward appearance of good health, and yet suffer such intense internal pain. The only advice he got was not to think about it and it would go away. As he confided to his diary, 'I would leave it behind fast enough if it would only abandon me'. He believed it was only his phenomenal powers of concentration that enabled him to carry on his work. The pain finally left him after three months, and then a stiff walk round the bay to Algeciras with a friend and a good meal at the *Casa de Pupilos* restored his spirits.[150]

* * *

The rest of 1863 was an exciting time for Warren. He was more than halfway through his Survey of Gibraltar; he was Master of a Masonic lodge; and, through the postal system, he was developing a long-distance relationship with Fanny Haydon. It was also the year he began in his spare time to assist in the archaeological work being carried out, unofficially, by Captain Frederick Brome, a former infantry officer who was governor of the military prison in Gibraltar.

The Darwinian theory of natural selection had stimulated a huge interest in the ancient bones of extinct species that abounded in numerous caves across Europe. And Gibraltar was no exception. Indeed, in 1848 a human-like skull had been found in a Gibraltan cave by Lieutenant Edmund Flint. It was only after a similar skull, found in Germany's Neander Valley in 1856,

---

[148] Lodge of Friendship, Attendance Book, 1862–64.
[149] Richard Ford, *The Handbook for Travellers in SPAIN*, 8th edition, Part II (Murray, London, 1892), p 420.
[150] Williams, *The Life*, p 34.

was analysed and the results published in 1864, that it was realised that Flint's 'Gibraltar Skull' was in fact the earliest discovered specimen of what is now known as *Homo neanderthalensis*. Had the 'Gibraltar Skull' been analysed and its results published in the 1850s, the Neanderthals might have been known instead as '*Homo gibraltarensis*'.

Early in 1863 Captain Brome began exploring Gibraltar's 'Genista Cave', entrance to which was gained through a small fissure on Windmill Hill Flats, not far from the barracks of the Royal Engineers. It is thus not surprising that Brome's work came to the attention of Lieutenant Warren. He and an artillery lieutenant, Alexander Burton-Brown, joined Brome in his excavation of the cave complex. Genista Cave had not been explored since the 1820s, from which it was known to hold an enormous number of ancient bones.[151]

The cave extended steeply down through several caverns to 200 feet below Windmill Hill, and the intrepid explorers only had candlelight to guide them. Initially they lowered themselves by rope, but in due course they built rope ladders so that they could bring their finds to the surface. Brome and his companions found huge deposits of bones belonging to large land mammals, apparently extinct forms of elephant and rhinoceros. But they also found, among the upper chambers, what appeared to be 'human remains … in great abundance', as well as artefacts: shards of pottery and sharp stone 'tools'.[152]

As an archaeological excavator, Brome was entirely self-taught, but he appreciated the need to precisely record, measure and describe everything he found, and in this he would have had the full support of Charles Warren. Genista was clearly a scientifically important site and, determined that Gibraltar would not be upstaged by subsequent discoveries elsewhere; they decided to draw up a full report and submit it to London for expert analysis. With this in mind, a plan and a cross-section of the cave were drawn, almost certainly by Warren, the engineer of the party; and in August 1863 these accompanied Brome's report, which, together with detailed drawings, descriptions and examples of their finds, was despatched to London.

The War Office referred the whole package to the President of the Geological Society, Professor Andrew Ramsay, for his opinion of its 'importance in the

---

[151] Charles Murchison (ed.), *Palæontological Memoirs and Notes of the late Hugh Falconer*, Vol II, 'On the Fossil Contents of the Genista Cave, Gibraltar' (Robert Hardwicke, London, 1868), pp 561–2; See also, Edward Rose and John Diemer, 'British Pioneers of the Geology of Gibraltar, Part 2: Cave Archaeology and Geological Survey of the Rock, 1863 to 1878', *Earth Sciences History*, 2014, Vol. 33, No. 1, pp. 26–58.
[152] Murchison, *Falconer Memoirs*, II, pp 559–61.

interests of science of following up the exploration, and for suggestions as to the manner in which it could be best conducted'.[153] Ramsay could see immediately the significance of the work, and at his urging the Secretary-at-War sanctioned the 'further exploration of the cavern by means of the labour of the military prisoners, under the able superintendence of Capt. Brome'.[154] And, for detailed analysis, Ramsay referred Brome's report, drawings and samples to Dr Hugh Falconer, the country's foremost authority on the archaeology of ossiferous caves. Falconer, who had excavated similar collections in South Wales and in Sicily, realised Genista was a cave of great scientific interest.

Meanwhile, that September, Warren was home again on leave, this time for just three weeks.[155] With the journey by sea taking five or six days each way, he would not have had long in England. His father was away in Belfast, and it is likely that the main purpose of the trip was to visit Fanny Haydon in Guildford.

He returned to Gibraltar to learn that prison labour had been authorised to assist the Genista excavations; and besides working on his ordnance survey, we can assume that Warren would have spent much of his spare time assisting Brome in recording and describing their finds. Examples were sent on a regular basis to Dr Falconer in London, 'carefully classified, by means of distinctive marks'.[156]

Warren was back in England the following February, 1864, this time for a month. By the end of this visit, if not before, he would have been engaged to Fanny. The marriage was arranged for that September. Warren spent the intervening months in Gibraltar completing work on the survey, after which Colonel Frome granted him nine weeks' leave, commencing 21 August.

Unable to get a berth on a regular troopship, the eager young bridegroom sailed at his own expense on the P&O screw steamship *Baroda*, reaching Southampton on 27 August.[157] Five days later, on Thursday 1 September 1864, Charles Warren and Fanny Margaretta Haydon were married in the Church of the Holy Trinity in Guildford. We can assume his father would have come over from Belfast for the wedding, although Billie was absent, still serving in Canada. The newly married couple went to Scotland for their honeymoon. They headed for the south-eastern Uplands, to the small village of Kirkmichael

---

[153] *Ibid.*, p 554.
[154] *Idem.*
[155] WO 17/1849.
[156] Murchison, *Falconer Memoirs*, II, p 554.
[157] *The Times*, 29 August 1864.

in Ayrshire.[158] Kirkmichael is a little off the beaten track, south of the town of Ayr, and Warren had probably found it while exploring the region with William Salmond two years previously. The village, consisting then of not much more than an inn, a church, a few houses and a small Elementary School, lies in a beautiful valley amid rolling hills with a stream running through. After a month in Scotland, Lieutenant and Mrs Charles Warren had two further weeks in which to visit family and friends before boarding ship for Gibraltar.

Warren was due back from leave by 25 October and he probably timed the journey so as to arrive a few days before. The Colonel's wife, Mrs Frome, who had at least two unmarried daughters with her, took Fanny under her wing and introduced her to their social circle in Gibraltar.[159]

* * *

One of the first things Warren would have learned on his return was that during the month he had been honeymooning in Scotland, Dr Falconer and the naturalist Mr George Busk FRS had visited Gibraltar at the invitation of the Governor, Sir William Codrington. Their visit had been financed by the British Association for the Advancement of Science. They had spent the best part of September examining the 'collections and collateral subjects' of Genista Cave. Falconer's report, submitted in the form of a letter of thanks to the Governor, praised Captain Brome's work and extended particular thanks to Colonel Frome and his Royal Engineers. Warren is not mentioned by name: Brome was the officer in charge of the excavation, and Warren was not present during Falconer's visit. But we can be sure that Colonel Frome would have told Falconer of Warren's involvement in the Genista excavation, and on Warren's return, he would have shown him a copy of Falconer's report.

Falconer praised the 'persevering energy and vigour with which [Brome had] followed up the enquiry', remarking that:

> the minute and scrupulous care with which he has discriminated and arranged the objects, is worthy of the highest commendation, and more especially so as the subject was new to him. We are inclined to believe that the labour of the prisoners was never better directed in the interest of science.[160]

Significantly for Warren, Falconer went on to remark that, although he had only had time for a 'cursory examination of the geology of the rock', he believed

---

[158] Williams, *The Life*, p 35.
[159] *Idem.*
[160] Murchison, *Falconer Memoirs*, II, pp 562–3.

it was of the greatest importance that a full geological survey be undertaken:

> Now that a complete topographical survey of the rock has been completed
> on a large scale, a geological survey would be a matter of comparative ease;
> and we would submit to your Excellency's consideration the expediency of
> an application being made for the services of an assistant from the Geological
> Survey of England, to be deputed for the purpose. The area is so compact
> and limited that the survey, including that of the surrounding bay, need not
> occupy much time.[161]

Warren had completed six years on the Rock: few stayed longer than that.
His Ordnance Survey had been formally signed off, and in this he had proved
himself a surveyor of high calibre. Realising his time in Gibraltar would soon
be drawing to a close, he identified a new role for himself. What could be
better than to follow up his topographical survey with the geological one?
He saw himself as the ideal man for the job. Realising he needed to bring his
name to the fore, he sat down to write a paper on the caves of Gibraltar for
presenting to the Geological Society. At the end of 1864 he sent his paper to
Professor Andrew Ramsay. In Warren's absence, it was read to a meeting of the
Geological Society in March 1865. In this paper he referred to the need for a
geological survey of the Rock and offered to place his services at the disposal
of the Geological Survey of England.[162]

Meanwhile, before he left the Rock that had become so familiar to him, he
was determined to show Fanny something of the Spain that he had enjoyed
so much. He realised this could not be a 65-kilometre-a-day hike, so he
proposed forming a small party and making an excursion on horseback to
Granada. He applied for two weeks' local leave. Colonel Frome liked the idea
and agreed that his daughter Nellie should go with them. William Salmond
was in England on sick leave and Warren persuaded a couple of fellow RE
lieutenants, Sturt and Bolland, to go with them. They hired some horses and
made their way up through the Ronda Mountains to Granada where they
stayed a couple of days before returning through the small fishing villages of
the Costa del Sol. It was judged by all to be a most successful holiday.[163]

* * *

---

[161] *Ibid.*, p 561.

[162] Charles Warren, 'Notes on the Caves of Gibraltar', *Quarterly Journal of the Geological Society*, 1865, Vol 21, p 371.

[163] Williams, *The Life*, pp 36–8, in which is quoted a letter from Nellie Frome to an aunt describing the journey.

On 9 July 1865 Charles and Fanny Warren set sail from Gibraltar, no doubt much missed by their numerous friends, and the Fromes promising to keep in touch. Leave for officers serving overseas was quite generous and Warren had a further two months owing to him. He was not due to take up his new position as Assistant Instructor in Surveying at the School of Military Engineering in Chatham until 17 September.

They arrived back in England in time for a reunion with Billie. *The Times* of the previous month reported that among those who were presented to HRH The Prince of Wales at a Royal Levée at St James's Palace on 7 June was Lt. William Warren of the 60th Rifles, newly returned from Canada.[164] Billie had not had a very eventful time in Canada. Unlike some in his battalion, he was not into hunting, the main off-duty pursuit of military officers. The most notable hunter in the battalion was a certain larger-than-life character, Lieutenant (later General Sir) Redvers Buller, who was to feature significantly in Charles Warren's life towards the end of their respective careers.

During these two months Charles and Fanny stayed with her family in Guildford. Warren probably got in touch with Colonel Sir Henry James, head of the Ordnance Survey Department in Southampton, where they had received his Gibraltar Survey and were preparing it for tracing and publication. He also contacted Professor Andrew Ramsay at the Geological Society in London.

Ramsay had been impressed by Warren's paper on the caves of Gibraltar and had apparently approached the War Office seeking permission for Warren to work with him on the Geological Survey of the colony. Indeed, according to Williams, Warren received an appointment for the job from the War Office that September. Things were working out just as Warren had hoped. He would soon be going back to Gibraltar. But the project ran into financial problems, it being undecided which department would shoulder the costs and Warren's plan for his future fell through. He ended up taking the teaching post in Chatham.[165] Professor Ramsay did not get to make the Geological Survey of Gibraltar until 1876, by which time Warren had moved on to other, much more exciting projects.

* * *

Charles and Fanny settled into the married quarters in Brompton Barracks and he began his new job as an Assistant Instructor of Surveying.

[164] *The Times*, 8 June 1865.
[165] Williams, *The Life*, pp 38–9.

In his nearly seven years of absence from Chatham, the Barracks had been expanded considerably. There was a whole new set of classrooms, and the accommodation blocks for officers and men had been extended by raising the roofs and adding a third floor.[166] In his teaching Warren would have made the most of his practical experience in the field, adding his own drawings and examples of problems to those provided in Frome's handbook, which was still the standard text, then in its third edition.

There had been a lot of change and infrastructure development in Britain during Warren's years in Gibraltar. Industry and housing were expanding rapidly and rail links now connected all the cities and most of the large towns in England. Rail expansion had even started going underground in 1863 with the opening of the world's first underground railway in London, the Metropolitan line. In the months before Warren's return hundreds of new limited-liability railway companies, taking advantage of the new Companies Acts, were floated on the London Stock Exchange. Share prices soared and the inevitable bubble burst on the original 'Black Friday', 11 May 1866. The appellation originated from the black margins printed on the newspapers reporting the crash the next morning.

Warren would have appreciated the advantages of being at the heart of the Empire instead of in the backwater of its smallest colony, not least for the wealth of information available from the national newspapers, delivered daily by rail to the Medway towns. He would have read in July 1866 of the *Great Eastern*'s successful laying of the first trans-Atlantic telegraphic cable, from Bantry Bay in West Cork to Trinity Bay in Newfoundland. And less welcome news: it was a hot summer that year and an outbreak of cholera killed 8000 people, more than 1000 being claimed in a single week in London.

Warren would have taken a liberal reformist view of the politics of the period. Prime Minister Palmerston's death in October 1865 opened the way for parliamentary reform, an issue that dominated political discussion through 1866 and split the Liberal Party. There were huge public meetings in London and other cities during the summer of 1866. And the Metropolitan Police Commissioner, Sir Richard Mayne, provoked a riot when he attempted to ban a meeting of the Reform League in Hyde Park in July. Twenty years later, Warren was to face similar problems when, for two and a half years, he was himself Commissioner of the Metropolitan Police.

---

[166] Peter Kendall, *The Royal Engineers at Chatham 1750–2012* (English Heritage, 2012), pp 118–22.

*Charles Warren's father, Major-General Sir
Charles Warren, KCB, in retirement in the 1860s.*
WARREN FAMILY COLLECTION

But in Chatham in the summer of 1866 a happier event focussed the attention of the Warrens, the birth of their first-born, a daughter. They named her Mary in memory of his mother and his infant sister, although she was known in the family by her second name, Violet.

It was about this time that Warren's father, who had been knighted in the New Year's honours list, moved with the 96th Regiment from Belfast to Colchester, just a few hours' journey away by rail from Chatham.[167] It was now possible for father and son to meet occasionally, perhaps for a day or a weekend. This was just as well, for on 27 October, on his 68th birthday,

[167] *Hart's Army List*, 1866.

Major-General Sir Charles Warren, KCB, died.[168] It is not known whether the death at this time was anticipated or preceded by illness. Williams does not mention it at all. But it would have marked a turning point in the life of his eldest surviving son who was now the head of the family. John, the eldest son, had died of his wound in Scutari; Margaret, who had married Lieutenant St. John in Gibraltar, had followed her husband to India and no more appears to have been heard of her; and Charlotte and Mary had died in childhood. That left just Charles and Billie of the original six siblings.

By this time events were already unfolding that would lead to what was to become one of the great highlights of Charles Warren's career, and which first brought his name to public attention, namely the archaeological excavation of Jerusalem.

* * *

Interest in the Holy Land, in Europe and North America, had been rising since the early 19th century as an increasing number of travellers, religious figures and artists brought back tales and images from Ottoman Palestine. Britain opened a consulate in Jerusalem in 1839 and this was followed by the consulates of France, Austria, Russia and others. In 1838 the leading American theologian and linguist Dr Edward Robinson visited the Holy Land and in 1841 he published a three-volume account of his journey and discoveries in Palestine, the most significant feature of which was the huge number of Biblical sites he had identified.[169] It was a time of awakening for Protestant Evangelical Christianity, especially in America where there was a strong emphasis upon the land of the Bible. In the words of archaeologist Neil Silberman, interest in the Holy Land 'reached fever pitch in the years that followed'.[170]

Three names were prominent in the rising British interest in the Holy Land: Revd Arthur Stanley, academic and Dean of Westminster (from 1863), George Grove, intellectual polymath and Secretary of the new Crystal

---

[168] I am grateful to Mr Richard Wigram, widower of the late Angela Rahilly Wigram, great-granddaughter of the younger Charles Warren, for providing me with a copy of the *Warren Family Tree*, from which the date of the father's death is drawn.

[169] Edward Robinson, *Biblical Researches in Palestine and Adjacent Countries* (Crocker & Brewster, Boston, and John Murray, London, 1841).

[170] Neil A. Silberman, *Digging for God & Country: Exploration, Archeology, and the Secret Struggle for the Holy Land, 1799–1917* (Alfred Knopf, New York, 1982), p 65.

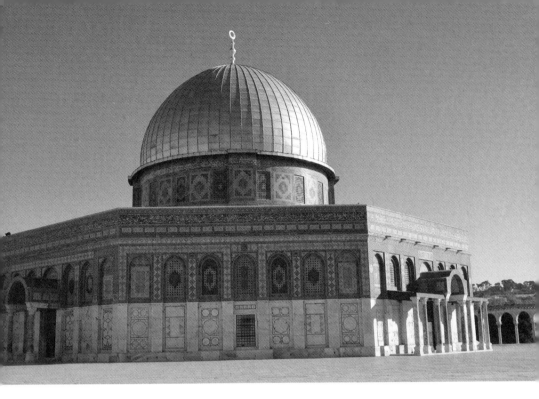

The Dome of the Rock.
KEVIN SHILLINGTON

Palace Company,[171] and James Fergusson, a widely travelled and renowned architectural historian who had made his name in India. Stanley had visited the Holy Land in 1852–53, and while working on the book of his researches,[172] he sought the assistance of George Grove. According to Grove's own recollection, he 'rubbed up [his] Hebrew' and 'plunged with delight into the sea of Biblical research'.[173] In 1856 Fergusson became General Manager of the Crystal Palace Company and brought displays of Asian art and architecture to this important cultural centre in South London. He and Grove became close friends and Fergusson expounded to Grove his controversial theory about two of the most important buildings in Jerusalem.

Jerusalem in the mid-19th century was mostly confined within the walls

[171] Charles L. Graves, *The Life and Letters of Sir George Grove, CB* (Macmillan, London, 1903), pp 37–40. The Crystal Palace Company had been formed to purchase the Crystal Palace that had housed the Great Exhibition of 1851 in Hyde Park. Under Grove's direction the Palace was dismantled and re-erected and expanded as an artistic and cultural centre on Sydenham Hill in South London.

[172] Arthur P. Stanley, *Sinai and Palestine in Connection with their History* (John Murray, London, 1856).

[173] Quoted in Graves, *Life and Letters of Grove*, p 48.

of what is now known as the Old City. On the eastern edge of this city stands a raised platform that covers the top of Mount Moriah. It is known to Jews as the Temple Mount and to Muslims as the Haram al-Sharif ('the Noble Sanctuary'). In the centre of the platform is the famous golden-domed shrine, known as the 'Dome of the Rock', which covers the peak of Mount Moriah. It is believed in Jewish and Muslim tradition that it was on this Rock that Abraham was prepared to sacrifice his son Isaac. And Jewish tradition holds that it was on or near this Rock that Solomon built the first Temple in the 10th century BCE. The Temple was subsequently destroyed and rebuilt twice; the second time by Herod the Great in about 20 CE. Herod enlarged the platform, creating the walls that, with much repair and restoration over the centuries, still stand today. The Temple and the upper part of the walls of the platform were destroyed by the Romans in 70 CE.

Muslim tradition holds that it was from the Rock of Mount Moriah, known to Muslims as the 'Sakhrah', that the Prophet Muhammad ascended into Heaven. Following the Arab Muslim conquest of Palestine in 636 CE, the Al-Aqsa Mosque was built near the southern edge of the platform of the Haram, and subsequently, the Muslim shrine of the Dome of the Rock was built over the peak of Mount Moriah, its golden dome, ever since, forming the defining image of Jerusalem.[174] Jews, forbidden to pray on the Haram itself, pray against the Western Wall of the platform, which is as near as they can get to what they believe to be the site of Solomon's Temple.

In 1861 James Fergusson published a pamphlet in which he challenged the validity of the holiest sites in Jerusalem for all three faiths, Christians, Jews and Muslims.[175] Fergusson had never been to Jerusalem, but he considered this irrelevant to his cause, since 'all the data for informing [his] opinion were available in this country', in the form of artists drawings and measurements and historic texts.[176]

Fergusson claimed that the Dome of the Rock, which clearly exhibited Byzantine influence, must be the church that the 4th-century Byzantine Emperor Constantine the Great had ordered to be constructed over the Holy Sepulchre, the burial chamber of Jesus of Nazareth. According to Fergusson,

[174] Simon Sebag Montefiore, *Jerusalem: The Biography* (Phoenix, London, 2012), pp 207–21.
[175] J. Fergusson, *Notes on the Site of the Holy Sepulchre in Jerusalem* (John Murray, London, 1861).
[176] J. Fergusson, *The Holy Sepulchre and the Temple at Jerusalem* (John Murray, London, 1865), p 62.

the widely recognised 'Church of the Holy Sepulchre', a twin-domed building in the western, Christian quarter of the Old City, did not display any Byzantine authenticity. It was of a much later style, obviously a Crusader church of the 12th century. Furthermore, it was situated *inside* the city walls, whereas it was well known from the Gospel of St John that Jesus was crucified and buried *outside* the city walls.[177] And if the Dome of the Rock were the true Church of the Holy Sepulchre, then it could not have been the site of the Herodian Temple of the Jews, which Fergusson boldly shifted to the south-west corner of the Haram, near the site of the present Al-Aqsa Mosque.

Fergusson's renown as a world expert on Asian and Muslim architecture ensured that his controversial theory gained many adherents, notable among them his personal friend George Grove. Dr Edward Robinson, however, dismissed the theory 'in less than half a page, [and] with a sneer'.[178] Most serious scholars of Palestine followed Robinson's lead. But Fergusson would not be put down. He held firm to his view and sought ever-greater publicity, contributing his theory to Dr William Smith's *Dictionary of the Bible*,[179] and publishing two lectures on the subject delivered at the Royal Institution.[180]

* * *

Meanwhile, in 1864 a group of prominent people in London, including Arthur Stanley and George Grove, formed the Jerusalem Water Relief Society to address the lack of clean water that was a potential health hazard to the increasing number of pilgrims to the Holy City.[181] The banking heiress and philanthropist Miss (later Baroness) Angela Burdett-Coutts contributed £500 to pay for a topographical survey of Jerusalem, an essential first step to building a satisfactory water supply system.

The British military establishment was always interested in mapping the world: one never knew where the Army might need to go next. The Ordnance Survey office in Southampton was prepared to lend equipment and to lend an officer and four sappers, one of whom, Corporal Henry Phillips, was a photographer. Captain Charles Wilson RE, who had proved his surveying

---

[177] *Holy Bible* (King James Version), John, Chapter 19, Verse 20: '... the place where Jesus was crucified [Golgotha] was nigh to the city'.

[178] Fergusson, *Notes on the Site*, p 67.

[179] William Smith (ed.), *A Dictionary of the Bible*, 3 vols (John Murray, London, 1863).

[180] Fergusson, *The Holy Sepulchre*. The lectures were delivered on 21 February 1862 and 3 March 1865.

[181] Graves, *Life and Letters of George Grove*, p 108.

skills on the North American Boundary Commission, offered his services, entirely at his own expense.[182]

Wilson's survey lasted from October 1864 to May 1865, during which time he had the full co-operation of the Ottoman Governor of Jerusalem, Izzet Pasha. This left him and his men free to conduct a full survey in and around Jerusalem. Furthermore, he gained the trust of the guardians of the Noble Sanctuary who allowed him to measure and draw large-scale plans of the Haram, the Dome of the Rock and the Al-Aqsa Mosque. He was even allowed to excavate down through the rubble that had accumulated against the Western Wall of the Haram.[183] He uncovered a large arch there, at right angles to the wall, which appeared to be the base of a walkway giving access

[182] C. M. Watson, *Fifty Years' Work in the Holy Land* (PEF, London, 1915), pp 15–16.
[183] C. M. Watson, *The Life of Major-General Sir Charles William Wilson, RE* (Murray, London, 1909), pp 41–53.

The Jewish Western Wall praying complex as it is today, with Wilson's Arch against the wall in the background.
KEVIN SHILLINGTON

to the top of the Haram. Known as 'Wilson's Arch', the hall beneath it today forms part of the Jewish Western Wall praying complex. Wilson also noted the existence of a broken off arch towards the southern corner of the Western Wall, which had gained the name 'Robinson's Arch', after the theologian who had observed it in 1838.

News that Wilson's survey was going ahead with the full co-operation of local authorities caused great excitement in England, and Grove proposed to his friends, Stanley, Fergusson, the MP Walter Morrison and others that they form a society to raise funds for the scientific exploration of the Holy Land.[184] A meeting of 25 prominent scientists, religious figures and MPs was held in the Jerusalem Chamber of Westminster Abbey in May 1865, with the Archbishop of York, the Most Revd William Thomson, FRS, FRGS, in the chair. They formed themselves into the Committee of an Association to be known as the 'Palestine Exploration Fund', the expressed purpose of which was to investigate 'the Archaeology, Geography, Geology and Natural History of the Holy Land'.[185]

At the first public meeting of the Fund, held in Westminster's Willis's Rooms on 22 June 1865, the Archbishop of York laid down the founding principles that would inform the work of the Fund. It should be based on sound scientific principles; it should abstain from controversy; and it should not be started or conducted as a religious society.[186] The latter was mostly to avoid being accused of religious sectarianism. Nevertheless, the setting up of the Fund was clearly to some extent a response to Darwinian theories of evolution. In effect, probably in the eyes of most of those present, the Fund would be bringing the backing of scientific evidence to the historical truths of the Bible. It was announced that Queen Victoria had agreed to become the Fund's Patron and numerous dukes, earls, bishops and MPs were signed up to become the Committee of the Fund.[187]

* * *

Lieutenant Charles Warren RE arrived back in England from Gibraltar a month later. There is no evidence he showed any particular interest in the new Fund, although he almost certainly would have heard about it from his

---

[184] Graves, *The Life*, pp 118–9.
[185] Palestine Exploration Fund (PEF) Archive: Minute Book; and Watson, *Fifty Years' Work*, p 17.
[186] Watson, *Fifty Years' Work*, p 18.
[187] *Ibid.*, pp 21–22.

Anglican and possibly Freemasonry connections. It was clearly the professional territory of his senior colleague, Captain Wilson RE, who, together with Lieutenant Anderson RE, was signed up by the Palestine Exploration Fund (PEF) in November 1865 for further work, a preliminary reconnaissance survey of Palestine beyond Jerusalem. Wilson and Anderson returned in April 1866 having completed much, but not all, of the reconnaissance survey. The five months' work had cost the PEF £1550 and the Fund's finances were at a low ebb.

The PEF clearly needed to raise its profile, and at a meeting of the committee in the new year of 1867, it was decided that the next exploratory expedition should be focussed on the Holy City. Wilson was engaged elsewhere and Grove appealed for an alternative young Royal Engineer to lead such an expedition.

Warren, possibly bored after teaching surveying at Chatham for eighteen months, volunteered as soon as he heard about it from his Colonel, despite being warned by friends that the Fund had no money and that the project would offer little chance of professional promotion.[188] But as both a religious man and a Freemason, Warren could not resist the opportunity.

Arrangements were quickly made. He was led to believe he would be receiving £200 a month for all his expenses and assumed this would be enough for his needs in Palestine. He selected three proven sappers to accompany him: Corporal Henry Birtles, who since Gibraltar had been attending a surveying course at Chatham, Corporal Henry Phillips, the photographer who had proven his worth on Wilson's 1865 survey, and Corporal Hancock whom Warren had probably come across on a course at Chatham.

On 1 February 1867, the eve of his departure for the Holy Land, Warren met with George Grove in the sitting room of the Charing Cross Hotel. Grove handed over £300 in cash with the promise of more to come, leaving Warren unaware that this was just about the last penny in the bank account of the PEF.[189] Grove gave him his final instructions, which included the determination of the position and dates of the principal religious sites in the Holy City, as well as the line of the walls of the ancient city as described by Josephus before the Roman destruction of 70 CE, and if possible the position of the even more ancient City of David.

[188] Charles Warren, *Underground Jerusalem. An Account of the Principal Difficulties Encountered in its Exploration and the Results Obtained* (Richard Bentley & Son, London, 1876), p 4.
[189] *Idem.*

It was clear to Warren, however, that the priority of his work, so far as Grove was concerned, was to provide archaeological evidence to back up the controversial theory of his friend James Fergusson concerning the sites of the Holy Sepulchre and the Temple of the Jews. Warren departed England on the assumption that Fergusson's theory was probably correct.

He was soon to change his mind.

Ottoman Palestine in the 1860s.

CHAPTER 5

Early Work in the Holy Land

The steamship *Charlotte* arrived off the Palestinian port of Jaffa on the morning of Friday 15 February 1867. A westerly gale was blowing which prevented any hope of an immediate landing and the captain, with a schedule to keep, turned his ship northwards for Beirut. It was a common enough occurrence; but on this occasion he did not get very far. There were a large number of passengers who wanted to disembark at Jaffa and they created such a clamour that the captain agreed to turn back. Besides Warren and his three corporals, Birtles, Phillips and Hancock, there were a number of local Arab and Jewish merchants, numerous deck passengers and a party of 35 Americans in first-class. Fortunately, by the time they got back to Jaffa, the sea had calmed and the *Charlotte* was soon surrounded by lighters that had rowed out to meet them.

The port of Jaffa at about the time of Warren's sojourn in Jerusalem. In the centre is a lighter, making its way out between the rocks. Boats such as these, rowed by up to eight men, conveyed Warren's party and their baggage from ship to shore.
CONTEMPORARY PHOTOGRAPH BY FÉLIX BONFILS: FROM THE COLLECTION OF JEAN-MICHEL DE TARRAGON, ÉCOLE BIBLIQUE PHOTO-LIBRARY, JERUSALEM

Warren's party, with their heavy baggage, was successfully loaded into the 'surf boats'. According to his own recollection, as the lighters shot through the surf into the inner harbour, Warren reflected that here was the ancient port where Hiram, King of Tyre, had landed the cedar trees from Lebanon that King Solomon used to build the Temple in Jerusalem.[190] If that is really what he thought at the time, rather than focussing on the safe passage of his valuable baggage, then Warren was already caught up in the romance of Biblical and Masonic history.

On landing, they were blocked by Customs officials who took one look at the red-jacketed soldiers and their surveying and mining equipment and declared it 'warlike'. Warren did not yet have his letter of authority, his *firmin*, from Constantinople; but the local British consular agent, Habib Kayat, came to his rescue and managed to convince the officials to let the men and their baggage through. One of Warren's trunks weighed 'half a ton' and, as he recalled, it had taken six English railway porters to lift it. But a shout for 'Said' brought forth the local 'Sampson' who managed to get it on his back and stagger up the steep and narrow stairway into the heart of the town, 'with a mob after him yelling in triumph'.[191]

That evening Mr Kayat began bargaining for mules to carry the baggage to Jerusalem, and with the matter still not settled, it was 10 pm before he and Warren retired to Kayat's house while Corporals Birtles, Phillips and Hancock were put up in the Greek convent. Habib Kayat had been appointed consular agent for Jaffa on the death of his father the previous November, and Warren was pleased to find him a widely educated Syrian gentleman from whose conversation he learned a great deal about the country and its people. In the morning the bargaining for mules recommenced and it was the afternoon before Warren and his men set off for Jerusalem with eight baggage mules and their muleteers.

They completed twenty kilometres that afternoon, reaching Ramleh by sunset. They put up at the Russian hospice, which was already crowded with Russian Orthodox Christian pilgrims. With the accommodation dirty and 'flea-ridden', Warren was thankful to be woken at 3.30 am by the Muslim call to prayer. Eager to get on the road, he roused his men, and by 7.00 am they had loaded the mules and got underway.

The wind was so intense and the rocky path so narrow and uneven that

---

[190] Warren, *Underground Jerusalem*, pp 24–5.
[191] *Ibid.*, p 27.

The final approach to Jerusalem. The road (bottom right) goes off picture to the right and returns to follow the line of the wall to Jaffa Gate, at the tower on the left of the picture.
PHOTOGRAPH TAKEN IN 1858: PEF – P5961 (BOX 101)

their heavily laden mules were regularly 'bowled over'. As a result, a journey that should have lasted five hours took them all of twelve. The light was fading fast by the time they came in sight of the Holy City. Determined to reach his destination with no further delay, Warren urged his men on and managed to reach the Jaffa Gate just before it was closed for the night. It took a while to manoeuvre the mule train through the 'L'-shaped gateway and then they 'clattered through the streets' towards the Muslim quarter where they put up at the Mediterranean Hotel, then situated a little to the south of Damascus Gate.[192]

The next morning, Warren left his men to unpack and sort the baggage

[192] Shimon Gibson, Yoni Shapira and Rupert L. Chapman III, *Tourists, Travellers and Hotels in Nineteenth-Century Jerusalem* (Maney Publishing for the Palestine Exploration Fund, Leeds, 2013), p 141.

A mid-19th-century view of Jerusalem from the east, showing the south-eastern corner of the Haram, with the Dome of the Rock to the right, the dome of the Al-Aqsa Mosque to the left, close to the southern wall, and centre distance, close to the horizon, the double domes of the Church of the Holy Sepulchre. The photograph was taken from the Mount of Olives, with the Kidron Valley in the foreground.
PEF, P2171

while he visited the British Consul, Noel Temple Moore, who lived near the hotel. Moore was a career diplomat who, unlike his charismatic predecessor James Finn, kept strictly to his brief and acted with extreme caution.[193] He was not a man to stick his neck out for Warren in any disagreement with civil or religious authorities. His attitude to the fact that Warren had not yet received his *firmin* from Constantinople was that he could not possibly commence work; but he agreed to introduce Warren to the Ottoman Governor of Jerusalem, Izzet Pasha.

Warren was hopeful of getting permission, based on the fact that Captain Wilson had found Izzet Pasha to be very amenable to his survey two years

---

[193] Mordechai Eliav, *Britain and the Holy Land, 1838–1914: Selected Documents from the British Consulate in Jerusalem* (Magnes Press, Hebrew University, Jerusalem, 1997), p 83.

previously. Wilson, however, was doing an overground survey, and one connected with supplying the city with clean water: clearly a worthy project. Wilson did in fact do some important excavation, but this was unofficial and in any case partly related to the underground water cisterns, and it was presumed by religious authorities that he was operating with the full approval of the Pasha. Although some of Warren's purpose in Palestine was to complete Wilson's reconnaissance survey of Palestine beyond Jerusalem, his instructions from the PEF, issued by Grove a week before his departure from London, informed him that the main object of his visit was to 'make discoveries in Jerusalem, more particularly in that portion of it known as the Haram Area which contained the site of the Temple'.[194]

Grove was basing these instructions on Fergusson's theory that the Temple was in the south-west corner of the Haram, where the Al-Aqsa Mosque had been built, and that the Dome of the Rock was in fact the Holy Sepulchre. Warren was not prepared to dismiss Fergusson's theory out of hand, as Robinson had done. His role was to solve the problem through proper scientific exploration, and in order to do this he must excavate.

Izzet Pasha cautiously welcomed Warren who assured the Governor that the British Government had communicated with the Porte in Constantinople and that his *firmin* should be arriving shortly. Acting on his own authority and on the understanding that he would not work directly *on* the Haram without the permission of the religious authorities, Izzet Pasha gave the British engineer permission to work 'about Jerusalem' while awaiting the arrival of his *firmin*.[195]

Warren, who had Wilson's full ordnance survey to hand, immediately began his own preliminary survey of the area around the Haram. The northern end was bordered by a military barracks and other buildings, so access from there would be very difficult, and the northern half of the western wall was wholly or partially blocked by contemporary housing, including the Pasha's Palace. The eastern wall formed the outer boundary of the city, and here the land fell away sharply to the Kidron Valley that separated Jerusalem from the Mount of Olives. At the southern wall of the Haram, the land sloped away more gradually. Here in the south the city wall abutted the Haram, about halfway along, level with the position of the Al-Aqsa Mosque above. The south-western corner of the Haram was thus inside the city boundary.

[194] PEF, JER/WAR/2, Grove to Warren, Crystal Palace, 26 January 1867.
[195] Warren, *Underground*, p 95.

Warren could see that the lower, more ancient courses of the Haram had been built with very large stones; those above, with smaller: presumably a more recent reconstruction. He knew that to construct anything on this scale, it must have been built on bedrock, and that meant digging deep below the current surface.

Among the many books that Warren had brought with him was a copy in translation of Flavius Josephus's *History of the Jewish War against the Romans*. In this book Josephus, a 1st-century Romano-Jewish historian, described both the city and the Temple of Herod as they were in the time of Jesus, and their destruction by the Romans in 70 CE. The Romans, who had no access to explosives, could only destroy the Temple and its surrounding walls by dismantling them from the top and casting their rocks down into the surrounding valleys. These would have quickly filled up with rubble, making a complete destruction of the lower walls impossible. For instance, within the city in Herod's time there had been a valley, the Tyropoeon, separating the Temple Mount from the rest of the city to the west. The depth of this valley was not known because it had been largely filled in by rubble and subsequently built upon. Many of these buildings were in turn destroyed and their rubble built upon again so that there was no longer any sign of a valley as such.

From his initial observation, two things became clear to Warren. He would have to start by sinking deep shafts through the rubble to find the original ground level, and then go even further down to reach bedrock. On the other hand, the fact that the lower walls had been buried for nearly 2000 years meant that what he did discover down there must, in his view, be the original walls of the Temple complex.

With specific instructions to 'carefully and minutely survey' the south and south-east area, Warren decided to sink his first shafts close to the southern wall of the Haram. Here, outside the city limits, there were no houses and his men would not be disturbed by the city population.

He hired Palestinian workmen from the nearby village of Siloam. Paying them a little above the local going rate, he devised a three-tier payment scale, placing in the top level those who were strongest or proved themselves the best workmen. The workers thought this most unfair, but were prepared to accept it once they saw that he would pay them cash in hand on a regular basis, rather than the more common practice of paying through a third party who would take a percentage. Dividing them into work groups, he placed members of the same family in different groups, so that one group would not work in competition or gang up against another. Discipline was a hard thing

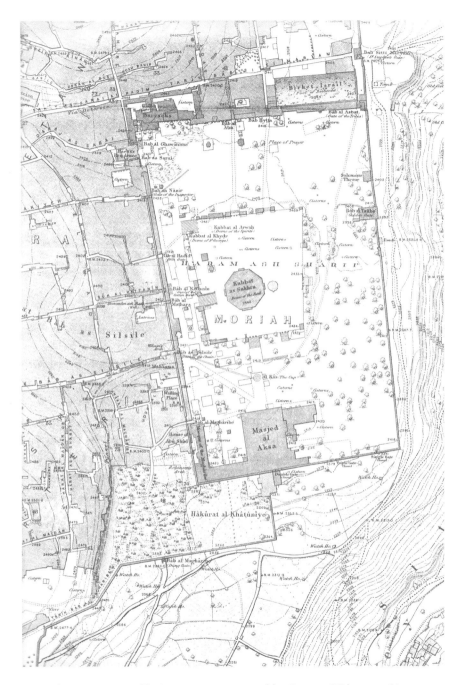

The Haram or Noble Sanctuary, as surveyed by Captain Wilson, 1865. PEF

to establish, but he had strict rules about safe operation below ground, and anybody who broke these rules and put others at risk was liable to dismissal. He also hired a small number of women, to carry water and to provide food and drink for the men who might otherwise depart to their village at mealtimes.

The next priority was to purchase large quantities of timber boards. A carpenter cut and jointed these into frames to shore up his shafts and tunnels as they would be digging through loose rubble rather than solid rock. In due course the shortage of timber in Jerusalem was to become a regular refrain in his reports to London, and he had to apply to Alexandria and Malta, and even England, to get enough sturdy planks.

Leaving Birtles to take charge of the digging, Warren made a round of diplomatic visits, doing his best to win over influential people to his project. He began with the Anglican Bishop of Jerusalem, Bishop Samuel Gobat, who was Swiss by birth and headed the Anglican-Prussian Mission. He represented all the Protestants of Northern Europe, of any nationality and no matter how divergent their creeds.

This lack of clarity did not appeal to Warren's ordered mind. He was already displaying something of an imperial mentality, which held that everything British was somehow superior, and the more the British could spread their culture and influence, the better it would be for all concerned. Warren admitted that he was personally impressed by Gobat, but he felt that if the Anglican Church was to win converts to the faith, which could only be a good thing for the people and the region, it should be separated from the other Protestant denominations and headed by an English Bishop. This would provide the necessary discipline in liturgy and hierarchy that would appeal to 'the Eastern mind', in contrast to the looseness of the Free Churches which only bred confusion.[196]

Next door to the Bishop's Palace, close to Jaffa Gate, lived Revd Dr Joseph Barclay LLD, a graduate of Trinity College Dublin, who headed the London Society for Promoting Christianity amongst the Jews. Warren took to him immediately, observing on reflection:

> ... from the time of my first visit to him until my departure from Jerusalem, he never failed to assist our work in every way in his power ... his personal influence was very considerable, and the Moslems and Jews looked at him with respect.[197]

[196] *Ibid.*, pp 97–100, and 103.
[197] *Ibid.*, p 100.

Warren and associates in Jerusalem, August 1867.
SEATED LEFT TO RIGHT *Lt Charles Warren, Revd Dr Joseph Barclay,*
Corporal Henry Phillips. RECLINING *Mr Eaton, a Jerusalem-based PEF*
associate. STANDING *Jerius Salome, dragoman (interpreter and general fixer).*
PHOTOGRAPHER: HENRY PHILLIPS. PEF/P/1315

At the Jewish Mission Society Warren met the medical doctor, Thomas
Chaplin, who ran a sanatorium for poor Jews, of whom there were many.
Warren was impressed that Chaplin made no attempt to convert his Jewish
patients while they were sick and was so beloved by them 'that they appeared
to forget he was not one of themselves'. In Warren's view, Dr Chaplin gave
Christians a good name among the Jews.[198] Through these two men, Chaplin
and Barclay, Warren managed to make many useful contacts, especially among
the Jewish religious authorities who took a keen interest in his work.

Meanwhile, after only four days, the work at the southern wall was
interrupted. They had dug two shafts, one of six metres, the other of five,
both of them alongside the Haram wall; but at that point the 'Military Pasha'

[198] *Ibid.*, p 107.

79

intervened and ordered them to stop work. Unfortunately Warren does not name this interesting gentleman who saw it as his role to protect the Muslim religious sites of the city. Warren went to meet him, and finding a cheerful man, hoped to develop a friendship between them. Unfortunately, the Military Pasha was convinced that digging next to the huge wall of the Haram would cause it to fall down and nothing Warren said would persuade him otherwise.

On the face of it Warren appeared to accept the Military Pasha's ruling. He moved his men back twelve metres from the southern wall, along what is known as the Ophel Hill that slopes away to the south of the Haram. He had them sink two new shafts, with a view to running horizontal galleries back towards the Haram. In this way he could continue with his original plan to examine the foundations of the structure, but without upsetting the Military Pasha. By this time the labourers were accustomed to their role and, under the direction of Henry Birtles, it was not long before they reached a depth of fifteen metres.

At this point they came across a stone construction about a metre thick. Warren ordered his men to dig further shafts, and from galleries extending from these Warren was able to trace the construction as an ancient wall that ran at a slight angle from the south-east corner of the Haram, southwards along the edge of the Ophel Hill. Part of the way along this wall was a turret, which suggested it was a former city wall. It was characteristic of Warren that he recorded it simply, in his detailed drawings, as an ancient former city wall, abutting the south-east corner of the Haram, and expressed no immediate opinion of its provenance.[199]

It later became clear that what Warren had found was in fact a Byzantine reconstruction of a much earlier wall,[200] what archaeologists today refer to as the 'First Wall' of the city of Jerusalem. According to contemporary Muslim sources, this wall had been abandoned after being fatally damaged by an earthquake in 1033 CE.[201] The wall is believed to have existed in some form or other since the time of David, who had, according to Biblical sources, captured the 'citadel of Zion' from the Jebusites in the 10th century BCE

---

[199] Warren to Grove, Jerusalem, 22 August 1867, known as Letter I, published: *PEF Quarterly*, September 1867, pp 7–10.
[200] Kathleen M. Kenyon, *Digging Up Jerusalem* (Ernest Benn, London & Tonbridge, 1974), p 19.
[201] Karen Armstrong, *Jerusalem: One City, Three Faiths* (Ballantine Books, New York, 1997), pp 262–3.

and made it his capital.[202] The name 'Zion' had been applied to other hills in Jerusalem, and, until Warren's discovery, the exact site of David's city remained unclear. What Warren had stumbled upon was a major archaeological find, for he was the first to reveal and excavate what is known today as the 'City of David', one of Jerusalem's largest ongoing archaeological sites.[203] And this was discovered in his first few weeks of excavation in Jerusalem.

Warren set his men to dig further shafts and galleries along the slopes below the eastern wall of the Haram, where Grove had instructed him to look for traces of a viaduct across the Kidron Valley to the Mount of Olives. Leaving these extended excavations in the capable hands of Birtles and his men, Warren decided to commence the reconnaissance survey work that Wilson and Anderson had not had time to complete the previous year. This was north-east of Jerusalem, as far as the Jordan River and the Dead Sea, and south-west of Jerusalem as far as Hebron in the south and Gaza in the west.[204] The aneroid barometers, required for measuring height above sea level, however, had been left behind during the rushed departure from England and Warren telegraphed for them to be sent out by P&O steamship. Nevertheless, he was eager to get out into the open country and took the opportunity to accompany Dr Sandreczki of the Church Missionary Society who was going on an excursion among the local Bedouin. Warren took the photographer Corporal Phillips with him.

Mounted on mules and carrying their own tents, they set off south for Bethlehem where they picked up a Church of England deacon who was running a school for Bedouin children. Together, they joined up with a Bedouin encampment and followed them around for the next ten days, going down east into the Jordan Valley as far as the Dead Sea, where the sheikh wanted to dip his sheep to cure them of the itch. While the two clergymen did their missionary work, Warren and Phillips explored numerous caverns, hills and ruins. Warren had always enjoyed the simple life: camping out, sleeping on the ground, and, despite being 'devoured by insects', he seems to have felt thoroughly at home among the Bedouin.[205]

On his return to Jerusalem on 31 March 1867 he found his surveying

---

[202] 2 Samuel. 5. V 6–9.

[203] I am grateful to Professor Gabriel Barkay for pointing out that this was one of Warren's many 'firsts': interview, Jerusalem, October 2014.

[204] Warren, *Underground*, p 111; and PEF, JER/WAR/2, Grove to Warren, Crystal Palace, 26 January 1867.

[205] *Underground*, pp 113–38.

instruments waiting for him; but no sign of any further money from Grove, beyond the original £300 he had been given in London. At first Warren could not understand this, for Wilson and Anderson had had a grant of £1550 to run their five-month survey the previous year, and his own excavation, combined with surveying, was a far larger undertaking. As instructed, he did his best to economise, but he had to commit himself to an expenditure of at least £200 a month.[206] It must have been a worrying time for Warren who complained to Grove that, besides his expenses in Palestine, he had a wife and child to support in England, though in reality Fanny's family money probably took care of that. Despite his complaints, however, Warren was by now totally committed to the project, and in order to keep the work on the road, to pay for stores and meet his wages bill, he ran up a considerable debt on his personal account.

On the positive side, his *firmin* had at last arrived. As he began to read through a translation of this document, he would have been pleased to see that the Porte in Constantinople called upon the local authorities to assist him in any way possible, and indicated that he was free to excavate anywhere, with the permission of the owners. But then followed the fateful phrase: '*with the exception of the Noble Sanctuary and the various Muslim and Christian shrines*'.[207] This more or less negated the primary purpose of Warren's presence in Jerusalem. Consul Moore was more supportive than he had been when Warren first arrived and advised him not to show it to Izzet Pasha, but just to use his own initiative as to how best to proceed. Warren observed that Christians and other 'infidels' were allowed ready access to the Haram and the Dome of the Rock, provided they paid the required fee to the religious authorities. This was confirmed by the then unknown young American journalist Samuel Clemens who visited Jerusalem in the summer of 1867 and, writing under the pseudonym of 'Mark Twain', observed:

> Up to within a year or two past, no Christian could gain admission to it or its court for love or money. But the prohibition has been removed, and we entered freely for baksheesh.[208]

Warren, however, spotted a way out of his dilemma. The Porte's *firmin* referred to the special permission that had been granted to The Prince of Wales to visit

---

[206] *Underground*, p 4.
[207] Quoted in Williams, *The Life*, p 42: *my emphasis*.
[208] Mark Twain, *The Innocents Abroad* (first published 1869; Signet Classics, Penguin Books, New York, 2007), p 449.

the 'Nobel Sanctuary', from which Warren was happy to conclude that the Porte must be confusing the Jerusalem 'Noble Sanctuary' with the far holier one at Hebron, which contained the reputed Tomb of Abraham, and had been visited by The Prince of Wales. Consoling himself with the thought that he was not acting contrary to his *firmin*, Warren decided to continue as though nothing had changed. But to be on the safe side, he would avoid showing the *firmin* to the Pasha for as long as possible.[209]

* * *

Leaving Birtles in charge of further excavation to the south and east of the Haram, Warren went down to the Jordan Valley to commence the reconnaissance survey. He managed to acquire the services of the Bedouin Sheikh Salah to act as guide, and on 3 April he set off with Corporal Phillips and a 'bodyguard' of ten porters and workmen. The Biblical 'road to Jericho' was now no road at all, being little more than a rocky path. There were signs that there had been a proper road in the past, but this had probably been destroyed by earthquake activity. On the way Warren climbed Kuruntul, the 1000-foot peak that was said to be the site of the 'Temptation of Christ'. From its summit he had a magnificent view over Jericho and the Jordan Valley, as far south as the Dead Sea.[210]

There were a number of 'tells' (mounds) within the Jordan Valley, with the largest one at Jericho itself. Most previous observers had dismissed these as natural features, but, having first viewed them from the mountain top, Warren took a military view and saw them as defensive towns, built on artificial mounds to provide protection from raids by mountain dwellers. He conducted a small excavation of the Jericho 'tell' and several others, and what he found seemed to confirm his theory. They were definitely artificial creations, on the top of which were ruins of buildings surrounded by mudbrick walls. He was careful not to expose too much as the ancient brick crumbled once it was exposed to the air. He found a lot of pottery, including some near-perfect jars, and in due course these were sent to England for the PEF's collection. He also drew cross-sections of some of the mounds.

He then surveyed northwards, up the west side of the Jordan, and had been in the valley for a little over a week when Salah, perhaps bored by the inaction and puzzled by the amount of physical labour undertaken by this

[209] *Underground*, p 146.
[210] *Ibid.*, p 202.

English officer, challenged Warren to a race. One of his men, he said, a well-built Nubian, could easily outrun him to a distant tree. Warren could not resist the challenge. The Nubian set off at a rapid rate, while Warren was content to follow at a steady pace. As they approached the tree the Nubian was forced to pull up from lack of breath and Warren sailed past him to win the race. He would have been pleased to have proved the wisdom of the fable of 'The Tortoise and the Hare'.

He went straight back to work, hot and sweaty in his shirtsleeves. That evening he developed a chill that became a fever during the night. The following morning he had a pair of abscesses at the back of his throat and could not eat. Finding no relief by the next day, he tried piercing the abscesses with his penknife, but this just filled his mouth with blood.

Later that day they were visited by Yacoob esh Shellaby, spokesman for a group of Samaritans who were camped on Mount Gerizim, near Nablus. Warren and his party were invited to the Samaritans' Passover feast that was being held in two days' time. Warren, weak from fever and lack of food, felt duty-bound to accept the invitation. Besides, he was interested to find out more about the Samaritans and it would be a good opportunity for Phillips to take some photographs.

On the appointed day they pitched their tents in the Samaritan's camp. Warren did not know how he was going to get through the feast until, as he recalled, 'a good Samaritan who hailed from Manchester and happened to be passing through Nablus, came to see me and sent me some beer'.[211] The so-called 'Samaritan' was an English theological student, Mr F. A. Reis, who had purchased a case of two dozen bottles of Bass beer that he had been surprised to find in a bazaar in Acre. Fortunately, he had not yet drunk any of the beer when, at the base of Mount Gerizim, he had met Corporal Phillips, on his way to Jerusalem to try and find some alcohol to relieve Warren's pain. As Reis recollected many years later, 'we took the Corporal to our tents and loaded him up with Bass. Captain Warren told us we had saved his life'.[212] The irony of finding a foreign 'Good Samaritan' in a camp of Samaritans was not lost on Warren, even in his enfeebled state.

They spent a week in the Samaritans' camp and through Yacoob's introductions, Phillips was allowed to take a number of excellent photographs of the Samaritan feast. Yacoob was very interested in the work of the Palestine

---

[211] *Ibid.*, p 211.
[212] Quoted from a recollection to Warren's grandson in 1927, see Williams, *The Life*, p 47.

Exploration Fund and, perhaps as a way of winning English support for his fellow Samaritans, he offered to present to the Archbishop of York as Chairman of the Fund an 18th-century *Book of Samaritan Prayers*, and for the Committee, a more recent copy of a *Book of Samaritan Hymns*. He explained that these were a gift, needing no payment, and to stress the point, he insisted that Phillips take a photograph of him handing the book to Warren.

For many years a large print of the photograph hung in pride of place in the archives of the PEF. It shows them sitting at a table in front of a tent, with Warren wearing a fez and looking somewhat worn and thin. Two years later Warren happened to meet Yacoob in Beirut and found him angry and resentful. He had expected to have received at least a letter of thanks from London. Despite Warren's urging, however, Grove had declined to send him one. Seeing that Yacoob seemed to be down on his luck, Warren gave him £5,

Warren receiving an 18th-century book of prayers from Samaritan Yacoob esh Shellaby at the Samaritan camp on Mount Gerizim, near Nablus. PEF, P886

which did not please him either as he expected at least £50. He made it clear that he had lost all faith in the English and the PEF.[213]

* * *

After completing his reconnaissance survey of the hills overlooking the western side of the Jordan Plain, Warren returned to Jerusalem at the beginning of May to find that Mohammed Nazif Pasha had taken over as Governor of the city.

In Warren's absence the new Pasha had summoned Birtles to the Palace and informed him he had no right to dig. In the manner that was to make Warren so proud of his colleague and assistant, Birtles had stood his ground and produced the temporary written permission that had been granted by Izzet, Nazif's predecessor. He then calmly informed the Pasha that he must take up the issue with Lieutenant Warren on his return to Jerusalem. In the meantime, Birtles continued with the excavation.

When Warren went to see the new Pasha, he was received in cordial fashion and offered a cigarette. Nazif said that Birtles had been stopped because he was digging near a cemetery; but Warren insisted that neither he nor his men had any wish to disturb graves and always avoided them. Warren had a long list of sites to excavate and he left the meeting determined not to let the Pasha interrupt his work. Each time he started digging a new shaft, however, Nazif found a reason to stop him. This did not deter Warren, who simply moved on and dug a shaft elsewhere. It developed into a game of cat and mouse and, as a number of the shafts were linked to each other by underground passages, the Pasha's officers never knew where Warren would emerge next. They referred to him as 'the Mole'.

Warren had another meeting with the affable Military Pasha, hoping to win him over. He found him very talkative, though most of his talk was utter nonsense. According to him, the Sakhrah ('Sacred Rock') that was covered by the golden dome lay on top of a palm tree from which flowed all the rivers of the world, and any disturbance of it would bring catastrophe.[214] Clearly his idea of geography had not advanced on those of the map-makers of medieval Europe.

---

[213] Warren, *Underground*, p 234. According to Warren's recollection this meeting was 'three years later', which would have put their meeting in 1870, but in fact the only time he visited Lebanon was in July 1869, as described in 'Our Summer in Lebanon', quoted in W. Besant, *Our Work in Palestine, being an account of the different expeditions sent out to Palestine by the Committee of the Palestine Exploration Fund since the establishment of the Fund in 1865* (Scribner, Welford and Armstrong, New York, 1873), p 238.
[214] *Underground*, pp 96–7.

At the end of May Warren returned to his surveying in the countryside, this time to the south-west of Jerusalem. He went first to Hebron and then west into Philistia where he stayed surveying until the end of June. On his return to Jerusalem he found that Nazif Pasha was still putting obstacles in his way, insisting they could not excavate any closer than 40 feet (twelve metres) from the Haram. Warren, however, had already worked out a way around this. As he explained, the Pasha was 'quite unaware of our powers of mining, and felt quite safe as long as we were not near the wall above ground'. By this means, they had already been mining right up to the wall of the Haram. What he decided to do was to write up a report on his excavation of the south-east corner, with drawings, and send it home to be published, knowing it would be seen in Constantinople. He could then claim in Jerusalem that his work was known to the Porte, no objection had been raised, and so custom had been established. The plan appears to have worked, and he moved closer than 40 feet in order to establish the next custom.[215]

By this time Warren was planning another surveying expedition and he instructed Birtles to sink shafts just outside the various city gates to get an idea of the nature and age of the foundations. He was also to dig further shafts in the valley of the Kidron, to discover the true bed of the river, and to confirm his earlier preliminary conclusions that the Kidron as it existed in the time of Jesus would have been far steeper than at present. In due course these excavations revealed the true bed of the Kidron Valley, which was twelve metres deeper and 27 metres further west, towards the Haram, than the current line of the valley. In other words, before the Roman and subsequent destructions filled the valley with so much rubble, the eastern wall of the Haram had towered above the nearly precipitous valley of the Kidron.

* * *

It was July 1867; Warren was in his fifth month in Palestine and had still not received any further money from Grove. It is probably from this period that there occurred the famous exchange so often quoted in which Warren recalled Grove's response for his request for money:

> 'Give us results, and we will send your money!' ... In vain I replied, 'Give me tools, materials, money, food, and I will get you results.' The answer was, 'Results furnished, and you shall have the money!'[216]

---

[215] Wilson and Warren, *Recovery*, p 43.
[216] Warren, *Underground*, p 3.

It was clear to Warren that Grove did not appreciate the amount he had already achieved during his short four and a half months in Palestine. It appeared that the PEF was living hand to mouth and needed dramatic results from the Jerusalem excavations to raise its profile and bring in more money from the public. Warren was to conclude that the problem probably stemmed from the strong influence of Fergusson on the Committee.[217] Had Warren found something that proved Fergusson's theory about the positions of the Temple and the Holy Sepulchre, Grove would have considered this a 'result', and the money may have been forthcoming. But, on the contrary, everything that Warren had discovered so far about the position of the so-called 'First Wall' and thus the size of the original Temple Mount, had been evidence tending to *disprove* Fergusson's theory.

In spite of this frustration and mounting personal debt, Warren was determined to complete the surveying in the countryside before returning to give his full attention to the Jerusalem excavations. He also recognised he would soon have to send Corporal Phillips home with his precious load of glass photographic negatives. But before that he had two further trips to complete. First he wanted to take Phillips to photograph the hot spring of 'Ain Jidy (Ein Gedi) near the southern shore of the Dead Sea that had most recently been described by Henry Baker Tristram in his *Land of Israel*, published in 1865. The second trip would be to make a reconnaissance survey of the hills and valleys on the far side of the River Jordan, in the present Kingdom of Jordan. Warren and Phillips were joined by Dr Barclay for the trip to the Dead Sea. They were accompanied by the Sheikh of the Ta'âmireh Bedouin, the 'protector' of the area, who brought 60 men, as the supposedly 'neutral' zone they were entering was threatened by bandits.

After visiting the delightful warm water spring of Ein Gedi, they made for Masada, the famous mountain fortress where nearly 1000 Jewish Zealots had heroically held out against the Romans before taking their own lives in 72 CE.[218] They stopped off to fill their goatskins at two freshwater springs along the route and reached the south-east end of Masada by 11.00 am on Tuesday 9 July. The Sheikh refused to accompany them round the other side of the mountain where there was water and an easy causeway up which to make the ascent. He argued that he was only contracted to take them to Masada. Undeterred, Warren decided to climb directly up the south-eastern face. He

[217] *Ibid.*, pp 16–17.
[218] *PEFQS*, No 4, pp 143–6.

began the ascent at 2.20 pm with Dr Barclay, three Bedouin and a small flask of water. They scrambled up a difficult path, and then:

> On getting close to the top we were nearly stumped: before us were two upright pieces of wall, of about fifteen feet [4.5m] in height without any apparent path; we found some toe-holes in these, and climbed up. A false step here would have been destruction: we arrived at the top at 5.20 pm and gave three cheers, re-echoed from below: we found we had landed on the middle of the eastern side of the flat surface of the fortress.[219]

Warren realised triumphantly that he must have travelled up the 'serpent' route mentioned by Josephus:

> … he that would walk along it must first go on one leg and then on the other; there is also nothing but destruction, in case your foot slip; for on each side there is a vastly deep chasm.[220]

Tristram, who had gone up the western route, had observed of the 'serpent':

> … the pathway itself is completely broken away; and it is probable that, for many ages, no unwinged [*sic*] creature has ever reached the fort from the east.[221]

Until, that is, the arrival of 'unwinged' Charles Warren!

Phillips came up the western route as the light was fading. As Warren and Barclay went down to rejoin the others, Phillips stayed on top for the night so he could photograph the ruined fortress in the early daylight. The Sheikh, meanwhile, feeling sorry perhaps for these 'crazy Franks', had relented and brought the mules round to the wady on the western side, where there was a 'beautiful stream of water in a deep gorge, where [they] could hide away from the sun'.[222]

The next day they were due to return to Jerusalem, but the Sheikh refused to allow his men to accompany them, protesting they would be going through bandit country. Warren decided to call his bluff and he and his party set off on their own. He calculated that the Sheikh and his men would follow, once they had had time to reflect that if 'the Franks' were killed, they would be blamed.

---

[219] *Ibid.*, pp 146–7.
[220] Quoted by Warren in *Idem.*
[221] H. B. Tristram, *The Land of Israel: A Journal of Travels in Palestine* (SPKA, London, 1856), p 306.
[222] *PEFQS*, No 4, p 149.

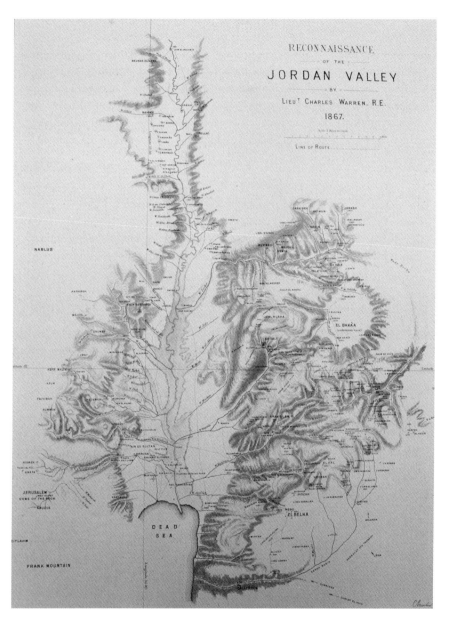

Warren's reconnaissance survey of the Jordan Valley, 1867.
FROM 'WARREN ATLAS' (1884): PEF

Sure enough, before they were out of sight, one of the men started to follow them and soon 'others came trailing in, and in a couple of hours we had a troop of some five-and-twenty volunteers at our heels'. Which was just as well, as a group of rival Bedouin trailed along parallel to them, occasionally in sight, to their south; but they reached Jerusalem without mishap.[223]

Warren did not stay long in the city, returning to the Jordan Valley in mid-July to conduct a reconnaissance survey on the eastern side of the river. This time he hired his own guide, the Bedouin Sheikh Goblan, whose territory lay in trans-Jordan. It was a tense time east of the river, with the Turkish Army attempting to enforce its authority over recalcitrant Bedouin. Goblan, who claimed to be 'Commander-in-Chief of the Bedouin Army', had to be careful not to stray into the territory of any of his enemies, but at the same time to avoid the Turkish troops, of whom a large number were said to be operating in the region.

Warren insisted on pushing as far north as Jerash, 30 kilometres east of the river and 40 kilometres north of Amman. Goblan, who was supposed to be protecting as well as guiding them, was nervous about venturing so far from his own familiar territory. As Warren understood it, he had 'upwards of 200 unwiped-out murders on his hands; among others, that of a Turkish officer and six men, whose throats he cut while they slept'.[224] Over the following weeks Warren completed extensive work on his reconnaissance survey, occasionally dodging Turkish patrols that were active in the area.

On his return to Jerusalem in mid-August, the weather was very hot and Warren, who could usually sleep anywhere – even on his horse – was getting little sleep in his hotel room. The walls, which were very thick, became damp in the winter, while in the hot summer months the moisture evaporated, rendering the bedrooms cold and stifling. He arranged with Dr Barclay for him and his men to camp for the rest of the summer in the grounds of the sanatorium at the London Society Mission. This was about half an hour's walk north-west of the city, close to the buildings of the Russian Mission. Warren would rise at dawn, walk down to the Mediterranean Hotel for breakfast and then start work in his room, which he kept on for use as an office.

---

[223] *Ibid.*, pp 149–50.
[224] *PEFQ* 1867, p 1, Letter I, Warren to Grove, Jerusalem, 22 August 1867.

CHAPTER 6

The Challenges of Work in the Field

While in trans-Jordan in early August 1867 Warren had received two letters from Grove pressing him for detailed plans of his surveys to be completed in the field and posted to London as soon as he got back to Jerusalem. This was too much for Warren who lost his cool. Grove had clearly no idea the pressure he was under. Responding from the field he wrote:

> The survey alone is as much as one man can do comfortably, and I have been nearly worked off my legs trying to keep all things square. When down in the plain I was, on an average, twelve hours in the saddle, besides observing at sunset and during the night; and although I do not take such long journeys here, still I can only keep up by working till after midnight – work all day and half the night in a semi-tropical climate, when continued for several months, is enough to knock up most men. I have also had to make all the arrangements for the excavations and read up the books of reference.

Then, in a sarcastic reference to the way Wilson had been treated, he added:

> I was not aware before that Captain Wilson sent any detailed plans home until he went home himself... I cannot promise any plans until I return to Jerusalem, when I will devote all my time to their preparation.[225]

By the time he returned to Jerusalem and was writing up his reports, Warren had had time to cool his temper and reflect on Grove's own situation. Clearly the PEF was in severe financial straits and he began to think of ways he could help in raising money. He spent the rest of August and much of September writing up his reports and sketching the drawings of his surveys in Philistia and Jordan. He had been the first person to conduct any sort of survey east of the Jordan River and in due course, after he had returned to England, the

---

[225] Warren to Grove, Ain Hemar, 4 August 1867, *PEFQ*, 1867, Letter III, p 14.

map he had produced of the valley and surrounding hills became the standard work for many years.[226]

From the end of August Warren began to send back regular reports for publication, so that Grove would have continual 'results' to publicise the work. The first batch of these reports, dated 22 August to 22 October 1867, was published in the *PEF Quarterly Statement* as 'Letters from Warren, Numbers I to XIII'.[227]

At the same time Warren found there were increasing numbers of visitors from Britain who were interested in his excavations. Although this was a distraction from his work, he decided to turn it to his and the PEF's advantage. He noted it was women in particular who expressed the most interest, and he saw this as a good opportunity for fundraising publicity. It was well worth spending the time and effort acting as a tour guide to the lady visitors as they, rather than the men, would be most likely to spread the word about his work and prompt their menfolk to donate to the Fund. He devised a chairlift to lower the ladies down to the bottom of his main shaft near the south-east corner. From here, by the light of magnesium lamps, they could make their way along the gallery to the base of the Haram where they were able to view the huge foundation stones on which he and Birtles had discovered some strange inscriptions.

Warren believed the stones dated back to the time of King Solomon, although it is now realised they were Herodian,[228] and that the inscriptions may have been made by the stonemasons themselves – a very exciting find for a keen Freemason. In due course, and in order to reinforce his publicity plan, he made a sketch of a cross-section of the shaft and tunnel, to which he added human figures in voluminous women's dresses, being lowered down and walking along the tunnel. He sent the sketch to the PEF and an etching of it was prepared for publication. Although it was 1871 before it was finally published, in Wilson and Warren's *The Recovery of Jerusalem*, clearly, Warren had an instinct for advertising.[229]

On 23 August 1867 he sent Corporal Phillips home with his precious

---

[226] Published as part of the 'Warren Atlas': Charles Warren, *Excavations at Jerusalem, 1867–70* (PEF, London, 1884).
[227] *PEFQS*, 1867.
[228] Eilat Mazar, *The Walls of the Temple Mount* (Shoham Academic Research and Publication, Jerusalem, 2011), pp 177–95.
[229] *Recovery*, p 26; also reproduced in Warren's, *Underground Jerusalem*, p 140; and on the front cover of the PEFQS for many years. For the publication history of this famous etching, see David Jacobson's editorial for the March 2013 edition of the PEQ Journal, Volume 145, No 1, pp 1–3.

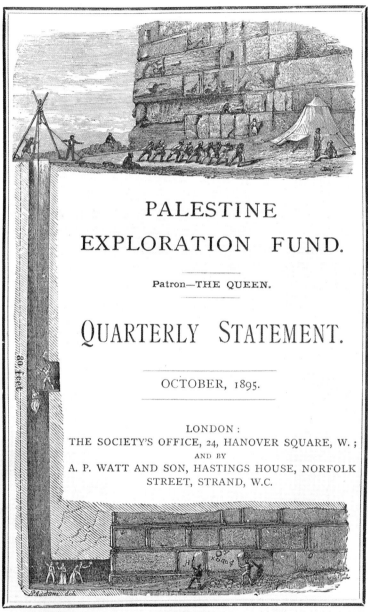

Warren's cross-section of his shaft to give access to the base of the south-east corner of the Haram, with a lift for visitors. The etching graced the cover of the PEF's Quarterly Statement for 50 years from 1872. PEF

cargo of photographic negatives, describing those from trans-Jordan as 'some of the most perfect negatives I have ever seen'.[230] He urged that prints be made available for sale to subscribers, and to the general public at a higher rate, while copyright was retained by the PEF. Prints should also be sent back to Jerusalem where there was a ready market for them among visitors. He pointed out that those from trans-Jordan were unique and ought to fetch a higher price.

Then, in September, a potentially critical event occurred that Warren was able to turn to his advantage.[231] While he was out of sight, working on his plans in his hotel room, the Pasha's constables tried to halt the excavation at a shaft by a building known as the Coenaculum,[232] just outside the south-west corner of the city. The loyal workmen had protested that they could not stop without orders from Henry Birtles, who by this time had been promoted to sergeant. Birtles was sent for and he insisted he could only accept orders from the Pasha if they came through the British Consul and Lieutenant Warren, at which point the constables arrested him.

Having refused to allow the arrest of his men, Birtles calmly accepted his own arrest; and he was publicly marched through the city to the barracks next to the Pasha's Palace. Here, in the privacy of the barracks where calmer counsels could prevail, Birtles pointed out that he was a British citizen, and consequently they had no authority to arrest him. Unsure of their authority, a senior officer ordered his release, an order which Birtles refused to accept unless it was officially authorised by orders from the Pasha. As Warren was later to observe:

> Sergeant Birtles acted admirably in the matter; he understood what I wished to a nicety [233] … I was fortunate to have a soldier with me who could carry out my wishes exactly as I required them.[234]

At the time, when Warren heard what had happened, he went straight to the Pasha's Palace with one of the British Consulate's constables and Consul Moore's official 'dragoman' (guide and interpreter). Moore was ill at the time, which suited Warren as the Consul might not have taken so firm a stand as himself.

---

[230] Warren to Grove, 4 August 1867, Letter III, *PEFQ*, 1867, p 13.
[231] Wilson and Warren, *Recovery*, pp 34–6; and *Underground*, pp 298–303.
[232] Coenaculum, the Latin word for the room in a Roman house, usually upstairs, where supper, the last meal of the day was taken. This Jerusalem building is traditionally accepted as the site of Jesus's 'Last Supper', as well as that of 'King David's Tomb'.
[233] *Recovery*, p 35.
[234] *Underground*, p 303.

From the beginning Warren took the attitude that 'firmness with "the Turk"' was the only way to proceed, and he recognised this occasion as a make-or-break point. 'Had I shown any disposition to coax [the Pasha]', he recalled, 'he would have stopped me at once'.[235] When Nazif offered him a cigarette and a chair some distance away, Warren declined the cigarette and remained standing. He had learned that cigarettes were only offered to 'inferior' suppliants: a foreign consul would have been offered a *chibouk* (a Turkish pipe) and a chair close to the Pasha. Accompanied as he was by the Consul's officials, Warren felt he should be treated with the same level of respect.[236]

Nazif Pasha, hoping to avoid an awkward clash of interests, ordered an officer to release Sergeant Birtles. But this did nothing to satisfy Warren who saw himself in a battle of wills that he was determined to win. He insisted that Birtles be given a written order, signed by the Pasha himself, indicating that he was being released with no charge against him. Having been so publicly marched through the streets and market, this was the only way to restore Birtles' reputation. When Nazif prevaricated and tried to avoid a direct reply, Warren settled himself in a chair next to the Pasha and made it clear that he would not move until he had satisfaction. And there they sat, side by side for some considerable time. Finally Nazif sent for *chibouks* and sweetmeats, and they smoked together for half an hour. Warren had won the first round in establishing his status. But if the Pasha had hoped this would mollify 'the Mole', he was bound to be disappointed. Warren continued to insist on his signed paper of release for Sergeant Birtles.

After a further two hours of inconsequential conversation and long silences, it was Nazif who blinked first. He agreed to draw up and sign the paper that evening. Warren recognised he would have to be satisfied with this. To have insisted any further would have been an open display of disrespect and distrust. Nevertheless, it was several days before Warren got his letter, and that was only after he had written to say he was sorry to hear that the Pasha could not keep his word. This was clearly overstepping the mark, but Warren did get his paper and for the next five months he and his men were left to continue their work, uninterrupted.

This, of course, is all just Warren's version of events; but it is entirely within his character. Like most Victorians of his class, Warren assumed an automatic superiority when dealing with 'foreign' officialdom: an attitude that

[235] *Ibid.*, p 7.
[236] *Recovery*, p 35.

would now be seen as imperial-minded arrogance, but was viewed at the time by other Europeans in Jerusalem as sensible firmness of purpose, exercised by someone who had the courage to maintain it.

From Nazif's point of view, the meeting was probably a minor embarrassment and a matter of saving face. His main concern at the time was the Jaffa-Jerusalem road that he had just started constructing, using forced labour, and he probably had his eye on Warren's 50 or so workers. In what may have been an attempt to establish a better relationship between them, he sought Warren's engineering advice on the construction. Warren pointed out the need to build a proper foundation for the road; but, having asked for his advice, the Pasha chose to ignore it and the road, without the foundations recommended by Warren, began to disintegrate after the first heavy fall of rain.[237]

For the rest of September and through October 1867 Warren worked with Birtles on the excavations. He focussed now on the western wall of the Haram, beginning at Robinson's Arch near the south-west corner where there were no buildings but a lot of 'prickly pear' cacti that provided some cover for their activities. He began by confirming Wilson's estimate on the breadth of the arc and sank shafts to find the first supporting pier.

It was very dangerous work, there being a large number of huge boulders to excavate through, many of them clearly fallen voussoirs from the arch itself. At times Warren used dynamite to blast his way through stubborn rocks such as the fallen voussoirs, probably causing damage to houses above. He reckoned it would be 50 feet (15 metres) down to bedrock, but in the end it was double that depth. At 50 feet he came to a pavement, but that was built on earlier rubble. He knew he had reached the original ground level when he came to what he referred to as 'red earth', the type of soil that had been fed by millennia of decaying natural vegetation. Just above, or within this soil he found numerous pieces of pottery, in particular what he called 'fat lamps': small clay lamps that had been fuelled by melted animal fat. They clearly belonged to an early period, and, although he had no way of dating them, he correctly recognised that some future researchers might find them of value. He saved and drew sketches of many of these lamps, showing their wide variation in style.[238]

He did not stop at bedrock, but cut through the initial soft rock until he found underground water cisterns and aqueducts that had been cut into the

---

[237] *Ibid.*, p 36.
[238] Reproduced in the 'Warren Atlas'.

*Robinson's Arch, jutting out from the southern end of the western
wall of the Haram, as Warren would have seen it when he started his
excavations nearby in 1867.*
CONTEMPORARY PHOTOGRAPH BY FÉLIX BONFILS:
FROM THE COLLECTION OF JEAN-MICHEL DE TARRAGON,
ÉCOLE BIBLIQUE PHOTO-LIBRARY, JERUSALEM

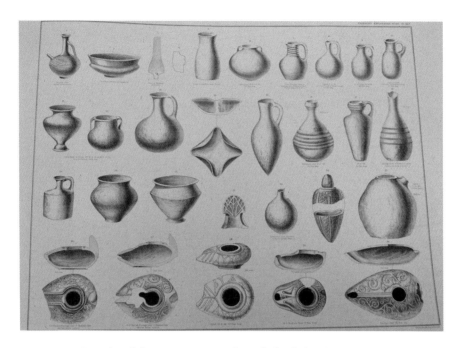

*Samples of the pottery Warren brought back for the PEF, with
(bottom row) what he called 'fat lamps'.*
FROM 'WARREN ATLAS': PEF

harder rock beneath. Some of these contained flowing water. As he worked elsewhere along the western wall and in due course under the Haram itself, he found many more water cisterns: indeed, the whole mountain on which the Haram was built was riddled with cisterns, some of them huge, and many containing water.[239] Some of the cisterns contained pebbles and these could be very dangerous to excavate for the pebbles were totally unstable. On one occasion the following year, when they broke into what may have been a large cistern below Robinson's Arch, pebbles poured out like running water and continued to flow for several days.[240] These moving stones were to be found throughout their digs and were an extreme hazard in the shafts and tunnels, for when they flowed, the wooden casing frames were left dangerously exposed with no support behind them. Warren had already issued strict instructions to

[239] See Shimon Gibson and David M. Jacobson, *Below the Temple Mount in Jerusalem: A Sourcebook on the Cisterns, Subterranean Chambers and Conduits of the* Haram al-Sharif (Archaeopress, BAR International Series 637, Oxford, 1996).
[240] Warren to Grove, 22 August 1868, Letter XXVII, *PEFQS*, 1868, p 67.

his Palestinian workers about how to observe safe practice in the shafts, with threat of sacking for anybody who did not obey his safety instructions. On one occasion a worker who tried, against Warren's strict instructions, to climb up the wooden casing, fell and broke his back, leaving him permanently disabled.

When Warren began the excavation of Robinson's Arch, he assumed, as Robinson, Fergusson and Wilson had before him, that it was the final support for a viaduct across the Tyropoeon Valley that carried a road linking the Haram to the upper city. Indeed, this was one of the assumptions that supported Fergusson's theory that the Jewish Temple had been in the south-west corner of the Haram because literary sources claimed that a viaduct ran from the upper city direct towards the Temple.

To test this assumption, Warren sank a series of shafts westwards, away from the Haram. In due course this revealed that after its initial great arch, the Robinson construction turned at a right angle southwards, from which Warren concluded that it actually supported a grand staircase. This would have given the public access to the Herodian cloisters, and not the Temple,

A contemporary painting of Warren emerging from a shaft such
as that sunk through the floor beneath Wilson's Arch.
ARTIST: WILLIAM SIMPSON IN 1869, FROM THE PEF COLLECTION

and as such, put another nail in the coffin of Fergusson's theory. Wilson's Arch, which had not personally been seen by Fergusson, was by far the better candidate to support the viaduct.

The first span of Wilson's Arch was complete, not broken off like Robinson's, and when Warren and Birtles squeezed through the small visible entry into the space below, they found themselves in a man-made cavern that today forms the northernmost part of the Jewish Western Wall Prayer Complex. They sank shafts through the floor of this cavern and found numerous underground rock-cut passages and cisterns.

* * *

Towards the end of October 1867, Warren came to the point where he felt he could no longer afford to accumulate any further personal debt. In the nine months since he had left London he had expended £2100. He had had occasional, erratic payments of £100 or £200 from Grove, but these amounted to no more than £1050, leaving him £950 in debt. Growing dispirited and frustrated by the injustice of it, he wrote to Grove and announced that he could personally support the project no longer. Consequently he would pack up and leave Palestine by steamer on 12 November.

The threat, perhaps combined with funds generated for the PEF by the publicity given to his work in Jerusalem, finally won through. A telegram arrived from Grove: 'Remain at Jerusalem, money will be paid into your account this week'.

Warren, who had been becoming increasingly dispirited and had, in his own words, 'lost elasticity' over the previous month, was immediately transformed. He conceded that in 'moments of enthusiasm' such as this he would 'stand on [his] head, run races on all fours, and go through other boyish tricks'.[241] Rejuvenated by the news from Grove, he headed out to joyously breathe in the fresh air beyond the city walls. He walked along the Ophel Hill whose fertile terraced gardens, now the site of the City of David Archaeological Park, grew such wonderfully huge cauliflowers for the markets of the city. Close to a terrace wall, below which was what the short-sighted Warren took to be a magnificent row of cauliflowers, he laid his handkerchief on the ground, bent down and stood on his head. At this point, looking upwards from ground level, he saw the row of 'cauliflowers' rise up and peer over the wall, followed by the olive-complexioned faces of a group of curious *fellahin*, below their white

[241] *Underground*, p 339.

101

'cauliflower' turbans! They politely made off; leaving Warren to speculate that while they prayed on their knees facing Mecca, they probably thought his was the curious religious pose of an English Christian![242]

In this spirit of exuberance he and Birtles decided to explore an underground passage that appeared to link the northern end of the Haram, near the Pasha's Palace, with the Sisters of Sion convent on the Via Dolorosa to the north. Wilson had noted it, but had not investigated as it was blocked by five feet (1.5 metres) of sewage. This, however, did not put off Warren or Birtles. Getting hold of three old, wooden doors, they laid them on the sewage 'and advanced along by lifting up the hindmost [door] and throwing it in front of [them]'.

After a while they found their way barred by a dam across the passage. Climbing over this slippery stone wall, with candles in their mouths, they found the sewage continued, two metres below the dam. Manhandling the doors over the wall, they continued their perilous journey. After a further fifteen metres, the sewage became so solid they were able to walk on it with the aid of poles. 60 metres from the beginning of the tunnel, they found the passage blocked by masonry. All the way along their perilous journey Warren was recording measurements, and after they had retraced their 'steps', he was able to draw what he referred to as 'a fair section' of the contour from the Palace to the Via Dolorosa, a sketch of which he despatched to London, showing himself and Birtles as little matchstick figures standing on their doors.[243]

Through November Warren's excavations focussed on finding a viaduct across the Tyropoeon Valley that would have linked the ancient Haram to the rest of the city. Sure enough, working westwards from Wilson's Arch, away from the Haram, his numerous shafts and tunnels revealed a series of arched vaults, which in fact formed a double viaduct: clearly the 'road' had been widened at some point. On 20 November, while crawling along a passageway that linked some of these vaults, he found a hole that led down through the roof of a particularly large and well-preserved vault. Lowering himself by rope, he found he was in 'a large rectangular vaulted chamber of ancient construction, with a column or pedestal sticking up from the centre'.[244] The floor was covered with several feet of earth and rubble; but the walls of the chamber were in good condition, with some of the original plaster remaining and evidence of mortar between dressed stone.

[242] *Ibid.*, pp 339–40.
[243] *PEFQS, 1867–8*, p 35, Letters XIV–XV, Warren to Grove, Jerusalem, 28 October 1867.
[244] *Recovery*, p 67.

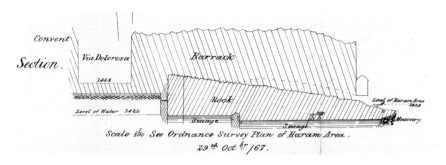

Passage through the sewage as drawn by Charles Warren. Little stick figures of Warren and Birtles can be seen manhandling their floating doors across the surface of the sewage.
PEF-DA-JER-WAR-60-2.6-SEWAGE

What particularly struck Warren was that single stone pillar with a broken top that rose up a few feet above the earth in the middle of the room. It reminded him of a Freemasons' myth that was incorporated into some of their Masonic ceremonies. It told of a Mason who lowered himself by rope into an enclosed cavern in the centre of which was a single pillar and beside the pillar was a piece of paper with some significant writing upon it. There was no such piece of paper in Warren's vault, but the similarity to the myth put the idea in his mind that perhaps this was a meeting place for Hiram's masons, the builders of Solomon's Temple. He had no way of dating the construction, so it was merely a fanciful idea, but in memory of that thought, he named the cavern the 'Masonic Hall'. The Freemasons are bound by secret oaths not to reveal anything that passes in their meetings, initiations and ceremonies, so it is interesting to note Warren's level of circumspection in his published account of the finding and naming of the chamber in which he says simply: 'This chamber acquired the name of the Masonic Hall from some circumstances connected with its discovery'.[245]

The 'Masonic Hall' was to become one of the favoured sites for Warren's regular tour of the excavations, and he fitted a ladder 'for the accommodation of the many ladies who visited it'.[246] Today it forms part of the Western Wall Archaeological Complex that is open to visitors. It retains the name 'Masonic Hall', although there is no evidence that it was ever used by masons. The

[245] *Ibid.*, pp 66–7.
[246] *Ibid.*, p 68.

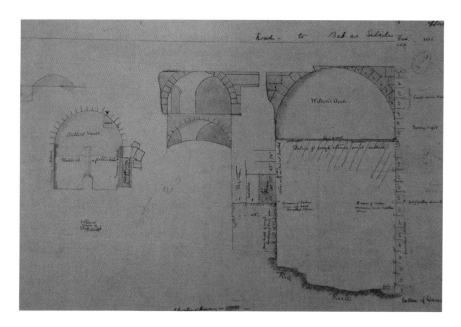

One of Warren's working drawings, indicating the position of the
'Masonic Hall', and the viaduct in relationship to Wilson's Arch.
PEF COLLECTION

earth has been cleared away to reveal a flagstone floor, and set into the wall
on either side are a pair of pillars. As Warren himself correctly surmised, the
capitals of these pillars would have formed a pair of arches that met in the
middle and were supported by the extended pillar in the centre of the floor.
The hole through which it is presumed Warren lowered himself is still visible
in the roof of the hall.

Towards the end of November 1867 fifty-one cases of mining frames arrived
and Warren was able to use these to open new excavations on the Ophel Hill.
Digging down into what is now part of the City of David Archaeological
Park, he investigated an ancient aqueduct that carried water between the
Fountain of the Virgin (Jacob's Well) and the Siloam Pool. And it was here
that he uncovered a vertical shaft that would have given access to the aqueduct
from within the Ophel 'City of David'. Uniquely, in archaeological practice,
he had excavated it upwards, from the bottom. To this day, the feature retains
the name, 'Warren's shaft'.

* * *

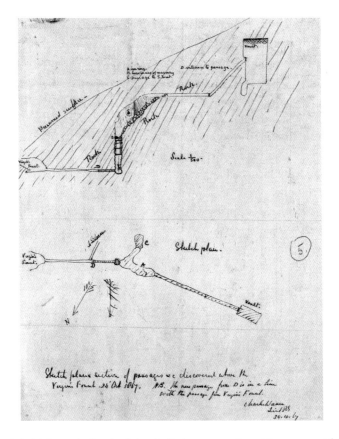

Warren's initial rough sketch of the shaft that was to bear his name, with (upper sketch, cross-section) a little stick figure on a rope at the bottom of the shaft.
PEF-DA-JER-WAR-62.20.2

In the new year of 1868 two additional sappers arrived. All seemed to be going well until Sergeant Birtles had a serious fall while climbing the wall of one of the vaulted chambers of the Wilson viaduct. He hurt his back so badly that 'he could barely crawl out into the open air'.[247] It was an accident that had been waiting to happen. Henry Birtles was as fearless as Warren himself; and like Warren, he led the workmen by example, never hesitating to risk life and limb in plunging down into unknown depths, often continuing work along passages long after they had run out of wooden casings. And all this amid the continuing danger of sliding shingle and underground running water,

[247] *Recovery*, p 66.

much of it mixed with sewage. Warren knew he was fortunate to have Henry Birtles as a partner – it was very much a partnership rather than an officer/subordinate relationship – and the injury to his back brought it home to the lieutenant that Birtles was irreplaceable. Fortunately, he was able to report on 2 February, 'Sergeant Birtles has recovered from the accident he met with, and is now about'.[248] That was what he reported to the PEF at the time, although he later admitted that Birtles suffered from his injury for several months.[249] Birtles, however, was the sort of man who would have claimed to be fine long before he had fully recovered.

Presumably with Birtles' accident in mind, Warren issued strict instructions that no unauthorised person was to approach the shafts or go underground without his specific permission. Indeed, he dismissed one working party for allowing an unauthorised guide to take some tourists down the shaft at Robinson's Arch. This impressed the workmen so much that when the Pasha himself came to the shaft and wanted them to show him what they were doing, they told him that he must send up to the hotel and get permission from Lieutenant Warren! Clearly Warren had acquired an 'authority' of his own in Jerusalem. The Turkish establishment generally were curious to know what 'the Mole' was up to, but on the whole were nervous about going underground. On one occasion Warren saw a Turkish military engineer approach Wilson's arch, clearly intending to go down one of the shafts on his own. As Warren reported in his next letter to the PEF:

> I passed in front of him, blew out my light, pushed off the ladies' ladder, and went down by the rope; hearing a crash, and seeing me suddenly disappear in the darkness below, he probably thought I had fallen, for he rapidly beat his retreat.[250]

* * *

During February 1868 they had 'the most miserable weather' – rain, sleet or snow almost every day – and Warren decided to take Birtles and some of the men down to Jericho for a few weeks to excavate the tells. Dr Chaplin accompanied them. Although the weather was drier in the Jordan Valley, the danger of fever was ever present. Sergeant Birtles' health suffered, although in Warren's opinion this was brought about by 'over exertion … in rendering aid to a lady who lay in a dangerous state from fever on the East of the Dead Sea'.

[248] *PEFQS, 1867–8*, p 59, Letter XXIV, Warren to Grove, Jerusalem, 2 February 1868.
[249] *Recovery*, p 66.
[250] *Ibid.*, p 60.

*Sgt Henry Birtles, Warren's partner in archaeological
discovery, emerging from a shaft in 1869.*
ARTIST: WILLIAM SIMPSON, FROM THE PEF COLLECTION

The lady appears to have been part of Dr Chaplin's party. The River Jordan was swollen and she could not get across to get help from Jerusalem, 140 kilometres away to the west. Birtles came to the rescue. He hurried back up to Jerusalem to get her supplies of food and medicine and returned with a mule-drawn palanquin to carry her back to the city. He then built a causeway on the East Bank of the Jordan so that they could get the patient into a boat for crossing the river. By the time this was completed, however, the lady had died, and it was her body that Birtles finally conveyed across the river. As Warren was later to acknowledge, the fact that their whole party escaped 'without further loss from fever was due in great measure to the majestic manner in which Sergeant Birtles carried out instructions given to him'.[251] While crediting Birtles with the physical work that he carried out, Warren could not resist taking the credit himself for giving the sergeant his 'instructions'. But it was all at the expense of Birtles' health, and on their return to Jerusalem in March, Warren decided his invaluable partner should be invalided home to England.

In his letters to London Warren had regularly praised the efforts of Birtles, and when the sergeant arrived home in April 1868, he was invited to attend a committee meeting of the PEF so that they could express their 'high opinion of his service' in the excavation of Jerusalem. As a mark of their gratitude they presented him with a testimonial to the value of ten guineas, the equivalent of about six weeks' wages.[252]

Warren found that during the absence of himself and Birtles in the Jordan Valley in February, the Turkish authorities had been trying once again to hinder his work. He suspected they were hoping to be bought off with *baksheesh*; but Warren viewed this as the thin end of a very long wedge and he refused to go down that path. At the same time, he felt he was not getting enough support from the PEF. He decided he needed to go to London to address the Committee in person, both to explain the reality of his work in Jerusalem and to get the financial arrangements sorted out: payment had returned to being infrequent and unpredictable. An additional motive for his return would have been to be reunited with Fanny and his infant daughter Violet. He arranged for work to continue in his absence on the uncontentious Ophel Hill, under the supervision of Dr Chaplin, and he booked passage to depart from Jaffa on 15 May.

---

[251] PEF Archive, WAR/JER/1870, Warren to Walter Besant (Sec. PEF), Brighton, 16 June 1870.
[252] PEF Archive, Executive Committee Minutes, 24 April 1868.

CHAPTER 7

'Jerusalem Warren'

Shortly before Warren's departure for England in May 1868, the Mediterranean Hotel received an important visitor, Revd Dr Robert Morris, a prominent American Freemason. As soon as Morris discovered there were a number of Freemasons in Jerusalem, he proposed holding an informal meeting of the brethren, which included Lieutenant Warren. They held two such meetings in a room of the hotel.

Warren appears to have told Morris about the underground quarry, the entrance to which Dr Barclay, or rather, Dr Barclay's dog, had discovered just outside the northern wall near Damascus Gate. It stretched for several hundred metres under the city in a southerly direction towards the Haram. It was clearly a quarry from which large building blocks had been carved by stonemasons, and it did not take much for Warren to convince himself that this was the work of King Solomon's stonemasons, the ancient precursors from whom modern Freemasons claimed to trace their origins. The quarry is now believed to have been last used in the early Ottoman period of the 16th century when the present walls of the city were reconstructed, although that is not to say that it could not also have been used by earlier masons. Certainly Warren liked to believe so.

At the time of Morris's visit there happened to be a British frigate in Jaffa and several of its Masonic officers were in Jerusalem. Dr Petermann, the German Consul, was also a Freemason. It was too good an opportunity to miss. They would hold a Masonic meeting in 'King Solomon's Quarry'.[253] Warren led them, 'with a good supply of candles', deep into the cavern, beyond any light emanating from the entrance.

> [They] found a chamber happily adapted to a Masonic purpose. It was a pit in the ancient cuttings, about eighteen feet square. On the east and west, convenient shelves had been left by the original workmen, which answered for seats. An upright stone in the centre, long used by guides to set their candles

---

[253] Now known as Zedekiah's Cave, after the last king of Judah before its conquest by Babylon in the 6th century BCE.

upon, served us for an Altar … We were perfectly [stilled] by silence, secrecy, and darkness, and in the awful depths of that quarry, nearly a quarter of a mile from its opening, we felt, as we never had before, how impressive is a place which none but the All-seeing Eye can penetrate.

Laying my pocket Bible open on the central stone, three burning candles throwing their lustre upon it, and the trowel, square, etc., resting near by [*sic*], a few opening remarks were made by myself, to the effect that never, so far as I knew, had a Freemasons' lodge been formed in Jerusalem since the departure of the Crusading hosts more than seven hundred years ago; that an effort was now in the making to introduce Freemasonry into this, the mother-country of its birth; that a few of us, brethren, providentially thrown together, desired to seal our friendship by the associations peculiar to a Masonic lodge; that for this purpose, and to break the long stillness of these ancient quarries by Masonic utterances, we had now assembled, and would proceed to open a Moot Lodge, under the title of Reclamation Lodge of Jerusalem.[254]

After prayers had been offered and the appropriate ceremonies completed, they each made a few personal remarks. When it came to Warren's turn:

This gentleman, in some extremely happy observations, expressed his pleasure at this meeting, called together under such singular circumstances, and was equally impressed with the importance of introducing Freemasonry, though cautiously and judiciously, into the Holy Land.[255]

Warren himself did not see fit to mention this Masonic meeting in any of his published letters or books. He preferred to stick with the Masonic tradition of secrecy, even to the extent of not mentioning that the meeting had happened at all.

* * *

Two days later, Warren left for England, arriving in Southampton on Tuesday 26 May 1868. His first priority was to be reunited with Fanny and Violet in Guildford where they would have been staying with her parents, Samuel and Fanny Haydon. Three days later he was in London attending a special evening meeting of the PEF's Executive Committee, held in the home of the recently appointed Treasurer, William Morrison MP.

---

[254] Robert Morris, LL.D., *Freemasonry in the Holy Land: or, Handmarks of Hiram's Builders* (Masonic Publishing Company, New York, 1872), p 463. I am grateful to Leon Zeldis of Herzliya, Israel, for allowing me to copy the appropriate pages from his copy of this book.
[255] *Ibid.*, p 465.

Warren had come to London determined to get the financial situation sorted to his satisfaction. Hitherto the armchair specialists of the Committee had had an easy time of it. People like Stanley, Grove and Revd Holland (the new joint Honorary Secretary) had all visited Palestine, published their observations and felt they 'knew' the Holy Land. But compared to Warren's time in Palestine, all of their visits had been fleeting and, although Grove was originally by profession a civil engineer and had made numerous sketches of the topography, none of them had any experience of surveying or excavating. James Fergusson, who to date had been so influential in the PEF's thinking, had not even been to the Holy Land. The committee's complacency was about to be challenged direct from the field by their principal officer, upon whom their whole project had come to depend.

For some time the committee had grown impatient with Warren's 'demands' and had even considered replacing him with a less demanding officer now that he had indicated his desire to return to England.[256] But they had misunderstood Warren's desire to come home. Having achieved so much in such a short time, and with so much more to do, he had no intention of giving up the project.

Over the past fifteen months Warren had learned the rewards of firmness, even in the face of higher local authority. And having experienced the responsibility of sole command in the field, he had developed an impatience with what he considered incompetence. If the Committee expected any humility or subservience on the part of their employee on account of his comparative youth and junior rank, they were soon to be disabused.

Warren would have been pleased to find that Morrison had taken over as Treasurer, and this would have boosted his confidence that the Fund's finances would now be put on a sound footing. That evening Warren had a lot to say about the general working of the Fund, quite apart from his ideas on the direction of the work in Palestine. Some members of the Committee were probably a little taken aback by his demanding approach. They needed a little time to take it all in. Warren was invited to put his proposals in writing and the Committee reassembled ten days later to discuss his ideas.

They agreed with his recommendation that a full survey of Western Palestine should commence as soon as possible, that an officer of the Royal Engineers and sappers be seconded for the purpose and special funds be raised to finance it. On the point of financing the Jerusalem excavations, Warren asked for a regular payment of £350, to be paid monthly in advance.

---

[256] Committee Meeting Minutes, 25 February 1868, PEF-EC-1 pp 44 and 46.

Grove argued against such a high sum, suggesting that Warren could manage without lining his shafts with expensive wooden casing, since he had, by sheer necessity, been managing without for several months. Clearly the Committee had no idea just how dangerous the excavations were. As Warren was later to remark, the loose stones in the diggings 'were not like the *fellahin* – subject to personal influence, and they continued to fall in spite of all our efforts'.[257] Fortunately, Warren had the support on the committee of the sporting adventurer, John 'Rob Roy' MacGregor. Eventually the figure of £300 was settled on, and it was agreed that decisions as to what should be excavated would be left to Warren's own discretion. It was also agreed that the Foreign Office would be asked to approach the authorities in Constantinople with a view to getting a more favourable *firmin* for Warren's work.[258]

The subscribers to the PEF, who had been reading about Warren's work through his published letters in the Fund's *Quarterly Statement*, were keen to hear from the man himself. Although he only had one further week in England before his return to Jerusalem, he addressed a public meeting at Willis's Rooms in Westminster. It was the first of many public lectures he was in due course to give on behalf of the PEF. His chosen subject on this occasion was 'The Great Rock-cut Aqueduct in the Kidron Valley', south of Siloam, south-west of the walled city.[259] When he discovered it, it was filled with a huge amount of silt, and he described to the meeting how he had cleared it out with shovels and wheelbarrows, much to the amusement of the workmen who had never before used a wheelbarrow. The aqueduct was steep and he concluded it was probably for carrying off sewage from the city.

* * *

He had just a few more days in England in which to prepare for his return to Palestine. This time he would be taking Fanny and two-year-old Violet with him. He had anticipated this before leaving Jerusalem in May, and had arranged to rent a house by the Russian compound just to the north-west of the walled city. He considered the fetid atmosphere of the Mediterranean Hotel to be unsuitable for his family. They left England on 16 June 1868, probably with neither of them then realising that during their three-week reunion, Fanny had fallen pregnant. On arrival at Jaffa they were able to make their way up Nazif Pasha's new road to Jerusalem in a single day. Warren

---

[257] *Underground*, pp 287–8.
[258] PEF Archive, Executive Committee Minutes, 29 May & 9 June 1868.
[259] *PEFQS*, No 5, pp 140–41.

settled his family into their rented house, and then went down to the Ophel Hill excavations that Dr Chaplin had been overseeing during his absence. His paperwork, books and artefacts had been left at the Mediterranean Hotel where he retained his room as an office.

He was pleased to find the Pasha far more amenable to his work and he put this down to the raised status of the British military after their defeat of the Abyssinian (Ethiopian) Army at the Battle of Magdala that April. The presence of the British fleet in the Eastern Mediterranean, and the regular visits of British naval officers and men to Jerusalem in this period further enhanced his own status.[260] Nevertheless, excavation in the hot summer months remained difficult and there was fever to be dealt with.

At the beginning of August Corporal James Duncan, who had joined the team in Jerusalem in January 1868, went down with a severe attack of fever and Warren must have wondered if he had made the right decision in bringing Fanny and Violet with him. But, having made the decision, all he could do during the fever months of summer was ensure they did not enter the walled city, especially since by this time it was clear that Fanny Warren was pregnant.

As Corporal Duncan's health deteriorated, Warren removed him to the relatively healthier atmosphere of his own house where he personally nursed him, presumably under the direction of Dr Barclay whose sanatorium was nearby. The English hospital in the centre of the city was considered too unhealthy. But in spite of the best care that Warren could give him, James Duncan died on 10 August 1868.

It was Warren's first and only fatality in all his time in Jerusalem and he took the responsibility hard. He personally assisted

The grave of Corporal James Duncan in the Anglican Cemetery, Jerusalem.
KEVIN SHILLINGTON

his men in digging a grave in the Anglican cemetery, and after engraving a headstone, he marked the grave with a Roman monopodium that he had excavated near the Western Wall. It remains in the cemetery to this day.[261]

[260] *Underground*, pp 394–5.
[261] My thanks to Professor Gabi Barkay for showing me round the Anglican Cemetery and pointing out the grave.

Inside Jerusalem's Jaffa Gate. Photograph taken in 1896 shortly before the entrance was widened to allow the entry of the carriage of Kaiser Wilhelm II whose state visit to Jerusalem occurred that year.
PEF, P5936

Warren would have been relieved a few days later to welcome back Sergeant Henry Birtles, who, like Warren, was accompanied by his wife.[262] Despite the class differences, Mrs Birtles would probably have been at least an occasional companion to Fanny Warren. The team, augmented in September by the arrival of four new corporals, now consisted of Sergeant Birtles and five corporals, one of whom, Lance Corporal J. Cock, would act as Warren's secretary, and did much of the drawing for him. Fever, however, soon took hold of the team and Warren had to close the excavation works through September and October. He was taking no risks with the men's health, and Corporals Hanson and Turner were both invalided home. Birtles, too, suffered from fever, but he had recovered from it before and was determined to stay put. Since their first arrival in Jerusalem, both Warren and Birtles had suffered numerous attacks of fever, although Warren himself appears not to have been affected on this occasion.

At the end of October the team's health was back to normal and they reopened the shafts. Over the next two months they continued with their excavations in the region of Wilson's Arch, along the Western Wall of the Haram, and below the Southern Wall. Warren also revived excavation along the Ophel Hill and in particular he worked on the detailed measurements and drawings for the aqueduct and the shaft that was to bear his name. He re-examined the rock-cut aqueduct south of Siloam and found a passage with running water near Bir Eyub (Jacob's Well). The water ran through a narrow passage, barely 1.5 metres high and half a metre wide, that had been cut through the limestone rock. What he had stumbled on was Hezekiah's Tunnel, cut by hand according to Biblical sources in 701 BCE to bring the waters of the Gihon Spring (the 'Virgin's Fountain') into the city at the time of a threatened Assyrian invasion. The aqueduct ran for 550 metres into the Siloam Pool, which would in those days have been within the walled city of Jerusalem. Today, walking through the tunnel in complete darkness, with water running above one's ankles, is a popular experience for visitors to the 'City of David'.[263]

* * *

Judging by the reports he sent back to the PEF, the pace of the work was not as frenetic as it had been in the first fifteen months of exciting new discoveries.

---

[262] PEF Archive, Executive Committee Minutes, 29 May & 3 July 1868.
[263] *PEFQS*, No 5, p 141. See also, *Chronicles* 32: 2–4; and for a virtual tour of the tunnel, see: http://www.cityofdavid.org.il/en/virtual_tour/hezekiah%E2%80%99s-tunnel-city-david.

During this period, from June 1868 to April 1870 when he finally left Jerusalem, the focus was on revisiting old workings and completing exploration and measurement, rather than venturing into completely new areas.

Previously, when Warren had camped outside the city in the summer of 1867, he would work in his office at the hotel until at least 9.00 pm when the Jaffa Gate closed for the night, and often later, once he had found where the gatekeeper kept the key. But now that he had his family housed outside the city, he seldom stayed late at the office. There seems to have been less frustration and anger in his letters; the Pasha was no longer being obstructive, the money was coming in and he had the expectant Fanny and Violet to help him keep things in perspective. Their second daughter was born in February 1869. With Dr Barclay on hand there was no reported problem with the birth. They named her Charlotte, after Charles Warren's elder sister who had died when he was six.

* * *

By this time Warren had developed a working relationship with one of the religious Sheikhs who was guardian of the Haram. Through his co-operation, with the help of suitable *baksheesh*, Warren was allowed to wander at will and take measurements more or less anywhere on top of the Haram, even inside the Dome of the Rock. Although he was not allowed to excavate on the surface of the Haram, he did occasionally manage to find a way down into its subterranean world. For instance, after a night of heavy rain, he saw that a hole had opened up near the northern end of the central platform on which the Dome itself was built. Watched by the anxious Sheikh, he plunged down into the depths beneath, and explored a huge cistern that appeared to be part man-made and part natural cavern, but clearly used for storing water.

In February and March 1869 he was visited by 'Rob Roy' MacGregor, who had just completed a canoe journey down the River Jordan. MacGregor was fascinated by the engineer's work and had been planning a visit ever since Warren's report to the PEF's Executive Committee the previous June. MacGregor wanted to see every bit of the excavations and on several days Warren and Birtles acted as his tour guide. On a visit to the Haram, MacGregor records:

> Mr. Warren … entered a small hole … where one could scarcely expect a terrier to go in, taking leave of us all, with a good-humoured joke to the anxious Sheikh, who forced a grim smile into his face … After 20 minutes of suspense we heard a cheerful ' Hallo!' far off and in a totally unexpected

*Warren at work in one of his galleries at the bottom of the
wall in the south-east corner of the Haram.*
ARTIST: WILLIAM SIMPSON, FROM THE PEF COLLECTION

direction, and there was Mr. Warren erect again on the surface some hundred
yards (91m) away, having traversed a new passage under the grass in total
darkness and creeping on his side. A bit of magnesium was given to the grave
Sheikh in reward for his easy guardianship.[264]

MacGregor repaid Warren's kindness by writing a detailed, vivid and poetic
account of the work being done. The report was published in *The Times* of 5
April 1869 and reprinted in an edition of the PEF's *Quarterly Statement*. He
praised not only the work, but also the 'management and diplomacy' that
Warren had had to use even to be allowed to open a single shaft in a place so
steeped in religious history and significance:

> Nor can we wonder that the Turk should refuse a stranger leave to dig quite
> close to his cherished *sanctum*. Even the Dean of Westminster, so valuable a

[264] *PEFQS*, No 1, p 20, ' "Rob Roy" on the Works at Jerusalem', first published in *The Times*,
5 April 1869. Magnesium was what Warren burned for lighting underground.

co-operator on the committee of the Palestine Exploration Fund, would be reluctant to allow a Turkish officer of Engineers to dig by the east buttresses of Westminster Abbey.[265]

On visiting Warren's excavations beneath Robinson's Arch, MacGregor observed:

> Tanks, cisterns, aqueducts, pavements, here open to us underground. Once we have got down we can scan by the magnesium light a subterranean city, the real city of Jerusalem. The labour of building this, and of now mining into it when buried, is forgotten in wonder as we gaze on the silent relics or wander about the caverns echoing a hollow voice. But for this we must be agile, like cats or monkeys, and follow Mr. Warren complacently crawling on his back through a dark crevice …[266]

Following MacGregor's visit, Warren spent quite a bit of his time taking visitors around the excavations, especially during the Easter pilgrimage period. He and Birtles handled parties of up to twenty at a time. A particular visitor of note was the famous wartime artist and illustrator, William Simpson. He was also a Freemason, which may have prompted Warren to pay him particular attention.

Simpson had gained his fame as an artist of the Crimean War, and he had been commissioned by the *Illustrated London News* to cover the official opening of the Suez Canal, which was due to take place that November (1869). Simpson decided to make the most of the travel expenses for his commission and spent at least a month in Jerusalem. He made a large number of sketches, quite a few of them including images of Warren at work. He later turned many of these into watercolour paintings, a number of which he donated to the Palestine Exploration Fund. Some he turned into etchings for publication in the *Illustrated London News*. It was all good publicity for the Fund, but also for Warren himself, whose name was coming to public attention in England in connection with Jerusalem. It was probably from this time that he gained the honorific moniker of 'Jerusalem Warren'.

* * *

OPPOSITE *Jerusalem Warren consulting a plan within one of his workings beneath the Old City.* ARTIST: WILLIAM SIMPSON, FROM THE PEF COLLECTION

[265] *Ibid.*, pp 20–21.
[266] *Ibid.*, p 19.

As the summer of 1869 approached, Warren was reminded of the health dangers of the previous year. This year he would have not only his men's health to consider, but also that of a second infant daughter. He and some of his men were already suffering attacks of fever in June. His problems were compounded by a shortage of timber. Wood shipped in from Alexandria and Malta had become prohibitively expensive and Warren decided he must close the works down altogether and leave Jerusalem for the duration of the hot summer period.[267] On 11 July 1869 he set off with his family and his complete team of sappers for Lebanon.

The long summer days and dry roads meant they need only travel for a few hours in the morning and again in the evening to complete a journey that in the winter would take a whole day. Warren, of course, did not miss any opportunity to observe and record, finding that with the 'under-vegetation being burnt up, any architectural remains can be examined without difficulty'.[268] They took no tents with them, but carried letters to Turkish Governors and introductions to Roman Catholic convents upon whom they could rely for accommodation that was more suitable for Fanny and her two small daughters than Warren's customary sleeping on the ground with or without a tent.

They travelled via Nablus and Nazareth before heading down towards the coast. They went a little out of their way to visit 'Hiram's Tomb', as Warren wanted to see if there were any Mason's marks on the stone:

> I could see only two: one is a Christian cross of the Byzantine type at the western end, of which I have got a squeeze; it appears to be ancient. The other consists of a square and compasses, very recently and rudely cut, apparently by some enthusiastic 'mason', who should have learnt the *proper* use of his chisel before he attempted such a task.[269]

They reached the coast at Tyre before proceeding north to Saida (Sidon) where they spent a day examining the castle and other buildings of the ancient city. On arrival in Beirut, after an eight-day journey from Jerusalem, they found that the British Consul-General had arranged for their party to occupy a house and compound in the cool of the mountains, where they spent most of the next three months.

During this period the party rested and generally recovered their health.

[267] *PEFQS*, No 4, p 131.
[268] *PEFQS*, No 4, p 136, 'Notes on a Visit to Saida in July 1869' by Captain Warren RE.
[269] *Ibid.*, p 138.

Warren enjoyed travelling around the hills, where he came across the remains of numerous 'heathen' temples, some of them Greek and Roman, but others that appeared to be even older. His observations prompted him to develop an interest in the orientation of heathen temples. He compared them in his mind with what he knew of Egyptian, Israelite and Assyrian temples. He wrote a paper on the subject entitled 'The Temples of Coele-Syria', which was published in the PEF's *Quarterly Statement* in 1870.[270]

Judging by his letters to the PEF, when he was not exploring the mountains of Lebanon Warren spent much of this time writing up reports and visiting Beirut. One particular piece of new excavation that he now wrote up was that of the north-east corner of the Haram, which he had explored for the first time in the spring of that year.

He had sunk several shafts near the north-east corner to reach bedrock and found it more than 30 metres below the surface. It was Warren's deepest shaft. Indeed, Charles Wilson in 1880 was to describe the depth of this shaft to be 'without parallel in the history of excavation',[271] and it meant that Mount Moriah, on which the Temple had been built, fell away sharply in the north-east towards the Kidron Valley. As a result, in order to achieve a flat platform on top of the Temple Sanctuary (the Haram), Herod had had to build a wall in the north-east corner that was 45 metres high. For Warren to sink shafts in this area, however, was particularly dangerous work as the ground was made up of loose rubble, and the excavators needed a lot of wooden frames to hold it back. As we have seen, a shortage of frames was one of the reasons behind Warren's decision to close the excavations for the summer.

The party returned to Jerusalem in November, this time travelling by ship to Jaffa. Warren's promotion had finally come through: he was a Captain of Royal Engineers.

* * *

Warren's time in Jerusalem was now drawing to a close. There was, however, one further piece of drama to act as a finale. It was the acquisition of the Moabite Stone. This reconstructed stele now stands in the Louvre in Paris. It has been dated to the 9th century BCE and contains 34 lines of Moabite script concerning the reign of the Moabite King Mesha. It has been described

---

[270] *PEFQS*, No 5, pp 183–92.
[271] Quoted in David M. Jacobson, 'Charles Warren: An Appraisal of his Contribution to the Archaeology of Jerusalem', *Bulletin of the Anglo-Israel Archaeological Society*, 2009, Volume 27, p 45.

as 'the most extensive document ever recovered referring contemporaneously to ancient Israel'.[272]

It was in the autumn of 1868 that Warren had first heard of a remarkable stone stele that had been seen in Moab, on the eastern side of the Dead Sea in what is today Jordan (see Map, p 70). The French missionary Revd F. A. Klein, of the Church Missionary Society, had been shown it by a local Sheikh near the town of Diban on 16 August 1868. It was half-buried in sand, a black basalt stone, measuring 71 x 71 cm, and standing 124 cm tall. It was inscribed on one polished surface in a script that Klein did not recognise. He copied parts of the script, hoping to have its language later identified. When he got back to Jerusalem, he showed his notes to Dr Petermann, the German Consul and Orientalist. Petermann thought the stone would be a valuable addition to the Berlin Museum. He contacted Berlin to find out how much they would be prepared to pay for it, and it was at about this time that Warren first heard about the discovery. His attitude was that so long as it ended up in a museum, it was not for him to interfere in another nation's acquisition.

When, the following year, he got back from his sojourn in Lebanon, however, Warren learned that the 'Moabite Stone' had still not been obtained for the Berlin Museum, and that it had in fact been deliberately broken up by the Bedouin. But what really shocked Warren was that to date, no attempt had been made to obtain a squeeze of the script. He felt the script was far more important than possession of the stone itself.

Petermann had apparently been authorised by Berlin to obtain the stone and he had made several attempts to purchase it, using Arab intermediaries. Once the Bedouin learned what 'the Franks' were prepared to pay for it, however, the price went up; and negotiations ran on through 1869. In the meantime, Petermann returned to Berlin and his successor decided to seek the help of the Turkish authorities in trying to acquire the stone. As soon as word of this got back to Diban, however, the Bedouin decided they would rather destroy the stele than have it fall into the hands of the Turks. They split it into many pieces by heating it over a fire, then dousing it with cold water.

At this point Warren and the French Consul, M. Clermont-Ganneau, both decided independently that they would try and retrieve the remnants of the stele and at the very least acquire squeezes of whatever script remained. They each sent a trusted Palestinian to Diban with squeezing paper and these returned on 15 January 1870 with fragments of the stele and some

[272] www.newworldencyclopedia.org/entry/Mesha_Stele (accessed 10 June 2016).

good quality squeezes. Warren and Clermont-Ganneau shared copies of the squeezes and sent back for more. The priority for both men was to get a copy of the complete script. In due course they got most of the stone fragments. As Warren said of their co-operation:

> I consider that our success in getting up the squeezes and part of the stone without hindrance from each other is due to the *entente cordiale* which existed between us.

In the meantime, Warren had written to Grove in London explaining what had occurred and what he was doing to try to retrieve the script. Unfortunately, Grove got carried away. He published a letter in *The Times*[273] in which he portrayed Warren as the discoverer of the Moabite Stone and the initiator of its acquisition. This caused Warren great embarrassment when copies of *The Times* reached Jerusalem. Clermont-Ganneau wrote a letter of protest to Grove, who felt obliged to publish a correction and a half-hearted apology in *The Times*. The *entente cordiale* in Jerusalem, however, never fully recovered, and according to Williams, Warren felt so let down by Grove that it contributed to his decision to leave Jerusalem.[274]

That month Warren wrote to the PEF Committee explaining that he had done all he could in the way of excavation, and in any case his health was suffering from long exposure to numerous untreated ailments. The Committee agreed he should wind up the excavations, fill in the shafts and return home.[275] It took a while to complete the closing of the shafts and then the whole party took the road down to Jaffa.

It would have been a sad parting for Warren and his family, moving on from the experience of a lifetime, especially one that in its latter years had been shared with Fanny. They departed the port of Jaffa to an uncertain future and Warren must have wondered if anything in his subsequent career would match the past three and a half years in terms of challenge and achievement.

* * *

They arrived at Southampton on 30 April 1870, and three days later Warren attended a meeting of the Executive Committee of the PEF. He made a

---

[273] 8 February 1870.
[274] Williams, *The Life*, p 74; *Underground*, p 542. For the full contemporary correspondence on the Moabite Stone, see *PEFQS*, No 5, pp 169–82; and *PEFQS*, No 6, pp 281–83 for Revd Klein's account of its discovery.
[275] PEF Minute Book, Exec. Committee Meeting, 2 March 1870.

point of praising the work of his NCOs, stressing in particular the work of Sergeant Henry Birtles, without whose dependable support he could never have achieved what he had in such a short space of time. The Committee agreed that Birtles should receive a silver aneroid (pocket barometer), suitably inscribed, and that two of the corporals should each receive a gift to the value of £2 or £3. Warren undertook to arrange the purchase of the gifts.

He was still in the pay of the PEF until the end of the year and he was commissioned to draw up a full report on his work in Palestine, which he did in collaboration with Captain Wilson who was by then a member of the Executive Committee. Entitled *The Recovery of Jerusalem*, it was published in 1871.[276] Warren himself became a member of the Executive Committee, and over the years that followed he toured the country giving lectures to raise money for the Fund. The enthusiastic reception he received on these occasions encouraged him to produce a personal account of his experiences in Jerusalem and Palestine. Published in 1876 under the title *Underground Jerusalem*, it sold well and increased the national stature of 'Jerusalem Warren'.[277]

However, it is for the quality and accuracy of Warren's *drawings*, together with the sheer range of his work, achieved in such a short time, that his name is so widely respected, not only within the PEF, but within the wider Jerusalem archaeological community, even to the present day. The drawings that he sent home during the course of his three and a half years in the Holy Land were, of necessity, mostly preliminary sketches, though accompanied by detailed records of precise measurements. In due course he worked these up into a set of final drawings that were published by the PEF in 1881, and are known as the 'Warren Atlas'. This publication still remains the standard baseline from which modern archaeologists of Jerusalem commence their own work. This and the sites named after him have helped to keep the name of Charles Warren alive and widely respected, even to the present day.

Warren was to maintain lifelong contact with the PEF, not only serving on its Committee, but always available, ready and willing to offer his help, suggestions and advice. He retained an interest in Palestine, too, though he did not return there. He published a pamphlet in 1875, *The Land of Promise: or*

[276] Capt. Wilson RE, Capt. Warren RE, *The Recovery of Jerusalem: A Narrative of Exploration and Discovery in the City and the Holy Land* (Appleton, New York, 1871).
[277] Charles Warren, *Underground Jerusalem: An Account of Some of the Principal Difficulties Encountered in its Exploration and the Results Obtained. With a Narrative of an Expedition through the Jordan Valley and a Visit to the Samaritans* (Richard Bentley and Son, London, 1876).

Turkey's Guarantee, in which he outlined his vision for the future of Ottoman Palestine.[278] He proposed that Britain should charter a private company to take over Palestine from Turkey in exchange for taking on some of Turkey's massive foreign debt. He envisaged a unitary Palestine in a colonial-style protectorate with the Palestinian peasantry forming the 'native' population, and the Jews forming a middle class of businessmen and merchants, who would, at some unspecified time in the future, gradually take over the administration from the British.

Land of Promise was a prophetic work that anticipated the foundation of the State of Israel, though not in the simple, peaceful and evolutionary manner that Warren had anticipated. The British did indeed take over the country from the Ottoman Turks, during the First World War, when General Allenby entered Jerusalem in 1917; but it was by conquest, not by peaceful exchange for debt, as Warren had originally proposed. And conflict has followed in its wake.

* * *

When he returned to England in 1870, after three and a half years in Palestine, Charles Warren was still only 30 years of age. His Jerusalem work for the PEF, which had brought him fame and respect, was undoubtedly the highlight of his young life thus far. Anything that followed was bound to be an anti-climax.

It had been an inspirational decision to take his wife and child with him for his final two years in the Holy Land. Fanny would have been a reliable anchor through all his excitements and frustrations, and the birth of their second daughter, Charlotte, would have helped him keep his life in perspective. And now, following his return to the relatively mundane life of a Royal Engineer on home posting, Fanny's supportive role would have been even more important. His various postings over the years that followed, to Dover Castle, the School of Gunnery at Shoeburyness and the Royal Gunpowder Mills at Waltham Abbey involved mundane work, compared with the freedom and challenges of Jerusalem; but it had the reward of five continuous years of sharing his life with Fanny, and experiencing together the growth of their young family. During this time two sons were born to them: Frank in January 1872 and Richard in February 1876. The years from 1870 to 1876 were the longest period during their childhood that their father was to spend at home with his family.

[278] Charles Warren, *The Land of Promise: or Turkey's Guarantee* (George Bell & Sons, London, 1875).

CHAPTER 8

Surveying the Diamond Fields

By 1876 Charles Warren had probably had enough of artillery and explosions, even experimental work, and like any young officer of his regiment, he was eager to get back to the excitement and challenges of fieldwork and to advance his career as a Royal Engineer.

His opportunity came in October 1876 with an invitation from the Secretary of State for the Colonies, Lord Carnarvon, for Captain Warren to serve as Special Commissioner for the survey and delimitation of a very sensitive boundary line between a British colony and a Boer republic in South Africa. Warren eagerly accepted in the expectation that he would be parted from his family for no more than six months. As we shall see, in the event he was away for three years, returning in 1879 with the rank of Lt.-Colonel.

On 26 October 1876 Captain Charles Warren RE departed Southampton aboard the Union Line steamer SS *Danube*. The contract for mail services between Cape Town and Southampton had just been awarded jointly to the Union Line and their rivals, the Castle Mail Packet Company. The competition this raised between the two companies produced ever-more rapid and efficient journey times. In the days of sail the journey would have taken about five or six weeks, and potentially far longer if they ran into inclement weather. The *Danube* took just three weeks and five days.[279]

Once he arrived in Cape Town, Warren wrote home regularly to Fanny and the children, at times in the form of a diary. Years later, when there was a particular interest in South Africa, he selected from these letters and combined them with his journals to publish a contemporaneous account of his first residence in South Africa.[280] In the absence of the original letters, this book, *On the Veldt in the Seventies*, is a particularly valuable source as it is clear from the style that his letters and journals were largely unedited. As such they provide a rare glimpse into the personality of the man as he recorded his first

---

[279] The two companies merged in 1900 to become the Union Castle line. In the 1970s when the Cape Town–Southampton service finally wound up, its ships completed the journey in twelve days – author's personal experience.

[280] Sir Charles Warren, *On the Veldt in the Seventies* (Isbister & Company, London, 1902).

impressions of the peoples of Southern Africa and their environment, as well as his own activities.

Warren was in high spirits on-board ship. He was travelling first-class, courtesy of the Foreign Office, as befitted the rank of Her Majesty's 'Special Commissioner'. His two NCOs, Sergeant Kennedy and Corporal Randall, would have travelled second-class. When he was not testing his field equipment with the NCOs,[281] Warren led an active and enjoyable social life on-board ship. His social circle included two lion hunters headed for the Zambezi, two brothers going to Basutoland, an engineer and two businessmen, Porges and Rube, en route to the diamond fields, and 'many others, mostly ladies'. They were an amusing lot and as Warren remembered them, 'the most amusing certainly was M. Porges [an Anglo-French gentleman] … He was the life of our party, and I saw a good deal of him'.[282]

They celebrated crossing the Equator by playing a charade for the gathered company. Porges proposed they perform the 'words' 'Don Quixote':

> Our engineer was turned into the 'Don' (Don Juan) and made to make love to two or three ladies at one time; the rehearsals were some of the most inexpressibly funny scenes imaginable; after much coaching, at which many of us assisted, he became an adept.
>
> In the last scene M. Porges was Don Quixote and shot me, a donkey dressed up as a lion. I brought down the house by an impromptu as I lay dead: pointing at Porges in his grotesque costume – 'Better a dead lion than a live donkey.' M. Porges was the more amusing because there was so much ponderous dignity mixed up with it, and while putting us forever on the grin he kept his own countenance severe.[283]

When he was not playing the fool with his fellow passengers, Warren had plenty to read. He pored over numerous books and official publications, learning as much as he could about the historical and cultural background of Southern Africa.

Of particular inspiration was his father's journal. As a young captain of the 55th Foot, his father had been stationed in the Cape Colony for several years in the early 1820s. He had served on the eastern frontier where a war with the amaXhosa, the colony's immediate eastern neighbours, had then recently concluded. The role of Captain Warren (senior) had been to man

---

[281] *UKNA*, CO 879/10, Confidential Print, p 159, No. 154, Warren to Colonial Office, Waltham Abbey, 14 October 1876.
[282] Warren, *On the Veldt*, pp 3–4.
[283] *On the Veldt*, pp 4–5.

and patrol the British forts in a 'neutral' zone between the Colony and the amaXhosa. At the end of his term of duty in June 1825, he had taken the opportunity of several months' leave, to head north into the interior, do a bit of hunting and explore the territory beyond the Vaal River. His inspiration for this may have been two recently published books: the journals of the British naturalist William Burchell, who had visited the Batswana north of the Vaal in 1812, before the arrival of the London Missionary Society; and the Revd John Campbell's account of setting up mission stations north of the Vaal. Both these books, published in 1822–24, would almost certainly have been available in the Cape Colony.[284]

Captain Warren (Snr) reached as far north as both Burchell and Campbell and visited the famous mission station of Kuruman, although Revd Robert Moffat was away at the time. He also ventured north-east of Kuruman, to the historic Batswana capital of Dithakong,[285] made famous by Burchell's portrait and description of the town. He found the place temporarily deserted, but he observed the ancient stone-walled animal enclosures that were to provide a strong defensive position when his son led an attack on it more than 50 years later.[286] Captain Warren kept a detailed journal of his experiences and his son, also Captain Charles Warren, now eagerly pored over this on his journey south to the Cape.[287]

∗ ∗ ∗

On four occasions over the last quarter of the 19th century, Charles Warren was to play a significant role in the affairs of Southern Africa. It was a period during which the conquest and subjugation of the indigenous African people was completed and the British attempted to bring the whole region under their control. Warren's role in this justifies a brief digression into the background of the Southern African situation into which he was about to become an active player. He would have learned a certain amount from his preparatory reading aboard ship; but that would have been limited to some extent by the social and political prejudices of the available contemporary literature.

---

[284] William J. Burchell, *Travels in the Interior of Southern Africa*, 2 volumes (Longman, London, 1822–24, facsimile reprint, C. Struik, Cape Town, 1867) and J. Campbell, *Travels in South Africa, Second Journey*, 2 volumes (Westley, London, 1822).

[285] *Dithakong* – 'place of stones'.

[286] See K. Shillington, *Luka Jantjie: Resistance Hero of the South African Frontier* (Aldridge Press, London, 2011), pp 11–14 for more on the southern Batswana at this time.

[287] Several extensive quotations from his father's journal are recorded in Warren's *On the Veldt in the Seventies*, pp 229, 344 and 352–5.

There had been a colony of European settlement at 'the Cape', the southern tip of Africa, for 200 years. It had been founded by the Dutch East India Company as a supply station for its merchant ships; but once it was realised that the sparse indigenous population could be readily conquered, it soon became a colony of ever-expanding settlement. The settlers were mostly of Dutch origin, but they included a number from Germany and France. They spoke a locally evolved dialect of Dutch, which by the 1870s, when Warren arrived, was beginning to be recognised as the distinct language of 'Afrikaans'. Those 'Boers' (from the Dutch for 'farmer') who settled inland were mostly hunters and pastoralists, grazing cattle and sheep. In the sparse grassland of the Western Cape region, they required a large expanse of land for a viable 'farm'. The regular size of their land claims was 3000 morgen (about 6300 acres or 2500 hectares). The Boers tended to have large families and each generation of Boer males carved out their own land claims from what they regarded as virgin land. They were only able to do this, however, by continual acts of conquest of the indigenous inhabitants.

Like the Boers, the latter were pastoralists or hunters, sparsely spread over the land, and in the initial century of conflict, the Boers had the military advantage of guns. The indigenous people, known in academic discourse today as 'Khoesan', were known derogatively to the colonists of the time as 'Hottentots' and 'Bushmen'. The former tended to herd cattle, and they were either robbed of their stock and incorporated into Boer society as subservient labour, or driven beyond the Colony, to seek refuge in the north. The so-called 'Bushmen' depended primarily upon hunting, and the Boers, treating them as subhuman, waged a genocidal war against them.[288]

The British seized the Cape Colony during the Napoleonic Wars and their possession of it was confirmed by treaty in 1814. By this time the eastern expansion of Boer settlement had been halted by the more densely populated kingdoms of the amaXhosa, a settled mixed-farming population of iron-working people who were not so easily conquered. What turned out to be a series of Eastern Cape 'Frontier Wars' had begun in the 1770s and, over the century that followed, erupted afresh every ten or twenty years.[289] It was in the aftermath of the fifth of these wars (1818–19) that Warren's father was stationed in the region. The British had provided military backing to

---

[288] Shula Marks, 'Khoisan resistance to the Dutch in the seventeenth and eighteenth centuries', *The Journal of African History*, XIII, 1972, pp 55–80.
[289] Noël Mostert, *Frontiers: The Epic of South Africa's Creation and the Tragedy of the Xhosa People* (Jonathan Cape, Cape Town, 1993).

the informal Boer commandos, which gave them a slight advantage; but the amaXhosa would not give up their land cheaply.

The northern boundary of the Eastern Cape at this time was the Orange River and by the early 1830s a number of Boers had begun to seek out new grazing land beyond the confines of the Cape Colony, on the 'Highveld' north of the Orange. What was at first a trickle of northward migration became a flood following the British decision in 1834 to, among other things, abolish slavery, upon which the Boer way of life so much depended. The subsequent Boer invasion of the Highveld, known in their historiography as 'the Great Trek', took about a third of the Boer population out of the Colony over a period of five years. Considering themselves now free of British overrule, they in due course established two republics, the Orange Free State, between the Orange and the Vaal Rivers, and the 'Transvaal', north of the Vaal River. In the 1850s the British reluctantly recognised the independence of these republics.[290]

The Boers had attempted to establish a similar independent settlement in the fertile south-eastern lowlands and foothills of the Drakensberg after they had won a major battle against the indigenous amaZulu. But their efforts were curtailed by British annexation in 1840, which established the British colony of Natal. Most of those Boers migrated back across the Drakensberg to join their fellows in the Transvaal.

In the west of the Orange Free State the Boers gradually extended their land claims westwards as far as the confluence of the Orange and the Vaal Rivers. This western boundary was disputed by the Griqua, a group of mixed-race immigrants from the Cape Colony who were led by their *Kaptijn*, Nicholaas Waterboer. They lived just north of the confluence; but their legal agent, David Arnot, claimed historic entitlement to much of the land within the confluence.

The British expressed no interest in the affair until, that is, diamonds were found in the territory, in large quantities from 1870. It was a turning point in the history of South Africa, and the British reaction could be considered as the opening gambit in the notorious European 'Scramble for Africa', which is normally ascribed to the 1880s.

The discovery of volcanic diamondiferous 'pipes' on land just south of the Lower Vaal, on what had hitherto been widely recognised as Free State territory, started a 'rush' of speculators and 'diggers', black and white, from all

---

[290] From 1852 the republic north of the Vaal was officially known as the *Zuid-Afrikaansche Republiek (ZAR)* ('South African Republic').

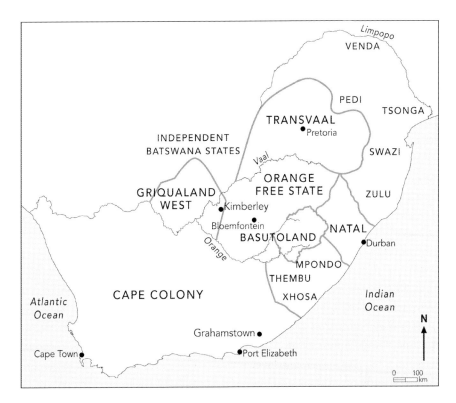

Southern Africa in 1876.

over Southern Africa and beyond. Free State Boers held titles to the three farms concerned and these were soon bought by merchant speculators from the Cape.

The British were determined to acquire the diamond fields. Having no legal claim to the territory, they supported the claims of Waterboer's Griqua and put the issue to a rigged arbitration which found in favour of Waterboer. He was persuaded to ask for British 'protection' and within days the Governor of the Cape, Sir Henry Barkly, annexed Waterboer's country as the Crown Colony of Griqualand West.[291]

The Boers of the Orange Free State and their President, Jan Brand, had refused to recognise the arbitration, and were furious at the British 'theft' of their territory. And then came the greatest embarrassment for Britain. When colonial surveyors began drawing up the new colony's boundary, it emerged

[291] Kevin Shillington, *The Colonisation of the Southern Tswana 1870–1900* (Ravan Press, Johannesburg, 1985), pp 35–60.

131

that the line claimed by the Griqua lawyer David Arnot as marking the limit of Waterboer's territory ran slap through the middle of what had by then become the diamond-mining city of Kimberley. If accepted, it would leave three of the four mines on the Free State side of the border.

There followed four years of delicate diplomatic negotiation before President Brand was finally persuaded to accept the British *fait accompli*. In July 1876 he agreed to a redrawing of the boundary line, just enough to leave the diamond mines on the British side, in return for £90,000 in compensation, a 'miserably inadequate'[292] sum considering the wealth of the diamond fields thus seized by Britain.

And it was this sensitive task of surveying and laying down the new boundary that had brought Captain Charles Warren to South Africa.

* * *

The SS *Danube* docked in Cape Town on the afternoon of Monday 20 November 1876. It was a hot and sultry day; in contrast to the cold sea breezes they had forced Warren to wear a greatcoat on-board ship. He found the docks small and chaotic, and he had a slight problem getting through Customs. He was carrying a silver presentation plate for Major Lanyon, the Administrator of Griqualand West. It was carefully packaged with plenty of padding, but when Warren presented the receipt, the Customs official insisted on opening the package and examining the plate. Warren had learned from his experiences in Palestine to be forthright and ingenious when dealing with minor officialdom. As he related in a letter to his family:

> I felt sure that they would spoil [the shine of the silver] with their rough hands, so I said I would rather kick it into the sea than have any more bother with it, and gave it a good kick. They gave in at once and said it could be of no value if I could kick it, and so I got it through without injury.[293]

He found Cape Town a picturesque town nestled beneath the curve of Table Mountain, spoiled only by the total lack of trees and the poor maintenance of its wide, unpaved streets. But he was pleased to find plenty of hansom cabs, expertly driven by Muslim Malays in tall straw hats.[294] He booked into St George's Hotel and was struck by 'the profusion of delicious fruit and

[292] *The Times*, 24 January 1927, from the obituary of Sir Charles Warren.
[293] *On the Veldt*, p 6.
[294] The so-called 'Cape Malays' were descendants of slaves brought from the Dutch East Indies in the 17th and 18th centuries.

vegetables of great variety which the hotel afforded'.

Warren had three full days in Cape Town before the next stage of his journey. On the first morning he paid his respects to the Governor, Sir Henry Barkly, who was also High Commissioner for Southern Africa and thus responsible for the separate colony of Griqualand West and other British interests in the region. Warren was able to present Barkly with a letter of introduction from his commanding officer, Colonel Peter Scratchley RE, who had written that he 'could not wish to come across an abler officer or a better fellow'.[295] Barkly assured him that provided he observed the main point that the Kimberley mines were to fall within the Griqualand Colony, he was free to use his discretion with regard to the precise detail of the boundary line.

Before leaving Cape Town on the next stage of his journey, Warren bought tents and other equipment suitable for fieldwork. He arranged for his two NCOs to travel by carriage with all the equipment and heavy luggage on the 1000-kilometre journey across the Karoo to Kimberley.[296] He himself travelled by the quicker, though more expensive route, aboard the *Danube* to Port Elizabeth, for the shorter overland journey by train and regular coach.

The *Danube* reached Port Elizabeth early on Sunday morning, 26 November. Warren and his fellow passengers were landed in surfing boats, which must have recalled his first arrival in Jaffa nearly ten years before. He put up at the Phoenix Hotel and bought tickets for Kimberley. Hearing the sound of church bells, he quickly changed into his uniform and made his way to a newly built church where an Anglican service had just begun. The church was filled with British colonists of all ages. He was impressed by the quality of the choir, the strength of the minister's voice and the sermon on the Second Coming. He left thoroughly refreshed from sharing the religious experience with fellow Anglicans: 'What a bond it is between us!'[297]

It was a hot day and Warren did not fancy returning to the hotel, so when he heard the sound of organ music coming from a fine-looking church down the high street, he headed in that direction. On entering the vestibule he saw a young man pumping away at the organ bellows while the organist played above. The 'pumper' looked ' at the last gasp' and Warren offered to 'lend a hand while he rested a bit'. The young man willingly handed over the bellows and left the church. The organ music continued for some time; the organ-blower did not

<hr>

[295] *On the Veldt*, pp 2–3.
[296] The Karoo is that semi-desert plateau that lies between the south-western Cape and the Orange River.
[297] *Ibid.*, p 10.

return; and Warren 'began to perspire very freely'. However, he did not like to inconvenience the congregation by stopping his pumping. Finally they filed out and as they did so, they looked at Warren as if to say, 'You are not one of us.' When the organist ceased his playing, Warren looked through the inner door 'and found it was a Roman Catholic Church'. He was horrified, 'and bolted!'[298]

In the afternoon he strolled round the town with his friend Porges. He was struck by the bright, clean clothes of the Muslim Malays, who inhabited their own quarter of the town. These were in sharp contrast to the amaXhosa, whom he referred to by the colonists' customary derogatory term, 'Kafirs'. They were scruffily dressed and had a 'very sullen look' which disturbed the young British officer. 'Everywhere else,' he commented, 'I have found the native looking upon the Englishman as his friend, but here [he] looks gloomily at us as his natural enemy'.[299] Warren had yet to learn of the level of dispossession and subjugation that the amaXhosa had suffered, much of it at the hands of British colonists. But his perception was prophetic, for in little over a year the amaXhosa would be in full rebellion, and Warren himself would be back with a volunteer force to help contain it.

They left early the next morning, by train to the end of the 75-kilometre line, and then by coach to Grahamstown, which they reached that first evening. It was to be another nine years before the rail line went all the way to Kimberley. For the next six days their coach covered about ten kilometres an hour for sixteen hours a day, with staging posts for fresh horses every 25 kilometres. They stayed in cheap wayside hotels that reminded Warren of the *ventas* of Spain, though 'not so amusing'. He was fortunate to have the amusing company of Porges, for he found the countryside 'dreary in the extreme' – flat, open grassland, punctuated only by small, flat-topped hills.

They arrived in Kimberley at dawn on Monday 4 December. Warren had been invited by Major Lanyon to stay at Government House, but not knowing Lanyon personally, and considering the early hour of the morning, he booked in initially at Mrs Jardine's Hotel, to get a wash and have breakfast. He was still at breakfast when Lanyon sent for him and 'wigged' him for not coming over to Government House immediately when he arrived. Lanyon, a fellow Freemason, was very hospitable and they established a good relationship.

Warren's opposite number and future colleague, Jos de Villiers, the Government Surveyor of the Orange Free State, had come over to meet him

[298] *Ibid.*, p 11.
[299] *Ibid.*, pp 12–13.

Kimberley mine in 1875.
MCGREGOR MUSEUM, KIMBERLEY, SOUTH AFRICA

and the following day they set off in De Villiers' Cape cart for Bloemfontein to meet the Free State's President Johannes ('Jan') Brand. The Cape cart was a lightweight two-wheeler with retractable hood, usually pulled by two horses. *En route*, they spent a night at De Villiers' home in Boshof. Warren liked De Villiers, and found his wife very welcoming. Professionally, the two men had much in common and the journey provided them both with the opportunity to discuss how they would work together on the survey.

Warren had heard that the Boers in general were difficult to get on with and some of them were outright anti-British. While that may have been true, and certainly was in the 1830s, they had reason to be distrustful of British motives, especially after the annexation of the diamond fields. By the 1870s, however, there had grown up a class of highly educated people of Dutch extraction, calling themselves 'Afrikaners', who, while emphasising their distinctive 'Afrikander' culture, were prepared to work within, or alongside, the British system. Brand was just such a man.

Johannes Brand came from a prominent Cape family: his father had been first Speaker of the Cape Legislative Assembly (1872–76). He himself had

135

studied law at Leiden in the Netherlands and was called to the English Bar before returning to Cape Town. He had practised in the Cape Supreme Court until his election to the Free State Presidency in 1863.[300] Having adopted the Free State, Brand became a staunch republican and it was his persistence over the diamond fields' dispute that won his country the £90,000 compensation. Nevertheless, Warren and Brand quickly established a relationship of mutual trust and respect, a position probably helped by the fact that Brand, like Warren, was a Freemason.[301]

Warren, however, gave Brand the credit for the success of their relationship. In a manner so typical of a Victorian English gentleman, he wrote to Fanny:

> I suppose he would not be offended if I say that he seems to be thoroughly English. We shall get on first rate together, I can see, he takes such reasonable views of everything.[302]

Being 'thoroughly English', however, was not necessarily an advantage from Brand's point of view. As Warren observed, some members of the Free State *Volksraad*[303] regarded Brand as 'too English' for republican tastes. In this respect, Brand was pleased to learn that Warren had discretion to make slight adjustments to the boundary line, for, as he pointed out, some of the border farmers had threatened to shoot those who laid down the line if it brought them into British territory.[304]

Warren stayed in Bloemfontein for the weekend. He attended Sunday service in the Anglican Cathedral and found Bishop Webb's sermon 'most impressive'. He spent the rest of that day in the company of members of the Anglican community. In very good humour, he caught the regular coach back to Kimberley early the next morning and found that his travelling companion was the Roman Catholic Vicar Apostolic for Natal, Bishop Jolivet.

There was generally considerable antipathy between the Anglicans and Roman Catholics in Victorian Britain, a position not helped by the conversion in mid-century of two prominent High Anglicans, Henry Edward Manning and John Henry Newman. Both were subsequently elevated to Cardinal by the Pope in 1875 and 1879, respectively. So it was a sensitive topic for Anglicans at the time.

---

[300] https://en.wikipedia.org/wiki/Johannes_Brand, accessed 24 January 2016.

[301] Macdonald, *WARREN! The Bond of Brotherhood,* p 82.

[302] *On the Veldt,* p 17.

[303] *Volksraad*: literally 'people's council', the legislative assembly of the republic.

[304] *On the Veldt,* p 17.

Warren's instinctive aversion to Catholicism had been revealed when he found himself inadvertently assisting at a Roman Catholic service in Port Elizabeth: he 'bolted'. And yet, here he was, for the next twelve hours, in the company of the most senior Roman Catholic cleric in South Africa. Warren, however, took people at face value. He judged a man by his character rather than by his background, and he found the bishop 'right good company, full of anecdotes, and most amusing'. A good sense of humour was high in Warren's list of social graces. Nevertheless, he was secretly pleased to hear the bishop complain at considerable length that the Bloemfontein Anglicans were gaining adherents at the expense of the Catholics. Warren silently approved: clearly the Anglicans were working hard, and 'getting ahead' of the Catholics there.

As they approached Kimberley, a large number of Roman Catholics came out to meet them. They had brought a carriage for the Bishop, who insisted that Warren join him, and together they 'drove into town in triumph'.[305]

* * *

Jos de Villiers was busy as a member of the *Volksraad* in Bloemfontein for a few days, and while Warren waited for his NCOs and equipment to arrive from Cape Town, he accompanied the Griqualand West Surveyor-General, Francis Orpen, down to Ramah on the Orange River, the southernmost point of the survey. During their journey, it soon became clear to Warren that although Orpen and De Villiers were both able and good surveyors, there had never been any agreement between them. They were 'a case of Box and Cox, they would never meet'.[306] They each did their own farm surveys and ignored those of the other. Over the next few days Orpen did his best to inculcate in Warren 'the English view', as an antidote to all the 'Dutch poison' he would be imbibing when working with De Villiers!

Warren had already drawn up a basic plan for the work, as agreed with De Villiers. The first job would be to fix the precise positions of the principal points of the agreed boundary. The line would run north-easterly from Ramah at the southern end; through David's Grave by the Riet River; to Tarentaalkop, a small hill just north-east of Kimberley. From there it would go westerly for a few kilometres, to clear the northern outskirts of Kimberley, before getting back on its north-easterly trajectory to Platberg, a large hill by

---

[305] *Ibid.*, p 24.
[306] *Idem.*; 'Box and Cox': to take turns, from a popular comic play of that name, about two lodgers who shared rooms but never met, one occupying the rooms by day, the other by night. http://www.phrases.org.uk/meanings/73300.html, accessed 20 January 2016.

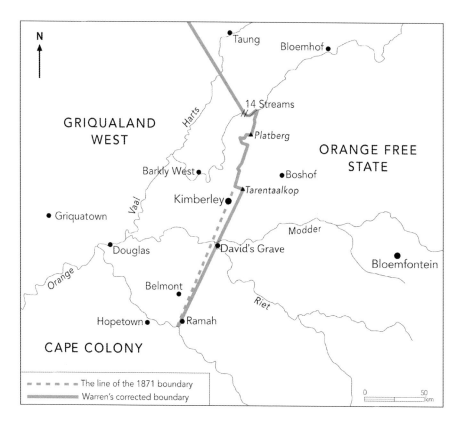

*The Griqualand West/Orange Free State boundary line
before and after Warren's survey.*

the Vaal. It would be necessary to fix the precise latitude and longitude of some point in the triangulation, and connect it with the farm triangulations near Kimberley, already done by Orpen and De Villiers. They would then be in a position to mark out an accurate straight line of stone beacons from one point to the next. De Villiers was already in agreement with Warren's plan. The only problem they anticipated was Orpen, who had a number of land claims in the region himself. He was keen to influence the work in favour of Griqualand West, and De Villiers would have been pleased to observe that Warren was having none of it.

Warren returned to Kimberley to find that Kennedy and Randall had arrived safely with the heavy baggage. For the next month Warren and his NCOs camped about a mile outside Kimberley, by a baseline previously used by Orpen for his triangulations. De Villiers, meanwhile, had returned from

Bloemfontein and began building stone beacons at the agreed trigonometrical points.

During this time Warren got together a wagon, a light cart, oxen, horses and other equipment and hired several servants, including an Indian cook. Getting and keeping reliable servants so close to the 'grog shops' of Kimberley was, however, a constant problem. Those he did get were not very attentive to their tasks, and kept allowing the oxen to stray. Warren wished he had 'some of our Syrian muleteers here, and even one of the most inefficient dragomans of that country, for there is no one who can act as a foreman to be got hold of'. He supposed that any man worth his salt was engaged in the diamond mines at high wages.

His Indian cook, Nerada, could do no more than make up a fire, so Warren taught him how to make bread ('in our way') and how to make an omelette, poach eggs 'and other little accomplishments, and now I suppose he will want to go'. And sure enough, he did, not to make more money in Kimberley as Warren supposed, but to his family in Natal where some of his children had died. Before leaving, however, Nerada introduced a replacement, named Balagaroo, but he had never cooked anything but rice. Fortunately, Fanny had supplied her husband with a little book on 'cottage cooking', which now proved very useful, as he proudly explained to her:

> I have made the dinner myself today, and the NCOs have pronounced it excellent. Minced beef with milk, salt, pepper, onions and Yorkshire Relish added, and boiled for twenty minutes.

He finally got an Indian cook named Sam, who really did know something about cooking, and for a while Balagaroo did the housekeeping.[307]

* * *

De Villiers came over after Christmas and the two of them worked together re-measuring Orpen's three-and-a-half mile baseline, which had become 'zigzag and wavy', probably from sheep using it as a path. As this was an international boundary, it was vital they got it absolutely right. By 22 January 1877 they had finished their work in the Kimberley area and Warren and De Villiers went down to David's Grave. They set up a joint camp and began their observations, building stone piles as markers.

The summer rains were late and the weather was very hot. Warren enjoyed

---

[307] *Ibid.*, pp 36, 41–2 and 51.

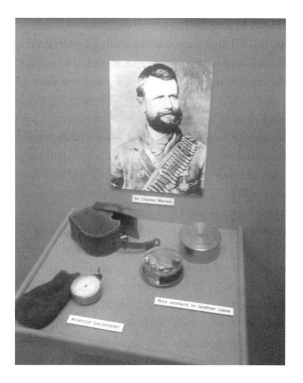

Warren's aneroid barometer and portable sextant.
MCGREGOR MUSEUM, KIMBERLEY, SOUTH AFRICA

the heat, but admitted it was difficult doing the calculations in the covered wagon, with daytime temperatures well over 100 °F (38 °C). In addition, the extreme heat and persistent drought distorted visibility and created mirages, so much so that they were only able to take accurate observations for ten minutes each morning and evening. This meant that, as they often had to make observations far from camp, they slept many nights out in the veldt.

Striking an accurate line south to Ramah over rough country, full of small hills, was quite a challenge; but, building on his considerable experience in Gibraltar and Palestine, Warren was full of innovative ideas, and De Villiers was happy to let him take the lead. They worked well together and put in long hours. He wrote to Fanny:

> Jos de Villiers and I only differ on one point in our work, and that is the rate of progress. He says I must be working piece work to wish to get on so fast.[308]

[308] *Ibid.*, p 68.

But Warren saw no reason to delay. There was no hunting to be had, little 'native life' to observe and no historic ruins to explore. Besides, he had promised Fanny he would only be away for six months.

Aware of the potential hostility of many Boers towards the British, Warren was keen to develop good relationships with them, especially those that he was now going to confirm would be on the British side of the new boundary. But Warren was a good communicator and was able to find a way round most potential problems.

Occasionally, when De Villiers was nearby and had shot a bustard (about the size of a goose), they would feast on that; but otherwise, their source of meat was sheep bought from local Boers. Often they refused to sell, despite having what Warren judged to be many sheep and very poor pasture. In typical Warren fashion, he stumbled on a way round this. On one occasion, with his party quite out of meat and the farmer refusing to sell, Warren simply said, 'Well, there is the money I shall give; now I shall go and take one'. Upon which, the farmer's attitude changed completely. 'Let me select it,' he said. It seemed there was a custom among them that if a starving man has the means to pay for food, the owner of the food must sell to him. Warren thought it quaint, but a useful custom, and from then on he had no problem buying food for himself and his men. On another occasion a man named Van Eck objected to Warren measuring from the top of a hill right next to his house. Warren, however, pointed out Van Eck's lack of hospitality when he entered his house to seek permission, so he had decided not to ask. Van Eck, duly shamed, became very hospitable and invited the young Englishman in for coffee.[309]

Warren credited his NCO, Sergeant Kennedy, in large measure with how well they got on with the rural Boers. Kennedy was a real asset. He was a big, powerful Irishman and Roman Catholic, who was always fit and healthy. He had a strong sense of duty, a good sense of humour, and a natural ability to get on with people.

* * *

The first of a series of periodic thunderstorms had begun late in the night of 27 January. In the morning the ground was damp and for a while the air was clear and cool, but in between the storms the heat returned and the problems of mirage were even worse. It was not until the end of February that the rains really set in and the mirages lessened, but then they had to dig trenches

---

[309] *Ibid.*, pp 95–96.

around their tents to prevent flooding.

In the damp weather Warren's horses started refusing to pull the spring cart, and as the oxen were much more biddable, he placed two oxen in front of the two horses. It was in this manner that he visited a Boer name Lubbe, who was one of those who had threatened to shoot the first Englishman who ventured onto his farm. As Warren drove up to the farm, Lubbe was so amused by the practicality of Warren's way of working reluctant horses that he was extremely civil, and by the time they parted he had quite forgotten his resolve to shoot Englishmen.[310]

At Mr Mager's farm north of the Modder River, a name later to become widely known as Magersfontein, the site of a major battle of the Anglo-Boer War, Warren received a delegation of lawyers, bankers and farmers from Kimberley. They were connected with a land speculation company and they wanted him to vary the line to ensure their property investments fell within British territory. According to Warren, despite many set speeches, he held firm, telling them he would treat them the same as other farmers along the boundary. The line would go straight and would not deviate just because 'they were an influential company with big people in England at their head'.

He did not get much support from De Villiers who was quite willing to give way on this, provided his own people on the Free State side would get the same concession. But Warren knew this would drive a coach and horses through his precious boundary. In the end the tenant of the farm where they were gathered, and which lay across the boundary line, got up and said:

> You have mistaken your man, you won't be able to persuade him; he will carry out the work as laid down by Lord Carnarvon, and will pay no attention to you or to anyone else except his chief.

With that, the gathering dispersed, promising to return in two days to press their case once more. As Warren observed in his journal with a wry smile, by then he would have reached Kimberley and the straight boundary would be laid down.[311]

On Sunday 18 March with the surveying party just five miles short of Kimberley, Lanyon came out to meet Warren. He was due to go down to Cape Town for a month's leave and to meet the new High Commissioner, Sir Bartle Frere. He warned Warren there was high feeling in Kimberley about the

---

[310] *Ibid.*, pp 93–94.
[311] Ibid., p 104.

inflexibility of the boundary, and he tried to persuade him to relent and make some compromises. The following day Warren went in to Kimberley where the local newspapers were agitating about a small piece of the road south from Kimberley that wavered across the line. They claimed this would damage the trade and traffic of the diamond fields. Warren thought it a ridiculous fuss as the 'roads' were only unmade tracks and a diversion could easily be cut through the veldt. Unfortunately, however, some local Free State officials had already started exercising jurisdiction over the road, and Warren decided he needed to pay a visit to President Brand to get his support. It might delay the work a week, but it would be worth it in the end.

The President was firmly on his side, recognising that it would never end if every interest group was allowed to interfere. There were just two exceptions, and these had already been agreed with Lord Carnarvon. The boundary would detour around the border farms of two prominent Boers who had strongly opposed Brand's agreement and had threatened violence if their farms did not fall within the Free State. As a result, Warren's straight line ended up with two westward kinks: a small one just north of Kimberley for the benefit of Commandant Gideon Joubert, and a larger one just short of Platberg for the group of farms belonging to Commandant Abel Erasmus. So far as the disputed road was concerned, Brand promised to order the local officials not to interfere with it. He was anxious to see the boundary completed before the next meeting of the *Volksraad* at the end of April, which put the pressure on Warren and De Villiers.

Fortunately, the Kimberley-Platberg line was a lot quicker to do than the southern portion, for Platberg could be seen from the top of a small hill near Kimberley. De Villiers was able to wave a flag from the summit of Platberg and Warren responded with a heliostat, flashed according to a prearranged code. He improvised his heliostat by scratching a small, circular hole in the reflective surface on the back of his shaving mirror. The mirror was attached to a stick and the back surface held up to the eye. Then, with the sun in the right direction, he could look through the hole and direct the reflected light accurately onto the desired point along the line. The mirror was not needed for shaving, for, as in Palestine, Warren grew a beard while working in the field.

Through late-March and early April 1877 work was 'incessant day and night', with Warren and his team more often than not sleeping out in the open. By 15 April they had reached the farm of Abel Erasmus, one of the strongest opponents of the boundary agreement. But once Warren was able to confirm that his farms were to be cut into the Free State side, he became very amiable. On Warren's first night at the farm, Mrs Erasmus laid on dinner and, according to Warren she told her husband to mind his language, warning him, 'That man talks "high English", he is not the same as those who come here and talk "low English", you must treat him properly'. Clearly Erasmus heeded his wife's advice, for Warren reported that the two of them 'got on splendidly'. Erasmus even allowed Warren to use his house as a base in which to do his calculations.

Three days later the line was ready for inspection. This began at Commandant Joubert's farm, near Kimberley. De Villiers and Warren were joined by two officials each from the Free State and Griqualand West. A number of others joined them unofficially and for the next five days they travelled along the line inspecting all the beacons north to Platberg and the Vaal, and then back over the same line to Tarentaalkop and from there south to Ramah.

Warren was proud to show off his beacons. There were 42 of them in all. They varied in height, according to how far apart they were. In the populated and cultivated area near Kimberley, he had placed them only about a mile apart, for he knew that this was where there was more likely to be land disputes. From a small hill twenty miles (32 km) south of Kimberley, looking north to Tarentaalkop there were fifteen beacons, and owing to the gentle slope of the ground, the top of one beacon appeared to nearly reach the base of the next, so that they had the appearance of a triangular-based straight stone wall cut through the veldt. They were so beautifully regular that, according to Warren, 'when the Boers first saw the line of beacons they exclaimed in Dutch "Allemachte, Lord Carnarvon himself could not have done it better!"'[312]

Erasmus had invited Warren to ride in his Cape cart for the duration of the five-day inspection. Warren was in high spirits after the completion of five months' intensive work and on occasion, to relieve the boredom, the carts raced each other across the rough veldt. It was the sort of dangerous sport that Warren thoroughly enjoyed. At one point Erasmus and Warren were in the lead when another cart collided with them and tipped over. Both carts suffered some damage. A long dispute ensued, with everybody calmly putting in their opinion as to who was to blame and thereby liable for damage. Eventually, a consensus was reached: Erasmus would get costs, as the other cart had come from behind and must have been responsible for the accident. Warren was impressed, for, as he observed, in England it would have gone to court.[313]

---

[312] *On the Veldt*, p 133.
[313] *Idem.*

On 24 April Warren formally handed over custody of the beacons to the Free State and Griqualand West authorities. He had a couple of weeks of paperwork to complete: some calculations and the drawing of a large-scale plan of the beaconed boundary line.[314] During this time he had the comfort of Government House to himself as Lanyon was still on leave in the Cape.

With time to reflect, Warren thought in the manner of a disappointed tourist:

> I am really disappointed in this country, there is so little to be seen; people have little information on any subject; they live only in speculation; but I have no doubt that when I get home I shall have plenty to say about the country. I wish, however, that there were any real natives here; the Kafirs are all imported, so that I have not seen a single native dance, or even a spear or a shield.[315]

He had been singularly unimpressed by the Africans he had met so far, mostly the marginalised and dispossessed, given to drinking and begging, and whom he referred to with contempt as 'mostly scum, and unfit to be classed with the people of any tribe'. His derogatory attitude was not helped by his frequent discussions with Boers, whose main refrain was complaints about the iniquities of their workers whom they flogged with impunity for any misdemeanour.

Warren's father had written positively about the Batswana he had met north of the Vaal in 1825, and Warren felt sure there must still in the 1870s be some 'natives' worthy of admiration. On one occasion while walking in the veldt he had heard the melodious singing of Christian hymns coming from a small building. On approaching, he realised it was a small chapel. He noted that there was no European missionary present, and he was pleased to observe that these 'natives' needed no outside supervision to indulge in 'civilised' Christian worship. Now, in his final weeks in Africa, he was determined to visit a 'real African' homestead. He made enquiries from the Acting Surveyor-General, Alexander Baillie, who took him to visit the home of Piet Manzana, an African from the Eastern Cape who had bought a farm in the Barkly District.

Manzana was a 'go-ahead fellow' who had a well-stocked farm and had built a dam. His homestead consisted of a group of traditional, African-style round thatched houses enclosed within a stockade. The enclosure was swept scrupulously clean and would have 'put the yard of any white farmer to shame'. But then, Warren noted, 'the white farmer [did] not have the

---

[314] A copy is held in the Royal Geographical Society's Archive, in London, Ref: South Africa D.119.
[315] *On the Veldt*, p 106.

assistance of several wives'. Warren and Baillie were treated to an excellent supper of chicken, roasted in a three-legged pot, and sour milk, all served spotlessly clean. That night Warren slept for the first time on the clean floor of a traditional African house.[316]

Before leaving Kimberley for the Orange Free State, Warren gave a public lecture on his favourite subject, Jerusalem. There were a number of Freemasons in Kimberley and it was probably they who invited him to speak. After the lecture the Acting-Administrator, Judge Barry, expressed a few words of thanks and remarked admiringly that Warren had 'gained the hearts of the Boers in the Province'.

Warren reflected that if this was true, all that had been needed was 'a little ventilation on the subject' of co-operation between Boer and Briton. He had been 'arguing with the Boers for four months' and he was confident he had helped 'rub aside some of their prejudices … They were all plain-spoken folk, and a little plain-speaking did a great deal of good'. He had of course been helped by the friendship of men like De Villiers, Erasmus and the Boers generally along the line. But he acknowledged that much credit must go to Sergeant Kennedy:

> I cannot help thinking that the meeting of the Boers with a soldier like Sergeant Kennedy had its effect. He is a man in a thousand.[317]

* * *

Warren completed his work in Kimberley on 7 May and spent the next week with De Villiers at his home in Boshof, making final checks on their calculations and drawing up a duplicate plan of the boundary between the British colony and the Boer republic. 'And so,' remarked Warren 'our work was concluded in five months' incessant hard work.' They proceeded to Bloemfontein where they formally handed over their plans for Brand's signature before forwarding a copy to England.

They were invited by the President to attend the annual *Volksraad* dinner. There was strong anti-British feeling among the members of the *Volksraad*, occasioned not just by the 'theft' of the diamond fields, but also by the recent British annexation, on 12 April 1877, of the Boer Republic of the Transvaal. On account of this hostile atmosphere, President Brand was concerned about allowing a toast to The Queen of Great Britain and Ireland, which would have

[316] *On the Veldt*, pp 135–6.
[317] *Ibid.*, pp 138–40.

been customary, in Warren's honour. Warren, however, reassured him that his reply to such a toast would allay any fears that he might have about its likely reception.

When the time came for Warren to reply he referred to, 'one of the principal products of their country of which nothing was ever said, but is worth all the gold and diamonds in the world'. He enlarged upon the subject, growing more and more expansive until in the end he explained that the product of which he spoke was the children that they reared. 'They were delighted … [and] as a result the toast was received with acclamation'.[318] Warren was clearly past master at schmoozing a potentially hostile audience. Before leaving Bloemfontein he received a unanimous vote of thanks from the Free State *Volksraad*.

Warren spent one final night with the De Villiers family in Boshof and arrived back in Kimberley early in the morning of Tuesday 22 May. He had only a matter of hours in which to make his final arrangements for he had booked a seat for himself on a coach departing from Kimberley that evening. The first thing he did was to arrange the transport for Sergeant Kennedy and Corporal Randall to travel south with all the heavy baggage to Cape Town. He himself planned to go via the Transvaal to Natal on the east coast where his old friend from Gibraltar days, Colonel Anthony G. Durnford RE, was stationed. From there he planned to sail up the coast to Zanzibar and home through the Suez Canal; but just before he left Kimberley, he received a telegram from High Commissioner Frere requesting that on reaching the East African coast, he catch a southbound steamer and report to him in Cape Town.

Meanwhile, Lanyon had returned from leave and the Griqualand West Legislative Council presented Warren with a formal vote of thanks, on illuminated vellum, thanking him for the speedy settlement of the boundary.[319] In due course the British Government was to honour him as Companion of the Order of St Michael and St George (CMG) for his successful work on the Griqualand West-Orange Free State boundary.

Warren had won many friends in Kimberley and when the Transvaal coach drew up at Government House that evening, a small crowd gathered to see him off, not knowing whether they would ever see him again.

[318] *On the Veldt*, p 139.
[319] *Ibid.*, pp 141–3.

CHAPTER 9

Return to Griqualand West

When Warren had arrived in South Africa in November 1876, the Transvaal was an independent Boer republic.[320] By the time he came to leave Griqualand West six months later, it had become a British colony.

The annexation of the Transvaal had come about as part of the British Secretary of State Lord Carnarvon's plan to unite the two British colonies and two Boer republics in a federation.[321] He had performed a similar feat in Canada in 1867 and he saw federation as the best way to strengthen 'British South Africa'. The remaining independent African kingdoms of the region were perceived to be a threat to the continued expansion of white settlement, and Carnarvon believed that, through federation, he would be able to bring all the Africans of the region under colonial control. Furthermore, the wealth of the diamond fields had made federation financially feasible. It was assumed that Griqualand West would become part of the Cape Colony, thus ensuring that the Cape would remain the most powerful state in the federation. Warren's border commission had been a necessary preliminary step to persuading the Orange Free State of Britain's good intentions. And in his relationships with individual Boers, Warren had unwittingly proven himself a good ambassador for the furtherance of British designs.

Although the Boer Republic of the Transvaal was known to be particularly anti-British, an unsuccessful war with the Bapedi in the mountainous Eastern Transvaal provided the British with a unique opportunity to forcibly intervene. Since the opening of the diamond fields, the Bapedi had been travelling to Kimberley to earn cash to buy guns for national defence. The Transvaal Boers saw this as a threat to their security and to their own labour supply, and in July 1876 President Burgers led 2000 mounted Boers against the Bapedi

---

[320] Known in Afrikaans as the *Zuid-Afrikaansche Republiek* or ZAR.
[321] Henry Herbert, 4th Earl of Carnarvon (1831–1890). See C. F. Goodfellow, *Great Britain and South African Federation, 1870–1881* (Oxford University Press, Cape Town, 1966); R. L. Cope, 'Carnarvon's South African confederation policy', *History in Africa*, 13 (1986), pp 11–34; and N. A. Etherington, 'Labour supply and the genesis of South African Confederation in the 1870s', *The Journal of African History*, 20 (1979), pp 235–53.

mountain stronghold. Bapedi resistance, however, was too strong and after a number of weeks the bulk of the Boer army deserted and returned home to protect their families and farms, leaving President Burgers with military defeat and a near-bankrupt government.[322]

In January 1877 Sir Theophilus Shepstone, a senior member of the Natal Executive, entered the Transvaal accompanied by 25 mounted police. He was on a special mission to persuade the *Volksraad* in Pretoria that in their weakened state, their best protection from the threat of both Bapedi and amaZulu invasion would be as part of a British federation. In March, having failed to get their agreement, Shepstone walked into the *Volksraad* and, as Warren described it when he heard the news in Kimberley, 'Like Oliver Cromwell he … told the Volks that as they could not govern themselves, he would do it for them'.[323] The British flag was raised and annexation formerly proclaimed on 12 April.

As Warren set off through the Transvaal six weeks later, he was keen to observe how the Transvaalers were taking to British overrule. The journey to the capital, Pretoria, took four days, with regular stops for change of horses. He did not encounter any overt hostility from the Boers they met, although he did observe some resentfulness at the sneaky way that Shepstone had 'stolen' their country. On the other hand, there was also appreciation that it would now be British soldiers who would be fighting their African enemies.[324]

When Warren climbed aboard the coach in Kimberley, he found the front three seats already taken and he had to squeeze into the back, alongside Auditor-General Ravenscroft, who was on his way home on leave before taking up a new appointment in Ceylon (Sri Lanka). By the time they reached Pretoria, the two young men had become firm friends. They booked in at the Masonic Hotel and the following day they were introduced to Administrator Shepstone. He invited them to take their meals in Government House where they met his Private Secretary, twenty-year-old Henry Rider Haggard, later to gain fame as the author of adventure stories set in Africa: *King Solomon's Mines* and *Allan Quartermain*.

Warren had planned to travel down to Durban in Natal; but then he heard about the road linking the small alluvial goldfields of the Eastern Transvaal with Delagoa Bay in Portuguese East Africa (Mozambique). It had been cut through 'lion veldt' and 'tsetse fly country', following the opening of the

---

[322] Peter Delius, *The Land Belongs To Us* (Ravan Press, Johannesburg, 1983), pp 181–216.
[323] *On the Veldt*, p 106.
[324] *Ibid.*, pp 150–51.

goldfields in 1873. But its staging posts had been attacked by the Bapedi during the recent war and the road had been closed for a year. The challenge was too much for Warren, who reasoned that the war was over and he would be doing a service to reopen the road. Ravenscroft agreed to go with him and the two of them paid for seats in a wagon bound for Lydenburg. This first stage of the journey took them six days, the latter part being through land laid waste by the war, so there was little food to be had and Warren forced a laugh at how cheaply they had been able to live.[325]

At Lydenburg they were eager to move on as their ship from Delagoa Bay to Durban left in ten days' time. They managed to buy a Scotch Cart and four oxen to carry their belongings. They hired a Griqua named Peet to guide them and two African servants to look after the oxen. The engineer in Warren could not be suppressed. He meticulously recorded distances and heights above sea level throughout the journey down from Lydenburg to Laurenço Marques[326] with a view to writing up a report for the interest of the British authorities.

They travelled day and night, snatching sleep when they could, and on the third day they began the steep descent down the eastern face of the Drakensberg. The road, such as it was, was so steep it was more akin to a flight of steps. They lashed the wheels of the cart and lowered it down in a controlled slide, descending 1200 feet (360 metres) in a single hour. Gradually the slope lessened and they passed through thick forest followed by tall grassland. Lions could be heard nearby and when they slept at night, they burnt a clearing through the grass and surrounded themselves and their oxen with thorn scrub and fires.

They began to pass through gently rolling country and came across a number of African settlements where they were able to purchase food. They were thankful to spend a couple of nights in African villages, sleeping on the floor of their huts. With plenty of lions about, fires were kept going through the night and they slept with guns at the ready. The Africans they met as they passed into Portuguese territory were well armed with guns from Delagoa Bay and consequently they were 'rapidly thinning the game and driving it away'.[327]

They reached the great plain near the Bay on 11 June, and with their steamer due the next morning, they drove their exhausted oxen on into the night. Cold and hungry, they pushed their way through mosquito-infested marshland, taking 'a little quinine to ward off the fever', and finally reaching the entrance to Laurenço Marques at 3 am. The guard at the entrance gate

[325] *Ibid.*, p 174.
[326] Today's Maputo, the capital of Mozambique.
[327] *On the Veldt*, pp 191–3.

was so astonished at seeing them that 'he lost his bayonet, and was some time before he found it stuck somewhere in his clothing'. They made their way to the only hotel and, leaving their servants to light a fire and settle down with the wagon and oxen in the middle of the street, Warren and Ravenscroft let themselves into the deserted hotel and grabbed a few hours' sleep on the dining room tables.

Rising at dawn, Warren was pleased to observe some Portuguese engineers constructing a road across the marsh and building a sea wall to protect the town from flood tides. He estimated there were about 50 Portuguese residents in the town, mostly men with African wives, in sharp contrast, he noted, to the Boers for whom an African wife was anathema. The Boers in Lydenburg and elsewhere had told Warren that the only way to gain the respect of his servants and other Africans he met was to treat them like dogs:

> … but this course we did not consider desirable. We sat down among them, fed with them, and joked with them, but always found them most deferential.[328]

* * *

Warren and Ravenscroft boarded the Union Company steamer *Natal* on 12 June and, after stopping briefly at Durban, reached Cape Town on the 26th. They had already booked their passage for England, departing on the 28th; but before paying for his ticket, Warren went to see the High Commissioner.

Sir Bartle Frere was full of praise for the way Warren had settled the Griqualand/Free State boundary. In fact he had pleased both sides so well that the High Commissioner wanted him to 'return to Kimberley as Special Commissioner on the Land Question, to arbitrate between the farmers'. Lanyon had apparently insisted that Warren was 'the only person competent to do the work in a satisfactory manner'.

This was the last thing that Warren wanted to hear. He had been looking forward to returning home to Fanny and the children. Besides, he knew it would be a hopeless task. The majority of land titles in Griqualand West were tied up in legal dispute. And, as he explained to Frere, despite the title of 'Special Commissioner', he would have no legal authority and would have to depend entirely on persuading the legal antagonists to give up some of their claims. Warren was under the direct orders of Lord Carnarvon, who had given him a single task, now completed. He was perfectly within his rights to decline Frere's request.

---

[328] *Ibid.*, p 197.

Frere, however, was determined to win him over. An essential part of the federation scheme was that Griqualand West, the richest colony in Southern Africa by virtue of the diamond mines, should become part of the mother colony, 'the Cape'. But the Cape Colony, which had been granted internal self-government in 1872, would never accept Griqualand annexation while the question of land titles remained unsettled. If left to the Griqualand Court of Appeal, it was likely to take several years to sort out, at great legal expense for both Government and claimants; and Frere was anxious to press ahead with federation. He did not explain these underlying political motives to Warren. Instead, he simply said that the future development of Griqualand West was being hindered by the legal quagmire of disputed land titles.

Flattery having failed, Frere appealed to Warren's sense of duty, adding that acceptance of this task would be viewed very favourably by the Home Government. According to the account that Warren sent home to Fanny, he 'did not feel in the least convinced and asked that [he] might have a few hours to think it over, fully intending to go to England'. The appeal to Warren's sense of duty, however, may have weakened his resolve, for when he called on Lady Frere, he was putty in her hands. As he explained to Fanny:

> She pointed out so clearly what I ought to do and settled it all so firmly that I felt I must give in. I was Sir Bartle's first selection, and there was no one so suitable for the work.[329]

When Warren called on the High Commissioner the next day, Frere said he had already written to Lord Carnarvon asking for Warren's services and explaining that for this work on the land question he needed 'a man with a backbone'.

Having been 'reduced to submission by Lady Frere', Warren could no longer resist her husband. He agreed to go back to Kimberley on the understanding that the work did not take more than six months. Warren loved a challenge, but his reluctance to accept this appointment was probably tinged as much by his conviction that it could not succeed as by his desire to return home to his family. He must have been pleased to receive so much praise of his worth, but he was fully aware of how disappointed Fanny would be in a month's time to receive a letter of explanation instead of a husband. That letter concluded: 'I have felt quite desolated for some hours but I must accept the appointment'.[330]

---

[329] *On the Veldt*, p 206.
[330] *Idem.*

*Fanny Margaretta Warren would have been very disappointed to receive
a letter rather than a husband home from Africa in 1877.*
WARREN FAMILY COLLECTION

Ravenscroft was sailing to England on the ship that Warren was to have taken and he carried Warren's letter to Fanny at their home in Wimbledon,[331] promising to go down and visit the family before his departure for Ceylon.

* * *

If subsequent entries in his journal formed the basis of further letters to Fanny, she must have noticed that her husband's 'desolation' did not last for long. Once he had seen off Ravenscroft and his NCOs, Warren's youthful exuberance returned and he was filled with the excitement of being on a new assignment. He could not set off immediately for Kimberley as he had to wait

[331] The house at 44 St George's Road, Wimbledon, South-West London, had been purchased by Warren, probably just before his departure to the Cape in 1876.

for Sir Bartle Frere to get Lord Carnarvon's authority for his commission, and it was almost a month before he left for Kimberley.

Although only a Captain, a relatively junior rank in military terms, Warren had the social advantage of being a Royal Engineer, unencumbered by the hierarchy of authority that characterised line regiments. He was in a privileged position: having come to South Africa the previous year as a Special Commissioner for the Earl of Carnarvon, he was not even under the direct authority of the Cape Governor and High Commissioner. He clearly enjoyed his position and made the most of it. He was of the 'gentleman' class – his late father a distinguished officer, his uncles rectors, and his grandfather a dean of a cathedral – and he moved at ease within the upper echelons of Cape society. Although he slept at the hotel in town, during the day he was a permanent guest at Government House, eager to fulfil any task that would please Sir Bartle or Lady Frere.

Warren's luggage had mistakenly been sent with Ravenscroft's from Natal to Zanzibar and Aden, and he had to purchase a second-hand suit while he was measured for a new frock coat and evening dress. He was amused to recall that one evening he was standing on a chair fixing a gas lamp for Lady Frere when John X. Merriman entered, dressed for dinner. Warren jumped down from the chair to shake hands with the distinguished parliamentarian, but Merriman put his hands firmly behind his back, mistaking Warren in his second-hand suit for a gas man who was being overfamiliar.[332]

Warren soon made himself socially known, however, when about a week after his arrival in Cape Town he gave a lecture on Palestine in the Library of Government House. 300 of the distinguished citizens of Cape Town were present, with the Governor in the Chair. With the sensibilities of his Afrikaner and British colonial audience in mind, Warren was careful to stress that his discoveries underneath the Holy City were all in accordance with the Bible.

With free access to the Governor's Library, Warren read widely on South African history and, at Frere's request, he wrote up a report on his journey from Lydenburg to Delagoa Bay. He detailed the nature of the road, indicating distances, altitudes and condition of the abandoned way stations. He discussed the possibility of railway construction, estimating its cost at between £1.8 million and £3 million. But he concluded his report by saying that in his opinion accounts of the Transvaal's wealth had been greatly exaggerated:

---

[332] *On the Veldt*, pp 207–8.

A land where horses, cattle, sheep, and fowls die suddenly of an incurable disease cannot progress very fast. The seasons are also most uncertain and the people indolent. A great influx of British might stir up the country, but otherwise *I cannot understand how it is to develop suddenly in the manner so often forecast*.[333]

Nine years later that 'sudden development' did indeed occur, as the largest goldfield the world had ever seen was discovered at the Witwatersrand ('white water's ridge') 60 kilometres south of Pretoria. And within five years Johannesburg had mushroomed into the largest city in Africa south of Cairo. But by then the Transvaal had reverted to being an independent Boer Republic, a State with which Warren was to have significant dealings. But all that lay in the future.

While Warren waited for his Land Commission assignment to come through, he made several exploratory trips around the Cape, including one with Lady Frere to the British naval base at Simonstown, on the south-east of the Cape Peninsula. The peninsula reminded him of Gibraltar, though on a much larger scale, but in contrast he was shocked to find Simonstown, the prime British military base of the Cape Colony, and indeed the Southern Hemisphere, so ill defended. A fortress was being built there in a hurry as it had only just been realised that if war were declared and the fleet not in port, a sea power could 'walk off with our Governor-General and the Admiral from Cape Town and Simon's Bay, and burn all our coal'.[334] From his Shoeburyness and Waltham Abbey experience, Warren recommended torpedoes as the best form of defence for the naval base.

At Frere's request, Warren went on an excursion up the line of rail to report on the prospects for the country around the railhead beyond Worcester and along the old wagon road. Warren and his companion Captain Nixon got off the train at Wellington, 70 kilometres from Cape Town, and while the train wound its way up the Hex River Valley, they walked the old wagon road up over Bain's Kloof some 450 metres above Wellington to arrive at Worcester three days later. Warren was refreshed by the invigorating walk, which recalled his earlier trips through Spain. He believed that farmers along the old road would soon lose out to those along the railway, although for the moment few

---

[333] *Royal Engineers Journal*, 2 May 1881, p 82, 'A Journey from Kimberley to Delagoa Bay', dated July 1877. *My emphasis.* The report as submitted to Frere was published as Confidential Print No. 135 (CO 879/11), Warren to Frere, Cape Town, 29 June 1877. It was later incorporated into his *On the Veldt in the Seventies*, published in 1902.

[334] *On the Veldt*, p 210.

farmers around Worcester appreciated the full potential of rail access to the markets of Cape Town.

* * *

A few days after Warren's return to Cape Town, he left for Kimberley, via Port Elizabeth on the SS *Nubia*. On boarding ship he found in the cabin next to him a young Englishman by the name of Cecil Rhodes.

It was the first time the two men had met, and at this initial meeting Warren was impressed by the younger man's energy and intellect. In due course, once Rhodes got into politics, Warren was to become highly critical of his policies. Rhodes was an undergraduate at Oriel College Oxford. With three more terms to serve, he was on leave for the summer holiday and had come out to South Africa to check on his diamond interests in Kimberley. Rhodes had just turned 24, to Warren's 37, and on the three days' sailing to Port Elizabeth the two men got on well together. Rhodes was in a garrulous mood and Warren learned all about his early experiences in South Africa.

Rhodes had arrived in South Africa in 1870 at the age of seventeen to join his eldest brother Herbert on his cotton farm in Natal. But by the time he arrived Herbert was away from home, busily becoming one of the earliest white prospectors on the newly discovered diamond fields on the Lower Vaal River. After a year on the farm, Cecil had joined Herbert in what had by then become the diamond city of Kimberley, and he began investing in diamond claims. He formed a business partnership with Charles Dunell Rudd and over the next few years they invested in several other businesses, including ice-making and a short-lived ice cream-making venture. During the rainy season of 1874 Rhodes and Rudd had won the highly lucrative contract to pump out water from the flooded Kimberley mine. But diamonds were the main business and by the time he first went to Oxford in 1873, Rhodes was already a very wealthy man.[335]

Unlike Warren, by all accounts Rhodes was not a studious undergraduate. He enjoyed the social life of those with wealth at Oxford. In 1877 he had just completed a year as Master of the University's Drag Hounds. He had joined

---

[335] The best full-length biography of Rhodes is R. I. Rotberg, *The Founder: Cecil Rhodes and the Pursuit of Power* (Oxford University Press, Oxford and New York, 1988, 2nd edition 2002). A much shorter account can be found in Kevin Shillington, *An African Adventure: A Brief Life of Cecil Rhodes* (Rhodes Memorial Museum and Commonwealth Centre, Bishop's Stortford, n.d.[1992]).

several exclusive clubs, including Vincent's and the Bullingdon.[336] He enjoyed the company of men: talking, trying out ideas and dining and drinking to excess. Warren, on the other hand, liked a cold beer in hot weather and an occasional brandy for 'medicinal purposes'; but he never drank to excess, considering it unbefitting of a true gentleman. Indeed, on the face of it, it is hard to find what Rhodes and Warren had in common.

An initial explanation may be found in the fact that just eight weeks before their meeting, Rhodes had been inducted into the University of Oxford's Apollo Chapter of Freemasonry.[337] That brotherhood of 'civilised men' appealed to both Rhodes and Warren, although their concepts of it differed. Warren saw Freemasonry as a means of binding good men together in a sense of duty to serve, particularly important in outposts of empire.[338] For Rhodes it was just one element in the pursuit of power. The Freemasons, as he saw it, wasted their potential as a secret band of brothers, although he was unlikely to have said as much to Warren, whom he would have realised took his Freemasonry very seriously. Rhodes had been attracted by the 'wealth and power they possess [and] the influence they hold'; but, writing on the same day as his induction, he observed:

> … I wonder that a large body of men can devote themselves to what at times appear the most ridiculous and absurd rites without an object and without an end.[339]

On the same day he was inducted into Freemasonry, Rhodes had drafted his 'Confession of Faith', his 'great idea' that was to guide his imperial ambitions and was incorporated into his numerous wills. As Rhodes saw it, 'we [the English] are the finest race in the world and the more of the world we inhabit the better it is for the human race'. The Freemasons may have provided him with the idea of a secret society, and the organisation and dedication of the Jesuits may also have been an influence, but Rhodes's concepts were merely a somewhat extreme version of the general jingoistic imperialism of 1870s Britain. Rhodes, however, went further than most in proposing the setting up of a secret society:

[336] Rotberg, *The Founder* (1988), pp 88–91.
[337] *Ibid.*, p 90; and John Flint, *Cecil Rhodes* (Hutchinson, London, 1976), p 248.
[338] Jessica L. Harland-Jacobs, *Builders of Empire: Freemasons and British Imperialism, 1717–1927* (University of North Carolina Press, Chapel Hill, 2013).
[339] Flint, *Cecil Rhodes*, p 249.

… with but one object the furtherance of the British Empire and the bringing of the whole civilised world under British rule for the recovery of the United States for the making the Anglo-Saxon race but one Empire.[340]

Rhodes does not seem to have entrusted Warren with his fantastical idea, although that August he talked of little else among his friends in Kimberley.[341]

In their initial conversations aboard ship, Warren was interested to find that Rhodes knew a good deal about the land problems of Griqualand West, and in this respect he proved a useful contact. On arrival in Port Elizabeth, he took Warren to 'the Club' where he introduced him to Judge Andries Stockenström, a distinguished young judge of the Eastern Cape Circuit. Stockenström had held a Land Court in Griqualand West the previous year, and it was from his judgements that had arisen all the appeals that Warren was supposed to sort out. Potentially, it was a politically sensitive meeting, between the Afrikaner judge and the imperial military officer who might well be unpicking the former's judgements. But Warren, as ever, managed to establish a respectful relationship with Stockenström and the two of them parted on good terms.

Warren and Rhodes travelled by train and coach to Grahamstown where Rhodes had some business, and as Warren wanted to explore the country around Queenstown where his father had been stationed, the two men agreed to meet up in Queenstown a few days later and continue their journey from there together.

Among the passengers on Warren's coach to Queenstown was a young African girl from a mission school. A couple of the adult passengers objected to an African being allowed on the coach, but as Warren observed, 'it was only a little girl and I think everyone was rather ashamed of saying much'. The incident seems to have prompted Warren to start thinking about the extent of racial prejudice in South Africa, such as he had not met elsewhere on his travels:

> The white folk in South Africa are very much down on coloured people. I do not think that in the whole of South Africa there is a single black man in high position. Not even a shopkeeper or innkeeper. There are no native merchants as there are on the west coast [of Africa] and at Gibraltar.[342]

---

[340] *Ibid.*, pp 248–9, with Rhodes's original lack of punctuation. The whole 'Confession of Faith' is reproduced as an appendix in Flint, pp 248–52.
[341] Rotberg, *The Founder*, pp 100–03.
[342] *On the Veldt*, pp 239–40.

After a few days exploring the Stormberg coalfields north of Queenstown, Warren rejoined Rhodes in the coach bound for Kimberley. During the journey Rhodes was learning by heart the Thirty-Nine Articles of the Anglican Faith, and Warren offered to hear him. They got on well until they got to Article XVII on 'predestination, and there we stuck'. The two men disagreed on the issue of predestination in Christianity and a lengthy argument ensued. As a devout Anglican, Warren accepted the concept that an all-knowing God necessarily knows our future and to that extent our life is predetermined: even if we exercise free will, God will know that and the way that we will exercise it. To that extent, he believed, we are fulfilling God's will. Rhodes, on the other hand, would not hold by this interpretation. He was the son of an Anglican vicar and knew his scriptures, but he interpreted free will as just that. Men were free to make their own choices and to determine their own lives, not dependent upon a path predetermined by God. To some extent their disagreement was a matter of semantics, but there was enough there to provide food for a vigorous philosophical argument that lasted for most of the rest of what would otherwise have been a very boring journey.

* * *

On arrival in Kimberley, Warren was a guest of Lanyon's at Government House for a few days while he sorted out his own accommodation and office. He rented a one-roomed building for his office, with a second building closeby for his sleeping quarters. They were both built of corrugated iron on a wooden frame with earthen floor; but from his experience of the previous year, he arranged to have the floor smeared daily with fresh cow dung to keep down the dust, and he had the walls and ceilings lined with canvas to help insulate against the heat.

The first thing Warren had to recognise was that as a colonial employee, he was now under Lanyon's authority and so lacked the freedom he had previously enjoyed on his imperial commission, where he was allowed wide discretion to act pretty much as he saw fit. Now he could only make recommendations rather than decisions, and these were subject to the approval of Lanyon and his Executive Council, and then of Frere and his officials in Cape Town. Clearly, the task he faced would need all his diplomatic skills, and patience, for which he was not well known. He was fortunate on his second day in town to hire a young magistrate's clerk, William Hutton, to act as his secretary. Hutton not only was familiar with Cape law, but also had been secretary to Stockenström's Land Court the previous year.

While Warren waited for his formal instructions to arrive from Cape Town, he read the papers of the Land Court – evidence and judgement – and a wide range of other relevant material. Few land claimants had been satisfied with Stockenström's judgement and 207 had appealed against it, most of the appeals being for multiple farms and overlapping claims. In the eighteen months since Stockenström's judgement, three cases had been settled by the Supreme Court and four were pending. At this rate, the remaining 200 cases would take years to settle. It was Warren's task to try and settle them out of court. But he was *not* an *arbitrator*. His only power was that of persuasion.

It seemed to Warren that the lawyers had the most to lose from an early settlement, for the longer the appeals dragged on, the higher would be their fees. So one of the first things he did was to meet with the lawyers. He pointed out that until all the claims were settled, there would be no market in land and precious little other economic activity in the colony, apart from diamond-mining. To his surprise, they came round to his point of view, and agreed that their clients must be prepared to compromise. The next step would be to study the paperwork of each claimant.

Warren decided that he must not pursue the claimants, but wait for them to come to him, so that if there was any later dissatisfaction, they could not place the blame on him. He joked to Hutton that they might be sitting in the office with nothing to do if nobody chose to trust him. But he did not have long to wait. His first supplicant was a Boer who had held an old Free State claim that was now in Griqualand West. He was confronted with a demand for a £5 annual quit-rent, whereas those who held Griqua titles from the time of British annexation were only charged £1. Warren got the Executive Council to agree that such cases should only be charged the original £1, although new landholdings from 1878 would be charged the higher rate. After this it did not take long for word of Warren's fairness to get round and claimants began to bring in their cases.

The largest claimant of all was Waterboer's agent David Arnot who claimed that the Griqua Chief had made over to him most of the land south of Kimberley, between the Free State border and the Lower Vaal. It took Warren two weeks of hard negotiation to persuade him to give up most of his claims, leaving him with a single farm, Eksdale, already allocated by the Land Court, besides the rents from some other farms and a pension of £1000 per annum in lieu of all other claims.

So far as the Batswana were concerned, 'locations', blocks of land around their principal settlements, had already been reserved for them. It had been conveniently maintained that African custom recognised *usage* rather than *ownership* of land and that therefore they should not have any individual title within these 'locations'. It was not part of Warren's brief to make recommendations on their behalf, although he did note that these 'locations' allowed little room for natural expansion of population. He also felt that 'civilised natives' – however that might be defined – should be allowed title to land, although with some protective restriction so that they could not straightaway sell to exploitative colonists or speculators.

The latter fate was exactly what had befallen most Griqua landholders. Waterboer had always maintained that he had only ever given over his land around the diamond fields to the British and that the rest of Griqualand was still under his authority. He had therefore continued to give out land titles to individual Griqua, for minor sums that he had treated as personal income. The British, however, maintained he had no such authority after British annexation in October 1871 and that Griqua titles issued after that date were therefore invalid. By the time Warren came along, most of these Griqua titles had been sold for a pittance to innkeepers and colonial speculators. Warren recommended a couple of small Griqua 'locations' for the landless; but this was too little, too late. There was mounting disaffection among landless Griqua that was to lead to open rebellion the following year.

By the end of 1877 Warren had persuaded all 200 claimants to withdraw their appeals. It was a remarkable feat of patience and persuasion and it only remained for him to write up his report, which he expected to complete by the end of January, pending a few queries and minor details.

Before he could complete the task, however, he was called to arms.

CHAPTER 10

Soldiering in South Africa

Once it was clear that Warren's Land Commission was nearing completion, he found himself in great demand. He was asked to write a report, based upon his professional opinion, as to the best way to work the Du Toit's Pan and Bultfontein mines, but he turned it down, being too busy with his own land report. He was offered the management of the Kimberley mine, for an enhanced salary, but he did not fancy managing that complex web of mining claims or bringing order to the demands of the unruly and avaricious claimholders. At about the same time, he received a letter from his friend Ravenscroft who had put his name forward to the Governor of Ceylon as the best possible man to make an archaeological exploration of two ancient cities there. Sir Bartle Frere, however, wanted him to go to the Transvaal to sort out the land problems there; and that looked his most likely next destination. Warren enjoyed being entrusted with such important responsibilities and it seems that his desire to return home to his family as soon as possible was no longer at the forefront of his mind. He was now prepared to go wherever duty called.

After spending a few days with Lanyon over the New Year at the old Vaal River diggings, and the two of them attending a Freemasonry gathering in Barkly West, Warren returned to Kimberley to find the talk was all 'over the Border!'

For some months the 'constant topic of conversation' around Kimberley had been the African uprising in the Eastern Cape. Everybody had an opinion as to its cause and solution. Warren's view was that the Cape's internal self-government was partly to blame. Because Afrikaners were in the majority amongst the white parliamentary electorate, the Cape Government pursued what Warren called 'the Dutch policy'. As Warren understood it, this allowed white settlement to encroach indefinitely on African land, with the Government relying on imperial troops when the policy provoked armed resistance. Warren believed that if the Cape's so-called 'responsible government' were to pay for the consequences of its own policies, it would not be so keen to disregard African land interests.[343]

Warren was a strong imperialist; but he saw British imperialism as a

---

[343] Warren, *On the Veldt in the Seventies*, pp 397–8.

benevolent and protective power, in contrast to the selfish interests of local colonists, British as well as Afrikaner, both of whom were happy to have imperial troops pick up the pieces 'as soon as they are in difficulties'. However critical he might be of colonial policy towards 'the native population', however, Warren was still a man of his time. Rebellion was rebellion, and he would gladly do his bit to help put it down. When the time came, Warren enjoyed the irony that the little imperial colony of Griqualand West should be going to the assistance of the great self-governing Cape Colony.[344]

On 7 January 1878 the call came through from Sir Arthur Cunynghame, Commander of Imperial Forces in South Africa. Warren was to gather a mounted volunteer force and proceed without delay to King William's Town in the Eastern Cape. Frere himself was already there and 'the Transvaal business' was postponed indefinitely. In the nineteen years that Warren had been in the Army, his work, at which he had distinguished himself, had been entirely related to the surveying and engineering skills for which he had been specifically trained. All of that was about to change. He was excited at the prospect: action in the Eastern Cape was much more enticing than another land commission. Like any soldier, he was keen to prove his worth.

Warren had been right to observe on the two occasions he had passed through the Eastern Cape that the African people there had appeared surly and 'unfriendly' towards the British. Conflict between amaXhosa and colonists – Boer as well as Briton and their African allies – had regularly flared up over the previous 100 years. The conflict that began in August 1877 was the ninth and, as it turned out, final Cape/Xhosa War.

Governor Frere was determined to end amaXhosa independence east of the River Kei and had intervened in what had initially been an intra-African conflict. But colonial forces suffered some initial defeats, which prompted Frere to order the disarming of all Africans under colonial rule west of the Kei. This merely escalated the war as thousands of amaXhosa fled their Cape 'Reserves' rather than be forced to disarm. Some spread out into the dense forest and 'Perie Bush' of the Amatole Mountains north and north-west of King William's Town, while others crossed the colonial boundary to join their fellow amaXhosa east of the Kei. This encouraged the latter to launch pre-emptive strikes into the colony, and it was at this point that the call went out for colonial reinforcements to assist the imperial troops who were conspicuously failing to crush the uprising.

---

[344] *Ibid.*, pp 398–9.

Warren's call for volunteers to form the 'Diamond Fields Horse' was responded to with enthusiasm by British, Afrikaner and other white colonists on the diamond fields. He drew some from previous volunteer groups, and he sent Captain D'Arcy, who had served in the Kimberley Light Horse, to Fauresmith in the Free State to hire horses and await his arrival there.

Within two days Warren had 120 volunteers. They were each equipped with a bandolier of ammunition and a Lee-Enfield rifle, not as accurate and long-range as the new Martini-Henry, but adequate for the short-range bush fighting they expected to experience. Warren kitted them out in light brown corduroy jackets, moleskin trousers and broad-rimmed felt hats.

The concept of troops wearing 'khaki' was an idea that was beginning to circulate among military commanders around this time. The word and colour originated in India where troops of Britain's Indian Army wore a dung-coloured overshirt to protect their red uniforms from the ubiquitous dust. Colonel Frederick (later Field Marshal Lord) Roberts, serving in the Bengal Army in the 1870s, was an early advocate of khaki as a form of camouflage. South African volunteer contingents normally wore a variety of casual clothing, some being survivals from previous military service. It is not clear whether Warren deliberately chose light brown clothing for the Diamond Fields Horse or whether this was all that was available in Kimberley at the time; but he was an early convert to the concept of wearing khaki for camouflage.

Warren's recruits were all civilians and, as he remarked of them:

> Everything was new to our men, there were none who could cook, very few knew anything about horses, and only one man besides myself knew anything about the use of a rifle in warfare.[345]

Warren himself had only of necessity learned to cook on the border survey the previous year, but he appreciated the need for adequate and wholesome food to keep the men fit and in good health. And so far as military training was concerned, at least Warren had been through Sandhurst and Woolwich where he had been drilled and had practised numerous war games; but that was twenty years ago and it had all been theory. Now he was about to embark on his first field command and he would have to use his instinct and initiative. It was just the sort of challenge on which he thrived. He probably recalled that from a very early age his father had inculcated in him the need to remain calm and authoritative under enemy fire.

---

[345] Williams, *The Life*, p 103, quoting from one of Warren's despatches.

Perhaps partly from their ignorance of the realities of warfare, combined with a typical colonial assumption about limited African fighting capability, Warren's volunteers' spirits were high. They probably assumed they would be facing disorganised bands of 'primitive natives', armed with spears and clubs, and that these would be no match for white volunteers, even those with no previous military training or experience. Warren knew differently. No easy assumptions could be made about any potential enemy. Warren's reputation for discipline and fairness was already well established on the diamond fields, and he knew he would have to use his journey south to give his men a crash course in military training and discipline.

Warren was still officially ranked a Captain. His gazetting to Major did not come through until 10 April. But General Cunynghame awarded Warren, as commander of a local field force, the local rank of Brevet Lieutenant-Colonel, entitling him to be referred to as 'Colonel'.

Thousands assembled in Kimberley on 10 January 1878 to cheer off Colonel Warren and the Diamond Fields Horse. Williams quotes one man in the crowd that day who wrote:

> With a tact that made itself felt among that band of men, the 'old man,' as he was familiarly called, made himself respected and revered.[346]

They covered the first stage of the journey, from Kimberley to Fauresmith, on foot, with such equipment as they could carry. They only had enough tents for one-third of the force, and Warren issued a rota, with himself included, for sleeping in the tents or in the open. He divided his men into three troops, appointing a captain and several lieutenants and sergeants for each troop, and in the several days it took them to reach Fauresmith, he taught them basic foot drill. Once they picked up their horses, it became clear just how limited was their riding experience: some had none at all. Warren had to recall his Woolwich training and teach them basic riding skills and how to look after their mounts. They finally moved off in some sort of order; but out of respect for the independence of the Free State, he could not commence proper military training until they crossed the Orange River into the Eastern Cape.

Once in the Colony, Warren was able to teach his three troops of volunteer horse-soldiers how to march in close order, how to vary pace, act under fire, dismount, take cover and return fire, not forgetting to tether the horses. He also stressed the importance of keeping their horses in good condition, ensuring they were regularly groomed, fed and watered. By the time they reached their destination, Warren was proud to report, '[We] arrived at King William's Town a well drilled body of Volunteer Horse ready for immediate duty against the enemy'.[347]

A few days after Warren's arrival a well-entrenched colonial force at Kentani Hill east of the Kei managed to beat off a mass assault by the main amaXhosa army. The British claimed this as a victory, although their subsequent withdrawal marked the end of any conventional warfare east of the Kei. The war now entered a guerrilla phase that would be fought among the densely covered hills and ravines in the Colony west of the Kei.[348]

Initially Warren was given command of the volunteer garrison outside King William's Town. His troops spent much of their first month in the field clearing rebels from caves in the rugged terrain north of the garrison. They often had to sleep out in the open, despite the heavy rain with which they were frequently assailed; but Warren kept the men regularly exercised, to which he ascribed the fact that 'their health was better than that of any other troops in the garrison'.

Because of the failure of the imperial troops to bring the war to a swift conclusion, General Cunynghame was recalled and replaced by Lieutenant-General Frederic Thesiger (later Lord Chelmsford). Thesiger arrived at King William's Town with imperial reinforcements on 4 March. Among the officers he brought with him were Colonel Sir Evelyn Wood, of the 90th Light Infantry, and Major Redvers Buller.

Thesiger set up his headquarters at the Pirie Mission Station, north-west of King William's Town, and began a concerted effort to clear the rebels from the Perie Bush and Amatole Mountains. He ordered Warren and two troops of the Diamond Fields Horse (DFH) to Bailie's Grave, on the west of the Perie Bush. It was mountainous country with steep slopes and ravines covered with a mix of dense scrub bush and forest trees, while the summits were open grassland. Commandant Edward Brabant's Horse had already reached the top of the Buffalo Range, and Warren was ordered to dismount his men and reconnoitre the thick bush for signs of the enemy.

It was unclear how long this would take and Warren had his men travel light, with only enough food and water for the day. As they advanced in skirmishing order, the rebels withdrew ahead of them and after several hours

[347] Quoted in Williams, *The Life*, p 103.
[348] For the Battle of Kentani Hill, 7 February 1878, see http://samilitaryhistory.org/vol056pg. html, accessed 11 May 2016.

Warren's men found themselves on the bare grassland summit. They had arrived just in time to aid Brabant's force that had come under sustained fire from well-armed rebels. Any notion that the African 'rebels' would be lightly armed with spears and clubs was rapidly expelled. They carried spears for close fighting, but many possessed guns, mostly muzzle-loading muskets, that they had acquired from the diamond fields. Furthermore, the amaXhosa were fighting on their home ground. They had generations of experience in guerrilla warfare as, for the best part of a century they had resisted ever-greater pressure from land-hungry colonists.

Although they drove back the rebels, Warren's and Brabant's troops were virtually trapped on the mountain heights. Warren's men had no blankets and only biscuit and coffee on which to subsist. Realising they needed both reinforcements and food, Warren took two volunteers back down through the dense bush to Thesiger's headquarters, managing to avoid enemy contact on the way. He reported to Thesiger, collected supplies and returned to the summit with the third troop of his DFH.

Thesiger ordered further reinforcements to the summit, bringing the total force on the mountain to about 400, with the plan that they should force their way down through the steepest bush, clearing it of rebels on the way. The manoeuvre was compromised, however, by Captain Brabant leading a majority of his men off in pursuit of some of the rebels' cattle. The capture of cattle was a regular feature of colonial warfare, both as loot to reward the volunteer troops and to deprive the enemy of their livelihood, for they subsisted on their milk.[349] After waiting a while for Brabant to return, Warren assumed command of the remaining 125 men and decided to descend in skirmishing order directly towards Bailie's Grave, as originally intended.

According to Warren's account, after about a mile through dense forest:

> … I was dangerously crushed by the fall of a forest tree upon my neck; after some minutes delay I was able to proceed supported by three men, still keeping command.[350]

The tree was probably deliberately brought down, it being an old amaXhosa trick to fell trees upon an enemy. Warren refused the use of a litter as it would seriously impede their progress.

[349] S I Blackbeard, 'Blaming Brabant: Another look at the so-called military 'disobedience' of Captain, later Major-General Sir Edward Yewd Brabant, KCB,CMG', *Military History Journal*, Vol. 14, No 6, December 2009.
[350] Quoted in Williams, *The Life*, p 104–107.

Soon afterwards they reached a precipice where they came under heavy fire from a concealed enemy, and a captain and a lieutenant were instantly shot dead. They were now in danger of being surrounded and Warren held a quick 'council of war.' It was decided they should return to their bivouac site on the mountain top, hoping to surprise the rebels who had occupied it into thinking they were the whole 400 returning to rout them. The ruse worked and the rebels withdrew, allowing Warren's severely outnumbered men to return by their old route down to Bailie's Grave, taking it in turns to carry their two dead on improvised litters.

In writing his report, Warren did not mention Brabant's pursuit of cattle; merely that he became separated from the rest. Warren's focus was on his own contingent and he deliberately underplayed his own injury in the incident with the tree. He probably felt a strong sense of responsibility towards his Kimberley volunteers; he was enjoying working with them, and he did not want to be invalided out of action. In reality it had taken three men some time to extricate him from under the tree. He had sustained a broken rib and a serious neck injury, referred to in another account as a 'near fatal injury'.[351] But Warren had proved before, in Gibraltar, that he could set aside pain through sheer force of willpower. The most that he might have taken for the pain would have been an occasional shot of brandy, laced, perhaps, with his favourite Worcester sauce! In fact, his injuries were to plague him for at least the next two years and, although he never allowed it to curb his activity in the field, it was eventually the cause of his being invalided home to England. The exact nature of the neck injury was never made clear, but according to Williams, doctors later told Warren that his trek up the mountain while the injury was still fresh 'had prevented lesion from taking place, which would have left him, at best, a permanent invalid'.[352]

In early April the rebels, now confined within a restricted area of bush, attempted to break out to the west, driving their cattle before them. On hearing this, Warren offered to lead 75 mounted men of the DFH at full gallop to cut them off.

After three miles Warren and his men suddenly found their way blocked by a large amaXhosa army. Warren estimated the force to be 1600 fighting men, divided into five regiments, each led by a mounted commander. Most

[351] C. Hummel (ed. & introduction) *The Frontier Journal of Major John Crealock, 1878: A Narrative of the Ninth Frontier War by the Assistant Military Secretary to Lieutenant-General Thesiger* (Van Riebeeck Society, 2nd Series, No 19, Cape Town, 1988), fn. 44, p 35.
[352] Williams, *The Life*, p 106.

Warren minding the horses while the DFH engage the enemy.
Illustrated London News

estimates put the enemy army's strength at 1200–1500 although Evelyn Wood, in his memoirs written many years later, claimed that Warren had grossly exaggerated for effect and the true strength of the enemy was only 500 men.[353] But Wood's memoirs were published in the aftermath of the Anglo-Boer War, by which time it had become fashionable to be critical of Warren. In any case, even 500 men attacking a thin line of 75, was still a formidable challenge. Warren was fortunate to find a narrow gulley running alongside the road that his men could slip into, facing the enemy 500 metres distant. An *Illustrated London News* report and illustration of the subsequent action depicts Warren lying on his back behind the gulley holding some tethered horses in one hand and a telescope in the other. The news report maintained that as a commanding officer, he was not allowed in the front line of fighting; although this had not stopped Warren in the past. It is probable that he

---

[353] Ibid., pp 106–7; and Hummel (ed.) *The Frontier Journal of Major John Crealock*, fn 44, p 35, referencing Field-Marshal Sir Evelyn Wood, *From Midshipman to Field Marshal*, Volume I (Methuen, London, 1906), p 311.

judged that from further back he would be better able to see the enemy and direct his men than if he were lying in the gulley with them. After two months of skirmishing in the bush, this was his first experience of anything like a conventional battle and he was determined to be in full control.

The amaXhosa made several rushes forward, each time discharging their guns before reloading and rushing forward again, ever closer. At the same time they sent out two 'horns' of men to encircle the gulley. Warren moved some of his men to the right to face the larger horn; and as the enemy came within 200 metres of the gulley, the DFH's Enfield rifles took devastating effect: the right horn was shattered. Many amaXhosa were killed and the attack was broken. When the commander of the army, Montgiso, was shot through the head, the amaXhosa withdrew, with some of the jubilant Diamond Fields Horse engaging the retreating enemy in hand-to-hand fighting.

After the action Warren's men counted 58 amaXhosa dead on the field, with many more assumed to have died of their wounds in the bush. Of the DFH, one trooper died of a spear wound sustained when, against Warren's orders, he pursued the enemy at the end, and two horses were killed. General Thesiger congratulated Warren and the Diamond Fields Horse on the success of this action, known as the Battle of Debe Nek, and Warren received the personal congratulations and thanks of Sir Bartle Frere, who happened to be in King William's Town at the time. For the rest of the month, Warren's troops were based at Debe Nek where they took part in numerous skirmishing movements that prevented any further breakout to the west.

On 30 April Warren and two troops of the DFH joined Colonel Wood's column in a systematic scouring of the bush on the Makabalekile Hills. According to one account, during this action Warren 'fell foul of Thesiger' when he brought into camp 600 amaXhosa women and children as prisoners. Warren's immediate rationale was that he was rescuing the women from starvation. A secondary reason was that they were searching for supplies and as such would have become 'a supply column for their fighting menfolk. He had them fed, escorted to King William's Town and handed over to the civil authorities to be later sent to Cape Town and apprenticed as domestic servants'.[354] The 'apprenticing' of non-combatant prisoners was a regular practice in colonial warfare and was an important source of labour for the colonial economy. Warren also brought in several thousand cattle, thus further depleting the amaXhosa of their commissariat.

---

[354] Hummel (ed.), *The Frontier Journal of Major John Crealock*, fn 44, pp 35–6.

It was probably during the manoeuvre in the Makabalekile bush that Warren first met Major Redvers Buller, an officer of similar rank with whom he was in due course to have important dealings.[355] Buller was just two months older than Warren and superficially the two men had much in common. They were both very physical: strong and tall, well over six feet (1.82m), and popular with their men, being happy to share all their hardships and physical work. Both were strict in military discipline, though forgiving of transgressions that did not endanger the men or the success of the task in hand. Beyond that, their backgrounds and personalities were very different.

Buller was born into a wealthy landed Devon family who sent him to Eton College for the most expensive education that money could buy. Unlike Warren, Buller did not take to academic work and, having failed the Sandhurst entrance examination, he purchased a commission in the 60th Regiment of Foot. In January 1859, just as Warren landed in Gibraltar, Buller set sail for India to join his regiment's 2nd Battalion in mopping up the last vestiges of the Great Rebellion (the 'Indian Mutiny'). In 1860 he fought in the Second Opium War against China, and the following year he was posted to Canada. He spent the next eight years there, seeing no real fighting, but thoroughly enjoying the hunting and other exploits of the Canadian wilderness. Whereas Warren enjoyed hunting, for food, Buller treated hunting primarily as a sport, the more dangerous, the better. Returning to England in 1869, he bought a captaincy and served under Colonel Garnet Wolseley, in Canada again, but this time to put down a rebellion in an adventurous piece of action known as the Red River Expedition. Although there was no real fighting, Buller gained great experience, and the admiration and trust of Wolseley who, subsequently, called Buller to serve with him in West Africa, as his Quartermaster-General in the Anglo-Ashanti War of 1873–74. Buller thus became part of 'The Wolseley Ring', a select group of officers, which included Evelyn Wood, whose careers Wolseley judiciously promoted.[356]

Buller had arrived in South Africa with General Thesiger in March 1878. After acting for some weeks as Staff Officer to a colonial volunteer brigade, he was appointed to lead the Frontier Light Horse, a large contingent of Cape Town volunteers, and it was in this capacity that he and Warren first met.

Although much later their relationship was to turn sour, it seems to have started on a jovial note. Buller does not appear to have recorded any memory

---

[355] Warren was gazetted Major on 10 April 1878.
[356] Geoffrey Powell, *Buller: A Scapegoat? A Life of General Sir Redvers Buller VC* (Leo Cooper, London, 1994), pp 4–28.

of this first meeting, but Williams records Warren's memory of it as an amusing anecdote:

> [Buller] was carrying a thick stick in his hand, and when Warren asked him what it was for, he said that it was for poking up his men in the bush, so Warren remarked, 'Take care you don't strike one of my men by accident or you may get shot!' At first Buller took strong exception to this remark, but Warren explained that his men were just as much Englishmen as the regular 'Tommy Atkins,' and would not stand being struck.[357]

According to Williams, the two men afterwards became firm friends although, quoting Warren, they 'often differed very much in opinion on many military and other subjects, but that did not interrupt our good relations but led to constant arguments and chaff'.[358] This, however, was probably written after they had fallen out in 1900, and may have been Warren's gloss on the affair.

On 14 May 1878 a telegram arrived in King William's Town requesting the return of Lt.-Colonel Warren and the Diamond Fields Horse to Griqualand West where a rebellion had broken out. By this time the back of the amaXhosa resistance had been broken and Warren was permitted to leave, with the thanks and congratulations of General Thesiger, who informed him that as a reward for his excellent service in the field his *local* rank of Brevet Lt.-Colonel was to be confirmed by the War Office. The promotion was formally gazetted on 11 November.[359] Thesiger further remarked on the good health and spirit of the DFH and, in particular, the good condition in which they kept their horses. Clearly, Warren's training on the journey from Kimberley to the Eastern Cape had paid off. That journey had taken them 25 days; but now, after four months in the field the men were well trained and their return was much quicker. With the urgency of rebellion back home, they were keen to get moving and they reached the border of Griqualand West in just sixteen days.

* * *

During Warren's absence, tension had been growing in Griqualand West, partly as a result of the perceived injustices of Warren's land settlement. The indigenous Griqua, Korana and Batswana had seriously missed out in the colonial land settlement that had followed British annexation. This had

[357] Williams, *The Life*, pp 103–4. The imperial troops ('Tommy Atkins') tended to look down on the colonials.
[358] *Idem.*
[359] *The London Gazette*, 11 November 1878.

been recognised to some extent by evidence to Stockenström's Land Court, but his judgement had merely stirred up a mass of appeals, mostly by white claimants. Many Griqua and Batswana had hoped for justice, as they saw it, from Warren's review of the land issue and, after their high expectations, they felt seriously let down. They saw very little justice, in the form of land, for any of them, though plenty for white men, most of whom were newcomers to the territory.

The catalyst that sparked rebellion, however, was a group of amaXhosa who, two generations previously, had settled along the Lower Orange River near the modern town of Prieska. In the 1850s they became victims of the colonial land grab that accompanied the Cape Colony's extension of its boundary to the Orange River. Under this pressure, the 'Prieska amaXhosa' moved their principal grazing grounds into what appeared to be unclaimed territory north of the Orange. In the settlement that followed the establishment of Griqualand West, however, their occupational rights there were ignored. Warren was their last hope and he considered they were not worthy of any consideration as the amaXhosa were not indigenous to the Griqualand area.

In March 1878, while Warren and his volunteers were fighting the main amaXhosa in the Eastern Cape, the Prieska amaXhosa, perhaps inspired by reports of the early successes of their remote cousins, began urging the Griqua and Batswana to rise up against their colonial oppressors. Disaffected Griqua did not need much urging and together in April they began raiding a number of colonial farms and trading stores in south-west Griqualand. They drove their stolen cattle and other loot off into the remote fastness of the southern Langeberge, a long, thin, steep-sided mountain range that stretched northwards across the border. The Langeberge had long held a reputation among colonists as a lawless sanctuary for cattle thieves and other bandits.

On 31 May Warren and his three troops of Diamond Fields Horse reached the border at Hopetown, where they crossed the Orange River by ferry into Griqualand West. Warren received a message from Administrator Lanyon to send one troop to Kimberley for possible northern border defence and to bring the remaining two troops to Griquatown where Lanyon had established a base.

After crossing the Vaal en route to Griquatown on 10 June, the Diamond Fields Horse were attacked by a mixed force of possibly as many as 200 Griqua and amaXhosa. Hardened by their experience in the Eastern Cape, Warren's men inflicted a sharp defeat on their attackers, killing 31 with no loss to themselves. As they drove captured livestock of 200 cattle, 850 goats and six horses towards

Lt.-Colonel Warren and officers of the Diamond Fields Horse.
MCGREGOR MUSEUM, KIMBERLEY, SOUTH AFRICA

Griquatown, a further message from the Administrator urged Warren to proceed straight to the Langeberge where he, Lanyon, would join him.

It was not recorded what happened to the livestock, but by the time Lanyon reached the Langeberge with 75 mounted men on 18 June, Warren had already begun an assault on the narrow valley of Paardekloof. Lanyon, besides being Administrator of the colony, had received his promotion to Lt.-Colonel earlier in the year and he outranked Warren in the field; but seeing that Warren had already begun the attack, he immediately placed his men under Warren's command and gave him full credit for the ensuing victory. It was Warren's first experience of fighting with a combination of light artillery and mounted infantry. He used the two nine-pounders to weaken the enemy and then, leaving the horses with the guns, he advanced with his men in skirmishing order. For the loss of one man, Warren's assault killed 35 rebels. He captured 100 women, together with a large part of the loot taken at the beginning of the rebellion: 37 wagons, 2000 oxen, 2000 sheep and 200 horses. The leaders of the rebels, however, slipped away northwards over the mountain to hole up in an even more precipitous Kloof known as Xoungs,

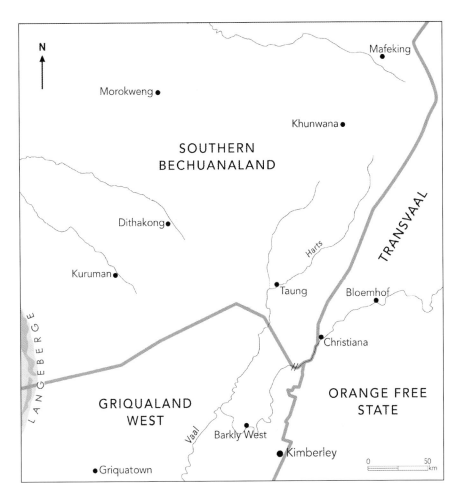

Griqualand West and Southern Bechuanaland, 1878.

where most of the women and children had taken refuge.[360]

Further reinforcements arrived from Kimberley, bringing Lanyon and Warren's combined force up to 230. Lanyon divided them into two columns, taking one northward to attack the rebel stronghold from the east, while Warren took the second column round to the western side of the mountain range to take the position in the rear. The attack from the west on 25 June took the enemy completely by surprise and with their combined forces Lanyon and

---

[360] *HCPP*, LII, Cd.2220 (1878–9), 'Summary of events in Griqualand West by General Thesiger, 30 July 1878', p 117.

Warren achieved a swift victory. Three rebel leaders were killed and among those captured were 80 men and 500 women and children.

By this time there were fears among the colonial authorities that the rebellion was spreading among the Batswana north of the Griqualand border. A colonial trading family named Burness, two brothers and the wife of one of them, had been attacked and killed in their store in the north of the colony, the attackers making off across the border into independent Batswana territory. Messages reaching Kimberley indicated that the 'Burness murderers' had gone towards Kuruman, putting that famous Mission Station and trading centre in danger. Lanyon left for Kimberley to assess the situation, leaving Warren to clear up any more resistance in the Langeberge.

On reaching Kimberley, Lanyon learned that a volunteer force of 30 untrained men, led by the distinctly unmilitary Surveyor John H. Ford, had crossed the border with the intention of 'relieving Kuruman'. Their intrusion was resisted by a small force led by Luka Jantjie, the son of a prominent Batswana chief. Ford suffered five men killed, his son mortally wounded and he himself wounded in the leg. His severely chastened 'relieving force' eventually limped into Kuruman where, ironically, they sought sanctuary in the Mission buildings. Lanyon regarded the Batswana defence of their territory north of the Griqualand colony as an act of war, and, gathering a further volunteer force in Kimberley, he set out for Kuruman.[361]

Warren reached Kuruman ahead of Lanyon, on 14 July, where he discovered that some of Ford's men, the 'Barkly Rangers', had been on a vengeful assault on a village, killing the first 25 Africans they came across. Warren restored discipline in the troop, and henceforth he ensured they worked in close collaboration with his own Diamond Fields Horse. It was characteristic of 19th-century colonialism, however, that neither Warren nor Lanyon considered charging any of the Barkly Rangers with murder for the 25 Africans they had killed, and yet, pursuit of the 'Burness murderers' was the official justification for their intrusion into independent Batswana territory.

When Lanyon arrived on 16 July, the local chief, Morwe, who had been threatening the Mission Station, protested his innocence of any involvement with the Burness affair and indicated a village to the north where the Burness killers were said to be hiding. Lanyon, eager 'to teach these natives a lesson', decided on an immediate attack on the nominated village, Gamopedi. Taking

[361] Kevin Shillington, *Luka Jantjie: Resistance Hero of the South African Frontier* (Aldridge Press, London, 2011), pp 89–105.

a six-pounder gun with them, he and Warren led their combined force of 300 men in an overnight march of 40 kilometres and arrived at Gamopedi at dawn on the 17th. With no preliminary attempt at negotiation, Lanyon ordered the immediate firing of six artillery rounds, which demolished much of the village. As the colonial troops then advanced, the chief and his men conducted a spirited defence in the hills beyond. According to Lanyon's report:

> The Diamond Fields Horse and Barkly Rangers, led by Colonel Warren, then gallantly charged after them, through a swamp and up the hills, where they dismounted and engaged on foot in skirmishing order.[362]

After an hour of hard fighting, the defenders, which included a handful of suspected participants in the Burness killings, fled westwards towards the Langeberge, leaving the colonial forces to loot the village and count the dead. They found 'more than 50' men killed, for their own loss of four dead and six wounded. There was no mention of women and children among the casualties, but there could have been a large number as the artillery barrage against the village had been launched at dawn with no prior warning. The loot amounted to twenty wagons, 600 cattle and 2000 sheep. There was some evidence of property taken from within Griqualand West, which to Lanyon's mind justified the operation.

The Gamopedi raid was a shameful affair as, despite the fact that some of the men hiding in the village were implicated in the Burness killings, there had been no attempt to save innocent lives. Lanyon had a reputation for this kind of raid, believing it was the only way that a handful of white men could project their power over an overwhelming black majority.[363] What Warren thought of Lanyon's policy to 'fire first with no negotiation' is not recorded; but his subsequent action showed that he was more inclined to offer a peaceful solution if that seemed possible. Besides, he would have been aware that the Gamopedi raid had failed to arrest the Burness suspects and other rebels from the Colony, who were now adding strength to the rebel stronghold in the northern Langeberge.

In fact the action at Gamopedi had merely stiffened the resolve of other Batswana to resist this 'colonial invasion' and they began to gather under the leadership of Luka Jantjie at the ancient Batswana capital of Dithakong, north-west of Kuruman. They were mostly experienced hunters, well armed

[362] *HCPP, LII*, Cd.2220, p 161.
[363] Shillington, *Luka Jantjie*, pp 86–7.

with a mix of muzzle-loading guns and rifles, and they took up a strong defensive position among ancient stone cattle enclosures along a ridge beyond the town.

Realising they now had a full-scale battle on their hands, Lanyon and Warren led their combined forces and three field guns to Dithakong. This time, however, when they were still a day away from Dithakong, and acting perhaps on Warren's advice, Lanyon sent a message demanding the surrender of 'the Burness murderers'. The Batswana, however, were full of confidence and sent back a message to the effect that 'what had been done had been done, and they would abide the consequences'.[364]

Lanyon opened the action with a three-hour artillery barrage aimed at the stone defences of the Dithakong ridge. He then divided his forces. While the Diamond Fields Horse, the Barkly Rangers and a contingent of amaZulu, who had been recruited from among migrant workers on the diamond mines, attacked the northern end of the ridge. Warren led the remainder in a charge against the Western Front. It was the kind of action in which Warren and his well-trained DFH were gaining considerable experience, and which they probably enjoyed: to ride up fast to near rifle range, dismount and advance in skirmishing order.

According to Lanyon's account, the Batswana were 'well armed and had plenty of ammunition. Being hunters, their fire was well directed, and had they been rashly attacked our loss might have been very heavy'. As it was, the colonial force suffered five killed and many wounded. The network of walls made it 'the most formidable place we have yet attacked.' After an hour of 'the hottest fire we have yet experienced', the colonial troops finally took the ridge with the Batswana 'fighting to the last in a most desperate manner'.[365] The survivors slipped away through the valley at the back, leaving the bodies of 39 of their compatriots among the stone walls. Luka Jantjie, with his father and brothers, escaped and made their way north into what is now Botswana.

Over the following few weeks Lanyon and Warren patrolled the region. They captured some of the Dithakong fighters whom they sent into Kimberley Gaol and took a large quantity of livestock, wagons and guns. These were sent to Kimberley for public auction. There was so much to be sold that the auction lasted a week. Leaving a small garrison at Kuruman, the two Colonels returned to Kimberley with the Field Force. On 22 August 1878 they rode in

[364] *Ibid.*, p 110.
[365] *HCPP, LII*, Cd.2220, pp 120, 161–2.

Colonel Charles Warren (seated left) wearing his CMG medal, sitting next to Colonel William Owen Lanyon with a selection of officers from their volunteer force in 1878.

MCGREGOR MUSEUM, KIMBERLEY, SOUTH AFRICA

triumph at the head of their troops down the Dutoitspan Road, accompanied by the Kimberley Light Infantry Band. Williams describes the scene:

> Addresses of welcome were read, and on entering Kimberley the two Colonels were chaired round the market square amidst the cheers of thousands of spectators. Special Masonic gatherings were held – for Warren was already a distinguished member of the Craft. Public dinners were given and a ball was held in Kimberley which was said to be the finest that South Africa had yet seen …[366]

It was the first break from active service that Warren and the Diamond Fields Horse had had since they left Kimberley for the Eastern Cape in January.

* * *

[366] Williams, *The Life*, p 113.

Warren was now locally gazetted Colonel Commandant of the Griqualand West Field Force and after a month's rest, he took them again into the field, the initial aim being to confront the mixed group of Griqualand rebels that had gathered now in considerable force in the northern Langeberge.

Warren approached the Langeberge from Kuruman with about 500 men, and one seven-pound Armstrong gun. The rebels had gathered in a wide valley on the western side of the range so that they had the impregnable mountain at their backs. Warren, who had already climbed and fought in the southern Langeberge, and had scaled the cliffs of Gibraltar, did not believe any mountain was impregnable. He started by reconnoitring the enemy's position, climbing the mountain from the east until he could look down into the rebel camp and assess its strength and disposition. He saw they had built their rock defences facing west, away from the mountain – clearly expecting an attack from the desert plain. Estimating their number to be about 1400 fighting men, Warren returned to base where he had left the wagons and divided his force into three columns.

Under cover of darkness in the early hours of 14 October 1878, his left and right columns climbed the mountain and moved into position behind the promontories north and south of the enemy's valley. Meanwhile, Warren himself led up the central column, dragging the field gun, so as to attack the enemy position from above, in the rear. He was in position by 10.00 am and signalled to the others by firing his gun at the enemy positions. At his signal his left and right wings began a slow, fighting descent. By firing his field gun left and right, just ahead of the two advancing columns, Warren crowded the rebels back down into the valley. In the rough and steep terrain, the advance was necessarily slow, but by 4.00 pm the battle was over. Warren's carefully planned method of attack ensured that his troops suffered no casualties, and leaving the western exit from the valley open allowed the rebels to escape rather than bottling them up where they might fight to the death and cause many casualties among his own men.[367]

They managed to capture a number of rebels and scatter the rest, the ringleaders having already fled into the desert. Among those captured were some of the Burness murder suspects, identified by having some of the trader's effects in their possession, including Burness's Masonic apron.[368]

Warren's conduct of this battle, especially the launching of the attack from

[367] *HCPP, LIII*, Cd.2252, p 2, extract from Warren to Lanyon, 2 November 1878.
[368] Williams, *The Life*, p 118.

the top of the mountain, was a remarkable achievement, especially considering that two decades later it was to take a much larger colonial army, of 2000 men, a six month siege and numerous assaults to defeat Batswana resistance, led by Luka Jantjie, in a similar valley in the northern Langeberge in 1897.[369]

In the days following the Langeberge battle Warren gathered all the local Batswana together 'against whom there was no charge':

> [He] registered them and detailed them to certain lands and villages with directions to commence ploughing at once, so that the season might not be lost.[370]

With these instructions, Warren had effectively taken over the role of an African chief. According to his report the Batswana expressed themselves pleased to be now under 'British protection' and to be rid of the amaXhosa and Griqua rebels.

In imperial terms, to take a people under 'protection' was to establish British overrule. This report of Warren's was the first official indication that the British had assumed political authority over Southern Bechuanaland. Warren's instructions from Lanyon were

> ... to take such measures as may seem to you advisable for the safety and protection of the province [of Griqualand West], and of Imperial interests beyond.[371]

Warren's action, therefore, was in line with 'Imperial interests', based on the principle that the failure of the Batswana chiefs to arrest some colonial murder suspects provided the justification for what was regarded as the inevitable expansion of white, British rule in South Africa. All that remained to be decided was which neighbouring British colony the territory should be joined to, Griqualand West or the Transvaal. These were issues that were to exercise Warren's mind over the following year.

* * *

During this time Warren got to know Revd John Mackenzie, the principal missionary at Kuruman. They hunted together down the Kuruman River and spent long evenings discussing the future of the country. They found that they were largely in agreement as to the policy that ought to be pursued. Both

---

[369] For the Langeberge War of 1897, see Shillington, *Luka Jantjie*, pp 215–62.
[370] *HCPP, LIII*, Cd.2252, p 2, Warren to Lanyon, 2 November 1878.
[371] *HCPP, LIII*, Cd.3635, p 9, Lanyon to Warren, 21 September 1878.

believed in the imperial project, the inevitable expansion of the white man in Africa; but they believed that this should be gradual and under careful control, with Africans treated fairly and with respect, under British 'protection' from the worst excesses of white colonial greed. They felt it could, under the right conditions, be achieved with the agreement and co-operation of the African people, who would ultimately have an equal share in their country's future.

Mackenzie was a forceful man. He had worked among the Batswana for nearly twenty years. His first ten years had been spent further north, in what is today the Central District of Botswana, where he developed a trusting relationship with the Christian convert Khama III, the King of one of the more powerful Batswana states. Mackenzie was fluent in the Setswana language and strongly believed that, once converted to Christianity, and literate, Africans could be the equal of any white man. Warren was gradually coming round to a similar view, although he restricted his concept of equality to 'the ordinary run of white man', thus presumably excluding the likes of himself and his class.

Neither Warren nor Mackenzie had any time for the crude Cape 'native policy' of conquer and dispossess, which, as evidenced in the Eastern Cape, led only to rebellion. The missionary also opposed restricting Africans to communal 'locations', as had recently, with Warren's approval, been done in Griqualand West. This, Mackenzie believed, provided no incentive for the people to improve themselves as individuals and would ultimately lead to resentment and unrest. Mackenzie's own scheme, with which Warren now largely concurred, was to confirm African farmers in the possession of their land, by offering them ten-year leases from the government, secure in the knowledge that the lease was renewable if they farmed the land well. At the same time a restricted number of white colonists, genuine farmers, would be allowed to settle the vacant land in between, in the belief that their farming practices would be a good example to their African neighbours. Something both Warren and Mackenzie were firm about was that 'land jobbers' and speculators would be excluded from the territory. Mackenzie contrasted his proposed policy to that of Lanyon's 'raid and fine':

> The one policy reminds one of the rude blow of a big, flat-headed hammer: the other is the quiet action of the thin wedge end of a crow-bar. The one smashes everything to pieces: the other moves & changes without destroying.[372]

---

[372] Mackenzie Papers, A75/2 (draft) Mackenzie to Lanyon, Kuruman, 1 February 1878. Quoted in Shillington, *Colonisation of the Southern Tswana*, p 154.

Although no doubt trying to avert the genocidal foundations of white rule in America and Australia being applied Southern Africa, neither Warren nor Mackenzie questioned the imperial project *per se* or the morality of the British deciding the settlement of land that was not theirs to give away in the first place. Both men merely aimed to manage the imperial project in what they perceived to be a practical and humane manner.

In due course, over the years that followed, Warren and Mackenzie were to get their opportunity to try to implement their ideas, working both separately and in conjunction, although they were to be opposed by strong vested colonial interests.

* * *

In the meantime, Warren needed to establish a British presence and ensure peace in 'Southern Bechuanaland', the land between Griqualand West and the Molopo River (the present southern border of Botswana). There were already signs that land speculators were entering the country and he issued an order that no sales of land or houses were to take place until the legal status of the country was established. He then prepared a proclamation, which he got Mackenzie to translate into the local language, Setswana, and to print copies on the Kuruman Mission printing press for widespread distribution.

The proclamation declared that the territory was now under British military occupation, the war was over and all who had fought against the British should surrender and they would be treated fairly. The ringleaders of the rebellion in Griqualand West and those who had committed murder must be punished; but other than that, 'The British Government is merciful, it seeks no revenge; it metes out justice, and desires all its children to have peace'. It continued in similar paternalistic vein, with an entreaty for those who had fled to return to their lands for the ploughing season was at hand, concluding in somewhat Biblical language that Christian Batswana would have appreciated, that if they delayed 'the season will be lost, and a famine will arise in the land'. To emphasise his point about his peaceful intentions, Warren employed a number of former rebels in positions of trust, looking after captured livestock and wagons, and this, he felt sure, created a favourable impression which helped his later work.

He planned to conduct a military tour of the area; but before he could do this, he received further instructions from Lanyon. He was to proceed at once to Taung, a major town beyond Griqualand West's north-eastern border. The local chief there, Mankurwane, was harbouring some of his own relatives who had entered the colony in June and killed a colonial farmer/trader named Francis Thompson.[373]

Leaving a small garrison at Kuruman under Major Stanley Lowe, Warren divided his remaining troops into four columns, each to advance on Taung by a different route, so as to create the impression among the wider populace that 'Warren was everywhere'. The columns rejoined just outside Taung. Under direct threat from Warren's army, Mankurwane surrendered his relatives, the alleged Thompson murderers; and these were sent into Kimberley to stand trial.

Over the following month Warren conducted a military tour of the principal Batswana towns of Southern Bechuanaland where he had his proclamation read out at large public gatherings. Mankurwane, at Warren's insistence, had provided a contingent of 100 men to accompany him, and this helped to persuade other chiefs to petition 'to be taken under British rule'. Nevertheless, a couple of chiefs refused to co-operate. Where this occurred, Warren issued a fine, in cattle, and appointed a more co-operative relative in their place. The more co-operative chiefs surrendered some of those who were wanted for attacks within Griqualand West, and these were arrested and sent to Kimberley for possible trial.[374]

In line with the policy he had discussed with Mackenzie, Warren left some of his most trusted officers as advisors to several of the more important chiefs. Their role was principally to advise on any dispute arising between Africans and Europeans. One of those appointed was Lieutenant Christopher Bethell, a cousin of Warren's wife, Fanny.[375]

It appears that Bethell, heavily in debt, though from a wealthy family in the North of England, had been sent to South Africa to escape his financial difficulties at home. His father appealed to Warren to find him something useful to do. He had reached Kimberley by May 1878 and Warren accepted him on his volunteer force against the Griqua rebels. He seems to have been particularly trusted by Warren who, when appointed Commander of the Griqualand West Field Force in August, had made Bethell his Head of Intelligence. Bethell appears to have learned some Setswana and was sent on several special missions to negotiate with Batswana chiefs. In November 1878

---

[373] Shillington, *Colonisation*, p 80. Thompson was known to have helped himself to at least a hundred wagonloads of firewood from across the border. Firewood, the principal fuel to drive the steam machinery for the diamond mines, was valued at £20 a load in Kimberley.

[374] *HCPP, XLIX*, Cd.3635, pp 3–4, Warren to Frere, Kimberley, 3 April 1879.

[375] Fanny's mother's maiden name was Bethell, and Christopher was a somewhat distant cousin.

Warren appointed him official advisor to Montshiwa, Chief of the Barolong, the principal Batswana group near the headwaters of the Molopo River (which today forms the border with Botswana). Bethell identified so strongly with Barolong interests that in due course he came to regard himself as 'Morolong' and some years later he married a Morolong woman.[376] The marriage had the strong support of Montshiwa, from which it has often been assumed she was one of his relatives. If she was, then this would have made Warren, via two marriages, a remote cousin of Chief Montshiwa!

In his visits to the country bordering the Transvaal, Warren witnessed the relentless progress westwards of Boer settlement, beyond the official border, into Batswana and Korana territory. It convinced him that the legal status of Southern Bechuanaland should be settled as a matter of some urgency, before its African farmers were totally despoiled and the eventual land settlement made infinitely more complicated, for someone like him to resolve.

Through December 1878 Warren wrote to High Commissioner Frere about his belief that the best destination for Southern Bechuanaland would be incorporation into Griqualand West, though with different legislation regarding African land interests. The British Government, however, had always intended that Griqualand West should become an integral part of the Cape Colony. Warren now proposed an alternative: a combined Griqualand-Bechuanaland could be treated as a separate province within a federated South Africa, rather than simply being incorporated into the Cape Colony, whose self-governing land policies Warren did not trust. He then went on to outline the plans for African land security in Bechuanaland that he had developed in discussion with the missionary John Mackenzie.[377]

Frere showed interest, but was non-committal regarding Warren's ideas. He was too busy planning the conquest of the Zulu Kingdom, which he regarded as an essential prerequisite for the security of white settlement in a federated South Africa.

Warren returned to Kimberley from his tour of the region on 1 January 1879. Nine days later he replaced Lanyon as Acting Administrator of Griqualand West, Lanyon having been promoted to Administrator of the Transvaal.

* * *

---

[376] Morolong = singular of Barolong.
[377] *HCPP, LIII*, Cd.2252, pp 41–2, Warren to Frere, 25 November 1878.

Warren was at Christiana in that undefined region between Griqualand West and the Transvaal when news reached him by relay despatch rider from Kimberley that the British invasion of the Zulu Kingdom had suffered a major defeat. On 22 January, fifteen kilometres inside the Buffalo River border, at a place called Isandhlwana, the Zulu army had overrun the main camp of the invading central column. The British lost 1329 men, a third of them Africans recruited in Natal. A whole regiment was virtually wiped out at Isandhlwana in what was the greatest British imperial defeat at the hands of a 'native' army. Ultimately, it finished Sir Bartle Frere's diplomatic career, along with British plans for a federated South Africa for at least a generation.

In the immediate aftermath of the battle there was panic in Natal where a Zulu invasion was expected at any moment. And throughout colonial South Africa it was assumed there would be a co-ordinated 'native rising', inspired by the Zulu victory.

Warren returned immediately to Kimberley and put the town on high military alert. The white population of the town was outnumbered by many thousands of Africans who came from all over Southern Africa to work at the diamond mines; but Warren's action was based more on a desire to reassure the white population than on any real belief on his part in the likelihood of another rising in Griqualand West. For a week all work at the mines ceased while the streets were patrolled by platoons of colonial volunteers.

Full of confidence in his own security, Warren sent a telegram to Frere offering to send a volunteer regiment of 100 men to assist Lord Chelmsford; but the offer was turned down as it was felt he needed all the men he could muster to defend his own colony. As it turned out, Warren's judgement was correct: the concept of a widespread African uprising was a figment of the colonial imagination. No such uprising was planned or took place, and the general white anxiety gradually subsided.

It was just as well that Warren had not felt impelled to conduct a mass arrest of potential rebels, for the Kimberley Gaol was already full to overflowing with 700 prisoners of war captured during his military occupation of Southern Bechuanaland. Some were being held for trial for the Thompson and Burness murders. Warren, acting on the advice of the Head of the Prison Service, but against the advice of his Attorney General, released the remainder of the prisoners. He believed in the importance of showing *trust* in those who had surrendered. In any case, having cowed most of the Batswana leaders north of the border, there was no longer the leadership likely to stir up further trouble.

There remained just one Batswana family of significance that had not submitted: that of Luka Jantjie, his two brothers and his ageing and ailing father. Following the Battle of Dithakong, they had sought refuge among the Batswana north of the Molopo River, in what is today the modern state of Botswana. In April the chief who had been harbouring them there decided it would be politic to give them up, and they were handed over to Chief Montshiwa where Lieutenant Bethell took charge of them. Montshiwa was paid £5 for his co-operation, and by the end of May 1879 Luka Jantjie and his two brothers were incarcerated in Kimberley Gaol.[378]

Attorney General Lord, who had been party to the decision the previous June to despatch the ill-fated Ford expedition, was keen that Luka should be charged for the death of Ford's son and the five other volunteers who had died at the hands of the Batswana chief and his men, as they battled their way through Luka Jantjie's territory towards Kuruman. Warren, however, judged there was no such case to bring against Luka. Although in his view the Batswana chief was 'a wild fellow who hates the English', he recognised that in this case he had been defending his independent territory against an uninvited military incursion. Warren and his Attorney General's disagreement on this matter became so intense that Lord was forced to resign. Warren recognised these were political prisoners, only being held in custody until their country was judged to be sufficiently settled for them to return. He still believed the extension of formal British rule over Southern Bechuanaland was imminent, which it was not. But Luka and his two brothers were released the following May (1880).[379]

The first confirmation that Griqualand West would simply be absorbed by the Cape Colony came in July 1879 when the Cape Parliament passed the Annexation Bill, although it was to be October 1880 before it was fully implemented. That put paid to Warren's plans for a united colony of Griqualand-Bechuanaland, separate from the Cape. And so far as the British 'protection' of Bechuanaland was concerned, that would take the return of Warren at the head of a large military expedition to implement six years later.[380]

---

[378] Shillington, *Luka Jantjie*, pp 117–22.
[379] *Ibid.*, pp 116–7 and 120. Luka Jantjie was to spend the next seventeen years trying to resist the colonial subjugation of his people and the seizure of their land. In the end he died a hero's death in a six-month war of resistance in the Langeberge in 1897. Luka's life of heroic resistance to colonialism was honoured in 2016 when the main administration building of the Northern Cape's new Sol Plaatje University in Kimberley was named 'Luka Jantjie House'.
[380] See Chapter 14, below.

By September Warren had tired of administering his little Crown Colony, as an interim measure before it was handed over to the Cape. He had had his fill of petty colonists making their incessant demands upon him. And while Kimberley's mining magnates were reshaping the city in permanent brick and tile, his own tin-walled and tin-roofed 'Government House' was an insult to his position as the Acting Administrator and local representative of Her Majesty's Government. His requests for something to be done about this were ignored by Cape Town where neither officials nor politicians saw any point in augmenting what was only a temporary post.

Warren had originally come to South Africa on a special mission that was expected to be completed in six months. He completed it in five, but that had been three years ago and Warren had had enough. To cap it all, he was still suffering from the injuries he had received eighteen months previously in the Eastern Cape. He had been able to put his injuries to the back of his mind while military duties had demanded his full concentration; but now, with the pressure off, they returned to trouble him. He applied to Frere for sick leave, which was granted, and in October he left for England.

He received a huge send-off in Kimberley with dinners, speeches and addresses of thanks. He had clearly won the hearts of the majority of the colonial population. And with his permission, the Freemasons of Kimberley established a Masonic lodge in his name.

CHAPTER 11

Chatham and Egypt

Brevet Lt.-Colonel Charles Warren, CMG, RE, was reunited with his family in England at the end of October 1879, on official sick leave, and with an uncertain future ahead of him.

He had been absent for three years and the first thing he would have noticed would have been how much his children had grown. Violet and Charlotte were now thirteen and eleven, respectively. They had always been close to their father and this had been the first time he had been away from them for an extended period. They knew him as a humorous father for whom they adopted the pet name 'Pip'.[381] The oldest son Frank, whom he had left at four, was now seven, and the youngest, Richard, who had been a babe in arms, was three and a half. Frank would have remembered little of his father, and Richard, nothing at all.

In his letters home, Warren had often included amusing anecdotes that he knew Fanny would read to the children, and these would have helped to keep his memory alive in the mind of Frank and create a jolly impression in the imagination of the youngest. For instance, he had related in great detail how he had been startled awake one night while camping out on the veldt. He could feel down his back what he thought was a cockroach, or at worst a snake. It took a good deal of thrashing around on his part before he realised it was his monocle which he had forgotten to remove. Attached to its cord, it had slipped round his neck during the night and was tickling his back.

He also related stories of cooks and food, and strange sayings of the local people. He made light of battles, in the same way that his father had when regaling his sons in Ireland with stories of his martial exploits.

* * *

Even when on official sick leave, Warren was not a man to sit still. In November he was elected a Fellow of the Royal Historical Society, to whom he

---

[381] The nickname 'Pip' was continued by his grandchildren, though its origins appear to have been lost over the generations.

had read several papers in the early 1870s concerning Palestine and Jerusalem. He re-established contact with the Palestine Exploration Fund, on whose Committee he served, attending their meetings, lecturing and offering his advice on current projects.

He found that during his absence in South Africa, James Fergusson had published another book, *The Temples of the Jews*, in which he repeated his controversial theory about the site of the Holy Sepulchre and the Herodian Temple, a theory that Warren considered his own work had thoroughly disproved. In the preface to this latest book Fergusson had written:

> … as the evidence at present stands, and is known to me, I can draw no other conclusions than those I have done, and I believe enough has been adduced in the various works I have published on the subject to convince any impartial and properly qualified person that the Dome of the Rock was built by Constantine, with all the consequences that inevitably follow from that admission.[382]

In other words, the Dome of the Rock was the Holy Sepulchre and the consequence Fergusson inferred was that the Temple must have been in the south-west corner of the Haram. There was no mention of Warren's conclusions that this positioning of the Temple was almost certainly not possible. Fergusson had clearly looked at Warren's work, but dismissed it as lacking in importance and clarity in a paragraph that clearly tested Warren's patience. In discussing Wilson's discovery of the Arch that bore his name, Fergusson had written:

> This was afterwards followed up by Captain Warren with his usual misdirected zeal and energy, and resulted in a series of vaulted chambers of various ages …

In Fergusson's view, Warren did not know what he was looking for:

> … and, what is worse, his discoveries were published only in so fragmentary and unscientific a manner that it is extremely difficult to [*sic*] others to make any use of them.[383]

To see his meticulous work publicly dismissed as 'fragmentary and unscientific' and his drawings prefaced with 'if accurate'[384] clearly tested Warren's patience. He sat down immediately and over the next two months wrote a book of

---

[382] James Fergusson, *The Temple of the Jews and the other buildings in the Haram area at Jerusalem* (John Murray, London, 1878), p xiv.
[383] *Ibid.*, p 172.
[384] *Ibid.*, p 168.

227 pages, *The Temple and the Tomb*, in which he methodically went through Fergusson's arguments step by step. Basing his responses on both his own work and on Fergusson's sources, which he knew virtually by heart, Warren listed 63 numbered 'misconceptions', all of which he comprehensively demolished, one by one.[385] His book was published by Richard Bentley rather than by John Murray, the preferred publisher of the PEF who had published Fergusson's work.

Warren also had to contend with criticism of his Jerusalem work from a fellow Royal Engineer whose work he had hitherto widely respected, namely Colonel Charles Wilson. In the January 1880 edition of the *PEF Quarterly Statement* Wilson published some notes on the construction of the wall of the Haram or Sanctuary which called into question the reliability of Warren's underground excavations in Jerusalem and some of the conclusions that Warren drew from his work.[386]

There was an air of professional rivalry that had probably been simmering between the two men ever since the original surveyor and excavator of Jerusalem, Charles Wilson, had been overshadowed by his junior successor who had been lauded with the honorific moniker 'Jerusalem Warren'. What particularly irked Warren, who responded in the next edition of the *PEF Quarterly*, was the

> … hypercriticism accorded to many of the measurements taken by myself and others, from which there is an inference that the measurements are not sufficiently accurate … and the comparison of measurements on unrevised plans with those that have been revised.[387]

Furthermore, Wilson had implied that Warren's work had been done 'in a somewhat perfunctory manner'.[388] In his turn Warren was able to show a number of inconsistencies in Wilson's own periodisation of the Haram Wall, concluding politely:

---

[385] Charles Warren, *The Temple or The Tomb. Giving further evidence in favour of the authenticity of the present site of the Holy Sepulchre, and pointing out some of the principal misconceptions contained in Fergusson's 'Holy Sepulchre' and 'The Temple of the Jews'* (Richard Bentley and Son, London, 1880).

[386] Col. C. W. Wilson, RE, CB, 'The Masonry of the Haram Wall', *PEF Quarterly*, January 1880, pp 9–60.

[387] Lt.-Col. Warren, CMG, RE, 'Notes on Colonel Wilson's Paper on the Masonry of the Haram Wall', *PEF Quarterly*, April 1880, p 161.

[388] *Ibid.*, p 164.

> … the ambiguity and obscurity of these and other affirmations will probably detract from the value of Colonel Wilson's notes.[389]

The criticisms of Fergusson and Wilson prompted Warren to prepare for publication the final revised copy of his complete set of Jerusalem drawings and his reconnaissance surveys of the Jordan Valley and Philistia. Known as the 'Warren Atlas', these were published in 1881 as part of the multi-volume *Survey of Western Palestine* that began to be published from that year.[390] The 'Warren Atlas' has remained a basic reference resource for archaeologists of Jerusalem ever since.

* * *

Having to his own satisfaction defended his reputation and dealt with Fergusson and Wilson, Warren now felt able to turn to his own future. By the new year of 1880 it was still not clear what future path his career would take and he contemplated a possible return to South Africa.

He had been offered a teaching post at Chatham, but he seems to have hoped for something more challenging, and perhaps he thought he could find it in South Africa. While travelling through the Eastern Cape in 1877 he had had an interesting conversation with an Australian geologist on what he described as 'my favourite subject, geology';[391] and now in January 1880 he wrote to the Secretary of the Royal Geographical Society (RGS), asking for introductions to the geographical authorities in the Cape.[392] If that was his plan, it, too, failed to materialise. Once again he fell back on teaching at Chatham, this time with a promotion, to Chief Instructor of Surveying at the School of Military Engineering (SME). He took up the appointment in February 1880, and he and the family moved into the married quarters at the headquarters of the Royal Engineers in Chatham.

Warren threw himself wholeheartedly into the new role. Since his time as Assistant Instructor in the 1860s, he had updated and expanded Frome's

---

[389] *Ibid.*, p 160.
[390] Captain Charles Warren, RE, *Plans, Elevations, Sections, &c. showing the results of the Excavation of Jerusalem, 1867–70, executed for the Committee of the Palestine Exploration Fund* (PEF, London, 1881), known as the 'Warren Atlas'; and Col. Sir Charles Warren, KCMG, RE and Capt. Claude Reigner Conder, RE, *The Survey of Western Palestine. Vol IV: Jerusalem* (PEF, London, 1884).
[391] Warren, *On the Veldt in the Seventies*, p 252.
[392] *RGS Archives*, CB6 1871–80: Warren to Secretary RGS, 3 Sermon Lane, St. Paul's, London, 23 January 1880.

textbook on surveying, he had conducted three reconnaissance surveys in Palestine, and he had made a detailed trigonometrical survey of the Griqualand/ Free State boundary. Now, as Head of the Department of Surveying, Warren was able to bring his knowledge and experience to a review of the curriculum. According to the official history of the SME:

> [Warren] laid great stress upon the necessity of distinguishing between military sketching, in which rapidity is the chief requirement, and surveying proper, in which accurate methods are essential, but rapidity of less moment.[393]

And he 'reorganised the system of instruction for RE Officers' in order to reflect this difference. He got the trainee officers out into the field, conducting coastal reconnaissances from Brighton to Pegwell Bay, each officer being allocated a few miles to reconnoitre before bringing back their sketches to Canterbury where they were pieced together. Nearly 30 years later, the official history observed that 'The present text book of military sketching [still] inculcates his teaching'.[394]

As already noted, from 1881 the Palestine Exploration Fund began publishing the *Survey of Western Palestine*. The work upon which this was based had been conducted by Lieutenants Claude Conder and Horatio (later Lord) Kitchener during the 1870s. Warren contributed, together with Lt Conder, most of the volume on the excavations at Jerusalem, which formed Volume IV of the *Survey*.[395] Warren was pleased to observe that the latitudes and longitudes of his reconnaissance surveys in Palestine, when compared with their trigonometrical survey, were only a few seconds out. He proudly published an article on it in the *Royal Engineers Journal*, which no doubt was compulsory reading for his trainee officers.[396]

Meanwhile, since 1872 the military had been experimenting with the possibility of using gas balloons for reconnaissance. Warren, with his childhood penchant for jumping out of windows, was naturally interested in ballooning. Familiar with the problems of surveying wide open countryside with its hidden dips, mounds and gullies, he saw that great advantage could

---

[393] Colonel B. R. Ward RE, *The School of Military Engineering*, 1812–1909 (RE Institute, Chatham, 1909), p 34.

[394] *Idem.*

[395] Volume IV (Jerusalem) of thirteen volumes, *The Survey of Western Palestine* (Palestine Exploration Fund, London, 1881–88).

[396] Col. Charles Warren, 'Limits of error in the latitudes and longitudes of places obtainable in a reconnaissance,' *RE Journal*, 2 August 1880, pp 174–5.

be gained from being able to observe from on high. Thus he would have enthusiastically welcomed the establishment of a balloon factory at St Mary's Barracks, Chatham, in 1882. Experiments were conducted there under Captain H. P. Lee, the officer in charge of the 38th (Depot) Company.[397]

Warren was soon to become a pioneer in the use of the gas balloon on a military expedition, but that was still in the future.[398] For the moment he had to content himself with making the most of his time at Chatham. If he was missing active service, which he almost certainly was, his chance came in the summer of 1882 with the British invasion of Egypt.

* * *

The background to the British invasion of Egypt can be traced to three factors in the 1860s, the most significant of which was the building of the Suez Canal, begun in 1859 and completed ten years later. Secondly, there was the development of Egypt as a major alternative source of raw cotton for British manufacturing during the American Civil War of 1861–65. Added to this was the desire of Egypt's ruler, the *Khedive* Ismail, to modernise the infrastructure of his country. All three of these factors provided the opportunity for the major bankers of Europe, mainly British and French, to rush in with overgenerous loans, in a manner familiar to relations between international finance and 'Third World' countries in the second half of the 20th century. Ismail used the loans to launch a vast programme of irrigation canals, railway building and modernisation of the port of Alexandria and, of course, the construction of the Suez Canal.

Ismail was persuaded that fees charged on the latter, which dramatically shortened the journey between Britain and her imperial possessions in India, would provide an important source of income for his country. In practice it became a millstone around the neck of the Egyptian State. The Canal was designed and built by the French. The financing was arranged so that European shareholders, who bore a quarter of the costs, took most of the profits, while the bulk of the costs were borne by Egyptian debt. Indeed, the schemes devised by the banking sector bore remarkable similarity to the financialisation of debt in the lead-up to the world financial crisis of 2008.

The bonds of Egyptian debt, on this project and others, were issued in a manner that was virtually fraudulent, the state often in practice receiving a

---

[397] Colonel C. M. Watson, 'Military Ballooning in the British Army,' *Royal Engineers' Institute, Occasional Papers*, Vol. XXVIII, 1902, Paper III, pp 44–7.
[398] See below, Chapter 14.

fraction of the debt levied while the bondholders were guaranteed a high level of interest. The bondholders included many within the British establishment, including Prime Minister W. E. Gladstone. Ultimately, the Canal and other loans bankrupted the Egyptian state and led directly to the British occupation of 1882.[399]

Bankruptcy was temporarily averted in 1875 by Britain's purchase of Egypt's share of the Suez Canal for £4 million, a mere fraction of its true cost to the Egyptian state. When, a year later, Ismail tried postponing interest payments on Egyptian government debt, the bondholders, supported by the British and French governments, virtually took over the running of the government of Egypt. British and French 'experts' ran various key ministries and set up 'dual control' of the country's finances. The government was now run in the interests of European bondholders. When Ismail tried to resist this effective 'colonisation' by dismissing some of his European 'ministers' in 1879, he was forced to abdicate in favour of his more pliant son, Tewfiq.

This aroused a wave of Egyptian nationalism, which soon spread to the Army, where it was led by the son of an Egyptian *fellah* (peasant), Colonel Ahmed 'Urabi, also known in British parlance as Arabi Pasha. He joined the civilian nationalists – intellectuals and Islamic reformers – in forming what became known as the 'National Party'. Their aim was to overthrow what they regarded as the autocratic rule of a corrupt Turkish and Circassian élite and replace it with a parliamentary constitution modelled along the lines of those in Western Europe.[400]

In response to this perceived threat to the status quo, Tewfiq's European 'advisors' ordered him to cut government expenditure by reducing the size of the Army, thus, hopefully, neutralising the nationalist threat within Cairo. A struggle for power ensued between Tewfiq's Administration and the Army.

'Urabi, who by this time had adopted the surname 'al-Misri' ('the Egyptian'), campaigned with the nationalists under the slogan 'Egypt for the Egyptians'. They had observed the French military occupation of Tunisia in May 1881 and believed a similar prospect faced Egypt if they did not stand firm. On

---

[399] The best critique of the British invasion of Egypt is to be found in John Newsinger's *The Blood Never Dried: A People's History of the British Empire* (Bookmarks Publications, London, 2nd edn 2013), pp 92–104. For a more detailed study, using Egyptian primary sources, see J. R. I. Cole, *Colonialism and Revolution in the Middle East: Social and Cultural Origins of Egypt's 'Urabi Movement'* (Princeton University Press, New Jersey, 1993).
[400] Wilfrid Scawen Blunt, *Secret History of the English Occupation of Egypt, Being a Personal Narrative of Events* (A. Knopf, New York, 1922), pp 129–32 for Blunt's interview with 'Urabi in December 1881.

9 September that year 'Urabi pressured Tewfiq into appointing Egyptian nationalists to key ministries. 'Urabi himself took the Ministry of War.

'Urabi's action was dismissed by contemporary Europe as nothing but an Army coup d'état, staged by an ambitious autocrat dissatisfied with cuts in the Army's budget.[401] In reality it is better understood as an attempt by 'Urabi and the National Party to form an independent nationalist government, answerable to Egyptians, and in clear defiance of European control.[402] Britain and France responded to the perceived 'Urabi 'threat' in a manner prefiguring their reaction to a later Egyptian nationalist, Abdel Nasser's nationalisation of the Suez Canal in 1956. They sent a combined naval fleet to blockade Alexandria in May 1882. As an attempt to bully the nationalists into submission, it failed. 'Urabi reacted by strengthening Alexandria's defences.

The European presence, their domination of all aspects of government and their racist contempt for the native Egyptians had been most overt in Alexandria. With Anglo-French navies threatening the city, Egyptian resentment erupted in a full-scale riot on 11 June 1882 that left 50 Europeans and 250 Egyptians dead. Invasion now became inevitable.

The killing of 50 Europeans was regarded in Britain as an affront to British prestige throughout the empire. It had to be avenged by massive force. The French, engaged in Tunisia, withdrew from the blockade and left it to the British. On 11 July British naval guns began a ten-hour bombardment of Alexandria that left the city in ruins and thousands of Egyptians dead. Two days later a naval force was landed in what was left of the port city, and Army regiments began to arrive from Malta and Cyprus the following week. It was not until 24 July 1882, rather late in the day, that Britain was put on a general war footing and the Reserves were called out.

* * *

At the School of Military Engineering (SME) in Chatham Lieutenant-Colonel Charles Warren had been carefully following events, and he saw the War Office call-out as an opportunity for action. With the permission of Sir Andrew Clarke, Commandant of the SME, he was quick to volunteer his services. A week later, probably as part of a plan to demonstrate his expertise and entice the War Office to offer him a significant assignment, he sent them a memorandum.

[401] *The War in Egypt, with Illustrations by Richard Simpkin and based on reports in The Times* (Routledge, London, 1883), pp 8–10.
[402] Cole, *Colonialism and Revolution in the Middle East.*

Warren realised that any army of occupation, no matter how short-lived, would need the support of local labour, and his memorandum contained proposals for 'arranging ... large scale working-parties and establishing discipline among Bedouin and Arabs'.[403] He had three years' direct experience of doing just this in Palestine; but to promote his chances of employment, he claimed he had 'passed ten summers in the Mediterranean and had extensive experience in such matters'. The time in the Mediterranean was true, but seven of those years had been spent in Gibraltar and had had nothing to do with organising 'Bedouin and Arabs'. Once again, Warren was prepared to stretch his CV to get what he wanted. He had after all spent the occasional week on leave in Morocco and would have observed some Arabs there.

His memorandum did not illicit an immediate response; but a copy was passed to the Admiralty. They had charge of military operations in the Eastern Mediterranean until the landing of the main body of the Army under General Sir Garnet Wolseley in mid-August. Once Alexandria had been occupied in mid-July, the main concern of the Admiralty was the safety of the Suez Canal, and on 27 July the First Lord of the Admiralty, Lord Northbrook, asked Warren to prepare a detailed report on 'the question of dealing with the Bedouin for the safety of the Suez Canal'.[404]

What Warren did not realise until later was that, two weeks before the bombardment of Alexandria, Northbrook had despatched a secret mission to Suez and Sinai to investigate the political affiliations of the Bedouin, especially those in the vicinity of the Canal. Warren himself had been briefly considered for the job, though not approached, and the man that Northbrook had settled on was Edward Henry Palmer, renowned Orientalist and linguist and Professor of Arabic at the University of Cambridge. He was the country's foremost authority on the Bedouin of Sinai, having served on two expeditions to the region for the Palestine Exploration Fund in 1868–70 and published an account of his travels as *The Desert of the Exodus: Journeys on Foot in the Wilderness of the Forty Years' Wanderings*.[405]

Palmer had jumped at the chance to undertake the mission. He loved adventure, was in financial difficulties and was hopeful that a successful outcome

---

[403] 'Notes by Sir Charles Warren on his connection with the Palmer Search-Expedition', printed as Appendix A in Alfred E. Haynes, *Man-hunting in the Desert: Being a Narrative of the Palmer Search Expedition* (Horace Cox, London, 1894), p 281.
[404] *Idem.*
[405] (Harper, New York, 1872).

might lead to some longer-term prestigious government employment.[406] On the face of it, Palmer seemed the ideal choice. He had detailed knowledge and experience of Sinai and claimed to have added every Bedouin dialect to his phenomenal linguistic range. He also claimed to be on good terms with the principal sheikhs of Sinai.

The trouble with the choice of Palmer was that he was temperamentally unsuited to the business of spying. In the first place he was indiscreet, telling his friends about his mission, including Wilfrid Blunt, a known sympathiser of 'Urabi and Egyptian nationalism. Secondly, he put out differing cover stories, changing them according to whom he met. And finally, the Bedouin politics of Sinai were fluid and changeable. As Warren put it, 'The tribes move on like the billows of sand in the desert'.[407] By 1882 Palmer's contacts and information were more than ten years out of date. Furthermore, Palmer's Sinai experience had been in a time of peace, when the British were viewed favourably. He would now be entering a country that was effectively on a war footing, with Britons like himself regarded as the enemy.

By the second week of July Palmer had travelled, via Jaffa, to Gaza from where he intended to make his way south-west through northern Sinai to meet up with British naval authorities, who were in warships anchored off Suez. The Bedouin were generally hostile to both Turkish and Egyptian control, and Palmer, on his own initiative, decided to expand his task. He would no longer simply assess the political affiliations of the Bedouin; he would actively engage with the sheikhs and assess whether, and at what price, they could be brought onto the British side. Travelling in disguise as 'Sheikh Abdullah', Palmer left Gaza with a handful of Bedouin just two days after the British bombardment of Alexandria.

By the time Northbrook asked Warren to prepare his report, nothing had been heard from Palmer for at least two weeks. It is possible that Northbrook saw Warren as a backup in case Palmer's mission failed.

Through his contacts in the Palestine Exploration Fund and the Royal Engineers (often used as intelligence agents in the field), Warren was up-to-date on the Bedouin of the Sinai, and he took a much more cautious and realistic approach to the situation, than had the self-advertised expert Professor Edward Palmer. He noted that the Turkish authorities were 'intensely jealous of the movement of English persons in Syria'. It would therefore be unwise, he

---

[406] David Sunderland, *These Chivalrous Brothers: The Mysterious Disappearance of the 1882 Palmer Sinai Expedition* (Chronos Books, Winchester, 2016), pp 68–71.
[407] Warren 'Notes', Appendix A, in Haynes, *Man-hunting*, p 285.

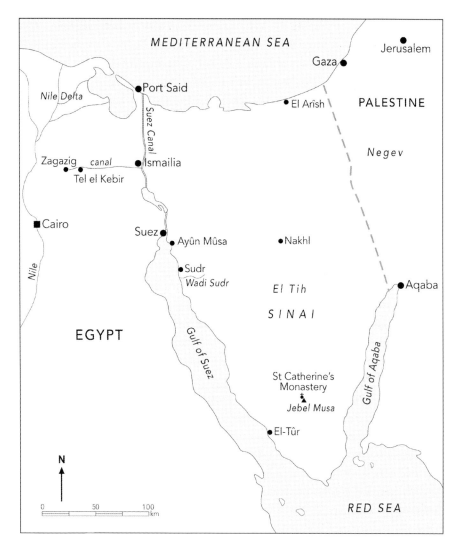

Egypt and Sinai in 1882.

informed Northbrook, to enter Sinai through the Turkish garrison at Gaza, or anywhere along the northern Sinai coast, which was exactly what Palmer had just done. If Warren were undertaking the task he would pass down through the Suez Canal and land on the Sinai coast some 60 kilometres south of Suez. The Sheikh of the Tiyahah Bedouin would be called to meet him there and he would form a Bedouin escort before proceeding into the interior. He advised strongly against sending in British troops.

Following the principle he had used with success in both Palestine and South Africa, he recommended displaying *trust* in the Bedouin as the best way to persuade them of Britain's benign intent. The principal risks for anyone leading such an expedition would be murder while sleeping or poisoning by an emissary of 'Urabi. He saw the former as the greater danger, especially at night. It was best guarded against by having just enough Europeans so that one of them could be awake at all times. And if Warren was undertaking the task, he would want men sufficiently known to him that he could totally rely upon them. Murder by either method would probably be attempted by a camp attendant,

> … and I would avoid this difficulty by having no camp-followers, and living among and eating among the Bedouin.[408]

* * *

While Warren was writing his report, Palmer emerged from the desert, reaching the British warships at Suez on 1 August. With the occupation already underway, the British naval captains were surprised to see the long-bearded, eccentric professor, dressed in Arab clothes, emerge unscathed from what was effectively 'behind enemy lines', and they fêted him as a returning hero, plying him with iced champagne.[409]

Palmer reported to Vice-Admiral Sir William Hewett, assuring him that, despite some sympathy for the 'Urabi cause, the bulk of the Bedouin could be bought, and brought onside. Palmer did not admit he had failed to go from settlement to settlement to converse with many sheikhs as he had proposed, but had relied instead upon a single contact that he had known previously, Sheikh Misleh, a man with a reputation for being anti-Westerner and a presumed 'Urabi sympathiser. Palmer, however, had supreme confidence in his understanding of the Bedouin and considered himself a man of powerful persuasion. He believed he had won over Misleh when the sheikh agreed that for £20,000 (an enormous sum by any standards) he would provide the British with 50,000 men to protect the Canal.

Palmer must have known there were not 50,000 men in the entire Sinai; but he made a firm agreement to this effect with Misleh, even though he had no authority to do so. In his official report, however, he did not admit to

---

[408] Warren 'Notes', in Haynes, *Man-hunting*, p 282.
[409] Sunderland, *Chivalrous Brothers*, p 21.

the agreement and merely implied that these were potential figures.[410] The Admiralty may already have had some doubts about the reliability of Palmer's grand assurances and large financial sums.[411]

The day after Palmer's arrival the Navy landed troops and occupied Suez, and for a few days Palmer was engaged as a translator in buying camels for the use of British forces. Palmer, however, had an agreement with Misleh that he must somehow satisfy and he indicated to Admiral Hewett that he needed to go back into the desert to meet with the sheikhs at Nakhl, a fortified town on the pilgrim trail in the centre of Sinai. This was authorised and he was entrusted with three small bags, each containing £1000 in gold coin, ostensibly to buy camels, but in reality to bribe the Bedouin.

By this time Captain William Gill RE had arrived in Suez on a separate secret mission to cut the telegraph wire that crossed the Sinai Desert and ultimately linked Cairo with Istanbul (Constantinople) whose Ottoman Sultan was the ultimate overlord of Egypt.

Gill was the man who had first introduced Palmer to Northbrook in June. He was a Royal Engineer of wide international experience, which included expeditions on behalf of the intelligence departments of both the War Office and the Admiralty.[412] He decided it would be a good cover for his mission to travel with Palmer and cut the wire at some remote spot in the desert where it could not easily be repaired. The Navy added Lieutenant Charrington RN to the party, to impress the sheikhs that this was an official mission and on 8 August the three men set off with Bokor Hassoun, the Jewish cook whom Palmer had hired in Gaza, and Khalil Atek, a Syrian Christian who had been Gill's attendant on a previous mission.[413]

They spent the first night at the town of Ayun Musa (Moses' Wells), fifteen kilometres down the Sinai coast of the Red Sea, where they met by prior arrangement with their guides, Meter abu Sofieh and his nephew. Sofieh had been introduced to Palmer as the Sheikh of the Bedouin who lived in that region. In fact, he was not a sheikh at all, but a minor figure, a clan

---

[410] HCPP, Cd.3761, *Supplementary Correspondence respecting The Murder of Professor E. H. Palmer, Captain Wm. Gill and Lieutenant Harold Charrington, RN*, pp 4–5: Palmer's Report on his journey through Sinai, Suez, 1 August 1882.

[411] Sunderland, *Chivalrous Brothers*, pp 31–2.

[412] Saul Kelly, *Captain Gill's Walking Stick: The True Story of the Sinai Murders* (I.B. Tauris, London, 2019), pp 2–4.

[413] Sunderland, *Chivalrous Brothers*, pp 33–5; and Tony Hadland, *Glimpses of a Victorian Hero: Captain William Gill, Explorer and Spy* (Hadland Books, Farringdon, 2013), p 76.

outcast who lived near Suez. More ominously, however, he was supposed to have arrived with a protective force of armed men and this he had failed to do. Nevertheless, Palmer determined to press on, with no protection.[414] The following morning, 9 August, the party set off into the desert, bound for Nakhl, accompanied by seven Bedouin cameleers to tend their numerous baggage camels.

* * *

Back home in Chatham, late in the night of Thursday 10 August, Warren completed his report on how best to deal with the Bedouin and despatched it to the Admiralty next morning. If Northbrook had not already had doubts about the wisdom of entrusting so important and dangerous a mission to someone of Palmer's background and character, he would surely have regretted his decision when he read Warren's report that Friday evening. Not only did Warren show Palmer's 50,000 available Bedouin to be a wild exaggeration – Warren put it at 5000 maximum – but he also then read Warren's fateful warning:

> Care would have to be taken to avoid Nackl [*sic*], where there is an Egyptian garrison [sympathetic to 'Urabi].[415]

If Warren's assessment was true, Palmer was walking straight into a trap. But the decision had been made and there was nothing the Admiralty in London could do about it now.

The following morning, Saturday 12 August, Warren was called to the Admiralty. It was only then that he learned of Palmer's mission and that there was no present prospect of his own services being required. Warren knew Palmer from their meeting in Jerusalem in 1870 and he appreciated his knowledge, linguistic skills and enthusiasm, but he would have been somewhat put out that a mere academic and amateur had been chosen over himself, when the mission clearly called for a military mind.

Northbrook probably realised by now that Palmer's mission was doomed, but he was more concerned with the apparent failure of Gill's mission. Nothing had been heard from any of the party since they had departed for the desert on Wednesday 9 August. General Wolseley's arrival in the Canal was imminent. Wolseley's plan was to launch an attack on Cairo from the direction of the

---

[414] Sunderland, *Chivalrous Brothers*, p 39.
[415] Warren's 'Notes' in Haynes, *Man-hunting*, p 282, 284.

Suez Canal, and the telegraph line that linked Cairo with Istanbul had still not been cut.

Warren heard nothing more until Thursday 24 August when he received a telegram from the Admiralty indicating that Admiral Sir Beauchamp Seymour, Commander-in-Chief of naval forces, had asked for his services and that he might be required to proceed immediately to Egypt. He attended Lord Northbrook at the Admiralty that afternoon, and was briefed on the situation regarding Professor Palmer's party. Nothing had been heard from them since they had entered the desert two weeks previously, and there were rumours they had been robbed. Warren was to proceed at once to the Suez Canal and report to the Admiral for services among the Bedouin.

In line with his recommendations regarding personal safety, Warren asked for three trusted men to accompany him. His request was granted and he chose, as clerk and storekeeper, Quartermaster-Sergeant Kennedy, that 'man in a thousand' who, as Sergeant Kennedy, had served him so well on the Griqualand survey. Kennedy was with the Ordnance Survey in Southampton and was immediately available. The other two were young lieutenants of the Royal Engineers: Lieutenant Alfred Haynes who was in Chatham currently attending Warren's surveying course, and Lieutenant Edmund Burton who had recently attended Warren's advanced course on military surveying and was currently serving in Ireland.

As Warren was later to observe, he was particularly impressed by Haynes' 'great talent for freehand sketching and military drawing, an excellent eye for country, a taste for geology, and considerable powers of observation, which, together with his liking for yachting and boating, marked him out as a man likely to be of service in any exploring expedition'.[416] This description of Haynes could have been of himself at that age and Warren seems to have treated Haynes as something akin to an adopted son. Kennedy and Haynes were immediately available for service and Burton was sent for from Ireland. Warren completed his arrangements that day and, bidding Fanny and the children goodbye, he, Haynes and Kennedy set off for the seat of war the following evening. Burton was to follow by the next night mail.

[416] From Warren's obituary of Alfred Haynes, *Royal Engineers Journal*, 1 September 1896, pp 202–3.

CHAPTER 12
'Man-hunting in Sinai'[417]

Warren, Haynes and Kennedy travelled by train to Brindisi in the heel of Italy, the fastest route to the Eastern Mediterranean, and there took ship to Port Said at the mouth of the Canal, arriving on 31 August 1882, a journey of just six days. Colonel Redvers Buller, Wolseley's Head of Intelligence whom Warren had known in South Africa, had arranged for Warren and his men to board another ship and be taken directly to Ismailia, halfway along the Canal, where Wolseley's army had affected a landing. They reached Ismailia on the evening of 1 September and Warren reported immediately to Admiral Seymour. He was told his mission was to discover the fate of Professor Palmer and his party, and no expense would be spared.

With the object of their mission now clear, Warren, Haynes and Kennedy travelled on down to the southern end of the Canal where they reported to Vice-Admiral Hewett in Suez on 4 September. There they were introduced to Osman Bey, *aide-de-camp* to the Egyptian *Khedive* Tewfiq. Warren was informed that Osman Bey had been specifically sent to Suez to assist in the search for Professor Palmer and he was to treat him as a colleague. Warren did not welcome the presence of an Egyptian political agent; he preferred to be in sole command; but he had to accept the diplomatic necessity.

Rumour had spread through the region that the British Army, which was advancing from Ismailia towards Cairo, had been thrown back by 'Urabi's army. The rumour was probably based upon news of an earlier British advance from Alexandria towards Cairo that had indeed been checked. Nevertheless, encouraged by the rumour of British defeat, some of the Sinai Bedouin had sacked the coastal town of Ayun Musa and driven out all foreigners. This was the point ten kilometres south of Suez at which Palmer had entered the desert, and but for its sacking it would have been the obvious starting point for Warren's investigation. However, some Greek families who had fled the

---

[417] Chapter title drawn from Alfred E. Haynes, *Man-hunting in the Desert: Being a Narrative of the Palmer Search Expedition (1882–1883)* (Horace Cox, London, 1894).

Bedouin attack had come into Suez, and Warren and Haynes were able to question them.[418]

The information Warren gathered from his Greek informants, however, ultimately proved unreliable. Bedouin names and places were mispronounced and misspelt and Warren was led to believe that Palmer's guide was Sheikh Musa of the Bedouin who lived in the vicinity of El-Tur, near the south-east tip of the Sinai Peninsula.

Acting on this misinformation, Warren and his men joined the steamer HMS *Cockatrice* that was going down the Gulf to El-Tur. The ship was carrying grain and other stores for the beleaguered Greek monks of St Catherine's Monastery on Mount Sinai (Jebel Musa). The monks were normally supplied from Alexandria, but the British bombardment had made that impossible, so the British accepted the responsibility of supplying them with food. The monks were usually on good terms with the local Bedouin, whom they supplied with food in hard times and who profited from the pilgrims that visited the monastery. It was hoped that the Greek Archbishop at El-Tur would be able to introduce Warren to Bedouin who would have information on the fate of the Palmer party.[419]

Initially Warren's party did not receive much help at El-Tur. Stories began to emerge, but most of them were contradictory. Warren tried to get in touch with Sheikh Musa, who had been wrongly identified as Palmer's guide; but the sheikh failed to respond, probably fearing that he was being lured into a trap.

Then a positive piece of news. An elderly Bedouin, claiming to have been a servant of Palmer's at the time of the Sinai survey of 1870, said that he knew Palmer was alive and was being held in a valley not far from El-Tur. At last Warren had something to go on. He wrote a letter to Palmer which he persuaded his informant to take to the place where he was being held. Warren tried to sound cheerful and encouraging:

Tor, Sept, 9th, 1882, Saturday.

My Dear Palmer,

I am here with English Consul (Mr West), looking for you; send word by the bearer, your old servant, how we can best assist you in getting back.

… Keep up your spirits! We will act as quickly as we can consistent with securing your safety. We only learnt to-day of your location in safety.

[418] Haynes, *Man-hunting*, pp 11–17.
[419] Haynes, *Man-hunting*, p 18.

I enclose paper and pencil for your reply. The Admiral is making all efforts for your recovery,

Your old friend, Charles Warren.[420]

Then in a postscript he told Palmer the latest news, that the British had occupied the Canal and were halfway to Cairo, and concluded:

If you cannot send a written reply send a token that you are well … a piece of cloth or string with three knots, one for each [of you], or some hair from your head or beard with three knots in it.

In retrospect, it is a pathetic letter, for Palmer's party had never been in the vicinity of El-Tur, and the old man had never been Palmer's servant. He had been servant to another Englishman, who had travelled through Sinai in 1875. And finally, Warren was writing to a man who had already been dead for four weeks. The old servant took his payment and never returned.

The *Khedive*'s political agent, Osman Bey, was not being at all helpful and was convinced by a story that Palmer had been captured and taken to Cairo. Warren, however, refused to believe it. He decided that if Palmer was alive and being held somewhere in the desert, he had better get some ransom money available. In order to get Osman Bey off his back, he gave him the task of returning to Suez to organise the ransom.

In the meantime Sheikh Musa had sent a message to the Archbishop of El-Tur indicating that he had heard that the Governor of Nakhl, acting on the orders of 'Urabi Pasha, had ordered that the Englishmen be killed, and that this had been carried out; although another version of the same story claimed they were still alive and held somewhere near Nakhl. Anxious to believe the latter version, Warren wrote again to Sheikh Musa asking for an escort to Nakhl where he hoped to negotiate their release. The Governor of El-Tur, offered to visit Sheikh Musa himself, and he set off, leaving Warren as Acting-Governor in his absence.

The following day a steamer arrived from Suez bringing Lieutenant Burton and the news that the Egyptian Army had been defeated at Tel El Kebir on 13 September, 'Urabi had been captured, and Cairo was in British hands. Warren sent a runner after the Governor with a copy of *Khedive* Tewfiq's proclamation of peace so that it could be read to Sheikh Musa. Then, as Acting-Governor of El-Tur, he assembled the people of the town in

---

[420] Quoted in *Ibid.*, p 27.

a courtyard and read the proclamation in English, after which his interpreter read it in Arabic. That evening the captain of the steamer brought champagne and other choice supplies up to the town and Warren and his companions had a great celebratory feast in the convent, with some of the monks joining in.[421]

Warren was anxious to pursue his investigations inland, but he could not do so without camels and so far he had failed to persuade any Bedouin to sell him camels or provide an escort. In an attempt to win Sheikh Musa's co-operation, Warren decided he needed to make a demonstration of trust. He, Haynes, Burton, Kennedy, his interpreter and a cook named Sala rode out on donkeys and camped away from El-Tur in the direction of Musa's camp. Warren's display of trust, however, appeared not to be reciprocated and after a frustrating two weeks of 'excessive heat, swarms of mosquitoes and rancid food' he was forced to strike camp and head back to El-Tur.[422] It later emerged that Sheikh Musa had in fact provided a small force of armed men who encircled Warren's camp at some distance to ensure that they were not attacked.[423]

Warren did not know this at the time and he returned to 'an exceedingly hot Suez' an extremely frustrated man. He had been a month in the field and had achieved virtually nothing, apart from picking up numerous rumours of doubtful authenticity. His preferred option of travelling under the protection of a Bedouin escort having failed to materialise, he asked the Governor of Suez for 30 soldiers to accompany him into the desert. The Governor, however, insisted that he would not be able to find 30 soldiers who could be trusted so soon after the defeat of 'Urabi's army.[424]

Meanwhile, Vice-Admiral Hewett, who now that the invasion was complete was due to return to the India Command, ordered Warren to Cairo to meet with General Wolseley. Leaving Lieutenant Burton to keep an eye on Ayun Musa, Warren and Haynes caught a freight train to Cairo. Wolseley agreed that Warren should continue his search for Professor Palmer and his party. He was authorised to draw up to £5000 of secret service funds through Admiral Seymour in Ismailia. He was to work as far as possible with Egyptian authorities and report to both the Admiralty and the Foreign Office.

Lt.-Colonel Charles Wilson, Warren's PEF rival concerning Jerusalem, was

---

[421] *Ibid.*, pp 36–7.
[422] Sunderland, *Chivalrous Brothers*, p 82.
[423] *Ibid.*, p 110.
[424] Haynes, *Man-hunting*, pp 51–2.

now Head of Intelligence in Egypt and he accompanied Warren to a meeting with Consul-General Sir Edward Malet who had been the senior British civil authority in Egypt since 1879. Between them they convinced Malet that he must insist on the replacement of the pro-'Urabi Egyptian Governors of both Nakhl and Aqaba, at the head of the gulf of that name on the eastern side of the Sinai Peninsula. Warren and Wilson then met the Egyptian Minister of the Interior, and the Minister recommended to them a sheikh who would provide Warren with an escort into the Sinai desert.

Warren and Haynes returned to Suez, and while waiting for the sheikh to gather his Bedouin escort, Warren decided to try a different tack. He would go south by sea, around the Peninsula of Sinai and up its eastern shore to see what he could discover at the fortress town of Aqaba.[425]

The Navy lent him the small warship HMS *Eclipse*. Leaving Burton in Suez to continue questioning witnesses, Warren left with Haynes and three minor sheikhs whom he hoped would testify to the truth of 'Urabi's defeat. The Government had not yet provided a replacement Governor for Aqaba, but Warren took with him Hassan Effendi, who was to be the new Governor of Nakhl. He also took his excellent interpreter, Selim Mosalli, a Syrian from Beirut who was used to guiding pilgrims and tourists. Mosalli was fluent in Turkish and Arabic, including Bedouin dialects, and had a reasonable command of several European languages. Warren always used an interpreter, even when he had a certain understanding of the language. As he later explained:

> … however well you may speak the language of another person, you are always at a *disadvantage*, being never quite perfect in it; while with an interpreter you have a distinct *advantage*, as you hear the reply in two languages, and get your own idea of it and that of the interpreter. Experience has taught me that a man who knows a little of a language and employs an interpreter, is better placed than one who knows a language pretty well and uses no interpreter … In fact I put very little faith in the results of interviews where a good interpreter is not employed.[426]

On arrival off Aqaba the passengers and crew of the *Eclipse* witnessed the hasty lowering of the green 'Urabi flag that had been fluttering above the 10th-century fort. The mudbrick town of approximately 1000 inhabitants lay behind the fort. Two cutters were lowered and rowed towards the shore.

---

[425] *Ibid.*, pp 104–5.
[426] Warren's 'Notes', in Haynes, *Man-hunting*, Appendix A, pp 285–6.

One carried Warren, Haynes and their interpreter Mosalli, as well as Hassan Effendi, the three sheikhs, Lieutenant Henderson RN of the *Eclipse* and twelve blue-jackets (naval soldiers). The other cutter contained twenty marines.

The Governor of Aqaba came down to the water's edge, accompanied by a large, threatening crowd of armed men. Anchoring offshore, Warren and his interpreter used a megaphone to tell the Governor about 'Urabi's defeat and that peace had been declared. The Governor got into a skiff and was rowed out to Warren's cutter to gain more details. He agreed to allow Warren and the non-military members of his boat to land. Warren ordered his cutter to approach the shore, while the other boat moved to the protection of an anchored dhow from where they could cover the landing party.

As Warren's party came ashore, they were surrounded by an angry crowd who threatened to shoot them. Warren coolly handed the Governor an Arabic version of the Khedive's proclamation and insisted that he read it to the assembled throng. The reading did not quieten them and one of the sheikhs that had accompanied Warren, convinced he was about to die, sank to his knees and began to pray loudly. Warren prodded the man with his foot and joked that the near-prostrate man, forgetting that he had travelled so far east, was facing the wrong way for Mecca. As this was translated, there was laughter and the tension was broken.[427]

Warren then got his interpreter to read the proclamation a second time and, with muskets still levelled at them, Warren told the Governor to send the crowd away so that they could sit quietly and share some coffee. The Governor seemed powerless to calm the crowd, but suddenly a tall man with a commanding presence appeared on the scene. He was Mohammed Gad, Sheikh of the Bedouin guardians of the Hajj pilgrims who passed annually through Aqaba. A wave of his sword and the crowd fell back.

The Governor tried to entice his visitors into the fort; but Warren was not yet confident of their safety and he declined the invitation. He was content to sit on the beach. The Governor knew that etiquette forbade him to refuse the sharing of coffee and eventually he gave way. Cushions and drinks were brought out from the fort and once they were seated in the shade of a palm tree, Warren showed the Governor a letter addressed to him from the Governor of Suez, along with some Arabic newspaper cuttings about 'Urabi's defeat.

---

[427] Haynes, *Man-hunting*, pp 77–8; Sunderland, *Chivalrous Brothers*, pp 105–6.

That evening Warren returned to the ship, leaving Hassan Effendi and the three sheikhs ashore. The following morning he and Haynes returned, this time accompanied by two ship's officers and two blue-jackets. As they approached the shore, the excited crowd levelled their guns at them once more. When Warren remonstrated with the Governor, the latter insisted that he could not control the crowd unless Warren's escort of the second cutter was sent back to the ship. Warren decided to risk it and ordered the marines away.

This time they entered the fort and as the great, iron-clad doors slammed shut behind them, they seated themselves on cushions in the courtyard and waited for coffee. The crowd outside, however, frustrated at being denied the chance to kill the strangers, struck up a huge racket, shouting and banging on the door, to such an extent that the gathering inside could not hear themselves speak. As Haynes recalled:

> … at last Colonel Warren decided to do a little shouting himself. So he commenced to harangue the Governor in a loud voice.

Pausing between phrases for interpreter Mosalli to translate, in an equally loud voice, he pointed out:

> … that if we met with any evil not one stone would be left upon another in the castle or houses; that … the Governor and his [police] could not possibly ever be employed again; that they would be outcasts among the Bedouin who hated them; that Mohammed Gad would cease to be sheikh over his tribe, and that his tribe would lose the care and lucrative custody of the Hajj pilgrims.[428]

This last had the desired effect and Gad and the police went out and beat back the crowd. Warren and his party were then invited into the cool of an inner room where a large meal of boiled rice and cooked spiced meat was laid on. They sat on their cushions and, as was customary, after washing their hands, they ate the meal in silence. Hassan Effendi, who had spent the night ashore, then indicated to Warren that he had learned during the night that the Governor had received an important letter from the Governor of Nakhl, and this Warren demanded to see. The Governor at first prevaricated, at which Warren, getting into his stride, told the Governor that the fort and town would be 'shelled out of existence' if he continued to support 'Urabi and did not co-operate.[429]

---

[428] Haynes, *Man-hunting*, pp 81–3.
[429] Sunderland, *Chivalrous Brothers*, p 107.

As Haynes explained:

> Colonel Warren had a theory that the best time for brow-beating an Arab host is just after he has fed you; when he thinks you ought to be satisfied with what you have eaten, and when he is himself well gorged and unable to resist your importunities. On this occasion the onslaught was successful; our host was taken aback by the sudden attack upon him, and began to assert his readiness to assist in anything in accordance with the orders of the Governor of Suez.[430]

The required letter from the Governor of Nakhl was finally produced and it proved to be the first piece of firm evidence that Warren had yet seen. The letter was written before the Egyptian defeat at the Battle of Tel El Kebir, from one 'Urabist governor to another, and neither imagined it would ever be read by their enemies. It claimed initially that 'Urabi had won a great victory, probably referring to the Egyptian blocking of the initial British advance from Alexandria. It then went on to reveal that the 'three Christians' – namely Palmer, Gill and Charrington – had been killed by Sheikh ibn Mershed of the Hawetat Bedouin, and that they had been killed in Wadi Sudr, a valley not far from where Palmer had set off into the desert.[431]

At last Warren had the evidence that cleared Sheikh Musa and his Bedouin. He had a named guilty party and he had the site of the killing. The only problem was that it ended all hope of finding Palmer, Gill and Charrington alive.

Armed with this information, Warren returned to Suez where he began to build up a list of men wanted for questioning. A number of sheikhs had finally arrived, with armed escorts, although it was not clear whether they would work together; and Sheikh Musa finally came in from southern Sinai. He was a tall, elegant man in a long, white robe and a white turban that made him appear even taller.[432] Now cleared of suspicion, Musa was most co-operative. He persuaded some of the potential witnesses to give evidence and he offered to escort Warren into the desert. He was to prove a reliable and trustworthy guide. Before departing from Suez, Warren ordered the taking of hostages from the families of the sheikhs so as to ensure his own safety and that of Haynes and Burton.

On 20 October they left Suez for Palmer's starting point of Ayun Musa where their escort and camels were assembled. The party consisted of Warren,

---

[430] Haynes, *Man-hunting*, p 83.
[431] *Ibid.*, p 85.
[432] Sunderland, *Chivalrous Brothers*, pp 109 and 275, fn.8.

Colonel Warren and his companions on the Palmer Search-Expedition, with
STANDING FROM RIGHT *Lt Burton, Colonel Warren and Lt Haynes (sitting), with
interpreter, Selim Mosalli (second left) and other guides and interpreters. Haynes is
seated because he was convalescing from sunstroke, suffered in the desert.*
FROM A. E. HAYNES, MAN-HUNTING IN THE DESERT

Haynes, Burton, Nakhl's new Governor, Hassan Effendi, two interpreters (Mosalli and Josef Raad, another Syrian) and a Turkish cook named Adam. They were accompanied by 50 sheikhs, 370 armed Bedouin and 200 pack camels (75 of them with grain and other stores for Nakhl). Warren retained the company of Sheik Musa and his escort, and sent the other sheikhs to investigate among their own people, announcing that he would be going straight to Nakhl. In reality, he intended to follow Palmer's route, slightly south via Wadi Sudr, the ravine that had been nominated as the site of Palmer's capture. Warren hoped to find evidence, especially journals and other papers there; but he did not want the other sheiks to know in case they went ahead and destroyed the evidence.

For their personal protection against violent assault on their journey through the desert, Warren, Haynes and Burton slept separate from the rest, on some cleared ground within a barricade of baggage.

As Haynes remembered it:

… we lay down side by side, with our rifles under our blankets, and revolvers, loaded in the last three chambers, fastened to our wrists. Our constant activity in the daytime precluded any attempt on our part to keep sentry-go at night … but we soon became extraordinarily light sleepers, and I have oftentimes been awake at night looking up into the star-bespangled sky overhead, and noticed that not a camel could grunt or shift his position near us, or, indeed, not a movement take place anywhere in the camp, without 'our Chief,' who appeared to be sleeping hard, and *was* to all practical purposes, at once lifting his head and fixing the cause of the disturbance.[433]

Warren had gained a reputation in South Africa for being able to sleep on horseback. So far as fear of poisoning was concerned, Warren had deliberately chosen his Turkish cook, knowing that his brother was one of the murder suspects; but as Warren reasoned it:

… the cook, knowing that he would be suspected, would take every precaution against *anyone else* poisoning us, and so I looked upon his being a safeguard instead of a danger.[434]

As Warren's party approached the appointed ravine they spread out, searching on foot for evidence of the attack. They found scraps of baggage, including some papers, and an envelope with the name 'Charrington' on it. They captured some Bedouin, including an old man who had a tobacco pouch marked 'H. Charrington'. He claimed it had been given to him by someone who had already been named as one of the attackers. In due course they were guided to the steep ravine at the bottom of which lay the remains of the five victims: Palmer, Gill, Charrington, the Jewish cook Bokor Hassoun, and the Syrian attendant Khalil Atek. Warren and Haynes were lowered down the ravine by rope; but what they saw was no longer identifiable bodies. After two and a half months, all that remained was some underwear and a scattering of bones, jumbled together, broken and chewed by scavenging wild animals. They gathered up all the remains they could find and put them together in a special box they had brought out with them from England.

They returned to camp and discussed the next step. Part of their mission had been achieved. The task ahead was to unravel the full circumstances of the killing, and arrest the guilty parties.

[433] Haynes, *Man-hunting*, p 120.
[434] Williams, *The Life*, p 146, quoting from a paper read to the Victoria Institute in 1917.

Wadi Sudr where the remains of Edward Palmer and his companions were found.
FROM A. E. HAYNES, MAN-HUNTING IN THE DESERT

The heat, the delays and the frustrations of Bedouin prevarication had brought out a harsh side to Warren's character. He was quite clear in his own mind that 'innocent blood [should] be avenged' and that this whole sorry tale could only conclude with 'the exaction of the death penalty'. This, he insisted, was expected according to Bedouin law – 'a life for a life' – and the Bedouin 'looked on with dread, but in a spirit of fatalistic expectancy'.[435]

Warren was determined to push on and the following day they headed for Nakhl. They halted in sight of the fort to allow the camels to close up, and

[435] Haynes, *Man-hunting*, pp 114–9.

Warren sent forward two men to say that he came in peace, and that they had brought the new Governor, Hassan Effendi. The outgoing Governor let them in and professed ignorance of the fate of Palmer and his party, a claim disproved by the letter he had written to the Governor at Aqaba. Warren had the Governor and his family arrested and sent under armed guard to Suez. After arresting a number of potential witnesses and subjecting them to harsh cross-examination and threats, Warren felt he now held pretty much all of the basic facts.

What he had learned was that Palmer and his party had proceeded, unprotected, at a leisurely pace, as though he were on one of his academic research trips. They had been attacked on the second day in the vicinity of Wadi Sudr. During the attack their guide, Sofieh, and his nephew had escaped, the nephew on Palmer's camel with the gold. The men had been stripped of their Arab clothing, down to their underwear, and held overnight under guard. The next day, their guide returned and tried negotiating a ransom with the attackers. With Palmer's agreement, he offered a relatively small amount of money and some camels, but not the £3000 in gold which might have saved them.

Palmer seems to have been convinced that he was at one with the Bedouin and they would never kill him. But the five prisoners were taken to the edge of the ravine, at which point it became clear they were going to be killed. Palmer called out a terrible Arabic curse upon his enemies, but to no avail. They were shot and fell into the ravine. Someone went down to finish off those who were

The fortress at Nakhl. Illustrated London News, *4 November 1882.*

not already dead.[436]

All that remained for Warren and his party was to arrest the culprits.

It was reported that Palmer's guide, Sofieh, had headed north across the desert to a small Napoleonic fortress to the east of the Canal. From Nakhl it lay north-west across 110 miles (176 km) of waterless desert; but Warren was determined to pursue him. While it was clear that the guide was not one of the killers, Warren believed that he was in league with them; that having deliberately led Palmer and company into their ambush, he failed to rescue them during the night when they were lightly guarded and he made only a feeble effort to arrange a ransom.

Leaving the precious remains of the victims and some Bedouin prisoners in the care of the new Governor of Nakhl, Hassan Effendi, Warren set off the next day with Haynes, Burton, Sheikh Musa and a Bedouin escort of about 100 men in what the historian David Sunderland has described as an 'extraordinarily reckless' expedition.[437]

In the rush to depart, some of the camels had not been properly watered. Warren had thought he could cover the distance in two days, yet by the end of the second day they had covered just 70 miles, with 40 still to go. On the third day they had seen their target, Sofieh, in the distance, and a fruitless attempt to capture him further exhausted the camels and wasted waterless hours. With camels and Bedouin dropping by the wayside, at dawn on the fourth day they reached water. As they rested by the water, with no shade, Haynes suffered sunstroke. He collapsed into delirium and thereafter had to be carried on a makeshift stretcher. It was only at that point that Warren abandoned the attempt to catch Sofieh and headed west, straight for the Canal.

It had indeed been a reckless attempt that had cost the lives of several Bedouin, and nearly that of the whole party. Warren appears to have become obsessed with catching Sofieh, whom he saw as the greater culprit as he had betrayed the trust of his employer, Palmer. The obsession seems to have affected his normal steady judgement.

They reached the Canal close to the town of Ismailia the following morning, and with Haynes still suffering high fever, Warren stayed by his side nursing him for the next five days. As Haynes loyally observed, '… it is

---

[436] Charles Warren, 'History of the Expedition of Professor Palmer', Alexandria, 21 February 1883, in HCPP, Cd. 3494, *Correspondence respecting The Murder of Professor E. H. Palmer, Captain Wm. Gill and Lieutenant Harold Charrington, RN*, pp 10–16.
[437] Sunderland, *Chivalrous Brothers*, pp 145–6.

undoubtedly to his kind attention that I owe my life'.[438] Ironic, considering that it was Warren's reckless lack of attention that had nearly cost him his life.

They arrived in Suez on 6 November to find that the object of their pursuit, Sofieh, had come in and surrendered himself. Initially under cross-examination he was considered to be 'shifty and circumlocutory'.[439] Warren, normally so steady, methodical and in control, lost all patience.

The root of his anger probably lay in their narrow escape from death in the desert, for which he would have held Sofieh, rather than himself, responsible; and for the first and only time in his subsequent cross-examination, Warren resorted to 'a little delicate manipulation' of the whip.[440] This loosened the guide's tongue and he finally admitted that he and his nephew had made off with the box of money, which they had concealed in a ravine a day's journey from Suez. He said he had tried to negotiate the prisoners' release, and added that he did not expect them to be killed as the orders of the Governor of Nakhl had been to capture the Christians and send them to 'Urabi. Since he knew they were to be captured, this was an unwitting admission by their guide that he knew he was leading them into an ambush.

Meanwhile, some visitors had arrived from England that Warren could have done without. They were Charrington's brother and sister, Spencer and Katherine Charrington, accompanied by Gill's brother, Robert, and his friend Edward Houndle. They were impatient at the slowness of the inquiry and insisted on being involved. In a letter home to his mother, Lt. Burton described Spencer Charrington as a 'babbling fool' and believed that he and his sister were indulging in a 'pleasure trip'.[441]

A few days later, with Haynes still convalescing, Warren and Burton returned to the desert with guide Sofieh to try and retrieve the money. Spencer Charrington and Houndle insisted on going with them. Once again the party was escorted by Sheikh Musa and some Bedouin. Sofieh retrieved the locked box from its hiding place. It contained, apart from some personal effects and £219 in English money, just one small bag of gold sovereigns amounting to £1000. Sofieh protested that he had not opened the box and knew nothing of the other £2000.[442]

Back in Suez Sofieh was returned to prison, a weak, confused and broken

438 Haynes, *Man-hunting*, p 143.
439 *Ibid.*, p 144.
440 Sunderland, *Chivalrous Brothers*, p 201.
441 *Ibid.*, pp 170–71, referencing Burton's private papers.
442 *Ibid.*, pp 146–8.

man. He was soon transferred to a hospital where he died shortly afterwards. Meanwhile, a large number of Bedouin potential witnesses and alleged culprits had been brought in, including Sofieh's nephew, who, like his uncle, protested that he had not opened the box and knew nothing of the missing money.

Warren began a systematic cross-examination of the witnesses, with special attention being paid to those believed to be the culprits. He was determined to extract confessions, for that, he felt, was the only way to guarantee their conviction. He would start by trying to befriend them, talking mildly and offering cigarettes. Then he would grill them thoroughly, going over and over the same ground until he tripped them up in a contradiction. In the absence of any forensic evidence, it was the standard method of police interrogation at the time, there or anywhere else. While Warren believed in 'hammering' and 'brow-beating' in order to get at 'the truth'; he professed not to believe in deliberate torture, for its results could not be relied upon.[443]

On 22 November Sheik Salami ibn Shedide, the senior sheikh of the Bedouin clan believed to be responsible for the killing, was brought in for questioning. At first he was unco-operative, but, 'by dint of continual hammering' and threats of dire consequences if he did not co-operate, 'he was reduced to a proper condition of subordination', and Warren soon had a complete list of 60 witnesses and suspects. Warren gave the sheikh one month to bring them all in; but by late-December he had sent in only 21 prisoners.[444] Dissatisfied with the slow rate of progress, Warren decided to pursue some of the suspects himself, and on 20 December he, Haynes, Burton and four naval officers returned to Nakhl, escorted once more by the faithful Sheikh Musa and his Bedouin.

Once in Nakhl, Warren conducted some 'tedious' cross-examination of the Bedouin prisoners being held there. According to Haynes, this lasted for several days until 'gradually their opposition would break down'.[445] Burton's unpublished private papers, however, reveal that on one occasion Warren broke with his conviction that torture produced unreliable evidence. He put four unco-operative witnesses outside in stocks in the face of a severe sandstorm – torture by any definition – after which they told him what he wanted to hear.[446] By the beginning of the New Year Warren appears to have felt he had sufficient evidence and witnesses.

✳ ✳ ✳

---

[443] Haynes, *Man-hunting*, pp 166–7.
[444] *Ibid.*, pp 162–5.
[445] *Ibid.*, p 167.
[446] Sunderland, *Chivalrous Brothers*, p 203.

As was his habit, throughout all his trips into the desert Warren had been making copious notes on the geography and geology of the country and on the Bedouin whom he met and learned about. He was storing up material for scientific papers that he would later write for the *PEF Quarterly* or other journals. He particularly wanted to see for himself the country of the Exodus, through which Palmer had travelled in the 1870s, and on 4 January 1883 he and his party set off south from Nakhl, across the Sinai Peninsula to St Catherine's Monastery, accompanied, as ever, by Sheikh Musa and some of his men.

On their way through various Wadis, Warren noticed that the few remaining acacia trees had been hacked down to stumps. He drew this to the attention of Sheikh Musa who explained that an Egyptian tax on charcoal had led to the people resorting to fresh timber for their firewood. The sheikh also remarked that he had noticed a fall in the amount of rainfall in recent years, at which Warren, the environmentalist, 'explained to him the relation of cause and effect, and urged him to stop the wholesale destruction of the trees … which, if persisted in, would make the country uninhabitable'. Haynes observed that 'The sheikh took his lecture very intelligently, and promised to bring the matter before his next Council of State'.[447]

No longer in pursuit of suspects and witnesses, Warren was able to enjoy introducing the naval officers to the country and the people. Meanwhile, he and his two lieutenants had grown used to the rolling gait of their camels. They found that the animal continued walking regardless of passenger, and one could sit forwards, sideways or even backwards, depending on which way the sand was blowing. As Haynes observed, 'on camel-back one had no trouble about reins; but can smoke, eat, or read, as comfortably as on the top of a coach'.[448] They slept at Bedouin encampments and, with winter snow on the high ground, they reached the monastery on 9 January 1883.

They pitched camp near the monastery and were gratefully received by the monks, who credited Warren with having ensured they received their stores from El-Tur in September. They brought out silver trays and Warren and his officers were presented with small glasses of *araki*, a local liquor distilled from dates, followed by a spoonful of jelly and a tumbler of ice-cold water – a treat indeed after five days in the desert. The effect, wrote Haynes, 'was excellent, and paved the way to thorough enjoyment of the convivial cigarette and coffee'. They spent a day at the monastery, during which Warren enjoyed examining its ancient

[447] Haynes, *Man-hunting*, p 189.
[448] *Ibid.*, p 180.

illuminated manuscripts and climbing Mount Sinai (Jebel Musa), believed to be the mountain on which Moses received the Ten Commandments.[449]

Warren then sent Burton into Suez to collect the Charringtons who wanted to visit the site of their brother's death while he and Haynes, accompanied by Sheikh Musa, headed straight for the fatal ravine. They arrived five days ahead of the Charringtons and were able to conduct a compass survey of the ravine and make a thorough search of the area. They found a number of personal effects, including part of Captain Gill's journal.

When the Charringtons arrived Warren showed them the site of the murder. He then read the funeral service and ordered the firing of three volleys into the opposite cliff, which startled the Bedouin who could not understand all this fuss over people who were dead and gone.

The Charringtons had brought an oak crucifix and insisted on the erection of a large cairn overlooking the ravine. Warren had to organise the quarrying of square-shaped stones out of the cliff, for the Charringtons were only satisfied when the cairn was four metres high. Charrington was the only man in the party who refused to assist in the building of the cairn. His sister inserted among the rocks a bottle containing a message, which Warren removed and discovered that it 'gave an account of her and her brother's journey to Egypt and suggested they had played a part in the capture of the murderers'.

By this stage Warren had had more than enough of the Charringtons. They had been trouble from the start. Spencer Charrington had insisted on standing in on some of the witness interviews, to which Warren had reluctantly agreed, on the grounds that otherwise Charrington would go back to England and tell all kinds of tales against us'. Charrington did this anyway, armed with criticism of Warren's 'bullying' methods of cross-examination. Now, on top of the cairn they inserted their large oak cross. The names of the three Englishmen were engraved on the front, with Harold Charrington spelt out in capital letters. On the reverse they had engraved the words 'Killed by the Bedouin', which Warren erased on the grounds that it was both incorrect and inflammatory.[450] He was glad to see the back of the Charringtons.

* * *

On his return to Suez there remained the matter of the trial of the twelve men implicated in the attack on Palmer. The British Government had decided the

[449] *Ibid.*, pp 194–5, and 197.
[450] *Ibid.*, pp 222–4; Sunderland, *Chivalrous Brothers*, pp 171–6.

case should be treated as a straightforward crime rather than the act of war that it clearly was. There can be no doubt that the Palmer party were British spies, acting in Egypt while that country was being invaded by Britain. If their capture and peremptory execution were accepted as an act of war, however, the arrested men were prisoners of war, and the war being over, they would have to be released. The British public and the press, however, were in full jingoistic mode and demanded retribution, and in Charles Warren, they had a willing accomplice. While it appears that 'Urabi's intention was that the Christians, clearly spies, should be arrested and brought to Cairo, Warren argued that the theft of money indicated that the killing was a criminal act, not an act of war. According to Burton's diaries, Warren wanted the men found guilty of incitement and murder and executed by Egyptian decree. He feared that if they were brought to trial they might retract their confessions, and the witnesses might not repeat their accusations.

After everything that he had been through over the previous five months, Warren was in a ruthless mood, determined not to be thwarted at the end. In a manner very different from his attitude in South Africa, he expressed a belief that 'as 'savages' they had no right to a defence council [*sic*]'.[451] He was conveniently adopting here what he interpreted as the Bedouin law of the desert, of which T. E. Lawrence was later to write: 'The desert did not afford the refined slow penalties of court and gaol'.[452] The British Government, however, insisted on going through the formalities of a trial, although it was neither particularly refined nor slow.

The court hearing began on 7 February 1883. In his *Life of Sir Charles Warren*, his grandson paid very cursory attention to the process of the trial,[453] and thus glossed over the fact that Warren was very closely involved in the proceedings. Having been the preliminary investigator, Warren was not allowed to be Prosecutor, so Burton stood in for him. Warren, however, was allowed to be the official British observer and from this position he virtually controlled the trial, advising Burton and giving direction to the Court President, whom Burton designated 'a fool' with little knowledge of court procedure or Egyptian law. Of the two Commissioners, one hardly spoke at all, and the other was absent from the third day. The prisoners were confronted with the statements of witnesses and then heard their own confessions read

---

[451] Sunderland, *op cit*, pp 197–8.
[452] T. E. Lawrence, *Seven Pillars of Wisdom* (originally published 1925, Penguin edition, Harmondsworth, 1962), p 29.
[453] Williams, *The Life*, p 143.

out three times. Each time they were asked to admit the truth of what they had heard. Most did, but even those few who did not had their confessions accepted anyway. They had no defence counsel. The proceedings were over in five days.[454]

The prisoners and their documents were sent to Alexandria where they came before a court martial, for according to Egyptian law, based on the Code Napoléon, the lower court did not have the power to pass a capital sentence. Warren played no direct part in the court martial, but there was never any doubt as to the outcome. Five were sentenced to death and executed two weeks later, in the presence of a sheikh and 32 selected Bedouin, two from each clan in Lower Egypt. Others were sentenced to lengthy terms of imprisonment while the ex-Governor of Nakhl was stripped of all office and sentenced to one year's hard labour.

The family of Palmer's guide were held responsible for the missing £2000, although ultimately they never paid back more than £100. Sunderland has argued that the missing money may well have been stolen by the near-bankrupted Palmer, who could have concealed two of the bags of gold coin before he left for the desert on his fateful journey.[455]

Straight after the court martial and before the executions were carried out, Warren, his two lieutenants and interpreter Mosalli left for El-Arish, a fortified town on the Mediterranean coast of Sinai that had been an 'Urabist stronghold during the war. Some personal items of Palmer's, including his pocket watch, had been recovered from there and Warren felt it was worth further investigation. The 'Urabist Governor of El-Arish had been replaced by a man named Mustapha Mamnoon who had taken advantage of his isolation to institute a reign of terror over his 'subjects'. When Warren arrived on 25 February Governor Mamnoon happened to be away, but had, without authority, installed his son as Acting-Governor. The son did nothing to curb the Egyptian soldiers' inclination to terrorise the townspeople with regular floggings and torture.

Warren found that by sheer force of command, he was able to dominate the son and, by informing Cairo, bring this abuse of power to an end. After a week at El-Arish, Warren heard that Governor Mamnoon was returning determined to restore his rule. Knowing that Mamnoon would have the backing of the soldiers, Warren staged what was in effect a *coup d'état*. At dawn

[454] Sunderland, *Chivalrous Brothers*, pp 198–200; Haynes, *Man-hunting*, pp 232–3.
[455] Sunderland, *Chivalrous Brothers*, pp 207–14.

on 5 March, the morning that Mamnoon was due to return, Warren entered the fort and demanded to inspect the soldiers on parade. He then confined them to quarters while he called the citizens into the courtyard, winning them to his side by promising that he was ending Mamnoon's reign of terror. Safe now behind the protection of the citizenry, Warren got telegraphic authority from Cairo, arrested the Governor as soon as he arrived, and sent him under armed escort to Cairo.[456]

Later that day, having found no further evidence concerning the Palmer Expedition, Warren and his lieutenants left El-Arish to return to Egypt, travelling overland with a small Bedouin escort.

They reached Cairo on 9 March where they learned there had been a debate in the House of Commons a few days previously in which Warren's integrity had been called into question and his methods of investigation severely criticised. The criticism stemmed from Spencer Charrington, who on his return to England had made complaints about Warren to the 'Urabist sympathiser Wilfrid Blunt.[457] Some days later the First Lord of the Admiralty, Lord Northbrook, spoke up for Warren in the House of Lords, saying that he was 'a very gallant officer who has done most excellent service for the protection of the Canal', clearly the first priority for the British Government:

> Colonel Warren, as soon as it was rumoured that Professor Palmer and his party were missing, volunteered at once to go out and assist in the search. He has pursued that search with gallantry, determination, good judgement and a perfectly judicial mind. He has taken the greatest care to ascertain who were the really guilty parties, and I must protest against the inference … that in prosecuting the murderers – for I can find no other term for them – there has been anything whatever done of which an Englishman can be for a moment ashamed. The inquiry has been conducted with the greatest care, and I am certain … that the men who were hanged deserved their fate.[458]

So it was official: Warren had done heroic work and deserved nothing but praise. As we have seen, Warren's methodical cross-examination of witnesses and suspects was harsh, but, apart from two occasions, was nothing different

[456] Haynes, *Man-hunting*, pp 247–58.
[457] For Charrington's vague and inaccurate accusations, see Wilfrid Scawen Blunt, *Atrocities of Justice under British Rule in Egypt* (Fisher Unwin, London, 2nd edition, London, 1907), pp 18–20.
[458] *Hansard*, House of Lords, statement, 11 March 1883, quoted in Haynes, *Man-hunting*, p 269.

from regular police methods of that time or for the best part of the following century. His determination that the arrested men should be treated as regular criminals rather than prisoners of war, however, betrayed his imperialistic bias.

On 16 March, a few days after Northbrook's defence of his behaviour, Warren and his colleagues sailed from Alexandria, bound for home with the precious box containing the remains of the five murdered men.[459] Warren's faithful interpreter, Selim Mosalli, accompanied them and Warren was able to find him a role at Chatham where he remained until ill health forced him to leave the service. At that point the British authorities, somewhat meanly, but in a manner familiar to a 21st-century audience, insisted that he be returned to Egypt.[460]

On 6 April 1883 the remains of the five men, three British Christians, one Syrian Christian and one Jew, were laid to rest in the City of London's great burial sanctuary for war heroes, St Paul's Cathedral. The funeral service was conducted in the crypt before a distinguished gathering that included, besides representatives from the families of Palmer, Gill and Charrington, Lord Northbrook and numerous admirals, generals and military officers, with, some way down the official list, Lt.-Colonel Charles Warren and Lieutenant Alfred Haynes. Representing the Palestine Exploration Fund were Walter Morrison MP and John 'Rob Roy' MacGregor. The box containing the mortal remains had been enclosed in lead and placed in an oak coffin. To the choral chant of 'Thy Will be done',[461] the coffin was lowered beneath the floor of the crypt, midway between the graves of Admiral Lord Nelson and the Duke of Wellington.[462] Nowhere in the proceedings or on the simple engraving on this very British tomb for heroes were the Jewish cook or the Syrian attendant mentioned, although they were included in the more detailed inscription on a plaque on the wall of the crypt.

In The Queen's Birthday Honours, on 24 May 1883, Warren, who already had a CMG for his work on the Griqualand West Border Commission, was raised to become a Knight Commander of St Michael and St George (KCMG). It was his first knighthood. In addition, he received the Egypt Campaign Medal and, from the Turkish authorities, the Order of the Medjidié. Lieutenants Haynes and Burton also received the Egypt Campaign

---

[459] Haynes, *Man-hunting*, p 279. Quartermaster-Sergeant Kennedy had been repatriated earlier.
[460] Sunderland, *Chivalrous Brothers*, p 245.
[461] *Hymns Ancient and Modern*, Hymn 264.
[462] *The Times*, 7 April 1882.

Medal and the Order of the Medjidié. In his official report to the Admiralty, Warren lobbied for Haynes and Burton to receive some additional recognition for bravery, arguing that their missions into Sinai were 'simply a question of absolute success or death'.[463] All he got in reply was a note to the effect that the Admiralty appreciated the work of his two lieutenants.

Warren gained more success from writing a glowing testimonial for Sheikh Musa. This won the faithful guide a gratuity of £20 and the official right to conduct travellers through Sinai, a role that would have provided him and his family with a substantial income. Before they left Egypt, Warren had donated £5 to the destitute family of the Jewish cook, to which Haynes and Burton had each added £2. Spencer Charrington, despite being the heir to one of the largest breweries in England, reluctantly offered a couple of pounds provided the gift was anonymous, an offer which Warren rejected with contempt. In due course the British Government awarded the family of Bakhor Hassoun, the cook, a generous annuity of £300 and the mother of Khalil Atek, Gill's Syrian attendant, an annuity of £200.[464]

In May 1883, after a month's well-earned leave at home, during which he wrote up various reports, Sir Charles Warren returned to his role as Chief Instructor of Surveying at Chatham. He was to remain there for the next eighteen months, before being called upon to lead another, very different expedition.

---

[463] *HCPP*, Cd.3637, Warren to Admiralty, 10 April 1883.
[464] Sunderland, *Chivalrous Brothers*, pp 244–5.

CHAPTER 13

Preparation for War

As the newly-knighted Sir Charles and Lady Warren settled back into family life at Chatham, his attention would have been drawn to a lengthy article in the April 1883 edition of the monthly literary review, *The Nineteenth Century*, entitled 'England and South Africa'. It was written by his missionary friend Revd John Mackenzie.[465] The article would have brought back memories of long discussions at Kuruman about the future of South Africa, and in particular about the best way to develop and incorporate Bechuanaland and its peoples into the protective fold of the British empire. Indeed, Mackenzie's article prompted Warren to gather together some of his official correspondence from his time in Southern Bechuanaland in 1878–9. Partly through Mackenzie's campaign on behalf of Bechuanaland, Warren was soon to be drawn back to Southern Africa.

Much had changed in the four years since Warren had left South Africa. Despite his promises to the Batswana chiefs of British 'protection', when Warren left Kimberley in 1879 Southern Bechuanaland had been left in limbo, an undefined territory lying between the British colony of Griqualand West and what had recently become the British colony of the Transvaal. In 1880 Griqualand West was absorbed into the Cape Colony and Bechuanaland was quietly allowed to slip from view.

Two months later the Boers of the Transvaal, who had never been reconciled to British overrule, raised the flag of rebellion and proclaimed the restoration of the Transvaal Republic.

The British were caught unawares and, in what was to become known as the First Anglo-Boer War, Boer mounted commandos inflicted a number of humiliating defeats upon the British, culminating, on 27 February 1881, in the Battle of Majuba Hill. In that iconic conflict, the British lost 230 men killed or wounded, to the Boer loss of just six men. Among the British killed that day was General Sir George Colley, Governor and Commander-in-Chief

---

[465] John Mackenzie, 'England and South Africa', *The Nineteenth Century*, XIII (April 1883), pp 700–28.

of British forces in Natal and High Commissioner for South Eastern Africa. It could not have been a more humiliating defeat, compounded by Liberal Prime Minister William Gladstone's decision to negotiate the withdrawal of British forces from the Transvaal.

At the Pretoria Convention of August 1881 the British handed control of the internal affairs of the Transvaal back to the Boers. The western border was redrawn, moving it further into Southern Bechuanaland (see Map 14.1, p 246). This increased the pressure on the valuable strip of arable land and its freshwater springs that lay just west of the new boundary. Intra-African conflict over this land broke out towards the end of 1881, and in the new year of 1882 white mercenaries from the Transvaal joined the fray. They laid siege to the two principal Batswana towns of the region, Mafikeng[466] on the headwaters of the Molopo River in the north, and Taung, north-east of the Griqualand West border in the south.

Both Batswana chiefs, Montshiwa of Mafikeng and Mankurwane of Taung, appealed to the British to make good the 'protection' promised by Warren in 1879, but the British had lost interest in the affairs of Southern Bechuanaland, and had even imposed restrictions on African access to guns and ammunition.

Mankurwane managed to hire some white mercenaries from Kimberley, but only on the promise of awarding them extensive farms and other land rights. Montshiwa hired few mercenaries, but he did still have the services of British advisor, Warren's cousin Christopher Bethell, who remained with and fought for the Batswana when the other British police were withdrawn.[467] As a white man, Bethell could purchase guns and ammunition in Kimberley, whereas the Batswana, as Africans, were barred from doing so.

From Kuruman, west of the zones of conflict, Mackenzie had sent letters of appeal to the British authorities in Kimberley and Cape Town, pleading that they enforce the new Transvaal boundary, protect the Batswana from this mercenary assault on their land and save the missionary and trading 'road to the north' from Transvaal annexation. But to no avail. While he was on long furlough in England from July 1882, Mackenzie campaigned avidly for the Batswana; but it was difficult to stimulate any interest in the fate of what were perceived to be 'a few natives' on the fringes of the Kalahari Desert. Besides, the British lion had all too recently been forced out of the Transvaal with its tail between its legs,

---

[466] Mafikeng, pronounced and spelt 'Mafeking' by the British.
[467] For the Bechuanaland Wars in this period see, Shillington, *The Colonisation of the Southern Tswana*, pp 123–48.

227

and there was no further appetite for challenging the Boers. Egypt and Ireland between them were demanding the British Government's full attention.

As a result of this neglect Mankurwane was forced to sign a peace accord in September 1882, at which point the white mercenaries on both sides of the conflict joined together in dividing up the spoils. They laid claim to a huge tract of the most fertile and best-watered land in the region and declared that this was now the independent 'Republic of Stellaland'.

Further north in Mafikeng, Montshiwa's Batswana held out against mercenary attack from across the Transvaal border, at least until Christopher Bethell's wagonload of ammunition from Kimberley was captured and looted while returning through 'Stellaland'. With that loss Montshiwa was forced to sign a peace accord with his enemies in October 1882. So far as Montshiwa was concerned, it was only a ceasefire. The mercenaries, on the other hand, regarded it as a conquest and declared a 'Republic of Goshen' across much of Montshiwa's best arable land. Ongoing Batswana resistance, however, meant that it was only ever 'a republic' on paper.[468] Fighting and cattle raiding continued in both war zones through much of the following year.

*　*　*

By the spring of 1883 the British occupation of Egypt was firmly established, Palmer's murder had been avenged, and the professor and his colleagues had been buried in their joint tomb for heroes. The decision by the editor of the prestigious *Nineteenth Century* magazine to publish Mackenzie's lengthy essay indicated that the time was right for the nation to shift its attention to other African matters.

Mackenzie had cleverly pitched his article to appeal to a sceptical British audience. He argued that the Africans being driven off their land by Transvaal 'freebooters' were no mere 'primitive savages'. They were literate Christian farmers, owners of ploughs and wagons. They wore Western-style clothing, and they grew irrigated crops for sale in the diamond-mining city of Kimberley. By the standards of liberal-minded imperialists, they could be termed 'civilised', thus deserving some of the rights of citizenship within the empire. Indeed, Mackenzie argued that they were worthy citizens of a future British Protectorate if the British Government would only accept its

---

[468] The 114 farms that made up 'Goshen' had in fact been marked out on a map by a Transvaal official as long ago as 1870, so the annexation of Barolong land had been a longterm goal of Transvaal officials, although at that stage there had been no attempt to occupy any of the 'farms': Shillington, *Colonisation*, p 140.

responsibility and enforce the boundary of the Transvaal as agreed at the Pretoria Convention of 1881.

Back in South Africa weight was added to Mackenzie's urging by Cecil Rhodes, the young Kimberley mining capitalist and up-and-coming politician. Rhodes, however, had no interest in African rights of citizenship. He was driven by his mining interests. His main concerns were firewood for steam machinery, much of it coming from Southern Bechuanaland, and African mine labour, which came to Kimberley from all over Southern Africa, but much of it passing through Southern Bechuanaland. And when Stellaland imposed a tax on the trade and labour passing through its 'republic' in June 1883, Rhodes urged the Cape Governor and High Commissioner, Sir Hercules Robinson, to press for Cape annexation of Southern Bechuanaland. The Afrikaners in the Cape Parliament, however, were not prepared to interfere with any new Boer 'independent republic', and Rhodes had to bide his time.[469]

The new President of the Transvaal, Paul Kruger, was encouraged by the British lack of action in Bechuanaland and in February 1884 he led a delegation to London to press for full independence from Britain. The British Government, hoping for a final solution to the 'Transvaal problem', agreed to its independence and to the extension of its western boundary further into Batswana territory, just short of the 'road to the north', but encompassing the eastern third of 'Stellaland'.

Southern Bechuanaland, including the rest of Stellaland, was to be brought under a minimal form of British protection. Revd John Mackenzie was seen as the ideal person to implement it, and it would get the increasingly strident evangelical and missionary lobby off the Government's back. Mackenzie accepted the appointment of Deputy Commissioner for Bechuanaland and sailed for South Africa with his wife and children in April 1884.

* * *

Meanwhile, President Kruger, having got what he wanted from London, made his way home via the continent of Europe, making a courtesy call at the German Chancellery in Berlin. Not much attention was paid to this in Britain at the time, but in hindsight it would be viewed as significant. In the same month that Mackenzie sailed for South Africa, the German Government declared a Protectorate over Angra Pequena, a small port on the southern coast of modern Namibia.

---

[469] *Ibid.*, pp 155–160.

The British did not at the time see this tiny German enclave as a threat to their interests; but before the year was out, it was revealed to be the first step in Germany's annexation of the whole of 'South West Africa' (Namibia). And with that stood the possibility of its seeking a territorial link across the Kalahari with the by now independent South African Republic (the Transvaal).

* * *

Colonel Warren, having himself been so closely involved in preparing Southern Bechuanaland for British overrule in 1879, would have followed closely the progress of Mackenzie's campaign. As a serving military officer, he would not have been allowed to participate in the missionary's hustings, but he was in complete agreement with Mackenzie's proposals; and he would have felt that Mackenzie's appointment vindicated his own efforts to bring peace and justice to the region.

Mackenzie reached Southern Bechuanaland in May 1884. Allowed only to recruit a small police force to back him up, he was unable to enforce the new Protectorate. His raising of the British flag in Taung was welcomed by Mankurwane; but the same ceremony received a mixed reception in 'Stellaland' and was treated with contempt by the Boers of 'Goshen', who continued their attacks on Montshiwa's Batswana the moment Mackenzie's back was turned. In one of these attacks, Christopher Bethell was shot dead as he lay wounded on the ground.[470]

Meanwhile, in Cape Town, the High Commissioner and Cape Governor, Sir Hercules Robinson was firmly under the influence of Cecil Rhodes. The one thing Rhodes wanted to avoid was the introduction of an imperial military force to bring peace to the region. He believed that any subsequent settlement would be influenced by the missionary lobby and would favour indigenous African land rights over those of colonial economic interests.

Rhodes saw the only way to achieve Cape annexation was to win the trust of the Afrikaner members of the Cape Parliament, and the very least they would require would be the unquestioning acceptance of the land claims of the Stellalanders and Goshenites. Rhodes was happy to arrange this. So far as he was concerned, the sooner Africans were landless labourers, the better. He had opposed Mackenzie's appointment from the start and from the moment Mackenzie headed north as Deputy Commissioner for Bechuanaland, he had done his best to undermine him. And when in August 1884 Mackenzie tried

---

[470] Shillington, *Colonisation*, pp 149–65.

to set up an inquiry into Stellaland land claims, it was at Rhodes's behest that Mackenzie was recalled to Cape Town and replaced as Deputy Commissioner by Cecil Rhodes himself.[471]

Urgency was suddenly added to the need for a settlement. That August, three months before the great powers of Europe assembled in Berlin for the conference that was to lay the ground rules for the 'Scramble for Africa', Germany proclaimed a protectorate over the coastal region of South West Africa north of the Orange River, later extended to the as yet undeclared boundary of Portuguese Angola. This confirmed Britain's need to establish firm control over southern Bechuanaland, from where she could extend her protectorate further north as the need arose.

Rhodes hurried north. He disbanded Mackenzie's land inquiry; and on 8 September 1884 he signed an agreement with one of the Stellaland leaders, G. J. van Niekerk. This became known as the 'Rhodes Agreement'. It stated that all Stellaland land claims would be recognised, without any further investigation. In return van Niekerk undertook to persuade the Stellalanders to accept Cape annexation.

Van Niekerk was the leader of the 'Harts River Afrikaners' of eastern Stellaland, his own farm, Niekerks Rust, lying within this region. In making his arrangement with van Niekerk, Rhodes completely disregarded the new London Convention boundary of February 1884, which placed eastern Stellaland and the Harts River Afrikaners within the Transvaal. He should not have been negotiating with these citizens of a foreign state at all. Rhodes was either ignorant of the new boundary, or he did not care; more likely the latter. He just needed somebody, urgently, to agree to Cape annexation.

Having easily settled, to his own satisfaction, the Stellaland issue, Rhodes moved north to meet the Goshenites. Here he had no such easy ride. He met their leaders at Rooigrond on the Transvaal border and found them distrustful of himself and the British. They preferred to rely on the Transvaal for their 'protection'. Rhodes was sent packing, and on 16 September President Kruger proclaimed the Transvaal's annexation of both Stellaland and Goshen.

Rhodes saw his precious fuel and labour supply and the road to the potential riches of the north blocked by an anti-British Boer Republic. But Rhodes was an eminently pragmatic man, and judging it by far the lesser

[471] *Idem; and Åke Holmberg, African Tribes and European Agencies: Colonialism and Humanitarianism in British South and East Africa 1870–1895* (Akademiförlaget, Stockholm, 1966), pp 89–91, 101–2.

of two evils, he urged Robinson to appeal for the immediate dispatch of an imperial military expedition.[472]

British Government ministers had hitherto been complacent about Bechuanaland, assuming that an ex-missionary with no previous administrative experience, and with no military backup, could bring peace to a region wracked by three years of war. Furthermore, they had been caught unawares by both the German annexation of South West Africa and Kruger's annexation of Stellaland and Goshen. It did not take Rhodes's report for them to see the potential for a link-up across Bechuanaland between the German Protectorate and the Transvaal. Such a hostile alliance would block British access to the trade, labour and potential riches of the Central African interior.

The British Government, seeing itself as the supreme power in South Africa, ordered Kruger to withdraw his proclamation. Kruger obliged, although he did nothing to prevent his burghers from continuing to cross the Transvaal's western border at will. It was clear that a military expedition would be needed to enforce an acceptance that Bechuanaland was British territory. The obvious person to lead it was Sir Charles Warren. Ironically, in the light of what was to happen, his appointment had been recommended by Robinson, at the suggestion of Cecil Rhodes.

* * *

Warren had been keeping himself up to date with the affairs of Africa, not only in Bechuanaland, but also in Sudan. Through the summer of 1884 the British public had been growing increasingly concerned about the safety of General Sir Charles Gordon, RE. He had been sent to Khartoum to evacuate Egyptian forces from the Sudan, much of which had been overrun by a Mahdist revolutionary army. Senior military figures discussed the options of sending a small relief force across the desert from Suakin on the Red Sea coast to reach the Nile at the small, riverside trading town of Berber, downstream from Khartoum, or sending a much larger force all the way up the Nile from Cairo.

Warren knew Gordon personally as a fellow Royal Engineer a few years senior to himself and he proposed a rescue mission that involved risking no British military lives at all, apart from his own. Warren believed that his

[472] *UKNA*, CO 417/2, Report by Rhodes and Graham Bower (Cape Imperial Secretary), 20 September 1884, in Robinson's Confidential Despatch of 24 September; and quoted at some length in J. A. I. Agar-Hamilton, *The Road to the North* (Longman Green, London, 1937), pp 356–8.

Sir Charles Warren in civilian dress.
MCGREGOR MUSEUM, KIMBERLEY, SOUTH AFRICA

reputation and influence among the Bedouin of the Lower Nile extended even into Sudan, and with his recent Sinai experience in mind, he offered to go himself in a private capacity and negotiate the raising of the siege. Bearing in mind that the Mahdi's forces were dominant in Western Sudan and along the Nile, he proposed approaching Khartoum from the east, through Abyssinia (Ethiopia) via the Red Sea port of Massawa. He believed that by working peacefully through the eastern Sudanese, he would be able to negotiate the raising of the siege, at least long enough for Gordon and the Egyptian forces and civilian personnel to be evacuated.

Warren was either incredibly brave or totally foolhardy: probably a mixture of the two. His scheme displayed a very high level of self-belief. That it was not completely implausible was shown by the support it had from his former commanding officer at Chatham, the Inspector-General of Fortifications,

233

General Sir Andrew Clarke.[473] But by mid-1884 the British public were in no mood for a quiet, low-key evacuation of the Sudan. British prestige was at stake and in July Gladstone finally authorised General Lord Wolseley, the ennobled hero of Tel El Kebir, to lead a large military force to the relief of Khartoum. In the event, Wolseley chose the long, slow route up the Nile and arrived too late to save Gordon.

* * *

With the War Office focussing its efforts on Wolseley's campaign, it was decided that the Bechuanaland Expedition should be a largely volunteer force and as such could come under the authority of the Colonial Secretary, Lord Granville. Warren was approached at the end of October 1884 and asked to draw up a proposal for the expedition.

Bearing in mind the mounted commando-style of Boer warfare, used with such dramatic effect in 1881, Warren indicated that he would need about 5000 officers and men, mostly mounted infantry, but including some field artillery and a small corps of engineers. If he could select his own officers from the regular Army, the bulk of the volunteer regiments could be raised locally in South Africa. The volunteers would all need to be on a regular payroll and so not dependent on loot, as was the case with the informal regiments normally raised in South Africa for 'wars against the natives'. Granville indicated a budget and gave him a free hand to organise it.

Warren was given the temporary rank of Brevet Major-General for the Expedition. He was allocated a small room in the Colonial Office where he gathered a team of trusted friends and family to undertake the initial planning and organisation. He started by hiring the ever-reliable Lieutenant Alfred Haynes, who was to act as his Private Secretary, and a non-military man, Ralph Williams, a relative by marriage to Fanny Warren. Williams' stepmother was a Bethell, daughter of the late Rt. Revd Christopher Bethell, Bishop of Bangor, and a relative to Lieutenant Christopher Bethell, who had just been murdered in Bechuanaland. Williams had recently returned from a tour of Southern Africa with his wife and young son. They had travelled through Bechuanaland, met Bethell at Mafikeng and had gone on through present-day Botswana and Zimbabwe, as far as the Zambezi and the Victoria Falls. Williams liked to boast that his wife was the first Englishwoman and possibly

[473] Williams, *The Life*, p 148.

the first white woman to visit the Falls.[474] In 1884 he was conveniently looking for employment at the Colonial Office. A man of his experience and initiative would prove useful to Warren who gave him the honorary rank of Captain and attached him to his Intelligence Department.

These two were soon joined by Colonel Frederick Forestier-Walker whom Warren had met during the Cape-Xhosa War of 1878 and whom he now made his Chief of Staff. Walker's younger brother, Montagu Forestier-Walker, became Warren's Assistant Military Secretary. The final member of the planning team was young Captain Sir Bartle Frere, son of the late Governor of the Cape who had recently died. Frere became Warren's *aide-de-camp*.

The Bechuanaland Field Force contained a number of regular Army units, including a squadron of the 6th (Inniskilling) Dragoons (a cavalry regiment that also fought on foot), a battery of field artillery, both on loan from Natal, and a battalion of Royal Scots, just returned from the West Indies. And from England Colonel A. G. Durnford RE, a former fellow subaltern from Warren's Gibraltar days, commanded a company of Royal Engineers and a Telegraph Company. Various other commissariat, transport and ordnance corps were supplied, together with a medical unit and several chaplains.

Beyond this, Warren selected the senior officers who would raise and lead their own volunteer regiments that would form the bulk of the Field Force. Most had recent South African experience, having served alongside Warren in the Eastern Cape, or under him on the Griqualand Field Force. If they were not already of the appropriate rank, they were temporarily raised to the rank of Lt.-Colonel. Among those invited to join him was Warren's old childhood friend, Colonel Fred Terry. Colonel Paul (later Field-Marshal Lord) Methuen raised an English volunteer regiment of 600 men, the 1st Mounted Rifles, known as 'Methuen's Horse'; but the rest of the volunteer regiments, mostly mounted infantry, were to be raised in South Africa. Captain Claude Conder RE, who had recently completed the Survey of Western Palestine for the Palestine Exploration Fund, was enlisted as the cartographer for the expedition.

Warren invited his younger brother Billie to join him, which he did in the capacity of a personal secretary. Billie had reached the rank of Captain in the 60th Rifles; but he seems to have experienced none of the exhilaration and excitement of military life that had been the good fortune of his elder brother.

[474] Sir Ralph Williams KCMG, *How I Became a Governor* (John Murray, London, 1913), pp 101–2.

He had retired from the Army in 1876 and it is not clear what he had been doing since. Sir Charles had a protective instinct and sense of responsibility towards his younger brother, whose name does not appear on the official list of officers. This was clearly a personal appointment, at the Expedition Commander's personal expense.

Warren was determined his force would not suffer the fate of those at Laing's Nek in January 1881, where a long line of scarlet-coated foot soldiers with mounted officers clearly identifiable were easily picked off by unseen Boer marksmen wearing clothes the colour of the veldt. Warren insisted that the whole of the Bechuanaland Field Force, officers and men, wear a uniform of mud-coloured corduroy tunic and pantaloons. Some of the English regiments wore khaki helmets, but the South Africans wore felt slouch hats. The uniforms were ordered in England and followed them out on a separate ship. It was the first occasion that an entire British force wore khaki in the field. Another of Warren's innovations was the issuing of a metal identity tag to be worn by all officers and men, around the neck under the uniform.

Warren had been observing the experiments in the use of gas balloons at Chatham and he was keen to take a detachment with him as he was sure it would be valuable for reconnaissance over the flat open country of Bechuanaland. Major Elsdale, Head of Chatham's Balloon Department, had hoped to accompany General Wolseley's Sudan Relief Column, but the equipment was not ready in time. It was, however, ready to join Warren's expedition in November: another first for Warren.[475]

Warren's official instructions, issued on 10 November, followed his own memorandum of 29 October in which he had listed the objects of the mission being first to remove the 'filibusters', that is, the recalcitrant Goshenites, from Bechuanaland; to 'reinstate the natives on their land, to take such measures as may be necessary to prevent further depredation, and, finally, to hold the country until its further destination is known'.[476]

In addition to these strictly military duties, Warren was granted a civil role regarding the immediate political administration of Bechuanaland. Sir Robert Herbert, Permanent Under-Secretary for the Colonies, wrote a letter to accompany Warren's official instructions, in which he clarifies this political role, indicating, 'You have also correctly defined the outlines of the policy to

[475] Colonel C. M. Watson, 'Military Ballooning in the British Army', *Royal Engineers Institute Occasional Papers*, Volume XXVIII, 1902, p 47; and P. W. L. Broke-Smith, *History of Early British Aeronautics* (Academic Reprint, 1968), pp 6–7.
[476] *HCPP*, LV, Cd.4227, pp 4–6.

Warren in the sort of uniform he prescribed for the Bechuanaland Expedition.
WARREN FAMILY COLLECTION

be adhered to, and your own duties as Special Commissioner'.[477] Warren took this to mean the Colonial Office's acceptance that the 'Mackenzian' system of 'territorial government' should be followed in Bechuanaland. In other words, the primacy of native interests over colonial ambition was to form the basis of the government of Bechuanaland. This was an important point and once he arrived in South Africa, it was to give rise to differences between himself and Rhodes, as well as High Commissioner Robinson.

✳ ✳ ✳

The khaki uniforms not yet being ready, Warren joined his officers at Paddington station for the train to Southampton wearing a topcoat, tall hat, low shoes and white cotton socks, looking, according to Ralph Williams, 'as little like a general leaving for active service as it is possible to conceive'.[478] They departed Southampton on the *Grantully Castle* on Friday 14 November 1884.

This was to be no cruise and, as Williams reported, Warren's thoroughness and untiring personal energy 'allowed no time for idleness aboard ship'. He formed his officers into 'committees of attack, defence, supply, laagering and all sorts of matters which were likely to crop up on an expedition of this sort'.[479] Warren impressed upon them the potential dangers of the expedition. They may be entering a region that he and many of his officers knew well, but under circumstances where certain Transvaal Boers had shown hostile intent. Laing's Nek and Majuba Hill were at the forefront of their minds.

On the second day out, crossing the Bay of Biscay, there was 'a lump of a sea', but the Sunday service was still held on the open deck. Ralph Williams related how the cleric on duty, enamoured of his own eloquence, preached an inordinately long sermon. As he got ever more eloquent, his congregation became ever more seasick. Finally, General Warren,

> … with a boldness which in church I have often since envied, walked up to him and said, 'I beg your pardon, Sir, but if you cannot bring your sermon to a close I must march my men off'.

The sermon came to an abrupt end, and Williams remarked, 'What a pity that home truths such as this do not oftener find their way to our pulpits'.[480]

---

[477] From a letter to Warren, 10 November 1884, quoted in Williams, *The Life*, p 155.
[478] Williams, *How I Became a Governor*, p 114.
[479] *Idem.*
[480] *Ibid.*, p 115.

Their arrival at the Cape Town docks on 4 December was greeted with the sort of triumphal celebration normally accorded to the successful conclusion of a campaign. It was a demonstration of imperial enthusiasm by British colonists eager to remind the 'Afrikaner Bond', the political grouping who dominated the Cape Parliament, that it was the British empire that ultimately called the shots. Mackenzie, who had been sidelined since August, was keen to demonstrate that his stand was finally being vindicated. He managed to make his way on-board ship to briefly greet Sir Charles before the general and his senior staff disembarked and made their way through the flag-waving crowds to Government House where the dining room had been set aside for them to use as an office.

At their first meeting, High Commissioner Robinson advised Warren to distance himself from Mackenzie, reassuring him that Rhodes had everything under control in Stellaland. As though on cue, Rhodes and his close ally, the Imperial Secretary Captain Graham Bower, entered the room with a draft for a telegram which Robinson urged Warren to sign. It was addressed to van Niekerk and it reassured him that all the arrangements regarding Stellaland made with Deputy Commissioner Rhodes would be fully accepted.

Warren was later to claim that he had only signed the telegram to van Niekerk against his better judgement, because he trusted Sir Hercules Robinson and did not wish to cross the High Commissioner at their first meeting. In fact he would have been aware of the terms of the Rhodes Agreement for it had been widely published. As for the Agreement's promise that the Stellalanders' land claims would all be recognised, Rhodes assured him that they were only laying claim to vacant, unused land. It should therefore not affect that part of Warren's instructions that stated he was to 'reinstate the natives on their land'.[481]

Over the next three weeks Warren was busy assembling his Field Force and making preparations for its advance into Bechuanaland. The line of rail had reached the south bank of the Orange River near Hopetown and he made at least two journeys to the southern boundary of Griqualand West which was now just two days' travel away from Cape Town. On the first of these trips he hired land for a base camp on the southern bank of the Orange. On a subsequent visit, however, the landowner tried doubling the rent. Warren promptly struck camp and moved it across the river to a farm known as Langford where the

---

[481] For a detailed account of the van Niekerk telegram of 6 December and its implications, see J. Mackenzie, *Austral Africa: Ruling it or Losing it* (Sampson Low, London, 1887), Volume II, pp 60–91.

landowner agreed a more amenable rent. And as the Field Force was assembled in Cape Town and Port Elizabeth, it was sent north to Langford.

The 2nd Mounted Rifles, known as 'Carrington's Horse', was raised by Colonel (later Major-General Sir) Frederick Carrington who had wide South African experience with local volunteer regiments. At the same time volunteers in Kimberley clamoured to be allowed to serve under General Warren, many of them from the former Diamond Fields Horse. A regiment of Kimberley volunteers, the 3rd Mounted Rifles, was recruited under Colonel Hugh Gough and, known as 'Gough's Horse', they joined the camp at Langford. Against considerable opposition Warren insisted on including in his Field Force a 'Native Contingent', under British officers. The opposition came from local colonists who felt that since the enemy they expected to face would be white men, it was inappropriate to arm Africans to fight them. Warren, however, wanted to make the point that the new British territory of Bechuanaland was to be for 'the natives' as well as for white colonists, and it was therefore fully appropriate that they join in the fight to save their land.[482]

During his time in Cape Town Warren oversaw the arrangements for equipment, commissariat and various legal issues. It was his first experience of being in charge of such a large project. He was used to being in direct control of every little detail on his former expeditions and he was not very good at delegation. As a result he was frequently frustrated by the slow pace and the pettiness of officialdom and it was probably from this time that he began to gain the reputation for being particularly bad-tempered. Ralph Williams recalled that Sir Charles was 'a trifle hasty in temper', in complete contrast to his secretary Alfred Haynes who was 'absolutely imperturbable'.

> I recollect [wrote Williams], one day the secretary taking a bundle of papers to the general, who, in a moment of temper, crumpled them up and then flung them hither and thither on to the ground. The secretary quietly walked back to his seat, on which the general thundered, 'Why don't you pick them up?' to which the reply was, 'Only the other day, Sir, you told me not to move any papers you put down.' The general looked fiercely at him and then burst out into a hearty fit of laughing, and peace was restored.[483]

Warren arranged for special trains to take his troops and stores north to the Orange River terminus, and this was done over a two-week period. On

---

[482] *Ibid.*, pp 46–7.
[483] Williams, *How I Became a Governor*, p 116.

22 December Warren himself departed Cape Town and arrived at the rail terminus on Christmas Eve. Captain Anstruther, commanding the telegraph section, had managed to offload the heavy ox wagons containing the telegraph equipment from their flat rail trucks; but they now faced the seemingly impossible task of getting them across the river.

Warren decided they should await the cool of the evening before making the attempt. The river level was unusually low and the wagons had to be slid down an almost perpendicular slope to the pontoon. The river was so low and wagons so heavy that the overladen pontoon was grounded halfway across. In what one of the officers involved described as 'an appalling manoeuvre', they 'had to take a second desperate plunge off the pont into the rocky bottom of the river'. They eventually made it safely across and joined the camp at Langford in the teeth of a dust storm.[484]

It was Warren's first experience of supervising the transport of heavy military equipment across a major river. Fifteen years later he was probably to recall this crossing when called upon to cross the Tugela River in north-eastern Natal in the face of Boer rifle fire.

Warren had hoped to treat the men to 'a good splash' on Christmas Day, but the whole of his personal baggage and supplies had been separated from his train at a siding on the way up from Cape Town, so the troops had a relatively modest Christmas celebration.[485] From Langford, Warren led his troops by a little-used road eastwards, avoiding the direct road to Kimberley which ran along the Free State boundary. Having surveyed the boundary, he knew personally most of the Afrikaner farmers on the Free State side and did not wish to upset their sensibilities by leading an imperial force so close to their land. In any case, he had no intention of marching his men through Kimberley, where he might lose many of them to the numerous bars and brothels of the diamond city.

Colonel Durnford had been sent ahead to set up base camp beyond Kimberley, at Barkly West on the north bank of the Vaal. The Field Force covered the 120 kilometres to the Vaal in four days, and after crossing the river by pontoon, they reached Barkly West on 31 December. The camp was pitched just outside the town and had been fortified by Durnford's engineers. Warren and his staff officers found quarters in Barkly West.[486] According to Mackenzie, who accompanied Warren, a number of Free State burghers came

---

[484] *Royal Engineers Journal*, 2 February 1885, pp 26–7.
[485] *Idem.*
[486] Mackenzie, *Austral Africa*, Vol II, p 88.

In camp, Barkly West, January 1885.
FRONT CENTRE WITH HAT IN HAND *Sir Gordon Sprigg, Prime Minister of the Cape Colony 1878–81.* REAR, LEFT TO RIGHT *Cecil J. Rhodes, Deputy Commissioner for Bechuanaland, 1884; Colonel Frederick Carrington, Commander of the Bechuanaland Border Police from 1885; Revd John Mackenzie, former Kuruman missionary and Deputy Commissioner for Bechuanaland, 1884; Major-General Sir Charles Warren, Commander of the Bechuanaland Expedition, 1884–85.*
RHODES MEMORIAL MUSEUM AND COMMONWEALTH CENTRE, BISHOP'S STORTFORD

to visit Warren at Barkly West. These probably included the Surveyor-General Jos de Villiers and Commandant Abel Erasmus, with both of whom Warren had previously developed a good friendship.

Robinson tried to restrict Warren's responsibilities to the purely military by sending Rhodes back to Bechuanaland as Deputy Commissioner to act as Civil Administrator. Warren did not approve for by this time he was fully aware he had been manipulated regarding the van Niekerk telegram on his first arrival in Cape Town. Indeed, according to Mackenzie, Warren gave Rhodes a lesson in geography, pointing out that the land claims of van Niekerk and the Harts River party lay within the Transvaal. The 'Rhodes Agreement' of 8

September 1884 was therefore irrelevant to the settlement of the remainder of Stellaland that lay within Bechuanaland.

Warren invited Mackenzie to join him as a special advisor, at which point Rhodes threatened to resign. Warren called his bluff; and Rhodes stayed for the time being. Although Rhodes was answerable directly to the High Commissioner, they both acknowledged that dual authority would never work and Rhodes agreed to accept orders from Special Commissioner Warren.

Thus both Rhodes and Mackenzie were present at the historic meeting that took place with President Kruger on 24 and 26 January 1885. Warren was convinced that this meeting would determine the fate of the expedition, whether there would be peace or war.

CHAPTER 14

The Bechuanaland Expedition

President Paul Kruger had written to Special Commissioner Warren suggesting a meeting at Christiana, a small township on the north bank of the Vaal some 30 kilometres inside the Transvaal. Warren saw that an early meeting with Kruger had the potential to head off open conflict and resolve most of the problems regarding the enforcement of the new boundary. But he refused to enter the Transvaal, taking the view that he was the representative of the supreme power in South Africa and therefore Kruger, as the supplicant, must come to him on their first meeting. He invited Kruger to meet him near Fourteen Streams, the main ford across the Vaal on the Griqualand-Transvaal border.[487]

Warren set off from Barkly West on Friday 23 January 1885, accompanied by his senior staff officers, together with both Rhodes and Mackenzie. Considering the contempt with which the Boers had treated their western boundary, Warren approached the Transvaal as though he were entering enemy territory. His prime concern at this point was to avoid provoking another Anglo-Boer War. Taking with him a squadron of Inniskilling Dragoons and a squadron of Methuen's Horse, he advanced slowly, sending his scouts out ahead.

As dusk approached Warren dismounted and, according to Ralph Williams, said simply, 'We will camp here'. He lay down on the ground and while the camp was being made ready, he got out his notepad and pencil and began writing notes 'as though in his office'. Warren knew the area well and what seemed to Williams a random selection of camping site had probably been deliberately selected well in advance. That night, Williams recalled, Warren borrowed his whisky flask because he was feeling unwell. As Williams produced the flask Warren said:

> 'Don't you know that I have issued orders forbidding anyone to carry spirits on this expedition?' He kept the flask that night, and in the morning he was much better and the flask was empty… Perhaps [speculated Williams wryly] it upset in the night.[488]

---

[487] The site of the present dam that feeds the Harts/Vaal irrigation scheme.
[488] Williams, *How I Became a Governor*, pp 119–20.

The Bechuanaland Field Force was not entirely alcohol-free. For reasons of discipline Warren had simply forbidden the bringing of liquor into the camp for sale. Instead, a regular allowance was permitted, three glasses of raw spirits a week. These 'half-ration nights' were very popular with the men and seemed to just about satisfy those who were seriously addicted to drink.[489] As Mackenzie was to observe regarding the several months the troops were stationed at Mafikeng, 'The sobriety of the men made [the Provost-Marshal's] duties very light'.[490]

Warren roused the camp at 4.00 am on Saturday 24 January – he was always an early riser – and they reached Brady's Farm on the north bank of the Vaal close to Fourteen Streams in time for a meeting that afternoon. Here the Vaal flowed across a hard, rocky surface and divided itself into fourteen separate streams. This feature enabled it to be used as a natural river crossing. On the south bank an Afrikaner was successfully developing an irrigation works, and on his farm a township had developed at what was in fact the junction of the roads from Mafikeng and from Pretoria. Since 1880 the township had been named 'Warrenton', in honour of the man who had so successfully laid down the Griqualand/Free State boundary and who had earned the respect of many Afrikaner farmers in the area.

President Kruger was at Blignaut's Pont on the north bank, a farm and pontoon owned by the Kruger family. It lay just inside the Transvaal boundary, and he invited Warren to join him there. But Warren refused to make the first move across the border and Kruger reluctantly gave way, coming over to the British side with a small bodyguard.

Kruger hoped through negotiation to prevent Warren's Field Force from proceeding into Bechuanaland. He had just come from Rooigrond where he had promised the Goshenites that he would do all he could to ensure that their land claims, which covered most of Montshiwa's territory, would be recognised. But Warren was having none of it. He had come to Bechuanaland to enforce the boundary agreed at the London Convention. The meeting broke up with nothing settled, and the next day being Sunday, the two parties agreed to meet again on Monday.

For the second meeting Warren was prepared to cross the border and meet Kruger at Blignaut's Pont. The President had insisted that no British troops should enter the Republic, a restriction that Warren ignored. He turned up

[489] Mackenzie, *Austral Africa*, Vol II, pp 304–5.
[490] *Ibid.*, p 302.

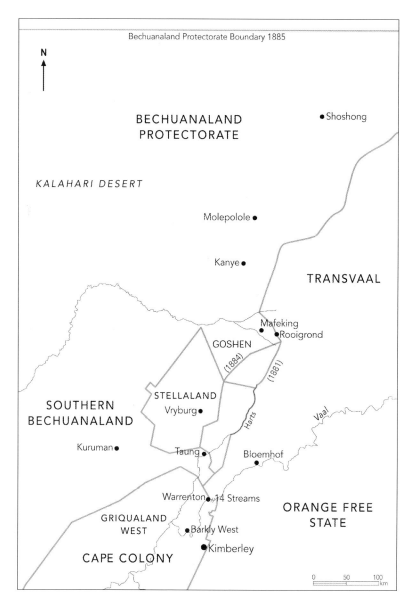

Bechuanaland at the time of the Warren Expedition, 1885.
The Transvaal boundary set by the British in 1871 was well to the east of Bloemhof.
By 1881 it was extended to the Harts River and by 1884 to well into 'Stellaland'.
Those 'Stellalanders' with land claims between the 1881 and 1884 boundaries
were known as the 'Harts River Boers' and it was these, who were now, in fact,
Transvaalers, with whom Rhodes signed his Agreement.

at the appointed venue escorted by his fully armed squadron of 'Skins', the Inniskilling Dragoons, the élite of his force. It was the first time British armed forces had entered the Transvaal since the Boer victory at Majuba four years previously. Rhodes, in a later attempt to discredit Warren, claimed that this 'display of military strength' was a gross insult to the Republic's President.[491] But Warren took the view that after Saturday's inconclusive meeting, he needed to impress upon the President his determination to carry out his Commission and, unlike Mackenzie, he had the military strength and the will to enforce it. The silent presence of Mackenzie at the meeting served to emphasise the point.

Kruger tried to argue that the Goshenites had acquired certain rights to land, by treaty with Montshiwa in 1882, to which Warren responded:

> I cannot recognise whites as being the people of any native chief; if they are so considered, they are liable to be put in native locations.[492]

Warren had made his point. By the end of the day Kruger had agreed to enforce the London Convention boundary and to order the Goshenite 'filibusters' to, in Warren's words, 'clear out of Bechuanaland'.[493]

Warren had been surprised to learn that no attempt had been made by either Briton or Boer to delineate the new Transvaal boundary in the eleven months since the London Convention. It was to Kruger's advantage to have no demarcation, as his burghers could continue their historic push westwards, as far eventually, they hoped, as the Kalahari. But Warren felt the main fault lay with High Commissioner Robinson who had failed to beacon off the new border as instructed in March 1884.[494] Indeed, Warren believed that had this been done there would probably have been no need for his Bechuanaland Expedition, for Mackenzie's Protectorate would have been respected, or could have been easily enforced by the small police unit, the Bechuanaland Border Police, that Mackenzie had been allowed to recruit.[495]

The meeting at Fourteen Streams was a triumph for Warren. It lay at the heart of the success of his Bechuanaland Expedition. He had succeeded in

[491] Basil Williams, *Cecil Rhodes* (Holt & Co, New York, 1921), p 84.

[492] Mackenzie, *Austral Africa*, Vol II, p 101.

[493] C. Warren, *Report of the Proceedings of the Bechuanaland Field Force* (War Office, London, 1885), p 13.

[494] *HCPP*, Cd.3947, p 60, Secretary of State to Robinson, 14 March 1884.

[495] C. Warren, 'Cecil Rhodes' Early Days in South Africa', *The Contemporary Review*, 1 January 1902, pp 649–52.

getting President Kruger to accept, on the spot in South Africa, the letter of the Convention that he had agreed to in London. In the opinion of Mackenzie, an admittedly very partial observer, Warren had shown that he

> … possessed other qualifications than those of a leader of irregular forces; and the results of the meeting at Fourteen Streams fully justified the action of Her Majesty's Government in also imposing on him civil and political functions.[496]

Warren returned to Barkly West to gather the main body of his 4000-strong force. He managed to acquire a mule-drawn former mail coach that had been used on the run between Bloemfontein and Kimberley, one of the ones in which he had shared that journey with Roman Catholic Bishop Jolivet in 1877. It was gaudily painted in red with the two destinations still emblazoned on the sides. Warren was to use it as his mobile office and for the use of any of his staff who was indisposed.[497] He himself preferred to travel on horseback.

He brought his main Field Force up to Fourteen Streams, and while he was there, Mankurwane came down to visit the General and find out the purpose of the British military presence. Seven years previously he had agreed to Warren's proposal that he come under British protection, but so far he had seen little effective evidence of it. He must, therefore, have been delighted to learn that Mackenzie's 'Protectorate' was to be upheld. The engineers, meanwhile, had extended the telegraph line as far as the border, and it was here on 6 February 1885 that they received the news of the fall of Khartoum and the death of General Gordon on 26 January. It was thus in a sombre mood that the Field Force crossed the Griqualand West boundary the following day and entered Bechuanaland.

Warren established his first fortified camp in Bechuanaland near Mankurwane's capital of Taung. While this was being constructed, he sent Rhodes and Ralph Williams on to Vryburg. They were to take possession of Stellaland's land certificates and other documents and to assemble van Niekerk and the Stellalanders in preparation for Warren's visit.

According to Ralph Williams it was during the week that he and Rhodes spent together at Vryburg that Rhodes evolved his scheme for pushing a railway northwards as far as the Lake Region of East Africa. He seems to have been a little vague as to the exact geography of the region, but he had

---

[496] Mackenzie, *Austral Africa*, Vol II, pp 107–8.
[497] *Ibid.*, p 107.

Mankurwane, Chief of the Batswana at Taung.
MCGREGOR MUSEUM, KIMBERLEY, SOUTH AFRICA

in mind the lakes in Northern Zambia where David Livingstone met his end. The aim of Rhodes's railway was to open up Central Africa to British domination and in doing so to prevent a link across the continent between German South West Africa and a potential German colony in East Africa.[498] It was well known that Carl Peters, a German explorer, had recently returned to Germany from a 'treaty-making' journey through mainland East Africa and

[498] Williams, *How I Became a Governor*, p 123.

was urgently pressing the German Government to declare a protectorate over the region.

At the time that Williams and Rhodes were formulating their imperial dreams in Vryburg, Chancellor Bismarck was hosting the Berlin West Africa Conference which was laying down the ground rules for the so-called 'Scramble for Africa'.[499] And immediately after the conclusion of that conference at the end of February 1885, Bismarck proclaimed the German East African Protectorate, just as Rhodes had feared.

It appears that until this moment Rhodes's dreams of colonial expansion northwards had been motivated primarily by his local mining and Cape political concerns.[500] Most early biographers of Rhodes, however, accepted unquestioningly his own boastful assertions that he had conceived his dream of a Cape-to-Cairo railway from his very earliest years in South Africa in the 1870s, and that he was the one who originated the impulse for British expansion northwards, which was to lead to his founding the colony of 'Rhodesia' in what is today Zimbabwe in 1890–93. As Warren was later to point out when writing about Rhodes in this period, assumptions concerning British northward expansion, at least as far as Northern Bechuanaland and the Zambezi, had been widespread in Southern Africa from at least the 1850s. There was nothing unique about Rhodes's ideas.[501]

* * *

Rhodes's sharing of imperial dreams with Ralph Williams was disturbed by the arrival of Warren at Vryburg on 14 February 1885. The Stellaland flag, which had previously been lowered by Mackenzie but had been raised again following Rhodes's intervention, was lowered once more and the British flag raised in its place. Warren retained the actual Stellaland flag and on his return to England had it sent to the Colonial Office for presentation to Queen Victoria. In due course she was to return it to him.

Warren realised that the white colonists of Stellaland whom Rhodes had gathered together were sharply divided into two factions: those who had

[499] For the best narrative account of this event from an imperial perspective, see T. Pakenham, *The Scramble for Africa* (Weidenfeld and Nicolson, London, 1991).
[500] Kevin Shillington, *An African Adventure: A Brief Life of Cecil Rhodes* (Rhodes Memorial Museum and Commonwealth Centre, Bishop's Stortford, n.d. [1992]), pp 26–9; Shillington, *Colonisation*, pp 155–65.
[501] Warren, 'Cecil Rhodes' Early Days in South Africa', *The Contemporary Review*, Jan. 1 1902, published a few months before the death of Rhodes.

accepted Mackenzie's Protectorate the previous May, and those Transvaal Afrikaners, headed by van Niekerk, with whom Rhodes had made his 'Stellaland Agreement'. As already noted, the land claims of the latter lay largely in what was now the Transvaal Republic. Warren took the view that Rhodes should have had no business dealings with these Transvaalers, let alone allow van Niekerk to speak for the whole of Stellaland.

About a week after arriving in Vryburg, Warren ordered the arrest of van Niekerk on a charge of conspiring in the murder of James Honey, a notorious cattle rustler and British citizen who had been killed in 1883. The murder had probably been carried out by Adriaan de la Rey, 'Groot Adrian', van Niekerk's Deputy; but evidence garnered since Mackenzie's first visit suggested that van Niekerk was in some way complicit. De la Rey was safely across the border in the Transvaal, with no hope of getting him extradited; but by charging van Niekerk, Warren hoped to demonstrate that British justice would now be upheld within the territory without regard to the prominence of the alleged perpetrator. In due course the case against van Niekerk fell through from lack of evidence. He was released and withdrew into the Transvaal.[502] But whether van Niekerk was in gaol or in the Transvaal mattered little to Warren. So far as he was concerned, he was thankfully rid of someone he regarded as a bad influence and whose land claims in any case were irrelevant to the future of Bechuanaland.[503]

In the absence of an alternative civil administrator of Stellaland, Rhodes being too closely associated with the Afrikaner faction, Warren proposed establishing military rule. This was accepted by the High Commissioner, but not by Rhodes, who had expected to have the civil administration handed to him. On 27 February, which happened to be Majuba Day, a day of great significance to all British military in Southern Africa, Rhodes resigned his Deputy Commissionership and retired to Cape Town. There he would be better placed to undermine the authority of Warren, whose continued presence in Bechuanaland, he now argued, was detrimental to the cause of Cape annexation.

Warren had grown to thoroughly distrust Rhodes. According to Ralph Williams, who had fallen under Rhodes's spell, 'Warren misconceived the character of Rhodes, deeming him a paltry land-grabber, working locally for his own monetary interests'.[504] Whether or not Warren's judgement of Rhodes was indeed this harsh, there is no doubt that Rhodes had his own agenda,

---

[502] Mackenzie, *Austral Africa*, pp 133–53.
[503] *HCPP*, Cd.4588, p 53.
[504] Williams, *How I Became a Governor*, p 125.

and Warren was pleased to have the Deputy Commissioner out of the way. He could now, with Mackenzie's advice, implement his own style of imperial protection, with its emphasis on the 'the restoration of the natives on their lands'.

Warren headed north from Vryburg on Friday 6 March and the following evening he reached the Setlagoli River, a tributary of the Molopo which today forms the boundary between Botswana and South Africa.

He had expected to stay at Setlagoli a few days while setting up a fortified camp, but the following morning he heard reports that the Goshenite filibusters were planning an attack on Mafikeng in a final attempt to drive Montshiwa's people from the land. On Monday 9 March he set off with two squadrons of the 2ⁿᵈ Mounted Rifles, under Colonel Frederick Carrington. They reached Sanie's village near Mafikeng in the early hours of the next morning, and soon after dawn Montshiwa's son and several headmen came out to Sanie's to greet their deliverer. Warren 'relieved Mafeking [sic] at noon the same day', Tuesday 10 March 1885.[505] This was only the *first* 'Relief of Mafeking', the *second*, far more famous one, was to take place during the great Anglo-Boer War on 17 May 1900. Chief Montshiwa was not at home to greet Warren. He was away at Kanye, 100 kilometres to the north in today's Botswana, where he was hoping to persuade the chief there, Gaseitsiwe, to form a defensive alliance against the Boers. Warren's swift move to Mafikeng, however, did away with the need for any such defensive alliance.

When he reconnoitred Rooigrond the following day Warren found that the Goshenites had melted away into the Transvaal with their wagons and tents leaving just a handful of people in the few houses that straddled the border. Back at Mafikeng he set up camp a few hundred metres from the African town and with troops from Vryburg arriving daily, he made preparations for establishing his headquarters at Mafikeng. The telegraph line that had been following them up through Bechuanaland reached Setlagoli by the end of the week and Warren was able to communicate across the intervening space by heliograph.

* * *

On Saturday 14 March Warren led a detachment of 'Royal Scots' to Rooigrond to exhume the body of Christopher Bethell. The Rooigrond residents denied

---

[505] Warren, *Report of the Proceedings of the Bechuanaland Field Force*, p 18. 'Mafeking' was the British spelling of 'Mafikeng'.

the truth of the story told by Israel Molema, Montshiwa's cousin that Bethell had been murdered while lying wounded. Molema had been wounded alongside Bethell but had played dead when the Boers approached. According to Molema, after exchanging a few words with Bethell, one of the Boers, whom Molema knew by the name 'van Rooyen', shot Bethell in the head. Warren now demanded of the handful of white men at Rooigrond that they show him where Bethell was buried. They pointed to a collection of 25 graves. Ralph Williams takes up the story:

> Warren questioned the Boers as to which grave it was but could get no satisfactory reply. 'Very well then,' he said, 'dig them all up.' And so grave after grave was opened and each coffin uncovered and examined. At one grave a Boer stepped forward and said, 'The girl there died of smallpox.' Warren was adamant and said, 'Open it,' and it was opened like the others. At last a Boer said, 'General, I will show you Bethell's grave,' and he did. There lay Christopher Bethell in his ordinary bush kit, six months buried, but as untouched at first sight as though he had been buried the day before, and there was the wound in the leg and the dastardly shot in the head, exactly as had been described to us by the natives.[506]

The body was placed on a gun carriage, covered by a Union Flag, and taken back to Mafikeng. That afternoon, in front of a huge African gathering, Revd John Mackenzie conducted the funeral service and the body of Christopher Bethell was reinterred with full military honours. Captain George Richard Bethell, a naval officer, had accompanied the expedition up from Cape Town and was present in Mafikeng for the reburial of his brother. Shortly afterwards he and Ralph Williams withdrew from the expedition and returned to England. Williams had felt at odds with Warren since the falling out with Cecil Rhodes.

On the same day as Bethell's funeral in Mafikeng, 14 March 1885, the British Ambassador to Berlin informed the German Government that the British Protectorate of Bechuanaland extended as far north as latitude 22 degrees south. This was intended not only to keep the Germans out of the Kalahari, but also to confine the Transvaal to the south and east of the Limpopo River, thus restricting their access to the north. A small party of Germans had already visited Shoshong in Northern Bechuanaland the previous year,[507]

[506] Williams, *How I Became a Governor*, p 126.
[507] Mackenzie, *Austral Africa*, p 253.

and in due course the British would find it necessary to extend the boundary of its Protectorate all the way north to the Zambezi.[508]

Warren spent the next two weeks in Mafikeng gathering evidence concerning Bethell's murder, setting up his headquarters and laying out the grid pattern of what was to become the European township known to the English as 'Mafeking'. Montshiwa arrived from Kanye with Chief Gaseitsiwe and his son Bathoen on 25 March. Montshiwa was delighted to see that 'his relative', General Warren, had arrived with a proper army to uphold Mackenzie's Protectorate. Gaseitsiwe, too, was glad to welcome Warren, for Kanye had also suffered attacks and cattle raids from the Goshenites.

The telegraph line reached Mafikeng on 2 April and Warren drew up plans to extend it further north and to dig a line of wells up the 'road to the north' as far as Khama's capital of Shoshong. The British Government failed to approve any large-scale expenditure north of the Molopo; but they did order Warren to proceed to the principal northern Batswana towns and get the chiefs' agreement to the extended British Protectorate.[509]

In the meantime the balloon detachment had arrived at Mafikeng, having travelled with its cumbersome equipment all the way from Cape Town by ox wagon. Major Elsdale RE, who commanded the detachment, was assisted by a Lieutenant and ten NCOs and sappers. The three balloons they had brought with them were made of a material known as 'gold-beater's skin', the internal membrane of an ox's gut. From experiments conducted in 1883 it was found to be far superior to silk, being 'practically impervious to the passage of hydrogen gas'.[510] They had brought the original skin balloon, the 'Heron', the largest at 10,000 cubic-foot capacity, and on 6 April it was filled with gas that had been brought out from England, compressed into specially constructed steel tubes. The basket of the balloon was just large enough to carry one person and Major Elsdale took the first flight up, with the balloon tethered to the ground by a long rope.

Warren insisted on making the second ascent. This time the balloon was tethered to an ox wagon that was driven around on the veldt, showing the extent to which the balloon could be manoeuvred. The thinness of the air at Mafikeng, which was 5000 feet above sea level, meant that the balloon could only rise 2000 feet above the ground, but even at this height it gave

---

[508] This was agreed by Anglo-German treaty in 1890.
[509] *HCPP*, Vol LVII, Cd.4432, pp 28, 101; and Warren, *Report*, p 20.
[510] Watson, 'Military Ballooning in the British Army', pp 45–6.

Trying out the military balloon at Mafikeng.
Illustrated London News, *20 June 1885.*

magnificent views across the flat, open veldt. For Warren, who kept up flag communication with the ground, the flight was not only significant for its military and scientific interest; it would also have been the fulfilment of a lifelong dream, stemming back to his schooldays at Bridgnorth Grammar.

Elsdale and Warren's flights were believed by those present to be the first-ever military ascents in the field of a gas balloon. In fact, unbeknown to Warren at the time, the first ascent had been carried out two weeks previously near Suakin on the Red Sea coast of Sudan, where the British Army was maintaining a small outpost.

Montshiwa was fascinated by the balloons, not only that they could go up, but also that they came down again. According to Mackenzie, the old chief and the Batswana generally, as well as a number of visitors from the Transvaal who had come over to view the balloons, were mightily impressed by 'the power of England'.[511] Montshiwa himself was persuaded to take a flight, much to the consternation of many of his people. And of this flight there can be no doubt: at 80 years of age, Montshiwa was not only the oldest person in the world to make an ascent in a gas balloon, but he was also the first African to do so.[512]

* * *

Leaving his Chief of Staff in command of the bulk of his force at Mafikeng and at his fortified camps between there and Barkly West, Warren set off for Northern Bechuanaland (today's Botswana) on 20 April 1885 accompanied by his brother Billie, Mackenzie, Alfred Haynes, his cartographer Captain Claude Conder and other senior staff. They were escorted by a squadron of Dragoons and a company of Carrington's Horse. Durnford's telegraph contingent had already begun laying the line northwards.

Warren arrived at Kanye on 22 April and camped at the foot of Kanye Hill on which the African town was built. He had a meeting the following day with Gaseitsiwe and Bathoen whom he had already met in Mafikeng. Warren did not focus on the Protectorate at this meeting as he knew he would be visiting Kanye again on his return journey. Instead he had 'a long conversation' on the iniquities of the liquor traffic and the amount of drinking that went on in Kanye. It would lead, he told Gaseitsiwe, to the ruination of his people. According to Mackenzie, the chief and his son, who were both known drinkers, were duly impressed, but they protested that the blame should not fall on the African drinkers, but on the white traders who refused to observe the restrictions on the sale of strong liquor to Africans.[513]

Warren then moved up to Molepolole where he met the old Chief Sechele, who in the 1840s had been David Livingstone's first and only convert to Christianity. Sechele and his sons, Sebele and Kgari, were ambivalent about

---

[511] Mackenzie, *Austral Africa*, Vol II, p 299.
[512] Williams, *Governor*, p 126.
[513] Mackenzie, *Austral Africa*, Vol II, p 233.

Warren's Protectorate. 'Who,' asked Sebele, 'are you protecting us from? We did not ask for it'. Sechele referred to the war that his people had fought with the Transvaal Boers in the early 1850s. After beating off that attack Sechele had travelled as far as the Cape to appeal, unsuccessfully, for the British to lift the restriction on the sale of guns to Africans north of the colony. When they needed protection then, the old chief pointed out, the British had failed to provide it. Warren left Molepolole with the chiefs indicating that they might be prepared to accept British protection if they saw that Montshiwa and Gaseitsiwe were actually benefitting from it.[514] For Warren it was a lesson in the political sophistication of the northern Batswana chiefs.

Warren's party reached Shoshong, the capital of the largest and most powerful Batswana state, on Friday 8 May. Mackenzie in particular was welcomed by the chief, Khama III,[515] with whom, as resident missionary at Shoshong in the 1860s, he had developed a close relationship.

During a period of leave in England in 1870 Mackenzie had published a memoir of his mission work in Southern Africa, *Ten Years North of the Orange River*.[516] It brought the name of Khama to the notice of the British public. Khama had been a Christian convert since 1858 and became undisputed ruler of his people in 1875. Mackenzie portrayed him as a noble man and wise ruler, and this reputation had only increased since then through the chief's periodic correspondence with the British High Commissioner in Cape Town and other British officials. He had frequently referred to the troubles he experienced from both Transvaal Boers and the amaNdebele with whom he disputed the border region between present-day Botswana and Zimbabwe.

According to Mackenzie, upon the arrival of Warren's party, the chief 'produced the most favourable impression upon every one by his quiet and sincere manners'.[517] Khama was pleased that Warren had come himself and not sent some more junior officer. The chief and the general had a number of informal interviews before broaching the subject of the Protectorate. Thanks partly to Mackenzie and his missionary colleague, Revd J. D. Hepburn, and to the presence of British traders at Shoshong, Khama viewed the British favourably and was prepared to welcome Warren's Protectorate. But he had a number of qualifications.

---

[514] *Ibid.*, pp 236-9; and *HCPP*, Cd.4588, pp 6–9.
[515] Grandfather to Seretse Khama, independent Botswana's first president (1966–80).
[516] Published by Edmonston and Douglas, Edinburgh, 1871.
[517] Mackenzie, *Austral Africa*, Vol II, pp 252–3.

There should be no sale or consumption of intoxicating liquor, by either white or black people. Any white person coming into Bechuanaland must be 'the right kind of English settler'; not hunters or passing traders, but people prepared to stay long-term and work the land. From these people the Batswana could learn and the country would develop. And there should be no freehold sale of African land. Finally, Khama and his chiefs must remain as rulers of their own people in accordance with their customs, although, he claimed, he was always willing to listen to the advice of the English.

Khama had a good understanding of international politics. He knew that the British would expect some payment for their 'protection' and he offered to make available a vast tract of land for British settlement: 200,000 square miles in the east of the country. This would provide a buffer between his people and both the Transvaal Boers and the amaNdebele of Lobengula.[518] In fact it was not really Khama's land to give and much of it was unsuitable for cultivation; otherwise, as one British official observed, it would have been taken by the Boers long ago.[519] But Warren was excited by this 'magnificent offer' as it fitted in with the ideas he was evolving.

On the last of their public interviews Khama presented Warren with a lengthy document of submission, laying out these terms. It had been translated and copied by Mackenzie who had been interpreter and note-taker throughout the several meetings that had been held in Khama's *kgotla* (public court). He had probably also acted as advisor to Khama and so it is hardly surprising that Khama's proposals were largely in line with Mackenzie and Warren's ideas for the best way forward for black and white in Southern Africa. Khama described the boundaries of his territory, mostly in relation to the rivers of the region, claiming outrageously that his rule extended as far as the Zambezi. But his specific detail formed the basis of a map that Warren's engineers were now able to draw up. The map clearly marked the land that was to be reserved for Khama's people and that which Khama was prepared to grant for British settlement.[520]

Armed with Khama's submission and map, Warren now turned south. He hoped that Khama's acceptance of the Protectorate and the terms under which he had accepted it would have a strong influence on the other Bechuanaland chiefs and this proved to be the case. In the interim at Molepolole *realpolitik*

[518] *Ibid.*, pp 253–68; and *HCPP*, Vol LVII, Cd.4588, pp 36–40.
[519] Shillington, *Colonisation*, pp 172–3.
[520] Mackenzie, *Austral Africa*, Vol II, pp 260–67.

had prevailed and Sechele, Sebele and the other chiefs decided to accept the Protectorate along the same lines that Khama had indicated. Warren's engineers drew up a map of the Molepolole Reserve and he obtained the chiefs' signatures on the submission document. This was repeated at Kanye.

By the end of May Warren and his party were back in Mafikeng where he drafted his proposal for the future of the country. Inspired by Khama's 'magnificent offer' of land, Warren proposed setting up a huge Crown Colony that stretched from Griqualand West to the Zambezi. It would be independent of the Cape and ruled along imperial and Mackenzian lines. He drew a sharp contrast between how this would be run and what would happen under Cape annexation:

> ... the Cape Government is quite incapable of dealing with the native question in these parts without causing strife and disturbances which must in a short time result in wars ultimately involving Her Majesty's Government in considerable expenditure, and bringing destruction and ruin to the native tribes. Bechuanaland under Cape Government will become a prey to land speculators and filibusters, and an area for fighting the battles of the Cape politicians, who would each attempt to catch the Dutch vote by bringing more and more Boers into the native territories.[521]

The British Government was horrified. It was not prepared to take direct responsibility for any new colony in Southern Africa. All along it had assumed the Cape Colony would take responsibility for Bechuanaland. Warren's military occupation was seen in London merely as a holding operation. The part of Warren's plan that most condemned it in the eyes of the Cape Government, however, was his report that:

> ... the native chiefs have stipulated that the settlers are to be English or English colonists, as it would be no protection for them were the settlers to be Boers of Dutch extraction; and they have also stipulated that the land is not to be sold, so as to prevent English speculators from coming in and selling to Dutch Boers.[522]

This created a great deal of animosity towards Warren among Cape Afrikaners in general. Even in London the political mood began to move against Warren and his independent ideas.

---

[521] *UKNA*, CO 417/5, No. 188, (copy) Warren to Robinson, 1 June 1885, marked 'NOT TO BE PRINTED'.

[522] *HCPP*, Vol LVII, Cd.4588, p 57.

From June the main concern of correspondence between High Commissioner Robinson and Secretary of State Lord Derby at the Colonial Office was how to get the Cape Government to agree to the annexation of at least part of Bechuanaland. They began to favour splitting the territory along the line of the Molopo River for there would be some chance of getting the Cape to agree to annex Southern Bechuanaland. The main sticking point was how much land would be reserved for Africans. The Cape Government wanted them to be allocated an absolute minimum, whereas a primary aim of Warren's Expedition had been 'the restoration of the natives on their lands', and the missionary lobby amongst the British public would not accept anything less.[523]

While this was being discussed, Warren appointed Mackenzie to chair a committee to inquire into the extent of African land use within Stellaland. This was the prime arable land of Mankurwane's people, where a large number of individual African farmers had used the numerous freshwater springs between Taung and Vryburg to irrigate and cultivate crops for market. Until 1882 the region had annually exported thousands of bags of wheat to Kimberley. Ironically, since 1884 and Mackenzie's urging of Africans to stop fighting and trust in British protection, the Stellalanders had managed to quietly eject these African farmers and take possession of their land.[524] The evidence collected by Mackenzie showed that if Africans were 'restored to their lands' within 'Stellaland', the white claimants would lose all of the most fertile land in the region.

This was too much for the High Commissioner who, with Rhodes's prompting took the view that the 'restoration of native lands' referred only to the Goshenite land claims and not to those of Stellaland. Robinson therefore proposed to the Colonial Office that the Warren Expedition should be withdrawn immediately and Southern Bechuanaland declared a separate Crown Colony. Mackenzie's committee would be disbanded and its papers submitted to a Land Commission that would be instructed to draw up a settlement that would satisfy colonial interests.[525] Robinson was confident that with a maximum amount of land reserved for white settlement, he would be able to persuade the Cape Government to take over responsibility for

---

[523] Shillington, *Colonisation*, pp 169, 172–3.

[524] *Ibid.*, p 173.

[525] For Mackenzie's land committee of August 1885, see, Kevin Shillington, *Luka Jantjie: Resistance Hero of the South African Frontier* (Aldridge Press, London, 2011), pp 147–48.

Southern Bechuanaland within a couple of years. In the meantime, Northern Bechuanaland would remain simply a 'Protectorate', with the Batswana chiefs in charge of their own affairs, and the minimal administrative cost of a Border Police force.

The British Government accepted Robinson's proposal and on 14 August Warren was informed by telegram from Lord Stanley that his force was to be withdrawn:

> Her Majesty's Government cordially recognize the great ability with which you organized the irregular forces, and the efficiency and good discipline which you have maintained in your command. The result has been that your expedition has met with no resistance from any quarter, and has achieved its objects in the most satisfactory manner...
>
> ... I have now only to acknowledge the zeal and ability with which you have discharged your important duties, and to convey to you the high appreciation of Her Majesty's Government.[526]

* * *

On 30 September 1885 Southern Bechuanaland, the territory south of the Molopo River, was formally proclaimed the Crown Colony of British Bechuanaland. At the same time, the territory north of the Molopo became the Bechuanaland Protectorate, with the intimation that it would suffer minimal colonial interference. British Bechuanaland was annexed by the Cape ten years later; but the Protectorate survived into the 20th century and went on to gain political independence as the Republic of Botswana in 1966. Significantly, the incoming Botswana government, led by Khama III's grandson, Sir Seretse Khama, chose the anniversary of the formal establishment of the Protectorate, 30 September, as their Independence Day.

Although most of the credit for the survival of the Protectorate and the achievement of independence lay with the Batswana themselves, Sir Charles Warren's preparedness to respect the Batswana Chiefs and actually *negotiate* the terms of the Protectorate enabled them to resist an attempt by Cecil Rhodes in 1895 to subsume the Protectorate into his colony of Rhodesia. Later, in the 20th century, a new generation of Batswana were able to use their ancestors' original *consent* to the Protectorate to avoid attempts to join the territory to apartheid South Africa. And finally, on 30 September 1985, the centenary of the establishment of the Crown Colony of British Bechuanaland

---

[526] *HCPP*, Vol LVII, Cd.4588, p 119.

The three Batswana Chiefs in London in 1896 to protest (successfully) against the British Government's proposal to hand their Protectorate, as negotiated with Warren, to Cecil Rhodes's colony of 'Rhodesia'. Here they visit Warren in Chatham, 13 November 1895. SEATED, FROM LEFT *Kwenaetsile (companion to Bathoen), Chiefs Bathoen, Khama and Sebele, General Warren, Warren's* aide-de-camp.
STANDING, FROM LEFT *Gohiwamang (Sebele's secretary/interpreter), Simeon Seisa (Khama's secretary/interpreter), Revd Willoughby (missionary/interpreter and general host to the visiting chiefs).*
MCGREGOR MUSEUM, KIMBERLEY, SOUTH AFRICA

and the Bechuanaland Protectorate, the *apartheid* 'homeland' Government of Bophuthatswana celebrated Warren's role in laying out the modern town of Mahikeng and saving the surrounding territory for Montshiwa's people by issuing a pair of postage stamps, one bearing a portrait of Montshiwa, the other a portrait of Charles Warren.

The success of Warren's 1885 Expedition can be traced in the first place to his meticulous military planning, and the firm but fair line that he took with President Kruger at Fourteen Streams. This was followed by a careful and steady advance through Bechuanaland, establishing fortified camps at Taung, Vryburg and Setlagoli, before reaching Mafikeng just four and a half weeks

Postage stamps to celebrate the centenary of the Warren
Expedition, issued by the Bophuthatswana postal authorities,
featuring General Warren and Chief Montshiwa.
WITH THANKS TO KIMBERLEY AFRICANA LIBRARY AND
MICHAEL NEW FOR COPIES

after crossing the Griqualand border. As a result he managed to expel the Goshenite filibusters without firing a single shot.

Warren's own assessment was that the avoidance of war with the Transvaal Boers, expected by many at the time, was due not only to the thoroughness of his organisation, the rapidity of his march north and the knowledge that there were several thousand good shots in the Field Force:

> … but the fact also that the officers and men were dressed alike, that the officers were armed with rifles, and that the dress of the troops had no distinguishing characteristics at a distance, were not only noticed by the Boers, but described by their papers to be unfair. The effect, however, upon [the Goshenite Boers] was described throughout South Africa as being the equivalent to a tremendous thrashing.

263

In his opinion, the expedition had 'restored to Englishmen the prestige which they had lost during the last six years'.[527]

Warren had 'restored the natives to their lands' – at least in the Mafikeng region, though not in Stellaland. He had negotiated a satisfactory settlement of the Bechuanaland Protectorate – satisfactory from both the British and the Batswana point of view. His troops had remained healthy, with no significant disease – there were just eighteen deaths, half of them from accidents. And his almost entirely mounted force of 4000 officers and men had lost less than two per cent of their horses to disease in a country where a loss of between ten and twenty per cent to 'horse-sickness' was the norm.

With Warren's withdrawal, a number of his staff officers remained behind to serve the new Bechuanaland administration. Lieutenant Alfred Haynes was to serve as secretary to the Bechuanaland Land Commission that began hearing evidence at Taung in 1886, while Colonel Frederick Carrington commanded the Bechuanaland Border Police (BBP) and went on to become the first Resident Commissioner of the Protectorate. Many from Warren's volunteer regiments joined the BBP and some of them, including Carrington, went on to form the military element of Rhodes's 'Pioneer Column' which began the colonisation of Zimbabwe in 1890.

As he made his way south in September 1885 Warren was accorded a triumphal reception in Kimberley. It was a city very much dominated by British mining and commercial interests, and he received thanks and congratulations from businessmen, municipality and the Freemasons. Warren's success in securing British access to the 'road to the north' and ultimately the wealth of Central Africa, gave a huge boost to imperialistic enthusiasm. The railhead had just reached Kimberley that month and special trains were laid on to convey the troops southwards. Warren himself had been invited to visit President Brand in Bloemfontein where he was received with great enthusiasm by the Free State Afrikaners. They had feared a clash between Britain and the Transvaalers which would have had the potential to set Afrikaner against Briton across the colonies and republics of South Africa. According to his friend Colonel Fred Terry, who accompanied Warren on the visit:

> At Bloemfontein, the capital of the Orange Free State, the ovation with which
> Sir Charles Warren was received was not merely of a private character, but was

---

[527] C. Warren, 'Our Portion of South Africa,' being a paper read to the Royal Colonial Institute at St James's Banqueting Hall, Regent Street on 10 November 1885, and reported in *The Times* the following day.

public – guns being fired and military guards of honour provided. The whole time Sir Charles Warren stayed at Bloemfontein he was fêted, and shouts of welcome greeted him wherever he went, the utmost satisfaction being expressed at the manner in which he had settled the Bechuanaland difficulties, had united the [white] races, and had brought about confidence in the future maintenance of peace.[528]

Warren then made his way south towards Port Elizabeth. At Grahamstown, which he reached on 15 September, this very British town had declared a public holiday and all businesses were closed. The streets were lined by the local volunteer corps, and the Mayor presented Warren with an address that had been signed by 1500 people. He was fêted for two days with concerts and banquets before boarding the train for Port Elizabeth. At this major port for the interior trade, he received similar public addresses and receptions and the particular thanks of the city's merchant houses whose access to the interior he had secured.

He boarded the steamer *Asiatic* and arrived in Cape Town on Monday 21 September. A horse-drawn carriage awaited him at the dock and as they passed through the dock gates, the horses were removed from his carriage and the shafts manned by a team of enthusiastic young men. They pulled the carriage to the Commercial Exchange where a platform had been erected, and where addresses were read and presented. Further addresses of gratitude and congratulations were sent from 23 of the districts and towns of the colony.[529] Among the various presentations made to him over the following days, Sir Charles was very touched to receive an album of South African photographs inscribed 'F. W.', for Lady Fanny Warren. At a luncheon hosted by Sir Richard Southey, former Lieutenant-Governor of Griqualand West (1873–75), Warren expressed his thanks to all those who had helped to make his expedition such a success. He singled out in particular his Chief of Staff, Colonel Forestier-Walker 'upon whose good sense and upon whose judgement I could always rely'.[530] Sir Hercules Robinson and Cecil Rhodes were both 'out of town' during Warren's few days in Cape Town; whether by design or by chance is unclear. But at the Castle of Good Hope the 'gallant General' was the guest of Sir Leicester Smyth, General Officer Commanding in South Africa.

---

[528] Quoted in Williams, *The Life*, p 188, from an interview Terry gave to a Sheffield newspaper in November 1885.
[529] Williams, *The Life*, p 179.
[530] *Royal Engineers Journal*, 2 November 1885, pp 254–5.

Perhaps because the Field Force had not fired a single shot in anger,[531] Warren found when he got back to England that the military side of the Expedition was greatly downplayed. Warren's field rank of Major-General was not confirmed and he reverted to his service rank of Colonel. Furthermore, no medals were struck for the campaign, although in their march through Bechuanaland the troops had proudly worn their identification tags on their chests, awarding themselves 'The Order of the Tin Pot of Bechuanaland'. Mackenzie recalled that in an evening's entertainment put on by officers and men in Mafikeng, a ballad of seventeen verses was recited, which contained the following:

> And O it was a goodly sight to see each gallant boy
> In his putties and cord breeches, and his coat of corduroy;
> But amidst this pomp and splendour, why, the thing that looked the best
> Was the medal of the B.F.F. each wore upon his breast.

> Aye, that was a medal surely, lad, – no bright and shining star,
> No bronze gew-gaw for marching that, and glittering from afar;
> But a simple tin-pot medal, with this touching legend stamped,
> The number of the tramper, and the corps with which he tramped.

> Thus you see, my lad, the medal that I once wore next my skin
> Is no blood-stained medallion – 'tis a simple bit of tin;
> But the sight of it reminds me how I wore it on my breast
> When I marched up thro' Stellaland, a chucking of a chest.[532]

$$* * *$$

---

[531] There is a tradition that one night while camped at Mafikeng a sergeant fired off his gun because he would be damned if he would serve on a military expedition that did not fire a single shot.
[532] Quoted in Mackenzie, *Austral Africa*, Vol II, p 303. Various other verses are quoted in Williams, *The Life*, pp 180–81; and numerous verses have appeared elsewhere.

CHAPTER 15

Politics, Freemasonry and Suakin (Sudan)

Sir Charles Warren arrived in Southampton aboard HMS *Spartan* on Thursday 15 October 1885. From there he caught a train to London where he would have changed to a suburban line to reach his home in Wimbledon, South-West London. Here he was briefly reunited with his family for the weekend before beginning a string of receptions and banquets where he was toasted as 'the saviour of Bechuanaland'.

On Wednesday 21 October he was guest of honour at a dinner hosted by the London Chamber of Commerce. Conscious that Rhodes had been briefing against him in the Cape, and aware that Rhodes was not yet well known in London, Warren took the opportunity of this high-profile meeting in the City to 'put the record straight'. He was careful to praise the High Commissioner, Sir Hercules Robinson, to the extent of crediting him with 'preventing the filibusters from swallowing up the lands of the natives from 1882 to 1884', when, in fact, Robinson had conspicuously done nothing of the sort.

Turning to Cecil Rhodes, Warren carefully placed him at the heart of any disagreement between himself, the High Commissioner and Cape Ministers. Rhodes had accused him of reneging on his agreement with van Niekerk; but Warren pointed out that 'Mr Rhodes's agreement was of fictitious nature', being made with the Stellalanders of the Transvaal, not with the Stellalanders of Bechuanaland, and therefore 'did not require endorsing'. He held Rhodes responsible for turning the Afrikaners of the Cape Parliament against him, and he was full of apprehension for the fate of 'the natives' of Southern Bechuanaland if their new Crown Colony were annexed by the Cape.[533] Warren's worst fears were in due course realised when, within fifteen months of being annexed by the Cape in 1895, 'the natives' of Southern Bechuanaland

---

[533] *Royal Engineers Journal*, 2 November 1885, p 255.

rose in rebellion.[534] Warren expressed similar sentiments at his other public engagements.

The success of the Bechuanaland expedition had made Sir Charles Warren 'one of the most distinguished and popular personalities of the moment for platform speeches, prize-givings, and so forth'.[535] He had clearly 'arrived' as a prominent national figure, more so even than when he was celebrated as 'Jerusalem Warren' in the 1870s. He was now a returning hero, seen in many eyes, including his own, as having scored a bloodless victory over the Transvaal Boers, just four years after the bloody humiliation of Majuba Hill.

He found himself courted by leading politicians and in the first week of November 1885 he was asked by the Liberals to stand as a candidate for the new parliamentary seat of Sheffield Hallam. Hitherto Sheffield had been a single, two-member borough, but the recent rapid growth of 'the steel city' had led to its division in May 1885 into five single-member wards. The general election in the autumn of that year was the first under the Representation of the People Act of 1884 (the 'Third Reform Act') which had extended the vote to 60 per cent of adult males. Warren's opponent would be the sitting Conservative MP, Charles Stuart-Wortley, who had the advantage of already being well known in the constituency. But there was now a whole new electorate and a feeling afoot that this was the beginning of a new era.

Warren had resigned his post at Chatham in order to lead the Bechuanaland Expedition. He was now on a colonel's half pay, possibly a little vexed at not being confirmed in his field rank of Major-General. He saw no immediate prospect of military employment, and was perhaps flattered by the invitation from the party of William Ewart Gladstone. He accepted with barely a second thought. He insisted, however, on standing as an Independent Liberal, for he did not like the party system. He felt it placed too great a restriction upon the judgement of individual MPs. He accepted no party funds and campaigned entirely at his own expense.

The election was scheduled for 24 November 1885, just three weeks hence, so there was no time to be lost. Warren threw himself into the campaign with his usual enthusiasm for a new challenge. He printed an election address, which made no reference to Gladstone or the Liberal Party's official policies. He preferred to lay out his own liberal principles.

---

[534] See Shillington, *Luka Jantjie*, pp 182–285.
[535] *RE Journal*, 2 November 1885, p 255.

He placed great emphasis upon education. The Education Act of 1870 had attempted to legislate for universal elementary education, with the state providing funds for schools in areas where none were provided by religious bodies. The Act of 1880 had made school attendance compulsory up to the age of eleven, but there remained fees and expenses that penalised the poorest. Warren urged that education in the Elementary Schools should be free for all and the money raised locally to pay for this. He believed that one of the principal aims of education should be to 'maintain the moral tone of the people at a high standard'. In this he urged the centrality of religious education, specifically that of Christianity, the basis of his own moral code. This should be imparted in such a way as to 'make instruction in the truths of Christianity real and effective'. In addition he placed an emphasis upon the benefits of physical training in Elementary Schools.[536]

More radically, he called for the immediate abolition of the laws of primogeniture for the inheritance of landed property and titles. He condemned inherited positions and pensions, and urged the reform of the House of Lords, although he did not spell out what this would entail. Furthermore, he called for Government to have 'a fixed colonial policy apart from party politics, and that an Empire Federal Parliament should be formed to strengthen the bond of union between the mother country and the colonies'.[537] Clearly he had in mind his own recent experience of distrust and conflict of interest between imperial policy and that of the local colonial government at the Cape.

Although he was standing as an Independent Liberal, Liberal supporters in the Hallam constituency organised for him a tight schedule of meetings and public speeches. No sooner had he started his campaign, however, than he was summoned to the War Office by Adjutant-General Lord Wolseley.

According to Watkin Williams, who appears to have had the only extant record of this meeting, Wolseley informed Warren that he was not at liberty to undertake a political campaign while he remained an officer on half pay. In response, Warren insisted that 'he was pledged to his electors; he was sorry, but he could not let them down'. Wolseley warned him that if he did not give up his candidature, he would never get another military appointment. But Warren stood firm. He was committed to his electors and 'he was honour bound to stand by them'.[538]

---

[536] Williams, *The Life*, p 184.
[537] *Idem.*
[538] *Ibid.*, p 183.

Wolseley, of course, was absolutely correct: the separation of military and politics was a basic element of the unwritten British constitution, and Warren should have thought of this before being swept up in the moment and accepting the Liberal invitation. He himself in some of his election speeches stressed the importance of the separation of Church and politics, condemning the tendency in the past for prominent figures of the Church of England to throw its support behind the Conservative Party.

After his conversation with Wolseley, Warren returned to vigorous campaigning. His speeches, as recorded by the *Sheffield and Rotherham Independent* and quoted by Watkin Williams, show a certain lack of focus and a rather rambling style, suggesting that he was speaking off the cuff. There was certainly none of the modern tendency to fashion 'soundbites'. He was very clear, however, when speaking about war, armaments and the colonies. He felt there was a tendency to go to war too readily when disputes could be settled 'by mutual consent'. He must have felt this was what he had achieved with Kruger in South Africa. Britain, he said, was in a somewhat peculiar position, having to maintain an army not only for the defence of the home country, but also for the defence of the Indian Empire and the colonies. He believed that 'the time was coming when we should not require troops for our colonies, but they would help us in cases of emergency'.[539] A prescient observation that was to be fulfilled in 1914.

At the height of his election campaign, he had not only to fight his incumbent Conservative opponent, but also to defend his reputation in the pages of *The Times*, where Cecil Rhodes had published a damning criticism of Warren's actions in Bechuanaland.

Rhodes had arrived in England in the first week of November and was promptly briefed by Ralph Williams on what Warren had been saying about him, in particular his criticism of Rhodes at the London Chamber of Commerce. The two men met at the Queen Hotel in Chester where Williams helped Rhodes draft a response to Warren. This was published over three columns in *The Times* of 11 November. Rhodes's letter happened to appear in the same issue that printed Warren's lecture, 'Our Portion in South Africa' that he had read to the Royal Colonial Institute the night before. Warren's paper was given primacy of place, which made Rhodes's letter look like an ill-mannered criticism of it. Warren responded in *The Times* the next day and thus

---

[539] *Ibid.*, p 186.

began a lengthy public and somewhat acrimonious correspondence between the two men, each accusing the other of misrepresenting the facts. Warren had the final word because Rhodes sailed for South Africa on 14 December, the day that Warren's latest contribution to the debate was published.[540]

While this was going on, Warren kept up his political campaign. There was no single voting day and results were not published in the early hours of the following morning as happens today. Voting began on 24 November and in the cities was generally finished in a day or two; but counting was slow and voting in the remote and rural areas took a great deal longer. As a result, the election was spread over a three-week period and the final results were not known until mid-December.

In the interim, Warren was summoned to Windsor Castle where on 1 December, and together with several other distinguished gentlemen, he was personally invested by Queen Victoria with the Grand Cross of the Order of St Michael and St George (GCMG).[541] This was the extent of his reward for the peaceful settlement of Bechuanaland. The awards that Warren had thus far received are known in popular parlance as 'Call Me God' (CMG, for the Griqualand/Free State boundary), 'Kindly Call Me God' (KCMG, for the Palmer Search-Expedition of 1882), and now 'God Calls Me God' (GCMG, for the Bechuanaland Expedition).

The election results were published on 15 December. Gladstone's Liberals won the largest number of seats, but were two seats short of an overall majority. That allowed Lord Salisbury to continue as Conservative Prime Minister, so long as he retained the support of the Irish Nationalists. In the Hallam constituency Warren lost to his opponent, although he did receive 46 per cent of the 7000 votes cast. The Liberal electors were clearly thrilled that he had given the sitting MP such a close run and they insisted on refunding his electoral expenses. Not only that, but they also presented him with 'an illuminated address and a handsome case of Sheffield plate and cutlery'.[542]

With Rhodes now on the high seas, the Bechuanaland chapter was firmly closed, at least for the time being. Warren was without a job and, as Wolseley had warned him, no prospect of further military employment. For his wife and children, it would have been a rare Christmas spent together. He enjoyed

---

[540] *The Times*, 11 November, 12 November, 26 November, 2 December, 14 December, 18 December 1885.
[541] *The Times*, 2 December 1885.
[542] Williams, *The Life*, p 190.

The Warren family on holiday in Brittany, December 1885 or January 1886, with friends and relatives. Left to right: Frank Warren, with waistcoat and watch chain; Violet Warren next to him; Charlotte Warren looking down; and Lady Fanny Margaretta Warren next to her. Second from right: Richard Warren, wearing a hat; and next to him in the background: Sir Charles Warren.

WARREN FAMILY COLLECTION

dressing up and playing charades, with himself taking the part of some Eastern potentate; but besides playing games with his children, he must have worried about what he was going to do next.

* * *

In the New Year Warren focussed his attention on the consecration of a new Masonic lodge specifically dedicated to Freemasonry research. He had maintained a keen interest in Masonic origins ever since his initiation into the Craft in Gibraltar. At that time there was a growing interest in Masonic journalism, with the *Freemason's Quarterly Review* in publication since the 1830s; but Warren wanted something more. In 1861, as a newly raised Master Mason charged with enthusiasm for everything Masonic, he had proposed to the Grand Lodge of England the setting up of a lodge for military personnel who were interested in discussing Masonic archaeology.[543] On that occasion he was discouraged by the Grand Secretary who perhaps felt that Warren, a newly raised Mason at the tender age of 21, was too young, junior and inexperienced to be taken seriously.

Following his Jerusalem experience, Warren had tried, with the artist William Simpson and the new Secretary of the Palestine Exploration Fund, Walter Besant, to set up a forum for discussing research papers on Masonic origins, but once he was posted to Dover and Shoeburyness, the idea withered on the vine. While he was engaged in Sinai in 1882, however, a group of five Freemasons, all of whom had published widely on Masonic historical research, discussed the idea of setting up a students' research lodge.[544] Despite their range of Masonic experience, they felt they needed a high-profile figure to lead them, and in 1884 they invited Sir Charles Warren, then at Chatham, to meet with them in London.

Since his early Masonic years in Gibraltar, Warren had not joined any further Masonic lodges during his various military postings, although at least one lodge, in Kimberley, had been named in his honour. Perhaps, he had lost interest in Masonic administration, although he was always happy to join the fraternity of Masonic gatherings as a guest. Involvement in a research grouping, however, was something else. The enthusiasm generated at this meeting led to the foundation of the Quatuor Coronati Lodge.[545]

The proposed title of the Lodge was in honour of the patron saints of Freemasonry. These were four stonemasons who suffered martyrdom during the Diocletian persecutions of 303–305 CE. Celebrated in the early Christian Church as the Four Crowned Saints or Martyrs, 'Quatuor Coronati', they were joined in Christian tradition by a fifth martyred stonemason, and four military officers who had also suffered martyrdom.[546] In order to honour the nine martyrs, Warren and his companions gathered together nine Masons, five civilian and four military, who would be founder members of the Quatuor Coronati Lodge.

The founders forwarded their petition for a Warrant of Constitution to

[543] Colin Dyer, *The history of the first 100 years of the Quatuor Coronati Lodge No. 2076* (Garden City Press, 1986), pp 6–7.
[544] *Ars Quatuor Coronatorum* (AQC), Vol I, pp 1–2.
[545] Dyer, *The first 100 years*, p 6.
[546] A. Woodford, 'The Quatuor Coronati', AQC, Vol I (1887), pp 59–60; and Dyer, *The first 100 years*, pp 8–9.

the Grand Lodge in the autumn of 1884. At the time Warren was in the midst of preparations for the Bechuanaland Expedition and it was clear that he would not be available to take up his post as first Master. In fact when the Warrant was issued by the Grand Master, The Prince of Wales, on 28 November 1884, Warren was on the high seas approaching South Africa. The founding members, determined to have Warren as their first Master, decided to delay the consecration of the Lodge until his return to England. Thus it was on Tuesday 12 January 1886 that the Quatuor Coronati Lodge was finally consecrated, Lodge No. 2076, by the Grand Secretary in Freemasons' Hall and Brother Sir Charles Warren GCMG was installed as the Lodge's founding Master.

In his speech thanking the consecrating officers Warren said:

> I have great faith in the benefits that the human race derives from Freemasonry, and I think this Lodge will supply a want that has been much felt. Every Mason has a craving to know something definite about the Craft, and … this Lodge will be the platform where literary Masons can meet together to assist each other in developing the history of the Craft.

And, in the presence of such noted historians of Freemasonry, he observed, 'I am only a novice in such matters'. There would, he said, be huge scope for scientific research into the antique foundations of Freemasonry. Hitherto the origins and history of Freemasonry had relied heavily upon oral tradition. These traditions, he said, need not be entirely set aside by scientific research: 'we have no desire to upset tradition. I am a firm believer in them'.[547]

Warren's claim that he was 'only a novice' in Masonic historiography has recently been called into question, it seeming implausible that a founder of a research lodge should himself be a novice in that research.[548] But Warren was aware that he was in the company of scholars who had devoted years to researching various Masonic issues. His research extended to the ancient temples of the Levant. He had his theory about their links to the temples of ancient Greece and Rome, and in due course he was able to present his paper on 'The Alignment of Temples' to a meeting of the new Quatuor Coronati Lodge. Beyond the writing of that paper, however, he had done no primary research, nor did he expect to do any, and in the company in which he now found himself, he considered himself a novice. In due course, Warren was

---

[547] *AQC*, Vol I, p 7.
[548] Bruce Robinson, *They All Love Jack: Busting the Ripper* (Fourth Estate, London, 2015), p 71.

to serve as Master for a second year, and the Lodge soon began the regular publication of a journal, *Ars Quatuor Coronatorum*, which survives today as a prestigious journal of Masonic research.

* * *

On Friday 15 January 1886, three days after the consecration of the Quatuor Coronati, Warren was a luncheon guest of 40 Cape Colony merchants living in London who presented him with some silver plate in grateful thanks for saving the Bechuanaland trade route to the interior.[549] He was accumulating quite a collection of silverware, but he could not live off silver plate, even if accompanied by luncheons and dinners. Nor could he live for much longer on his reputation as the saviour of Bechuanaland. Although his colonel's half pay had not yet been rescinded, in line with Wolseley's threat, it might be at any moment. But salvation came in the form of a telegram that afternoon. He was summoned to attend the War Office on Monday morning.

There he learned that he was, after all, to be offered another military appointment. According to Watkin Williams it was, surprisingly, on the recommendation of Lord Wolseley himself. In reality it should not have been very surprising. Wolseley probably regarded it as a favour for a fellow Freemason, who was in any case in public favour with The Queen. Wolseley would have felt it impolitic not to have offered something to the hero of Bechuanaland. In line with his earlier warning to Warren, however, he made quite sure that the appointment would not be viewed as a promotion. Warren was appointed Commander of Military Forces and Civil Administration at the remote outpost of Suakin, on the Red Sea coast of Sudan. And his rank would be no more than Brevet Major-General, meaning that he would still be on a colonel's pay. But at least it was full pay.

As he had done throughout his military career, Warren accepted whatever fate had to offer and gave himself to the appointment wholeheartedly. Bidding farewell to his family once again, he departed from Charing Cross that Friday, 22 January 1886. From his experience in Sinai, he was familiar with the route by train and ship, and he reached Suakin two weeks later.

After the fall of Khartoum to the Mahdist revolutionary forces at the end of the previous January, a skeleton force had been maintained at the Red Sea port of Suakin, the only part of Sudan still nominally held by British-occupied

---

[549] *The Times*, 16 January 1886.

Egypt. The town was dominated by the garrison and protected by three forts, strategically placed to the north, south and west of the port. It also contained a small but long-established merchant population that in the past had played an important role in connecting the trade of Berber on the Nile and of Eastern Sudan with that of the Red Sea with its links to Egypt, the Persian Gulf and India. For the past couple of years the victorious Mahdist State had cut off Berber and more or less brought the Sudanese end of this trade to a halt.

For the most part the residents of Suakin, military and civilian, clung to their little outpost and hoped to survive any Mahdist onslaught that might be coming. And to remind them of the precariousness of their position, they were nightly subjected to pot-shots from the Hadendowa, the dominant grouping of the indigenous Beja people of the Eastern Sudan.

The Hadendowa had allied themselves with the Mahdists and had established outposts in the hills to the west of Suakin. British troops nicknamed them the 'Fuzzy-Wuzzies', from their curly hair, traditionally worn long and bushy. It was a name that was to pass into military legend, assisted by the ballads of Rudyard Kipling. To the wider British military they were known as 'the dervishes', from an ascetic Sufi Muslim sect that was widespread in the region. The British classed them 'religious fanatics' because of their willingness to die in battle and never surrender. On the same basis, British military regiments could well have been termed 'imperial fanatics'. The Hadendowa were led by the notorious Sudanese slave trader Osman Digna ('Uthman abu Bakr Diqna') who was believed to have been born in Suakin.

For Warren the Suakin posting was no sinecure. He was not going to sit in this backwater and be thankful that he had military employment. He would make his mark, even here. He set himself two tasks: to strengthen the garrison enough to enable it to drive back the enemy; and to strengthen the civilian government by re-establishing Suakin as an important centre of Red Sea trade. He decided the troops needed reorganising. They consisted of three nationalities: a detachment of British Cavalry, a troop of Egyptian Mounted Infantry and, from India, a detachment of Madras Cavalry. Each worked to its own set of regulations. In his first days in the post, Warren drew up a single set of regulations, to be observed by all three military units, and he then set about using his troops as a united force to drive back the Hadendowa and thus end the nightly rifle fire that was undermining troop morale and unnerving the civilian residents of Suakin.

The local Beja of the immediate hinterland had used to profit from the Red Sea trade, selling cattle, camels and goats in exchange for guns and other modern essentials of the desert. They resented Hadendowa interference in the region, and Warren found that they would be prepared to assist in any action that might drive back the Hadendowa and lead to the restoration of their trade. These local Beja were known in simplistic British colonial terminology as 'friendlies'.

By Saturday 13 February 1886 Warren, who had only been at the garrison for a week, was ready for action. He assembled 270 local Beja on rising ground at the westernmost fort in front of Suakin. Most were on foot, but a few were on horseback and 50 rode camels. He placed them in the vanguard, under the command of Sheikh Mahmoud Ali. When Warren gave the signal, the mounted Beja advanced rapidly through the bush, followed at a fast pace by their infantry. Warren followed with a second attacking wave consisting of the Egyptian Mounted Infantry and the Madras Cavalry. He left the British Cavalry to guard his rear and protect Suakin. He believed that it was important that the Beja lead the attack so that to them would go the honour of victory.

The advance went according to plan. The mounted Beja reached the Hadendowa camp fifteen kilometres from Suakin undetected and caught them unawares. But the Hadendowa, who were superior in numbers, rallied and drove back the mounted men onto their advancing infantry. They had begun to press back the whole line when Warren, who had arrived on the scene, brought into the action two small field guns as well as the Egyptian Mounted Infantry and the Madras Cavalry.

> The 'friendlies', seeing that they were supported, made a fresh charge, and the rebels were dispersed, leaving some twenty men killed. The 'friendlies' lost two killed and three wounded.[550]

After the battle Mahmoud Ali's men rounded up 306 Hadendowa camels and 31 cattle which Warren allowed them to keep as a reward for their services.[551]

Warren was satisfied that, with the local Beja emboldened by their success, the Hadendowa had been taught not to interfere in the affairs of the coastal region. He began, somewhat ambitiously, to plan the opening of trading links as far as Berber on the Nile. He believed that the restoration of 'normal' trading relations would help break down the Mahdists' hostile instincts. In the meantime he visited the small Red Sea ports north and south of Suakin where

---

[550] Williams, *The Life*, pp 192–3, quoting from an unnamed contemporary newspaper report.
[551] *The Times*, 15 February 1886.

he encouraged the re-establishment of salt works and other industries. He believed that this would invigorate their commercial prosperity, and thereby the economic and political stability, of the whole region. He informed the authorities in Cairo what he was doing, expecting to get their enthusiastic support, but he got no reply. According to Williams, he soon discovered that 'they did not wish to encourage trade by Suakin, as it would reduce that going through Cairo'.[552]

There seemed little more that Warren could do to enliven his remote posting when on 13 March he was rescued from potential boredom by a telegram from the Home Secretary. He was being offered the appointment of Commissioner of the Metropolitan Police.[553] In his customary style, without a second thought, he accepted the appointment that fate had thrust upon him.

Warren had made quite an impact in the five weeks he had spent at Suakin, and on announcing his departure, he received a grateful address from the merchants of the town who appreciated the efforts he had made to increase their security and revive the coastal and interior trade.[554] He left for England the next day to take up an appointment that would present him with one of the greatest challenges of his professional career.

[552] Williams, *The Life*, p 193.
[553] Contemporary documents often referred to the post as 'Chief Commissioner', when it was officially, simply 'Commissioner', there being only one. Originally, when the police force had been set up by Robert Peel in 1828, there had been two Commissioners and it may have been from this that the prefix 'Chief' was customarily added when there was only one Commissioner, but several Assistant Commissioners.
[554] Williams, *The Life*, p 193.

CHAPTER 16
Constabulary Duty[555]

On 29 March 1886, just two weeks after leaving Suakin, Sir Charles Warren arrived at Dover by special steamer. He docked at 9.15 am, just in time to catch the 9.30 train to Charing Cross.[556] He reported immediately to the Home Office where he met the new Secretary of State, Hugh Childers.

The Government had changed hands during Warren's brief absence from the country. The minority Conservative Government had been defeated in the House of Commons and without an election Gladstone had returned as Liberal Prime Minister on 1 February 1886. This time, Gladstone had the support of Charles Stewart Parnell's Irish Parliamentary Party, for he had committed himself to Irish Home Rule. On 6 February he appointed Hugh Childers Home Secretary. Childers had been Secretary of State for War (1880–82) during the occupation of Egypt and was thus familiar with Warren's search for Professor Palmer and the hunting down of his killers. He had also recently served as Chancellor of the Exchequer; but he had no experience of the Home Office.

Childers' first day at work had been an inauspicious one. It was Monday 8 February 1886. He arrived at his office at 11.00 am for an introductory meeting with his Permanent Under-Secretary Godfrey Lushington and the Commissioner of the Metropolitan Police, Sir Edmund Henderson. During the meeting Childers received a note from his wife from their home in Piccadilly reporting that there had been some smashing of windows in the street – 'Our windows have escaped, but those of our neighbours have suffered,' she reported.[557]

Commissioner Henderson was aware that a public meeting had been called in Trafalgar Square; but it had been twenty years since there had been

---

[555] From Gilbert and Sullivan's *The Pirates of Penzance* (1879/80): 'When constabulary duty's to be done, to be done, A policeman's lot is not a happy one, happy one' (www. gilbertandsullivanarchive.org/pirates/web-op, accessed 31 August 2016).

[556] *The Times*, 30 March 1886.

[557] Lt. Colonel Spencer Childers RE, *The Life and Correspondence of The Rt. Hon. Hugh C. E. Childers* (Murray, London, 1901), p 238.

any serious disturbance in Central London. He was confident the police could handle any difficulty and he continued his meeting with Childers at the Home Office. The Commissioner was thus out of touch with his force when the two rival meetings of the London United Workmen's Committee and the Social Democratic Federation (SDF) gave way to rioting. Both gatherings had been called to protest against high levels of unemployment, and were possibly deliberately timed to coincide with Childers' first day in office.

After fiery speeches in the Square, the SDF were persuaded by the police to lead their supporters to Hyde Park and a crowd of up to 5000 proceeded along Pall Mall and through St James's where they responded to insults hurled at them from the Carlton Club by smashing the windows of London's most prestigious clubs, and what had started as a peaceful protest now became a full-scale riot.[558] After gathering in Hyde Park, the protesters marched down Oxford Street, smashing more windows and looting shops.[559]

74-year-old District Superintendent Robert Walker, whom Henderson had left in charge, was isolated in Trafalgar Square where, in civilian clothes, he had his pockets picked.[560] To add to the humiliation, the police reserve of over 500 men had been misdirected to 'The Mall' where they stood idly guarding Buckingham Palace while windows were being broken half a mile away in 'Pall Mall'. There was huge material damage, and after the rioters were eventually dispersed, Mayfair looked like a war zone. The next day and all that week the newspapers resorted to their default position and blamed the police.

Childers hastily set up a committee of inquiry, 'most improperly chaired by himself'.[561] The satirical magazine, *Punch*, which had published a cartoon of Sir Edmund Henderson asleep in his office above the caption 'The Great Unemployed', commented, 'We trust Mr CHILDERS will be afforded every opportunity of sitting on himself'.[562]

The committee assembled the following Monday and after four days the chairman reported to himself at the Home Office that the main fault lay with

[558] Sean Creighton, 'From Revolution to New Unionism: The impact of 'Bloody Sunday' on the Development of John Burns' Politics', in Keith Flett (ed.) *A History of Riots* (Cambridge Scholars Publishing, Newcastle, 2015), p 16.

[559] Douglas G. Browne, *The Rise of Scotland Yard: A History of the Metropolitan Police* (Harrap, London, 1956), pp 199–200; and David Ascoli, *The Queen's Peace: The Origins and Development of the Metropolitan Police, 1829–1979* (Hamilton, London, 1979), pp 155–6.

[560] Ascoli, *The Queen's Peace*, p 156.

[561] *Idem.*

[562] *Punch*, 20 February 1886, pp 91 and 102.

"THE GREAT UNEMPLOYED."

(The Chief Commissioner of Police, Feb. 8, 1886, the first Day of the Rioting.)

Cartoon of Metropolitan Police Commissioner Sir Edmund Henderson, asleep while rioting takes place outside the window. Punch, *20 February 1886.*

the lack of proper organisation and communication between senior police officers. According to his son Spencer Childers, writing in 1901: 'Police stations were not connected, as they ought to have been by electric telegraph or telephone.... Had Mr Childers' advice early in 1880 been acted on, these electric communications would long before 1886 have been properly installed; and that would have made the extension of the riot impossible'.[563] Apart from the fact that the telephone was only just beginning to come into

[563] Childers, *The Life of Childers*, p 238.

public use in the early to mid-1880s, the son was determined to establish that no blame could be attached to his father or the Home Office. He appears to have overlooked the fact that Childers had been Chancellor of the Exchequer for four years between 1882 and 1885 – plenty of time to have funded these reforms.

While giving evidence to the committee, Commissioner Henderson saw which way the inquiry was going and that he was to be made the scapegoat. To save his reputation after seventeen years of good service, he resigned immediately, leaving Childers to cast around for a replacement while the inquiry was still sitting. On the last day of the inquiry, Thursday 18 February, Childers wrote to his son Francis:

> I offered the Chief Commissionership first to Sir Redvers Buller, and Lord Charles Beresford, but they in turn declined it. I have not had any other important H.O. business.[564]

Meanwhile, Godfrey Lushington, Permanent Under-Secretary at the Ministry, was anxious to protect the reputation of the Home Office. He wrote a critically important memorandum in which he warned Childers that he must disabuse the public of the notion that the Home Office was in any way responsible for 'Police Orders, detailing Police arrangements for the maintenance of order at public meetings'. That responsibility lay fully with the Commissioner and not with the Secretary of State. The Commissioner, wrote Lushington, issues orders on his sole authority and sends copies to the Home Office 'for record only'.

> It is essential that the Commissioner should feel that he has a free hand, that he must rely solely upon himself, and be exclusively responsible for the result.[565]

It was a position that Lushington was quick to reverse when Warren, as Commissioner, tried exercising just such a 'free hand'; but it is important to bear in mind that this emphasis upon the independence of the Commissioner was the attitude imparted to Childers, and thus to Warren, at the time of the latter's appointment.

---

[564] *Ibid.*, p 241. Buller had just been promoted Major-General, was in Ireland at the time, and had a promising military career ahead of him without getting into what was widely perceived to be a dead-end job at Scotland Yard. Beresford was a popular naval captain and MP for Marylebone East.
[565] Childers, *The Life of Childers*, pp 242–3.

Lushington went on to advise Childers on the sort of person he should be looking for as Commissioner of the Metropolitan Police:

> What has to be done is to make a quasi-military arrangement for the preservation of order. The Commissioner is usually a soldier; at all events accustomed to handle [*sic*] bodies of men. He has experience of dealing with crowds ... [566]

Over the following three weeks Childers approached some other unnamed candidates, but none was willing to sup from the poisoned chalice. The one man locally available who would have been prepared to accept it, indeed expected to get it, was the head of the Criminal Investigation Department (CID), Assistant Commissioner James Monro. He was the most experienced police officer of his rank in the Metropolitan Police, although most of that experience, until his appointment to the CID in 1884, had been in India, which may have prejudiced some minds against him. In any case, in light of the February riot, Childers favoured a military man for the post.

On 13 March he alighted on Sir Charles Warren, who suddenly seemed the obvious man for the job. He fitted the requirements as laid down by Lushington, and, what is more, isolated as he was in Suakin, Warren was only too pleased to accept the challenge.

Warren's appointment received a warm welcome from *The Times*. The recent Bechuanaland Expedition had demonstrated his 'capacity and power of organisation and resolve in the face of difficulties'; but the paper considered that the good work he had done before that in South Africa, 'civil and quasi-military', made him even more 'directly qualified for the Chief Commissioner's Office'. And that was not forgetting the satisfactory resolution of the Palmer case in Sinai. In the opinion of *The Times*:

> If we are to have a soldier as Chief Commissioner of Police, no better choice could have been made than of a man of the wide and varied experience which Sir Charles Warren has gone through.[567]

Even that bane of the Metropolitan Police, *The Pall Mall Gazette*, welcomed the appointment of such 'a stern, just, incorruptible, religious man'.[568]

Warren's honeymoon with the popular press, however, was destined to be

---

[566] *Idem.*
[567] *The Times*, 17 March 1886.
[568] Ascoli, *The Queen's Peace*, fn 1, p 160.

short-lived as *The Pall Mall Gazette,* in particular, soon resorted to its default mode of open hostility to the police. The public attitude towards the police, as expressed through the popular press, was that they indulged in unwarranted interference in people's private lives, an attitude with which Warren in fact had some sympathy.

* * *

After his initial meeting at the Home Office, Warren had two days to spend with his family at their home in Wimbledon before taking up his duties as Commissioner on Wednesday 31 March 1886. It was probably around this time that Warren and his family moved house from Wimbledon to take up residence at 14 St George Street, Belgravia, in the fashionable West End of London.[569] In the meantime, for his first day at work he is likely to have commuted from Wimbledon by train, arriving at Charing Cross station, near the south-east corner of Trafalgar Square.

From there he would have taken a short walk down Whitehall, past an archway on the left that led into Great Scotland Yard, and taken the next left into Whitehall Place. His office was on the left at No. 4, a three-storey Georgian building, formerly a private residence, but converted, together with the building next door, into the offices of the Metropolitan Police. The rear of No. 4 had been extended back, via labyrinthine passages into an adjoining building in Great Scotland Yard. Here there was a divisional police station which in effect formed the back entrance to the Metropolitan Police offices. It also contained the head office of the CID. Unless they had come to meet the Commissioner or one of his Assistants, the general public wishing to contact the police used this back entrance in Great Scotland Yard, and thus the whole headquarters of the Metropolitan Police became known in the public mind as 'Scotland Yard'.[570] Sometime after the move in 1890 to the new premises of 'New Scotland Yard' on the Victoria Embankment overlooking the Thames, the old buildings of Great Scotland Yard and Whitehall Place were demolished and completely rebuilt. No. 4 no longer exists, but a blue plaque on the wall of No. 3 Whitehall Place indicates where the original headquarters of 'Scotland Yard' were situated.

[569] http://www.ghgraham.org/charleswarren1840.html, accessed 14 July 2016: 1891 *Census*, RG12-74.
[570] C. T. Clarkson and J. Hall Richardson, *Police!* (Leadenhall Press, London, 1889), pp 127, 133. There had originally been a medieval palace on this site, built for the Kings of Scotland for those rare occasions when they came to pay homage to the Kings of England.

SIR C. WARREN,
UNDER THE CHIMNEY-POT.

Commissioner Warren designed his own uniform of dark blue tunic and chimney-pot hat, the latter so he would be easily seen and identified.
FROM THE WARREN FAMILY SCRAPBOOK

Warren's relations with the Home Office were destined to be fractious from the start. This was not helped by the fact that three months after he began work as Commissioner, the Gladstone Government fell and Childers was replaced by the Conservative Home Secretary Henry Matthews. Most historians of the Metropolitan Police of this era place the blame for the subsequent bad relationship between the Commissioner and the Home Office upon Warren who, they point out, was a military man, not a policeman.[571] Historian of the Metropolitan Police David Ascoli took this further with his opinion that much of the fault for Warren's fractious relationship with the Home Office lay with his 'abrasive … arrogant and opinionated' character.[572]

Furthermore, Ascoli claims that Warren wrongly assumed his role was 'to reorganize and re-inspire a demoralized public institution'.[573] But this was exactly the role that was expected from Warren when he was first appointed. Even *The Times*, in welcoming news of Warren's appointment, had observed that 'in no safer hands could the promised reorganisation of the London police be placed'.[574] And within days of Warren's taking up his post, Home Secretary Childers set up a special committee, of which the new Commissioner was a member, to consider what administrative reforms should take place within the Metropolitan Police in order to rectify the organisational shortcomings identified by the previous committee.[575] Indeed, once Warren got going on his reforms of the police, the fact that he was not a professional policeman could be seen as an advantage, for he brought a fresh look to the service.

When not sitting on that committee and contributing his ideas on police reform, Warren spent his first few months in office getting to know his area of responsibility. The Metropolitan area, originally defined as within ten miles of St Paul's, had by the 1880s been extended to within fifteen miles of Charing Cross. For policing, it was divided into four districts and subdivided into numerous divisions. Warren visited all four districts and many of the police stations within the divisions. Originally there had been a

[571] The idea seems to have been started by Clarkson and Richardson, see their *Police!*, p 82.
[572] Ascoli, *The Queen's Peace*, p 158; see also Stefan Petrow, *Policing Morals: The Metropolitan Police and the Home Office 1870–1914* (Clarendon, Oxford, 1994), p 61.
[573] Ascoli, *The Queen's Peace*, pp 157–8.
[574] *The Times*, 17 March 1886.
[575] HCPP (1886), Cd.4894, *Disturbances (Metropolis). Report of the committee appointed by the Secretary of State for the Home Department to inquire into the administration and organisation of the Metropolitan Police Force.*

A contemporary cartoon on Warren's supposed choice for the new Chief Constables.
FROM THE WARREN FAMILY SCRAPBOOK

District Superintendent for each of the four districts, but under Henderson these had not been filled as vacancies arose. By 1886 there were just two District Superintendents and they were mostly based at the Commissioner's headquarters in Whitehall Place. As a result of his tour of the stations, Warren discovered that in some districts little or no inspection by senior officers had taken place for some time and consequently the discipline of the service 'had seriously suffered'.[576]

As a result of Warren's recommendations, a higher rank of Chief Constable was appointed to each of the four districts, with an additional one placed at Scotland Yard. It was recommended that they be of the gentleman class, preferably a former Army or naval officer. Below them the senior police officers were increased in number and a hierarchy of Superintendents, Inspectors and Sergeants was established within each division along the sort

[576] *Ibid.*, p 4.

of military lines to which Warren was accustomed. This gave rise to an unwelcome feeling among the constabulary that they were being militarised.

In order to improve communications throughout the force, the Chief Constables and District Superintendents were tasked with maintaining a system of regular communication between the districts and police headquarters at Scotland Yard. A telegraph system connecting the Commissioner with every police station in the Metropolis had been established in 1867;[577] but there was no way of communicating electronically between police stations within a district or between districts. Warren rectified this, establishing a system of telegraphic links between individual stations and providing a telegraphic code for every senior officer. Warren had three codes: CC for himself, CO for his office, and CX as a spare in case the others were busy. The codes for other senior officers were, where possible, their personal initials.[578]

The Commissioner had 13,000 men under his command and from the beginning Warren paid particular attention to discipline. As he saw it, the main cause of ill discipline was drunkenness. He issued an order that drinking while on duty was forbidden, which caused considerable resentment among the constables. They had been used to receiving free drinks from public houses in return for laxity in enforcing the licensing laws.

Blackmail by police officers, especially in the fields of licensing and prostitution, was a deep-seated problem. This was highlighted by the satirical magazine *Punch*, on learning of Warren's appointment: 'As he distinguished himself in South Africa, it might be naturally supposed that WARREN would know more about blacking than the blues. No doubt Sir CHARLES will deal summarily with the black mail'.[579] It was a problem that Warren was determined to root out through enhanced discipline within the force.

On his first day at work the new Commissioner wrote out a 'Police Order' for the 'preservation of order' on the occasion of the Oxford and Cambridge Universities' Boat Race on Saturday 3 April 1886. The annual boat race between Britain's two premier universities was a hugely popular piece of live entertainment, particularly as it was the only major sporting spectacle that was free to view by the general public. Warren's Police Order placed 754 officers of all ranks at key points along the Thames from Putney to Mortlake. Nobody was allowed on the newly reconstructed Hammersmith Bridge, the

[577] Brown, *The Rise of Scotland Yard*, p 132.
[578] UKNA, MEPOL 7/49, 5 June 1888.
[579] *Punch*, 20 March 1886, p 133.

first of several future upgrades.[580] Since the bridge had just been strengthened to cope with 'heavier traffic', it is likely that Warren's decision to close it to spectators was due to the tendency of some within the crowds to throw missiles down upon the crews as they passed underneath. It is not recorded whether Warren watched the race; but it was described in the official boat race history as 'thrilling' and 'sensational' as Cambridge came from two lengths down at Barnes Bridge to win by two-thirds of a length.[581]

As printed Police Orders were sent out to all divisional police stations in the capital, Warren began to use them as a regular method of communicating directly with the force under his command. He reminded constables of best practice, such as the importance of 'civility' in apprehending suspects. He insisted this be taken very seriously, and its importance particularly impressed upon new officers. 'Forbearance and moderation,' wrote Warren, 'will always be understood and appreciated by the public, the magistrates, and the Commissioner'.[582] A few days later he felt the need to remind constables that even when pursuing people fleeing arrest, they were not allowed to enter private premises without a warrant. Forced entry by the police was one of the greatest causes of public complaint against them.[583]

Rabies was endemic in London, especially during the hot days of summer, and Warren used his Police Orders to call for stricter enforcement of the Dogs Act. Rabid or suspected dogs 'not being under the control of any person' should be seized and disposed of and the person responsible, if known, to be fined up to twenty shillings (£1). Dogs on leads should be muzzled to protect the public from potential dog bites.[584] Warren was to be mercilessly mocked by the popular press for his attention to dogs, to which it was claimed he paid greater attention than to the apprehension of thieves. Indeed, the Warren family have in their possession a postcard dated 17 September 1886 addressed to 'Charles Warren, Dog Muzzler in Chief".[585] Undeterred by the

---

[580] Concerns about the safety of the original bridge had been raised as long ago as 1870 when 11,000 people had crowded onto it to watch that year's boat race. The rebuilt bridge of 1886 was subsequently officially opened by The Prince and Princess of Wales as part of the celebrations of The Queen's Golden Jubilee on 22 June 1887.

[581] G. C. Drinkwater and T. R. B. Sanders, *The University Boat Race: Official Centenary History* (Cassell, London, 1929), p 88.

[582] MEPOL 7/48, 144, 18 June 1886.

[583] *Ibid.*, 146, 21 June 1886.

[584] Clarkson and Richardson, *Police!*, p 254.

[585] Thanks to Isabella Warren, widow of the late Revd Christopher Warren, great-grandson of Sir Charles Warren, for showing me this card.

*Warren came in for a considerable amount of press mockery for
what was perceived to be his obsession with dogs.*
FROM THE WARREN FAMILY SCRAPBOOK

mockery, Warren kept on with the theme in his Police Orders, insisting that dogs should 'at all times [have] free access to fresh water', and healthy stray dogs should if possible be sent to the 'Home for Lost and Starving Dogs' in Battersea where they could be reclaimed within three days on production of a valid dog licence.[586]

By August Warren was getting into his stride. Following public complaint about police abuse of their powers of arrest, he sent out an eighteen-page Police Order detailing revised instructions on the apprehension of offenders, especially regarding when and where warrants were necessary. He also brought together into a single Police Order all the legislation relating to arrestable offences dating back 60 years to George IV and combined it with subsequent Home Office instructions and Acts of Parliament.[587] It was in effect a basic rule book outlining a constable's powers of arrest, and as such it was probably appreciated by the general constabulary.

Not so the even longer document he produced the following week. On 25 August he published a 24-page Police Order concerning the reintroduction of squad drill to the police force, with a special focus on constables in training. Warren believed that drill would not only impress the public with the discipline of the police force, but it would also enhance the efficient movement of large numbers of police in cases of civil or other emergency. The public, however, and the press in particular, condemned it as the militarisation of the police force. Nor did it impress the officers who had to enforce it, or enhance Warren's reputation among the constables.

* * *

The Metropolitan Police had been 'primarily founded to maintain order';[588] and with the riot of February 1886 a recent memory and the occasion of his predecessor's resignation, the maintenance of public order was always at the forefront of Commissioner Warren's mind.

By the time of the first anniversary of the February 1886 riot, the plight of the unemployed and homeless in London, which had been at the heart of the demonstration that had sparked the riot, had still not been addressed and the police had difficulty preventing a large anniversary meeting in Clerkenwell Green from turning into a riot.

---

[586] MEPOL 7/48, 142, 16 June 1886.
[587] *Ibid.*, 196, 18 August 1886.
[588] Brown, *Rise of Scotland Yard*, p 140.

The meeting in Clerkenwell Green, February 1887.
FROM THE WARREN FAMILY SCRAPBOOK

Warren decided it was time to instruct his officers in what constituted a 'riot' and how the police were to deal with large crowds in potential riot situations. His emphasis was upon the dispersal of unlawful gatherings *before* they caused trouble. If a crowd should become large and disorderly, the police were to 'act with vigour and disperse the crowd and apprehend the offenders', noting that 'in a large and tumultuous meeting *force may be necessary* to disperse it'.[589] For a large demonstration in Hyde Park on Easter Monday (11 April 1887) Warren flooded the surrounding streets with 4000 police, and doubled patrols all over Central London. The demonstration passed off peacefully and Warren seems to have concluded that a high police profile was enough to discourage most potential rioters.

He was aware, however, that with large gatherings there was always the potential for things to get out of hand, and he turned his attention to a constable's only real defensive or offensive weapon, the truncheon. These had traditionally been two feet long (0.6m), made of wood and liable to break if wielded too enthusiastically, which they often were. Warren ordered they

[589] MEPOL 7/48, 12 February 1887, his emphasis.

be shortened to fifteen and a half inches (0.4m) and concealed in a special pocket built into a constable's trousers or cape. They were to be made of a much harder and more durable wood and in the light of what was to happen in Trafalgar Square towards the end of the year, it is interesting to note the special instructions he issued for their restricted use. Constables were only to use them to protect themselves from violent attack:

> If a Constable is likely to be overpowered he may draw his truncheon and use it, taking care to avoid striking anyone on the head. The arms and legs should be aimed at to disable a prisoner, as parts of the frame least likely to suffer serious injury. The use of the truncheon is not to be resorted to except in extreme cases, when all other attempts have failed, and a prisoner is likely to escape through the Constable being ill-used and overpowered.[590]

The major public order occasion that he had to anticipate in his second year in office was Queen Victoria's Golden Jubilee in June 1887.

Her Silver Jubilee in 1862 had not been celebrated as The Queen was in mourning for her late husband Prince Albert who had died only six months previously. She had continued in deep mourning for more than a decade, rarely and then only reluctantly appearing in public, and she wore black for the rest of her life. She made a gradual return to public life during the 1870s; but with the popularity of the 'absent queen' declining, the government and palace officials, having missed out on a Silver Jubilee, were determined to mark the Golden Jubilee with a very public celebration. It was proposed that The Queen should host a banquet in Buckingham Palace for the royal heads of Europe on the actual anniversary day, Monday 20 June. The following day she would ride in a procession through the streets of London, ending with a service of thanksgiving in Westminster Abbey. The success of this second day would weigh heavily upon the shoulders of the Metropolitan Police.

The greatest potential threat to public safety at this time came from the 'Fenians', an 'Irish Republican Brotherhood' committed to the use of violence to win Irish independence.[591] They were mostly financed by Irish Americans whose families had fled the Famine in the late-1840s. The Fenians had first come to public attention in London in 1867 with the bombing of Clerkenwell Prison, an abortive attempt to rescue some of their members that left six innocent bystanders dead and 126 injured. After a period of quiet, an

---

[590] MEPOL 7/49, 11 January and 4 February 1887.
[591] The name 'Fenian' was taken from the '*fianna*', Celtic warriors of mythical renown.

intense bombing campaign had begun in March 1883 and had led directly to the founding of the Special Irish Branch within the CID. The following year the CID office in Great Scotland Yard was destroyed by a Fenian bomb.

By the end of 1885, however, the Fenians had been well infiltrated by British agents and most of them had been rounded up in Dublin and in London. But the potential threat remained. Indeed a plot to bomb Westminster Abbey while The Queen was present during the Jubilee celebrations was uncovered in the early months of 1887 and only thwarted on the eve of the Jubilee itself. Ironically, it was found to be a plot devised by a British double agent.[592]

Warren had had several opportunities to rehearse the policing of the Jubilee during 1886, starting with The Queen's opening of the Colonial and Indian Exhibition in Hyde Park on 4 May. For that occasion Warren had cancelled all police leave and ordered 3127 officers of all ranks to police the park and surrounding roads, detailing the exact numbers of constables to be at each specific junction and the positioning of sergeants and senior officers. He also brought in 30 men from the mounted department, a division of the force that consisted of about 1000 men. Until now they had been mostly used for patrolling the lengthy beats of the outer suburbs and this was one of the first occasions they were to be used for crowd control. From January 1887 Warren was to bring many more of the mounted division into Central London where they were trained specifically for that purpose.[593]

By the time of the Jubilee Procession on Tuesday 21 June, the police were well used to Warren's methods. On this occasion 8000 police were on duty. The whole of the month of June had been exceptionally hot and dry and huge crowds gathered to see The Queen pass by in an open landau with an escort of Indian cavalry. The Commissioner stated exactly how many constables should be on every road and junction, where the sergeants should be positioned and how many reserves should be held at particular points. The procession passed from Buckingham Palace, through Trafalgar Square and the City to the East End where she was cheered by an enthusiastic crowd in Whitechapel, ironically, the stalking ground the following year for the world's most notorious serial killer. Needless to say, The Queen proceeded only along the main street, which had been cleaned up for the occasion, and

[592] Sir Robert Anderson, *The Lighter Side of my Official Life* (Hodder & Stoughton, New York and London, n.d., a reprint of a series of articles from *Blackwood's Magazine*, 1909–1910), pp 117–120. See also, C. Campbell, *Fenian Fire: The British Government Plot to Assassinate Queen Victoria* (HarperCollins, London, 2002).
[593] MEPOL 7/49, Police Orders for 8 January, 29 January and 3 February 1887.

Queen Victoria's Jubilee procession through Whitechapel, 21 June 1887.

she saw nothing of the sordid and putrefying conditions in the backstreets and alleyways, among the worst in the capital, in which the people of Whitechapel were obliged to live and work.

The Queen returned through Whitehall to Westminster Abbey where she attended a service of Thanksgiving. Warren was proud to publish The Queen's subsequent letter of thanks from Windsor Castle for 'the wonderful order preserved on this occasion'.[594] A special Golden Jubilee Medal was struck for all the Metropolitan Police to mark the occasion, and The Queen saw fit to confer upon the Commissioner a further knighthood. Warren became a Knight Commander of the Bath (KCB), an order of chivalry that had been awarded to his father shortly before his death.

[594] *Ibid.*, 27 June 1887.

CHAPTER 17

'Bloody Sunday'

Warren's efficient policing of the Jubilee parade may have given the outward impression of contented and loyal subjects of the great Queen Empress;[595] but all was far from well in the imperial capital. There were in effect two Londons, one reflected in the wealth of the rising middle classes, mostly living in the expanding suburbs, and the other reflected in poverty pay rates, insecure jobs, high levels of unemployment and homelessness – the world of crowded slums and the workhouse, where life was short and far from sweet. Those in factory employment commonly worked ten or twelve hours a day, six days a week in dangerous conditions, and all for pitiful wages. The match-making women at the Bryant & May factory in Bow in East London went on strike for better terms and conditions in June 1888 and won their case after a three-week campaign, helped by the socialist journalist and campaigner Annie Besant.[596] Their success provided a great boost to the emerging trade unionism and working men and women everywhere; but the unemployed and homeless had nothing but their visible presence in Central London to protest their condition.

Homelessness in the capital had been aggravated by the transformation of Central London through large-scale railway construction and the slum clearance associated with the construction of major thoroughfares such as Shaftesbury Avenue, completed in 1886. The new roads and railways benefitted the middle classes, but pushed low-income housing out of Central London, mostly to the already crowded East End and left many of the unemployed to sleep on the streets.

During the long, hot summer of 1887, the homeless and the unemployed became ever more visible in Central London. As shopkeepers and private clubs objected to their hanging around and sleeping in doorways and the police kept moving them on, many began to congregate in Trafalgar Square. Here they were able to drink water and wash in the fountain pools, sit on the

---

[595] Victoria had been proclaimed Empress of India under the Royal Titles Act of 1877.
[596] Louise Raw, *Striking a Light: The Bryant and May Matchwomen and their Place in History* (Bloomsbury Academic, London, 2011).

The poor and unemployed, sleeping on the streets of Central London, with (from top left) the Embankment, London Bridge, Trafalgar Square and Covent Garden.
FROM THE WARREN FAMILY SCRAPBOOK

steps and sleep around the statues. The Square was close to Covent Garden where some were able to get casual work podding peas and sorting fruit in the predawn preparations for the morning market, and others were able pick up some discarded food.

The high visibility of such poverty in Central London offended the

BY MATTHEWS' ORDERS.

Chief Warren's got his warrant; so   He muzzled dogs a while ago—
It's now as it was then :   To-day he'd muzzle men.

(See Verses Page 2.)

Cartoon critical of Warren's 'muzzling of free speech'.
FROM THE WARREN FAMILY SCRAPBOOK

sensibilities of the well-to-do. Warren and his police came in for a lot of criticism in the press and in Parliament for not clearing away the 'unsightly masses'. A number of middle-class philanthropists took pity on the poor squatters and provided soup and clothing which, in the opinion of their critics, merely encouraged more to gather. Warren was slow to act. He had no powers to move them if they were not causing a disturbance and within the Square they were not blocking any thoroughfare. Besides, he was well aware they had nowhere else to go. Moving them on from such a highly visible site would merely shift the problem to different venues where they might not be so easily monitored.

By early autumn thousands were gathering in the Square, camping out for days at a time. The socialist political grouping, the Social Democratic Federation, took up their cause and organised demonstrations and processions around the streets of Central London. Warren found himself in an impossible situation. Criticism was heaped upon him by the 'respectable' establishment, but while the demonstrators remained peaceable, there was little he could do. Despite having a somewhat sympathetic attitude towards the unemployed, by late-October Warren was becoming increasingly anxious. The main problem as he saw it was that 'a number of roughs and thieves' were attaching themselves to the gatherings in the Square, their only object being 'to promote disorder for their own purposes'.

Acutely aware of how quickly the gathering of February 1886 had got out of hand, Warren temporarily cleared Trafalgar Square on Monday 17 October, judging the situation to be 'on the verge of a riot'.[597] The following morning 5000 returned to the Square and a socialist harangued them from the steps of the National Gallery:

Men of England! ... Will you be slaves?[598]

He was arrested after a scuffle with police. The Square was cleared again and, despite not yet having the authority to do so, Warren kept it closed for the rest of the week, hoping that tempers would cool. He liaised with the local Poor Law Union who found beds in 'common lodging houses' for many of the homeless. Over the following week and with the co-operation of the police, the Union issued up to 450 boarding house tickets a night for the homeless of Trafalgar Square.

[597] Williams, *The Life*, pp 209–10, quoting from a letter, Warren to Secretary of State, 22 October 1887.
[598] *The Pall Mall Gazette*, 18 October 1887.

The right-wing press supported Warren's action in closing the Square, the *Standard* condemning the 'mobs which throng our squares'. *The Pall Mall Gazette*, on the other hand, pointed out that these were merely 'demonstrations of the unemployed' and should not be banned simply because the better-off considered them 'a nuisance'.[599] The Social Democratic League responded by giving notice that they would retake the Square on Sunday 23 October. Warren, remembering that his predecessor had lost his job when a similar gathering had turned to riot, appealed to Home Secretary Matthews to back him in banning all meetings within a mile of Trafalgar Square. This would keep them out of Pall Mall, Mayfair, Oxford Street and Parliament Square, but allow demonstrators to assemble in Hyde Park. The Home Secretary prevaricated while Warren held firm. He kept the Square clear that weekend and the Social Democratic League's meeting took place peaceably in Hyde Park.[600]

Warren allowed the Square to reopen on Monday 31 October, but kept a number of constables on permanent duty around Nelson's Column, at least two police under each lion.[601] He complained to the Home Secretary that he had to employ 2000 men shepherding processions through the streets of the West End and the situation was escalating.[602] By this time Warren was clearly losing patience and in line with the headlines of *The Times*, he began exaggerating the threat posed by these meetings, referring to the demonstrators as 'the mob'. He protested to Matthews:

> It is the highest degree impolitic to allow a hostile mob to perambulate the streets day after day, even under police supervision … They will soon get out of hand.

And two days later he observed in another memo to Matthews:

> It appears that the Commissioner of Police and the Secretary of State take a totally different view of the state of affairs.[603]

To make matters worse, Warren learned that Gladstone, smarting from the failure of his Irish Home Rule Bill and his consequent loss of the Premiership, had made a speech lamenting that 'the wrongs of Ireland would never be

---

[599] *Idem.*; the *Standard* was quoted in the same issue of the *Gazette*.
[600] Williams, *The Life*, p 210.
[601] *The Pall Mall Gazette*, 4 November 1887.
[602] Browne, *Rise of Scotland Yard*, pp 203–4.
[603] MEPOL, 2/182.

THE TRAFALGAR SQUARE LIONS.

SIR CHARLES WARREN.   MR. HENRY MATTHEWS.

The Two Lions: Police Commissioner Warren and Home Secretary Matthews.
FROM THE WARREN FAMILY SCRAPBOOK

addressed without the use of force'.[604] As if Warren did not have enough on his hands with the socialists, the unemployed and their attendant 'roughs', without the Leader of Her Majesty's Loyal Opposition raising the spectre of more violence in the cause of Ireland's woes. It was only two years since the Fenian bombing campaign had been contained. And still Matthews failed to take responsibility.

On the morning of Friday 4 November a large crowd gathered again in Trafalgar Square. They were addressed from the steps at the foot of Nelson's Column by William Morris, poet, artist, textile designer and intellectual socialist. So far all was peaceful, but then James Allman, one of the more articulate unemployed, mounted the steps and, in his own words, 'went on

---

[604] Browne, *Rise of Scotland Yard*, p 204.

to abuse Sir Charles Warren in the regular Trafalgar Square style'. Interviewed later by *The Pall Mall Gazette* and asked to explain what he meant by the 'Trafalgar Square style', Allman replied:

> Well, using violent language, which is justifiable on the part of the unemployed men who have been violently treated by the police. I talked about that 'arch cut-throat Sir Charles Warren,' who was solely responsible for these occurrences, and said he would not be so successful in bludgeoning unemployed workmen as he had been in bulleting and bayoneting the semi-civilized savages of South Africa … I continued speaking, abusing Sir Charles Warren, when I was suddenly seized by the collar from behind.[605]

Allman was arrested, along with several others and the Square was cleared again. Warren observed that gatherings in the Square and at nearby Charing Cross were becoming increasingly organised.[606]

That weekend Home Secretary Matthews finally caved in to pressure, not only from Warren, but also from London businessmen and parliamentarians, and with the agreement of the Office of Public Works, which managed the Square on behalf of The Queen, he authorised Warren to issue a Police Order prohibiting all meetings, gatherings or public speeches in the Square. It was the Home Secretary's decision to close the Square, but the proclamation was issued under Warren's name and so it was universally regarded as 'Warren's ban'. Before dawn on Tuesday 8 November the printed Order was pasted up all over London. The notice claimed that the ban was motivated by a desire to 'preserve the Peace' and it warned that 'all necessary measures' would be taken to uphold that peace 'and to supress [*sic*] any attempt at the disturbance thereof'.[607]

That evening Warren attended the Annual General Meeting of the Quatuor Coronati Lodge at which he relinquished the Chair following his second year as Master. He apologised for the infrequency of his attendance at meetings of the Lodge over the past two years, claiming pressure of work and adding 'I have had a good many difficulties to contend with in the last few days … in securing the safety of the Metropolis'.

On Thursday 10 November William Sanders, former Liberal MP,[608]

[605] *The Pall Mall Gazette*, 4 November 1887.
[606] Rodney Mace, *Trafalgar Square: Emblem of Empire* (Lawrence & Wishart, London, 2005), p 177.
[607] *Ibid.*, p 178.
[608] William Sanders (1823–95) was Liberal MP 1885–86 and 1892–95.

member of the Progressive Party and co-founder of the sensationalist Central News Agency, gave notice of his intention to test the ban peacefully by delivering a speech in Trafalgar Square on Friday 11 November.[609] He duly appeared in the Square with the Christian Socialist Revd Stewart Headlam, and as soon as he tried to deliver his speech he was arrested.[610] *The Times* supported Warren's action asserting that it was 'an absurdity' to claim that the prohibition of demonstrations in this particular place was a general assault on freedom.[611] *The Pall Mall Gazette* took an opposite view and reported Sanders' arrest under the headline 'Charles Warren the Law-Breaker'. The paper's editor, W. T. Stead, influential pioneer of investigative journalism and founder member of the new Law and Liberty League, considered Warren's ban had created a political crisis. He declared that 'something must be done, and that at once, to defend the legal liberties of the Londoner from the insolent usurpations of Scotland Yard'.[612] That 'something' was to be a large-scale and direct challenge of the ban.

The Metropolitan Radical Association and the Law and Liberty League issued a call for a public meeting in Trafalgar Square on Sunday afternoon, 13 November. It has been argued that if Warren had had a freer hand earlier, he might have 'nipped the trouble in the bud';[613] but he alone could not have prevented the crisis from exploding in the way it did. The root of the problem lay with the Government's failure to heed the needs of the unemployed and the homeless. As it was, battle lines had been clearly drawn and Warren prepared accordingly.

On Saturday 12 November 1887 he issued a further order, which prohibited any procession from approaching Trafalgar Square on Sunday the 13th. He cancelled all police leave and ordered 3800, all ranks, to various positions on the Sunday morning. Half of these were to close the streets on the approaches to Trafalgar Square to all traffic except horse-drawn buses and cabs. The rest were to assemble in and around the Square itself.

* * *

They were all in position by late-morning. The foot police provided what

[609] The Central News Agency was to play a role in the 'Jack the Ripper' case the following year.
[610] *The Pall Mall Gazette*, 11 November 1887.
[611] Mace, *Trafalgar Square*, p 178.
[612] *The Pall Mall Gazette*, 12 November 1887.
[613] Brown, *Rise of Scotland Yard*, p 204.

looked like an impenetrable barrier around the Square and 30 pairs of mounted police patrolled the Square on all sides. The mounted police were not permitted to carry swords, but they were armed with truncheons. Warren himself, dressed in his self-styled uniform of dark blue frock coat and tall 'chimney pot' hat, arrived in the Square at 12 noon, mounted on horseback. Armed with a memo pad and, accompanied by a small team of 'despatch riders', he adopted the appearance of a regular general about to do battle. He sent a memo to the Secretary of State, who was in his office awaiting news. It was the first of a series of contemporaneous memos which provide a valuable insight into Warren's view of events on that fateful afternoon:

> 12 Noon. The police are in possession of Trafalgar Square and all is quiet. A number of Socialists and extreme Radical clubs have announced their intention to march to Trafalgar Square in the afternoon at about 2.30 pm.[614]

Warren's top priority was that 'Trafalgar Square should be kept clear without riotous proceedings' and at 1 pm he requested the General Officer Commanding Troops in London to move four Squadrons of Life Guards with two magistrates from Regent's Park and Hyde Park to Horse Guards Parade, behind Whitehall. There, near the Admiralty corner, they would be 'ready to show themselves in case of emergency'.[615] The cavalry squadrons were fully armed and armoured, with breastplates, helmets and sabres.

At about 2 pm groups of demonstrators began to congregate at agreed points around the city. Up to 5000 men and women, the unemployed and their supporters, assembled at Clerkenwell Green. They were addressed by William Morris and Annie Besant before beginning their march towards the Square, accompanied by the band of the East Finsbury Radical Club. Some were armed with sticks to defend themselves if necessary, but all was peaceful until they turned south into St Martin's Lane, leading directly towards the Square. By this time it was about 3.45 pm and a similar procession from Paddington and Notting Hill had reached Waterloo Place near its junction with Pall Mall, little more than 100 metres from Trafalgar Square. Meanwhile a large number of contingents from various points in South London converged on Westminster Bridge and began to cross the river on their way to Parliament

---

[614] *Metropolitan Police Heritage Centre*: Trafalgar Square 1887, File D769, Commissioner of Police of the Metropolis to Secretary of State Home Office (hereafter 'Warren Memorandum'), 13 November, noon.
[615] 'Warren Memorandum', 13 November, 1 pm.

Street. In all three cases the demonstrators marched into the massed ranks of the police, who were headed by mounted units.

Warren reported:

> 3. 45 pm. Large crowds are now approaching Trafalgar Square and there are signs of considerable disorder amongst them – many of them are armed with sticks and they have stated their determination to take Trafalgar Square.[616]

William Morris and most other eyewitnesses had a very different perception. According to Morris, mounted police rode out from side streets lining St Martin's Lane and attacked the orderly procession. At the same time a large force of foot police approached from the south end of the Lane and 'struck right and left like what they were, soldiers attacking an enemy'.[617] Some of the demonstrators fought back, but the procession as a whole was quickly broken up into small units. Some retired from the scene, but others remained, determined to break through into the Square.

There were similar confrontations at Waterloo Place and at Westminster. As the south Londoners crossed Westminster Bridge and reached the Big Ben clock tower alongside the Houses of Parliament, they were charged by mounted police who tried to disperse them. But the procession pressing up from behind was so huge, an estimated 10,000 in total, that those at the front could not turn back. The sheer weight of numbers pushed the police back, enabling the demonstrators to make their way round into Parliament Street – ahead lay Whitehall and their goal, Trafalgar Square.

At 3.45 pm Warren was confident he had sufficient police to hold the line. Twenty minutes later he was not so sure. The police were struggling at all three points and he ordered up two squadrons of Life Guards to relieve the pressure on Trafalgar Square where a number of individuals were managing to break through the police cordon. He sent a further squadron to Waterloo Place, 'where I'm told there was a serious riot occurring'.[618]

At that moment a group of 400 demonstrators appeared from the Strand and challenged the inner cordon of police.[619] They were headed by the radical socialist and Liberal Party MP Robert Cunninghame Graham and the Social Democratic Federation leader from Battersea, John Burns. Cunninghame

---

[616] *Ibid.*, 3.45 pm.
[617] *Illustrated London News*, 18 November 1887; quoted in Mace, *Trafalgar Square*, p 187.
[618] 'Warren Memorandum', 4.05 pm and 4.30 pm.
[619] Creighton, 'From Revolution to New Unionism', in Flett (ed.), *A History of Riots*, pp 11–37.

Magistrate Marsham and Life Guards arrive in Trafalgar Square.
FROM THE WARREN FAMILY SCRAPBOOK

Graham and Burns were immediately arrested, the former receiving a severe beating about the head with truncheons.

As their leaders were dragged away, the crowd remained defiant, shouting abuse at the police; but they soon found themselves surrounded, 'kettled' in modern police parlance, as the first squadron of Life Guards rode up from Whitehall. The squadron divided into two troops and encircled the police cordon around the Square. The sight inspired a correspondent from *The Pall Mall Gazette* to heighten the sense of menace by commenting: 'They moved like a machine … in the failing light their breastplates suggested, in an uncomfortable way, cold steel'.[620]

A second squadron of Life Guards remained in the middle of Whitehall.[621] At the same time 400 red-uniformed infantry, the Grenadier Guards, emerged from behind the National Gallery and formed a line in front of the Gallery, rifles at the ready with fixed bayonets.[622] The police proceeded to truncheon the trapped demonstrators, supposedly to 'disperse' them, but there was

---

[620] *The Pall Mall Gazette*, 14 November 1887.
[621] Mace, *Trafalgar Square*, p 188.
[622] 'Warren Memorandum', 4.30 pm.

The confrontation at its height.
FROM THE WARREN FAMILY SCRAPBOOK

nowhere for them to go. Many were injured and a number arrested.

By 5 pm Warren was confident that 'matters [were] quieting in Trafalgar Square'; but 'a new mob [had] come into Parliament Street'. They appear to have come armed with sticks, and some with knives. Warren sent the Whitehall squadron down to hold the line, but a police constable was stabbed in the back and a mounted man had his reins cut before the turmoil was brought under control.[623] By 6 pm most of the demonstrators had been dispersed and half an

---

[623] *Ibid.*, 5 pm and 5.15 pm.

hour later Warren was able to report: '*All quiet*'. The cavalry were returning to Horse Guards and the streets were returning 'to normal'.[624]

Some 200 people received hospital treatment for their injuries that day. And in the coming weeks two of them were to die; whether or not as a direct result of injuries they received that day is not clear.[625] But those who had taken part and survived had no doubt: they were martyrs of Trafalgar Square's 'Bloody Sunday'.[626] It should be noted that very few of the injured were policemen, and only 50 people were arrested for 'riotous behaviour' or 'assaults on the police'.[627]

Warren's normal restrictions on the use of the police truncheon as a weapon of last resort, for personal defence and for use against the arms, legs and torso only, had not been applied that day. Whether this was with his sanction, or was simply the result of spontaneous police anger, whipped up by intemperate language that regarded the demonstrators as a 'hostile mob', is not clear. It was at times a straight fight between club-wielding demonstrators, or 'roughs', as Warren would call them, and truncheon-wielding police; but the vast majority of the demonstrators were unarmed and, throughout, the police had the upper hand. They had their mounted men and the backing of the troops. The Life Guards do not appear to have drawn their swords or been much involved in actual fighting. Their role was to intimidate and the demonstrators tended to keep their distance from them. And there were no reports of anybody being seriously stabbed by the bayonets of the Grenadier Guards, although they were said to have wielded their rifle butts to drive people back.

Warren managed the whole proceedings like a general at a battle and must therefore bear full responsibility for police brutality that day. Banners and flags were seized from the demonstrators like trophies from a battlefield. At no point did Warren express any regret about the way the police held the line and one can only assume that he approved their actions. It should be observed that similar confrontations between police and mass demonstrations were to occur at various times in Britain over the subsequent century. Warren appears merely to have set the pattern.

So far as Warren and the police were concerned it was a tough but

[624] *Ibid.*, 6 pm and 6.20 pm.
[625] Mace, *Trafalgar Square*, p 189.
[626] This was only the *first* 'Bloody Sunday'. Later ones include St Petersburg, Russia, in 1905, Selma, Alabama, in 1965, and Derry, Northern Ireland, in 1972.
[627] 'Warren Memorandum', 6 pm.

necessary day's work. They upheld the law in preventing an assembly in the centre of Trafalgar Square. Warren received the thanks of *The Times* and the establishment generally,[628] although history has condemned him as the perpetrator of 'Bloody Sunday'. And that reputation was reinforced by what happened the following weekend.

Anticipating further protests, Warren began an energetic campaign of swearing in thousands of special constables. And with Home Office approval, on Friday 18 November he issued a Police Order indicating that the ban on meetings in Trafalgar Square was to remain 'until further notice'.[629] The radicals and socialists had given notice of an 'indignation' meeting to be held in Hyde Park the following Sunday (20 November) and Warren mobilised 5000 special constables and a similar number of regular police to hold Trafalgar Square and other Central London venues.[630]

After the meeting in Hyde Park many of those who had attended walked down to Trafalgar Square 'to see if Sir Charles Warren's display of strength was really as great as rumour had it'. It was. And as the crowds gathered, no doubt shouting abuse at the police, the mounted officers began charging at them, 'in a fashion,' wrote William Morris 'with which London is now so familiar'.[631] On the edge of the Square Alfred Linnell, 'a radical law-writer', fell and his thigh was crushed by a police horse. He was rushed to Charing Cross Hospital, but died two weeks later.

After two post-mortems and much contradictory evidence, the jury at Linnell's inquest returned an open verdict. To the radicals and socialists, however, he was another martyr of 'Bloody Sunday', and they exploited his funeral accordingly.

The funeral of Alfred Linnell took place on Sunday 18 December. The organisers wanted to start the cortège on the edge of Trafalgar Square where Linnell had fallen, but this was prohibited by Warren. Instead they started in Great Windmill Street, just north of the police cordon at Piccadilly Circus. An estimated 120,000 mourners lined the streets and joined the procession to Bow Cemetery in the East End. The coffin was draped with the green flag

---

[628] *The Times*, 14 and 15 November 1887.
[629] MEPOL, 7/49, 18 November 1887.
[630] Creighton, 'From Revolution to New Unionism', p 22; and Mace, *Trafalgar Square*, p 192.
[631] From William Morris, *Alfred Linnell, killed in Trafalgar Square, November 20 1887* (R. Lambert, London, 1887), quoted in Mace, *Trafalgar Square*, p 192. Income from sales of Morris's pamphlet went towards a fund for Linnell's wife and children.

of Ireland, the red flag of the socialists, and the green and yellow flag of the radicals.[632] A large shield on the front of the hearse proclaimed 'KILLED IN TRAFALGAR SQUARE'. The pall-bearers were the prominent socialists Herbert Burrows, Cunninghame Graham (who had been gaoled for three weeks and had recovered from his head injury), William Morris, Annie Besant and Frank Smith of the Salvation Army. The sixth pall-bearer was the editor of *The Pall Mall Gazette* and bane of the Metropolitan Police, W. T. Stead.[633]

There were a number of demonstrations in the streets and in Hyde Park over the next couple of weekends, but no further serious attempts to defy Warren's ban and occupy Trafalgar Square, and the Commissioner was able to gradually relax the heavy police presence in Central London.

The 'Battle of Trafalgar Square' was, in the view of one historian, 'the most serious public confrontation the Metropolitan Police had faced in the sixty years of its existence'.[634] And yet, in his Annual Report for 1887 Warren appears to have played down the significance of the conflict:

> During the Autumn attempts were made by unruly mobs to riot in the streets and Trafalgar Square, which proceedings were successfully coped with by the Police.[635]

It has been implied that Warren made light of the affair, 'obsessed' as he was by his confrontation with the Home Office and his determination 'to be sole master in his own house'.[636] But the number of times he referred to it in subsequent correspondence makes it clear that the 'riotous behaviour' of 1887 *was indeed* a big issue for him. A prime concern for a commanding officer was loyalty to his men, and the best way to understand Warren's laconic entry in the Annual Report is as an answer to the criticism that had been levelled at him and his men by the press and by many parliamentarians. He refused to be put on the defensive. He did not consider their criticisms worthy of response, and in this case, omission spoke volumes.

The ban on the use of Trafalgar Square for public meetings had started as a political decision, albeit at Warren's urging and it now reverted to being a purely political issue. It remained in force and became the subject of a debate in the House of Commons in March 1888. It was not finally lifted, with

[632] Creighton, 'From Revolution to New Unionism', p 22.
[633] Mace, *Trafalgar Square*, p 193.
[634] Ascoli, *The Queen's Peace*, pp 160–61.
[635] Quoted in Ascoli, *The Queen's Peace*, p 162.
[636] *Ibid.*, p 162.

certain restrictions, until after Salisbury's Conservative Government had fallen in 1892, by the Liberal Home Secretary and future Prime Minister, Herbert Henry Asquith.[637] Those restrictions remain in force today, with no large-scale 'static demonstration' being allowed in Trafalgar Square without prior police permission. Warren's methods of police crowd control, too, have to some extent been followed to the present day: using mounted police to control the movement of particularly large crowds – though without the Life Guards – and isolating ('kettling') those deemed to be potentially hostile to police control.

---

[637] *Ibid.*, pp 195–200.

CHAPTER 18

A Policeman's Lot[638]

During his first eighteen months in office, Sir Charles Warren had not been popular among the uniformed rank and file. As Robert Anderson, soon to become Assistant Commissioner in charge of the CID, remarked: 'The Police cannot tolerate military discipline,' and initially there was 'a dangerous want of sympathy between the Commissioner and the rank and file'. As Anderson went on to observe, Sir Charles 'was not the man to make things smoother in such a case'.[639] By the close of 1887, however, Warren had largely won over the rank and file by the way he stood up to the Home Office when they and some MPs criticised their actions around Bloody Sunday. By the time Anderson became Assistant Commissioner CID at Scotland Yard in August 1888, Warren's 'popularity with the uniformed Force was established'.[640]

For much of 1887, however, and throughout the remainder of his tenure through 1888, his relationship with two particular senior colleagues at Scotland Yard and with senior civil servants at the Home Office was dire. For most of his professional life Warren had been used to being in sole charge of whatever mission he was on. He had been fortunate, like many Royal Engineers, in that he had never felt the indignity of being a middle-ranking officer in a line regiment, with his decisions always needing the approval of senior officers. He had not been 'tamed' by the protocols of officialdom. Now, as he saw it, he had been appointed by Parliamentary Statute and, as such, was answerable solely to Parliament through the Secretary of State at the Home Office. He was thus not an employee of the Home Office.

He was thorough and efficient, and was in sole command of the police. His position allowed him to give full rein to the less tolerant side of his disposition. As a historian of the Metropolitan Police, David Ascoli, has observed, not too

---

[638] From Gilbert and Sullivan's *The Pirates of Penzance* (1879/80): 'When constabulary duty's to be done, to be done, A policeman's lot is not a happy one, happy one' (www. gilbertandsullivanarchive.org/pirates/web-op, accessed 31 August 2016).
[639] Robert Anderson, *The Lighter Side of My Official Life* (Hodder & Stoughton, London, 1910), pp 127–8.
[640] *Idem.*

unkindly, Warren was 'an abrasive character … opinionated, and determined to have his own way', although, as Ascoli admitted, he 'was at least as much sinned against as sinning'.[641] There is no doubt that Sir Charles Warren was intensely frustrated by the feeling that his freedom of action to manage the police in the best way he saw fit was being restricted and undermined whichever way he turned.

It was a period of huge expansion in the strength of the police force, as well as its modernisation with new technology. This was in line with the rapid growth of London itself, from a population of 5 million in 1870 to 7½ million by 1901, as illustrated by the extent of late-Victorian housing in the middle suburbs of modern London. As a result many new police stations were built or old buildings converted and updated. Through all this construction, the annual estimates and choice of contractors were a constant source of friction between the Commissioner and the Receiver.

The Receiver was the man who held the purse strings of the Metropolitan Police. In Warren's day the Receiver was A. R. Pennefather. Like Warren, his office was at 4 Whitehall Place and he regarded it as his mission to control the Commissioner. Indeed, he often acted as though they shared a dual authority at Scotland Yard. Warren's attitude, on the other hand, was that the Receiver was merely an accountant, there to assist the Commissioner who alone was responsible for the smooth running of the police force. The Commissioner was the one who would get the blame if things went wrong. He was therefore ultimately responsible for the correct expenditure of his budget and *he* should be the one who decided spending priorities. Warren felt the choice of contractors for new works as well as maintenance of old should be subject to his approval. In his opinion Pennefather often signed contracts for work that was not necessary.

It was clear that in terms of personality the two men were totally incompatible. Pennefather was no Lieutenant Haynes and could not cope with a man of Warren's temperament. He complained that Warren was 'aggressive'; but he himself could be just as stubborn. Some of their arguments were petty and Warren brought some of his problems upon himself by insisting on having a say in everything, from how to dispose of old truncheons, to the size and siting of new offices in the 'New Scotland Yard' building being constructed on the Victoria Embankment.[642]

---

[641] Ascoli, *The Queen's Peace*, p 158.

[642] The headquarters of the Metropolitan Police moved from Whitehall Place/Great Scotland Yard to this 'New Scotland Yard' in 1890, which was after Warren's time as Commissioner.

Things came to a head in March 1888 as Warren complained to the Home Secretary that the Receiver had 'acquired a control in administration which paralysed the efforts of the Commissioner, and at the same time prevented him for exercising any check on the expenditure and led to extravagance'.[643] The Home Secretary tried to smooth things over by setting up an inquiry into the statute responsibilities of Commissioner and Receiver.[644] The inquiry dragged on through the summer and ultimately settled nothing, for it was found that their statute responsibilities overlapped and were bound to clash when there was a stickler for detail such as Warren as Commissioner.[645]

The situation was not helped by the fact that there was a parallel row going on between Warren and the Under-Secretary of State (today's Permanent Secretary) at the Home Office, Godfrey Lushington, who insisted on treating Warren as though he were an employee of the Home Office. Warren had no time for civil servants. In his opinion, they were there to hinder decision-making and block the smooth running of the state.

His conflict with Lushington came to the fore in the summer of 1887. That July Warren issued a Police Order withdrawing police from watching suspected brothels on behalf of vestries (the Victorian equivalent of modern borough councillors).[646] As Warren explained to the Home Office, it was not 'the strict duty of the police to be taken from their beat to undertake this work', when they could be better employed elsewhere.[647] Lushington saw his chance and sent Warren a memo to the effect that it was not for the Commissioner 'to determine the policy to be observed towards brothels'.[648] A further Police Order, in which Warren codified soliciting for the guidance of police constables, elicited an even more restrictive response from Lushington: the Commissioner had 'no power to issue a general order without 'the approbation' of Home Secretary Matthews'.[649]

This was in complete contradiction to Lushington's previous minute to Home Secretary Childers in the weeks before Warren's appointment in which

[643] *UKNA*, HO 247/12, Commissioner to Secretary of State, 20 March 1888.
[644] See *ibid.* for the voluminous submissions to the Enquiry; and MEPOL 5/306 for copies of correspondence between Warren and Pennefather.
[645] See the report by Mr Knox, Treasurer-General at the War Office, in HO 247/12.
[646] MEPOL 7/49, 20 July 1887.
[647] Quoted in Stefan Petrow, *Policing Morals: The Metropolitan Police and the Home Office, 1870–1914* (Clarendon Press, Oxford, 1994), p 150.
[648] *Idem.*
[649] *Ibid.*, p 134.

he stressed that the Commissioner must have a free hand to act as he saw fit.[650] Warren saw Lushington's position now as a direct attack on his ability to independently communicate with his force. If he had realised this restriction on his freedom to act, he told Lushington on more than one occasion, he would never have accepted the appointment.

In Warren's opinion while there was public demand among men for prostitutes, brothels 'will exist in spite of vestries and the Vigilance Societies, and the more they are driven out of their brothels in the back slums, the worse it becomes for law and order and decency'.[651] Lushington responded that '*public opinion* will not allow the matter to be left entirely alone'. But this was bringing politics into it. Warren was not interested in 'public opinion' unless it affected 'law and order'.

The subject of prostitutes, how to identify them and what, if anything, to do about them had arisen the previous year and on that occasion it had caused huge embarrassment for the Metropolitan Police. On 29 June 1887, the week after the Jubilee parade, Elizabeth Cass, a nineteen-year-old milliner who lived in Southampton Row, had ventured out just as it was getting dark to buy a pair of gloves and to view the Jubilee illuminations in Regent Street. No sooner had she arrived in Regent Street than she was arrested for soliciting by Police Constable Endacott, a man who had a reputation for arresting prostitutes. On the charge sheet Endacott described Cass as a 'common prostitute'.[652]

Cass denied the charge and at Marlborough Police Court the next day her landlady Mrs Bowman vouched that she was 'a respectable girl'. Magistrate Newman was obliged to acquit, but he then compounded the injury to Cass's reputation by issuing her with a formal caution not to walk alone in Regent Street at night or face a fine or imprisonment. In doing so he confirmed a widespread belief among 'the respectable classes' that an unaccompanied woman on the street at night was by definition a prostitute, making it clear he did not believe the witness.[653]

The case was raised in Parliament; even The Queen showed an interest in support of Elizabeth Cass; and *The Pall Mall Gazette* enjoyed mocking the police.[654] Under pressure from the Lord Chancellor, Warren set up an inquiry

[650] Childers, *The Life of Childers*, pp 242–3. See above, Chapter 16, p 282 for the circumstances under which Lushington expressed a contrary opinion.
[651] Petrow, *Policing Morals*, pp 150–1.
[652] *Lloyd's Weekly Newspaper*, Sunday 25 July 1887.
[653] *Idem.*
[654] *The Pall Mall Gazette*, 21 July 1887.

at Scotland Yard which found in favour of Cass.[655] Endacott was made the scapegoat for the Met's embarrassment. He was suspended and charged with perjury, although the case against him was eventually dropped and he was quietly reinstated as a police constable.[656]

On the day of the Scotland Yard Inquiry, which had been chaired by Warren, the Commissioner issued a Police Order which he hoped would ensure there would be no future embarrassments such as that caused by the overzealous actions of PC Endacott. The police, he declared, 'are not justified in calling any women a common prostitute, unless she so describes herself or has been convicted as such'. Although a police constable 'may be perfectly convinced in his own mind that she is such [he should] not assume that any particular woman is a common prostitute'.[657]

The establishment's obsession with curbing prostitution, however, continued into 1888 with the vestries pressuring the Home Office to allow the police to enter and search any house in which they suspected prostitutes may be plying their trade. The Home Office simply passed the matter on to the Police Commissioner at Scotland Yard.

Warren protested that he had 'the very strongest view of the privacy and inviolability [of] every private house'. He disapproved of the principle of police spying. If it turned out they were spying on a respectable house, there would be a public outcry against the police. Vestries 'wanted the police to exercise "a surveillance over citizens which I trust the police will never be able to exercise in this country" and which had no legal sanction'.[658] Vestries, he went on, seemed to want the police to regulate brothels and 'confine them to certain localities … [which was] tantamount to licensing and regulating them!'[659]

* * *

By this time Warren was complaining at a more general level of Home Office interference in his role as Commissioner of Police, and combined with restrictions imposed by the Receiver, he tendered his resignation on 8 March 1888. He was called into Downing Street where he was told that his resignation could not be accepted. It was at this point that the inquiry was set

[655] *Lloyd's Weekly Newspaper*, Sunday 25 July 1887.
[656] *Ibid.*, pp 133–4; and Browne, *Scotland Yard*, p 205.
[657] *UKNA*, HO 45/9964, x15663, 19 July 1887.
[658] Petrow, *Policing Morals*, p 151, quoting HO 45/9678, Warren to Home Office, 22 March 1888.
[659] Petrow, *Policing Morals*, p 152.

up to look into the responsibilities of the Commissioner and the Receiver, and Home Secretary Matthews seems to have hoped that the inquiry would also resolve the issue of the freedom and limits to the power of the Commissioner with respect to the Home Office. As we have seen above, the inquiry resolved nothing. Like so many official inquiries, then and now, it was more of a delaying tactic than a determined attempt to resolve existing difficulties.

Finally, there was an ongoing conflict between the Commissioner and the Head of the CID, James Monro, who was of Assistant Commissioner rank, but refused to recognise Warren as his superior officer.

The Criminal Investigation Department had been founded under Commissioner Henderson in 1878. Sir Charles Howard Vincent had been appointed the first Director of the CID. Howard Vincent was a former soldier and barrister who had just completed a report on the Paris detective department. The new post was at the equivalent rank of Assistant Commissioner. Under Howard Vincent's leadership the Metropolitan CID became a well-organised service under its own hierarchy of control.

There was, however, from the beginning, a certain resentment of the CID among the uniformed force. In the first place they were not subject to the same disciplines as the uniformed constables, and they received enhanced rates of pay. Furthermore, the CID were based within each division, but operated without reference to the uniformed branch, whose officers were responsible for that division. This sense of separation extended right to the top. As Ascoli has observed, the CID 'had always tended to be a law unto itself'.[660] Howard Vincent was an efficient lawyer and Henderson had allowed him to operate the CID as virtually a separate service. And when Monro succeeded Howard Vincent two years before Warren became Commissioner, he continued to run it as though it were a separate department.

Monro had extensive legal and police experience in India, ending his service there as Inspector-General of Police for the Bombay Presidency.[661] When he took over as Head of the CID in 1884, it had been at the height of Special Branch's operation against the Fenian bombing campaign, for which Monro had a special source of funds from the Home Office, outside of the regular Metropolitan Police budget.

Monro may have felt passed over when the outsider, Warren, was appointed Commissioner. It was certainly a wide assumption within the force that

[660] Ascoli, *The Queen's Peace*, p 164.
[661] See Martin Fido and Keith Skinner, *The Official Encyclopedia of Scotland Yard* (Virgin Books, London, 1999), p 168.

Monro would succeed Henderson, and it is clear that Monro was determined to keep Warren out of the CID's business.[662] Even after the downgrading of Special Branch's anti-Fenian campaign, Monro maintained a direct line of communication with the Home Secretary, bypassing the Commissioner. Monro allowed an idea to float around his department that he was protecting the CID from Warren's interference.[663] Monro's *de facto* independence had ironically been helped by a Fenian bomb a few years earlier. The bomb that exploded in a public urinal in the basement of Great Scotland Yard on 30 May 1884 had destroyed Monro's CID offices at the back of 4 Whitehall Place. Subsequently, the offices of Scotland Yard's Detective Department moved to the far end of Whitehall Place and across the road to No 15, physically beyond the direct oversight of the Commissioner.

Warren has been criticised for being 'uninterested in criminal investigation'.[664] This seems to have stemmed from the fact that he failed to mention the activities of the CID in either of his two Annual Reports. It is true that Warren regarded crime *prevention*, through a conspicuous police presence on the beat, as more important than *investigation* after the event. But his failure to mention the CID in his Annual Reports can perhaps be better understood as Warren's response to Monro's conspicuous attempts to keep the running of the CID beyond the critical eye of the Commissioner.

The quarrel between the two men reached crisis point in the summer of 1888. In May Warren complained that Monro had written direct to the Home Office, without reference to the Commissioner, recommending a candidate for the new appointment of Assistant Chief Constable CID. Matthews and Lushington, who seemed to enjoy playing the two protagonists off against each other, replied directly to Monro. Warren demanded that direct communication between Home Office and Monro must end, and in August, to put the pressure on, he once more offered his resignation. Monro, knowing how the Home Office felt about Warren, countered by offering his own resignation. Matthews could not afford to lose both men. At the moment he had no obvious replacement for Warren and he accepted Monro's resignation. This was done without any communication with Warren, a further cause of grievance for the Commissioner, who only heard about the resignation through the grapevine.[665]

---

[662] Ascoli, *The Queen's Peace*, p 157.
[663] Fido and Skinner, *Encyclopedia*, pp 168–9.
[664] Brown, *Rise of Scotland Yard,* p 196.
[665] *The Times*, 13 November 1888, p 10.

Matthews, meanwhile, retained the services of Monro as Director of 'Section D' (Special Branch) at the Home Office, where he had an office labelled 'Director of Detectives'.[666] From there, on behalf of Matthews, he was able to keep an eye on the operations of the CID.[667]

The man Matthews now promoted to Assistant Commissioner CID was Robert Anderson, a secret intelligence officer responsible for running an anti-Fenian spy network for the Home Office. Once more Warren was not involved in the decision. Anderson later recalled that he found the CID at Scotland Yard demoralised by the resignation of Monro, who had encouraged a belief among his men that Warren was trying to undermine them, and militarise them as it was believed he had done with the uniformed branch.

Monro's notice officially expired on 31 August, but he seems to have vacated his office before that date and Anderson unofficially began attending the CID offices in Whitehall Place in the last week of August. Warren came over to meet with Anderson on several occasions that week and this added to the belief in the CID that the Commissioner wanted to control the Department.[668] In fact, Warren was going abroad on leave for the first week of September and it seems natural that he should want to discuss matters with his new Assistant Commissioner, who would officially take over the CID during his absence. He may also have wanted to discuss the murder of Mary Anne 'Polly' Nichols, whose savagely mutilated body had been found at 3.40 am on Friday 31 August in Buck's Row, in London's East End district of Whitechapel.

* * *

There had been two earlier murders of women in Whitechapel that year, the first being Emma Smith, the apparent victim of a gang assault, in April. The second had occurred on 7 August when Martha Tabram was repeatedly stabbed on a first-floor landing in George Yard. Inspector Edmund Reid, in charge of CID 'H' Division (Whitechapel), investigated both murders. An unidentified soldier was the chief suspect in the Martha Tabram killing, but by the end of August both murders remained unsolved.

Mary Anne Nichols, murdered on 31 August 1888, was thus the third victim of what became known and filed as 'the Whitechapel murders'. Following this latest murder, and while Warren was away, Anderson seconded Chief Inspector

---

[666] Fido and Skinner, *Encyclopedia*, p 169.
[667] www.casebook.org/police_officials/po-monro.html, accessed 21 September 2016.
[668] Anderson, *The Lighter Side*, pp 133–4.

Frederick Abbeline from Central Division to Whitechapel. Abbeline had extensive experience of the district, having served as Inspector in charge of Whitechapel CID for fourteen years before transferring to Scotland Yard in 1887. None of the modern forensic techniques were available to the detectives, and Abbeline, Reid and their team of officers focussed their investigations on interviewing known associates of the victims and searching for witnesses who could help build up a picture of the last known movements of the deceased.

Continuity of investigation did not get off to a good start for Anderson was suffering from exhaustion during the first week of September and was ordered by his Harley Street doctor to take two months' sick leave. Thus, on Friday 7 September, the day Warren returned to his office, Anderson departed for a month's rest in Switzerland.

At 5.30 the following morning, Saturday 8 September, a fourth woman, Annie Chapman, was murdered in Whitechapel's Hanbury Street, her body being discovered at about 6.00 am. Her throat had been cut and her body mutilated in much the same manner as that of Mary Anne Nichols. The similar *modus operandi* of the two latest killings suggested very firmly that they were the work of the same man. The police had a serial killer on their hands, one obsessed with the killing and mutilation of women who appeared to be sleeping and/or working at night on the streets and alleyways of Whitechapel, one of the most deprived and overcrowded areas in the whole of London.

Warren appreciated the urgency of the situation. Realising that with Anderson away he must take charge, he sent a memo to the Home Secretary:

> I believe that the Whitechapel murder case can be successfully grappled with if it is systematically taken in hand. I go as far as to say that I could myself unravel the mystery provided I could spare the time & give individual attention to it. I feel therefore the utmost importance to be attached to putting the whole Central Office work in this case in the hands of one man who will have nothing else to concern himself with.[669]

Considering that the infamous murder mystery was to remain unresolved for more than the next 100 years, it seems, with hindsight, an amazing show of hubristic self-confidence that Warren should assume he could 'unravel the mystery' on his own if only he had the time to devote himself entirely to it. He was probably thinking of how he solved the Sinai murders, but there

---

[669] Warren to Secretary of State, Home Office, 8 September 1888, quoted in www.jack-the-ripper.org/swanson.htm, accessed 21 September 2016.

he had been able to arrest any suspect and all witnesses and cross-examine them indefinitely until they cracked – a method then in common use on the continent. But in London, with *habeas corpus* preventing random arrests, and the press, parliamentarians and civil groups on guard against police abuse of civil liberties, such methods were out of the question.

As with modern investigations of murder, Warren appreciated the need for a central point where all intelligence could be collated, sifted and interpreted. Whatever he may have thought of his own abilities, however, Warren was no detective and he gave the job to a man who was. He chose the most senior detective available in Scotland Yard in Anderson's absence, Chief Inspector Donald Swanson. Swanson was given his own office at CID headquarters, down the road at 15 Whitehall Place, and Warren instructed that 'every paper, every document, every report, every telegram must pass through [Swanson's] hands. He must be consulted on every subject'.[670]

Even while Warren was making these arrangements, the press went to town on police incompetence. *The Pall Mall Gazette* that Saturday evening captured the theme most clearly:

> The triumphant success with which the metropolitan police have suppressed all political meetings in Trafalgar-square contrasts strongly with their absolute failure to prevent the most brutal kind of murder in Whitechapel.[671]

A stage play of Robert Louis Stevenson's novella, *Strange Case of Dr Jekyll and Mr Hyde*, first published in 1886, was being performed at the time in the Wyndham's Theatre in London's West End, and the *Gazette* could not resist commenting, 'There certainly seems to be a tolerably realistic impersonification [*sic*] of Mr Hyde at large in Whitechapel'. The popular press in general did not hesitate to publish every gory detail of each murder case, with sketched illustrations, and speculated wildly about who 'the fiend' might be.

A number of additional detectives had been drafted into Whitechapel; but, Warren complained, 'the reporters of the press are following our detectives about everywhere in search of news & cross-examine all parties interviewed so that they impede police action greatly'.[672]

Warren had never had much time for the press. The popular press, as he saw it, besides entertaining the public with a lot of nonsense, was dedicated to

---

[670] *Idem.*
[671] *The Pall Mall Gazette*, 8 September 1888.
[672] UKNA, HO 144/221, Warren to Ruggles-Brise, Private Secretary to the Home Secretary, 19 September 1888.

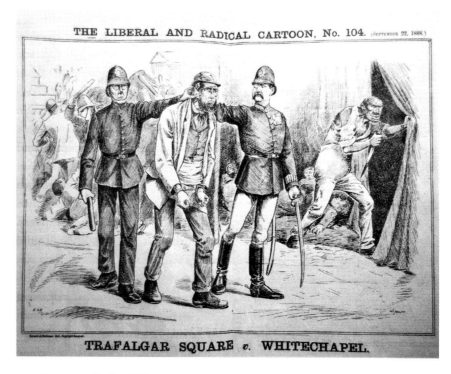

THE LIBERAL AND RADICAL CARTOON, No. 104. (SEPTEMBER 22, 1888.)

TRAFALGAR SQUARE *v.* WHITECHAPEL.

Cartoonists had a field day depicting police incompetence, here showing Home Secretary Matthews (L) and Commissioner Warren (R) arresting a Trafalgar Square demonstrator, while the Whitechapel killer slinks off, stage right.
FROM THE WARREN FAMILY SCRAPBOOK

criticising, undermining and impeding the work of the police; and he ordered his men not to give any information to newspaper reporters. This of course tended to make the press even more critical of 'police incompetence'. Even the drafting in of an extra contingent of uniformed police to double the patrols of the Whitechapel streets at night was mocked by *Punch*.[673] Warren's antipathy towards the press, however, hindered what might have been a more successful investigation of the murders, if every press report of potential witnesses had been followed up.

On 27 September the Central News Agency received the first of a series of letters and postcards purported to be from the killer himself. It was addressed to 'Dear Boss', apparently aimed at the Commissioner of Police, and it was

[673] *Punch*, 22 September 1888.

signed 'Jack the Ripper'. The Agency forwarded the original to Scotland Yard on Saturday 29th and spent the weekend organising the sale of copies to various newspapers.

It had been three weeks since the last murder and the police were no nearer to identifying the culprit; but Warren, together with most of the police, believed the letter to be a hoax. It mocked the police's abject failure to find him and it forecast more murders with the chilling phrases, 'I am down on whores and I shant [*sic*] quit ripping them till I do get buckled', and 'I love my work and want to start again'.[674] Even if it was a hoax, it was a safe bet that a serial killer who had not been caught would strike again. But whether or not it was indeed from the killer, he had provided the moniker by which he would gain worldwide notoriety, 'Jack the Ripper'.

And in the early hours of the following morning, Sunday 30 September, he struck again, twice. Elizabeth Stride was killed in Berner Street, off Commercial Street, at 1.00 am and Catherine Eddowes in Mitre Square, just inside the boundary of the square mile of the City, at 1.45 am. There appeared to be no doubt that both were victims of the one serial killer. Stride had had her throat slit and, although she had not been mutilated like the other victims, police believed this was because the killer had been disturbed and the body discovered just after she had been killed. Catherine Eddowes, on the other hand, had been mutilated in a most savage fashion.

Further drama was added that night by the discovery of part of Eddowes's bloodstained apron by the open porch of a house in Goulston Street. And on the inside wall of the porch, clearly visible from the street, was a cryptic message written in chalk. The writing had not been there earlier in the evening, and with the proximity of the bloodstained apron, the police immediately associated it with the murders. The message read:

> The Juwes are
> the men That
> will not
> be Blamed
> for nothing

Warren was roused, probably by telegram at his home in Belgravia, and told about the double murder within a couple of hours of the bodies being

---

[674] Facsimile reproduced in Stewart Evans and Donald Rumbelow, *Jack the Ripper: Scotland Yard Investigates* (Sutton Publishing, Stroud, 2006), pp 138–9.

discovered. He immediately made his way to Whitechapel, going first to Commercial Street police station and then to Leman Street station where he arrived shortly before 5.00 am. From Chief Inspector Arnold he learned more about the two bodies and the writing on the wall. Arnold had placed police at all three sites and there were also City police at Mitre Square. Since the writing on the wall seemed to clearly implicate Jews, Arnold had sent an officer to Goulston Street with a sponge to wipe it out, but with instructions to await his arrival. He was about to go there now and Warren accompanied him.

According to Warren's own account, he was worried that Jews were being implicated in the murders. There were a lot of Jews living and working in the East End of London at the time, many of them recent immigrants from pogroms in Russia and Eastern Europe. At least one had already been arrested in connection with the murders, but had been released for lack of evidence. In their subsequent reports Warren and Arnold both indicated their fears that the writing on the wall could be the spark that would set alight a fire of anti-Semitism and riot.

A photographer had already been sent for to record the writing before it was rubbed out, but he would not be there before it was light enough to take the photograph. By that time people would be about, preparing for the morning market. Warren made a hasty decision. He could have covered it up and left a couple of constables to guard it until the photographer arrived, but he decided that was too risky. Instead, he made a copy of the writing in his notepad, exactly as it was written (see above), and then ordered it to be erased. He then went to see Colonel Fraser, Commissioner of the City of London Police, to explain what he had done.

Warren was to come in for a great deal of criticism from the press for this action, as it was alleged that he had erased a vital clue in the hunt for the killer. But Warren was no detective. His focus was on maintaining public order and the prevention of riot. It does not seem to have occurred to him that a photograph would have enabled the handwriting to have been compared with that of the 'Jack the Ripper' letter and so have settled the issue of whether the letter was genuine or a hoax.

Hysteria about the case reached fever pitch the following day, Monday 1 October, when various newspapers published the 'Dear Boss … Jack the Ripper' letter.

Warren had 10,000 leaflets published and circulated around the East End asking for information about the killings of all four 'Ripper' victims, clearly discounting the two earlier murders from being his handiwork. Virtually all modern writers on the case have followed this assumption. The popular press, led by W. T. Stead of *The Pall Mall Gazette*, were not assuaged by Warren's leaflets. They had never forgiven him for Bloody Sunday and were out to exact revenge by turning him into 'a national hate figure'.[675] The speed with which the popular press can build up a national hero and then knock him down may be familiar to modern readers, but it was a relatively new phenomenon in the 1880s.

Warren was clearly out of his depth, although he would never have admitted it to himself or to the Home Secretary. Matthews was in fact receiving just as much criticism as his Police Commissioner and was coming under increasing pressure, including from The Queen herself, to catch the Whitechapel murderer. Matthews decided to recall Robert Anderson from his sick leave on the continent and telegrammed him in Paris, where he had just arrived after three weeks in Switzerland. Anderson had been reading about the murders in the continental newspapers, and by 3 October he was back in London where he met for 'several hours' with Matthews and Warren at the Home Office.[676]

Years later, Anderson was to recall that the Home Secretary greeted him with the words, 'We hold you responsible to find the murderer'. To which Anderson carefully and wisely replied, 'I hold myself responsible to take all legitimate means to find him'.[677] Anderson was then briefed by Warren as to what action had been taken so far, including, in particular, the doubling of uniformed patrols at night to ensure the protection of women on the streets of Whitehall. Anderson described this as 'wholly indefensible and scandalous'. Soliciting on the streets was illegal and the extra police patrols meant that 'these wretched women were plying their trade under definite Police protection'. Far better, he argued, that the police of Whitehall arrest 'every known "street woman" found on the prowl after midnight'.[678]

Warren could not accept this. Not only did he believe that prostitution could not simply be removed from the streets, but also the 'street women', as Anderson called them, would simply move to a different district, for prostitution would continue just as long as there was a demand from men, and so long as women were desperate enough to satisfy that demand.[679]

[675] Evans and Rumbelow, *Scotland Yard Investigates*, p 146.
[676] *The Daily Telegraph*, 4 October 1888.
[677] Anderson, *The Lighter Side*, p 136.
[678] *Idem*.
[679] Petrow, *Policing Morals*, pp 150–52.

Warren would also have referred Anderson to the case of Elizabeth Cass, a 'respectable' milliner whose arrest for soliciting in Regent Street the previous year had caused such embarrassment to the Metropolitan Police. On that occasion the charging of the arresting officer with perjury had been a warning to all constables to be very wary of taking any action against street prostitutes.

Warren and Anderson therefore agreed that the only recourse was to warn street prostitutes that the police could not protect them. Double patrols, however, were to be maintained, leaving the prostitutes to act as bait for the murderer, who it was hoped must soon be caught by vigilant police on the beat.

During this time the press, and Scotland Yard, received a huge number of letters from the public, each with its own idea about who the murderer was and how best to catch him. Anderson, writing in 1910, commented:

> When the stolid English go in for a scare, they take leave of all moderation and common sense. If nonsense were solid, the nonsense that was talked and written about those murders would sink a *Dreadnought*.[680]

One suggestion was that bloodhounds should be used to track the murderer. *The Times* and *The Pall Mall Gazette* both initially supported the idea, and the very fact that it was seriously considered for a while makes it clear that another murder was anticipated, for only then could the hounds follow the scent of the killer. A Yorkshire breeder of champion bloodhounds was induced to bring two of his dogs to the capital for trial. The bloodhounds Burgho and Barnaby were tried out in Regent's Park and the initial trials declared successful. Warren himself attended a further trial in Hyde Park and typically undertook to act as prey. He set off at a brisk run fifteen minutes before the hounds were released. After a mile or so he mounted his horse, but the hounds, which were free-running, eventually caught up with him. Warren took this as a sign of success as the hounds had managed to track him even after he had mounted his horse.

In contrast, the press took it as merely another opportunity to mock the Commissioner, wasting his time playing with dogs in the park. Warren ignored his critics, though the cost of purchasing the hounds became an issue. Warren appears to have thought they might be loaned, but the owner insisted

[680] Anderson, *The Lighter Side*, p 135. Anderson was writing in 1910 and HMS *Dreadnought*, launched in 1906, was at that time the largest, fastest and most heavily armed warship in the world. It revolutionised naval warfare and its name became synonymous with anything that was huge and very heavy.

The Penny Illustrated Newspaper'*s view of Burgho and Barnaby.*
FROM THE WARREN FAMILY SCRAPBOOK

on a handsome sale, or nothing.[681] The scheme was dropped when some wise head pointed out the very different conditions that existed between London's largest open park and the streets and alleyways of Whitechapel with the footprints of thousands of pedestrians constantly criss-crossing each other.[682]

A more plausible suggestion was that a reward should be offered for information leading to the arrest of the killer. The Lord Mayor of the City of London offered a £500 reward after the Mitre Square murder. The idea was supported by the Whitechapel MP Samuel Montagu and the Whitechapel Vigilance Committee. Warren was in favour and even suggested the informant should be offered immunity from prosecution. But, despite a lengthy correspondence on the subject between himself and Matthews, he was unable to persuade the Home Secretary to agree.[683]

---

[681] *The Times*, 10 October 1888.
[682] *The Pall Mall Gazette*, 6 October 1888.
[683] *Ibid.*, 2 October 1888; and Evans and Rumbelow, *Scotland Yard Investigates*, p 95.

Despite failing to support Warren on the idea of a reward, the Home Secretary still expected the Commissioner to track down the serial killer, by whatever means possible. There appears to have been a suggestion that the police should conduct a mass raid on all houses in the district, it being widely assumed that the killer lived locally. The politicians in the Home Office seemed unaware that the police had no authority to enter any house without reasonable suspicion that a crime was being committed or that a fugitive was in hiding there.

Warren wrote to Mr Ruggles-Brise, Matthews' Private Secretary, pointing out that as Commissioner he was 'quite prepared to take more arbitrary measures'; but the Secretary of State must take full responsibility, and the Government must officially 'authorise [him] to do an illegal act'. Otherwise he and his constables would be held directly responsible. And 'if we did not find the murderer … [it] might band the Social Democrats together to resist the Police and we might be then said to have caused a serious riot'. With frustration leading to hyperbole, Warren declared that he was not prepared to risk any one of his 12,000 men '[who] might be hanged if a death occurred in entering a house illegally'.[684]

As Warren was writing this note to the Home Office, *The Pall Mall Gazette* reported on a meeting of the Whitechapel District Board of Works which called upon the Commissioner to strengthen the police presence in Whitechapel. Warren had already drafted in as many extra police as he felt he could spare from elsewhere, and he felt compelled to respond to the *Gazette* to try and dispel the commonly held belief that he had a surfeit of constables sitting around doing nothing.

His letter smacks of exasperation at the way he and his police were being unfairly criticised by armchair detectives who had no idea of the difficulties of policing the metropolis. 'Statistics show,' he claimed, 'that London in comparison to its population is the safest city in the world to live in'. It is unlikely that comparative statistics were available, but even if they were, he was indulging in a blatant misuse of a statistical average, for while Central London, the West End and the suburbs where people of his class lived, may have felt very safe, Whitechapel clearly was not. He then resorted to unfairly blaming the victims who 'collude' with the murderer by taking him to a secluded spot.[685]

[684] *UKNA*, HO 144/221/A49301C, Warren to Ruggles-Brise, 4 October 1888.
[685] *The Pall Mall Gazette*, 4 October 1888.

In writing thus, Warren, under pressure no doubt from all sides, was breaching his own code of conduct in assuming that a lone woman on the street at night was necessarily a prostitute. This not only appeared to make it a less serious crime, but also totally overlooked the fact, as revealed by Hallie Rubenhold's study, that most of these women were not prostitutes at all, but were merely down-and-out victims of poverty who, in drowning their personal and economic misery in alcohol did not have the sixpence to pay for a night in a seedy boarding house.[686] In fact the only confirmed prostitute among them was the fifth and final victim, and she was murdered in her bed. Furthermore, the assumption by Warren and the police, press and general public that the victims were prostitutes overlooked the point that street prostitution was by its very nature a life-risking occupation only engaged in by women driven to it from dire necessity; and that it was men, not wanting to be recognised, who sought out the poorly lit backstreets and alleyways of Whitechapel.

* * *

There were no more murders in Whitechapel that month and with Anderson now in overall charge of the investigation, by mid-October Warren felt able to reflect on the current state of the Metropolitan Police. As he saw it, his one failure had been his inability to catch the Whitechapel murderer, for which he accepted full responsibility. But he never directly complained about the plethora of insults regularly hurled at him and he never publicly laid off any blame upon his constables or the Detective Department. Indeed, he defended them in the most public way possible, by writing an article on 'The Police of the Metropolis' for publication in the influential *Murray's Magazine*.

Warren composed his article in the second half of October 1888 and it was published in the November issue of the magazine. It can best be read as his assessment of his two and a half years' work as Police Commissioner. Warren had never intended to make a long-term career in the service, as his two predecessors had done. He had come into the post with a view to reforming the police service. In his opinion that had been achieved and he was now ready to leave. He had offered his resignation twice that year, in March and August, and it had not been accepted. It is probable that, following the publication of this article, he was planning to offer it again.

The article started with a strong defence of police action in the 'Battle of

[686] Hallie Rubenhold, *The Five: The Untold Lives of the Women Killed by Jack the Ripper* (Doubleday, London, 2019), pp 337–348.

Trafalgar Square'. In this he was appealing to his middle-class audience and he adopted the language of the establishment, portraying it as a conflict between 'law and order' and 'the mob'. He praised the behaviour of the uniformed police, contrasting it with the demoralised force that had failed to contain the riot of February 1886. Since that time the police had been transformed through administration and discipline into a force that could uphold the law, even in the face of a mob mobilised by demagogues.[687]

He then gave a brief history of policing in England as a background to describing the current structure, duties and workings of the police of the metropolis. Proud of his achievements, he referred to his two years of 'great labour' that had brought all relevant information and legislation concerning the duties of the police together in such a way that it '[could] be found in sequence without difficulty'.

This was all innocuous enough and should not have created any difficulty. But he then went on to describe his own role as Commissioner and to list the duties and powers that the appointment conferred upon him. This included a long list of regulations that he might at any time impose, and the various licensing powers that he possessed. To the uninitiated, it may have seemed uncontroversial, but to the Home Office it was a deliberate tilt at them and their attempts to rein him in.

With reference to the CID, a subject he could hardly ignore in the light of the still unresolved Whitechapel murders, he stressed his well-known position on the primacy of prevention over detection. This would have been seen by Monro, now at the Home Office, as an oblique put-down of the Detective Department. Warren claimed that the uniformed and plain-clothed police worked well together; but he then went on to write that the 'real' detectives were the public, working in conjunction with the uniformed branch.

The Home Office were incensed. One can imagine Monro leaping to the defence of his former department. But Lushington and Home Secretary Matthews interpreted the whole tone of the article as an out-of-control Commissioner asserting his independence. How dare he publish something about a Government Department without prior authorisation! But that struck at the heart of the whole conflict between them. As Warren had so often asserted, the Commissioner was not subject to the strictures of the Home Office. He did not need prior authorisation for his actions. But he could not have been surprised at the Home Office's reaction. Indeed, he must have expected it.

---

[687] *Murray's Magazine*, Vol IV, No. XXIII, November 1888, pp 577–9 and 589.

Relations between Commissioner and Home Secretary had been becoming increasingly fractious since the resignation of Monro and the virtual control of the CID that the former head of the Detective Department exercised from the Home Office, despite Warren's protests. Indeed, according to Warren, every morning in the recent weeks of the investigation of the Whitechapel murders, Anderson had been meeting with Monro and Matthews in the Home Office while he, the Commissioner, was only being supplied with 'information … of the scantiest character'. The Home Secretary's censure of Warren's article in *Murray's Magazine* merely 'completed the rupture'.[688]

The article was Warren's swansong. Since the Home Office would not accept his freedom to publish without their authorisation, he once more offered his resignation. This time, Matthews had somebody who, from his point of view, was ideally suited to replace Warren – James Monro – and on Thursday 8 November he accepted Warren's resignation. In the event, Monro, who had been heavily involved in the Whitechapel investigation from the start, was no more successful than Warren in catching 'Jack the Ripper' and once he was in Warren's shoes, Monro found Home Office interference intolerable. His tenure as Commissioner was likewise short-lived.[689]

In the meantime, before Warren's resignation had been made public, the Whitechapel serial killer struck again. On the morning of Friday 9 November the savagely mutilated body of Mary Jane Kelly was discovered in her room off Dorset Street. Many who have studied the 'Jack the Ripper' murders regard this as his final victim.

News of Warren's resignation was withheld until Monday 12 November when the Home Secretary announced it in the House of Commons. Not even Scotland Yard knew of it until Warren's personal books and papers were cleared from his office at 4 Whitehall Place on that Monday morning.[690] Senior police officers deeply regretted his going and Superintendents Draper and Fisher led a delegation of them to his private house in Belgravia. From the first, they told him, 'they had felt confidence in him as a leader, and he had reciprocated that confidence'. They knew he always had their interests at heart and that his main concern was 'to render the service more efficient'. In response, Warren told them he attributed his resignation to 'the interference of Home Office subordinates in what he considered the routine work of his department', adding that he had never disputed 'the absolute veto or control

[688] *The Times*, 13 November 1888, p 10.
[689] Browne, *Scotland Yard*, pp 212–15.
[690] *The Times*, 13 November 1888, p 10.

of the Home Secretary'. Referring to his two and a half years' work at Scotland Yard, he felt confident he had put the organisation of the Metropolitan Police 'on its proper footing'. He had made many friendships, which he valued, but he had 'never tried to make himself popular. He had worked hard himself and had expected others under him to do so'. In conclusion he remarked that he had 'never come across a body of men who had better or more zealously and indefatigably done their duty, and he thanked officers and men most heartily and sincerely'.[691]

The establishment press were supportive in their evaluation of Warren's record.

The Times was not surprised to receive the news of Warren's departure, considering that for some time relations between Sir Charles and 'his official chief' had 'not been of an entirely pleasant or harmonious nature'. *The Times* dated this to 'the Trafalgar-square riots', for which incident the paper placed most blame on the Home Secretary. Commissioner Warren 'clearly knew his own mind and how to carry out a definite policy', whereas Mr Matthews 'did not know his own mind and showed no capacity for action'.[692]

The Telegraph took a similar line, reserving its strongest criticism for the Home Secretary. The paper considered the role of Commissioner needed a combination of soldier and lawyer. Warren suffered from 'the defects of his qualities': he was too much of a soldier and not enough of a lawyer. Matthews, on the other hand, was too much the lawyer and possessed nothing of the soldier.[693]

The popular press, on the other hand, had no sympathy for Warren. They condemned him primarily for his ban on demonstrations in Trafalgar Square and his handling of the consequent 'Bloody Sunday'. They also criticised him for forcing the resignation of James Monro as Head of the CID.[694]

Interestingly, although one cartoonist saw Whitechapel as the final cause of Warren's downfall, the contemporary press in general did not use the occasion of his resignation to blame him for the failure to catch the Whitechapel murderer. By contrast, Warren's resignation has commonly been portrayed by subsequent writers on the Whitechapel murders as a sacking for his failure to

[691] A report of this meeting was quoted in Williams, *The Life*, p 225. As such the report was probably drawn from Warren's contemporaneous notes.
[692] *The Times*, 13 November 1888, p 9.
[693] *The Daily Telegraph*, 13 November 1888.
[694] See *The Pall Mall Gazette*, 10 November 1888, quoting the views of *The Standard, Daily News, Morning Advertiser, Daily Chronicle* and *The Morning Post*.

One contemporary cartoonist saw a link between Trafalgar Square, dogs, Home Secretary Matthews, the Whitechapel murders and Warren's downfall.

FROM THE WARREN FAMILY SCRAPBOOK

catch 'Jack the Ripper'. But this is far from the truth, as any understanding of Warren's ongoing relations with the Home Office should reveal. It is true that the press criticism over the Met's failure to catch the serial killer would not have encouraged Warren to stay at his post, but it was not the cause of his departure. The root cause of that lay with the ongoing conflict between Commissioner and Home Office as to who was ultimately in control of the Metropolitan Police.

Historical judgement on Warren's time as Commissioner has undoubtedly been tainted by the infamy of 'Bloody Sunday'. But the failure to identify and catch 'Jack the Ripper' has had far more traction over the years. 'Bloody Sunday' has faded from public consciousness, and been superceded by other subsequent 'Bloody Sundays'; but the Ripper story has been kept very much alive by the plethora of literature on what was to become the world's most infamous unresolved murder mystery. Indeed, all around the world to this day where Warren made an impact and his name is known locally for some local reason, the one thing that people know about him beyond their immediate field of interest is that he was the man who failed to catch 'Jack the Ripper'.

A strange genre of literature, known as 'Ripperology', developed during the 20th century, much of it focussing on the identity of the killer, some of it outrageously speculative. The genre received a huge boost from the opening of official police and Home Office files in the late-1980s. These files, like most of those in the Public Record Office (now the National Archives), had been weeded, leaving no way of knowing what may have been excised. However, a website dedicated to the case has copies of most of this material and more besides.[695] There are tours and walks around Whitechapel that keep the prurient interest alive, and there is even a 'Jack the Ripper Museum' and a 'Jack the Ripper' opera.

In the absence of direct evidence concerning the possible identity of the serial killer, most authors have developed a theory based on a chain of circumstantial evidence combined with much gory detail about the actual killings and mutilations. Few have shown much interest in the five women as anything other than victims.[696] In much of this literature, where Warren is considered at all, he is at best dismissed as an incompetent military martinet, more used to directing troops in Trafalgar Square than detecting a serial killer. At worst, on a couple of occasions he has been condemned for being part of

[695] www.casebook.org, accessed August–September 2016.
[696] The most notable exception is Hallie Rubenhold's *The Five*.

some huge Masonic conspiracy to conceal the identity of 'Jack the Ripper'. A recent book on the subject, *They All Love Jack: Busting the Ripper*, by the actor, scriptwriter and film director Bruce Robinson, places the ball very firmly in Warren's court.[697]

Robinson has argued that his is not a work of 'Ripperology', which genre he mostly dismisses with contempt. His book, he claims, is different in that he finally nails the killer and, by virtue of Masonic conspiracy, explains why he was never identified or caught. The killer, according to Robinson, was the Freemason and music hall singer, Michael Maybrick, who, confident in his Masonic protection, taunted Warren in the 'Dear Boss' letters and postcards that he sent to his fellow Freemason, the Police Commissioner. Robinson finds every murder and mutilation pregnant with Masonic symbolism. He takes particular issue with the spelling of the word 'Juwes' in the writing on the wall that Warren recorded and then rubbed out. Most contemporaries, and writers since, have assumed that it was merely a misspelling of the word 'Jews'. Robinson, however, has maintained triumphantly that the spelling was deliberate and referred to three mythical Masonic murderers whose names all began with 'Ju …': Jubela, Jubelo and Jubelum. These three were alleged to have murdered King Solomon's Master Mason, Hiram Abiff, and suffered terrible, mutilating executions as a result. The mutilations of the Whitechapel murderer's victims were, maintains Robinson, in imitation of this, and as such were a clear sign to any well-educated Freemason that the murderer was a fellow Mason. Warren was thus, according to Robinson, bound by Masonic oath to protect him, which he did by covering up the evidence.

In order for this theory to convince the reader, Warren, on his first introduction in the book, must be severely denigrated. As already noted, most Ripperologists portray Warren as inappropriate for the job of Commissioner of Police: primarily a military man and an incompetent detective. Robinson goes much further. He writes off Warren, the man of principle and duty, as 'a lousy cop and a worse soldier'. He draws the latter conclusion from a brief passing opinion expressed by a biographer of Prime Minister Lord Salisbury with reference to the Battle of Spion Kop, one of many battles lost in the Anglo-Boer War more than a decade later. Warren at that time was made the scapegoat for the loss, but was later vindicated by public inquiry after the war.

Robinson goes on to describe Warren as 'an aggressive authoritarian who imagined all social ills could be solved with a truncheon'. In 1887, according

---

[697] Bruce Robinson, *They All Love Jack* (Fourth Estate, London, 2015).

to Robinson, 'he went berserk on the back of a horse in London's West End, and shafted the riff-raff as if he was up a delta in Matabeleland'.[698] In these two sentences Robinson reveals both his extreme bias against Warren and his ignorance of Warren's life before the autumn of 1888. Quite apart from his total distortion of Warren's behaviour on 'Bloody Sunday', Warren was never in Matabeleland, in which in any case there are no deltas.

Not satisfied with this, Robinson goes further in seriously libelling Warren by claiming that Prime Minister Lord Salisbury, whom Robinson tells us 'didn't have a lot of time for ethnics', recalled Warren from Bechuanaland in 1885 because the 'continuance in power [of this aggressive authoritarian] was a real danger'.[699] The clear implication is that Warren was committing excessive violence against Africans; whereas in fact, as a previous chapter here and any volume on the Bechuanaland Expedition would reveal, Warren was doing exactly the opposite. He was recalled because of his 'overzealousness' in protecting the Africans of Bechuanaland from a South African colonial land grab driven by Cecil Rhodes.

Having decided that Warren, an 'obsessive Freemason', was a ruthless and aggressive man inured to violence, Robinson portrayed him as someone who would think nothing of covering up the identity of a serial killer simply because he was a fellow Freemason.[700] Warren, as a youth, had taken an oath of loyalty to all Freemasons; but he had been attracted to Freemasonry by its code of honour, duty and fraternity. And as a military man, he had also, before becoming a Freemason, taken an oath of loyalty to The Queen. As Commissioner of Police he was duty-bound to do his utmost to protect the public, even prostitutes, for whom he had in fact shown some sympathy. And the idea that he would resign his position so as not to expose himself as the man who had protected 'Jack the Ripper' – while at the same time leaving that sadistic serial killer free to continue his gruesome work – is simply preposterous.

It is not the place here to critique Robinson's argument in detail. That would require a whole book and no doubt it will stimulate other Ripperologists into writing another one. Suffice it to say that his careless and often flippant use of sources does not fill one with confidence when it comes to his arguing

---

[698] Ibid., p 61 and fn.2 p 807, quoting from Andrew Roberts, *Salisbury: Victorian Titan* (Weidenfeld & Nicolson, London, 1999), p 752.
[699] Robinson, *They All Love Jack*, p 61.
[700] *Ibid., passim.*

the case for conspiracy, especially with his tendency to convert circumstantial evidence into proven fact.

Robinson has defied Ripperology convention by insisting that Michael Maybrick – against whom on the face of it he makes a plausible case – went on to commit numerous other murders. Not all police were Freemasons, and if there were a great Masonic conspiracy, it defies belief that the secret would be maintained once the *éminence grise* of the conspiracy, the great protector Sir Charles Warren, had removed himself from the scene. Ultimately, all Robinson's book proves is that the art of Ripperology is alive and well in the second decade of the 21st century.

CHAPTER 19

The Singapore Command

Relieved of his duties as Police Commissioner, Warren was able to celebrate Christmas and New Year with his family at home in Belgravia. Violet and Charlotte, aged 22 and nineteen, respectively, were as yet unmarried and living at home. The photograph of Sir Charles, Lady Fanny and Violet playing charades, supposedly depicting the British Empire, dates from about this time, with Sir Charles posing as an 'Eastern potentate' and Violet as 'Britannia'.

The younger son, Richard, was twelve and probably attending boarding school, while Frank at sixteen had graduated from Sandhurst and was under training at RMA Woolwich. Warren probably visualised his eldest son following in his footsteps, and Frank must have felt under considerable psychological pressure from his high-profile father. It is doubtful that Frank had the enthusiasm for mathematics, science and engineering that had carried his father so rapidly through training and into the Royal Engineers. Nevertheless, he applied himself assiduously and was rewarded at the age of nineteen with a commission in the Royal Artillery in 1891.

Warren's income as Police Commissioner lasted until the end of November 1888. After that he reverted to half pay in the Army. Despite holding the Brevet rank of Major-General for both the Bechuanaland Expedition and the Suakin Command, Warren's official rank when not thus employed was still that of Colonel, and it was at this rank that he now received his half pay. At Army headquarters in Horse Guards, Lord Wolseley was still Adjutant-General and with Sir Redvers Buller as Quartermaster-General, Warren was confident that some posting would soon be found for him, a confidence enhanced by the fact that all three were Freemasons, and he had done a favour for Buller when the latter had been posted to Dublin as Under-Secretary for Ireland, 1886–87.

In the summer of 1887 Warren had been invited to Ireland to address a scientific society in Limerick, a city in which he had spent nine months at the age of seven. In passing through Dublin, he paid a courtesy visit to Under-Secretary Buller at his office in Dublin Castle, the scene of Warren's childhood explorations in 1848.

Warren was planning to spend a week or more in South West Ireland,

The Warren family playing charades with, L TO R, *Sir Charles Warren, Lady Fanny
Warren, Violet Warren (as Brittania) and Emily Carey (family friend).*
WARREN FAMILY COLLECTION

visiting the Lakes of Killarney in County Kerry, and Buller asked him to
make some enquiries for him while he was there. Buller was interested in the
activities of the so-called 'Moonlighters', followers of an eponymous 'Captain
Moonlight' and a reworking of the 'Ribbonmen' of Warren's childhood. Their
agrarian terror tactics had been revived in the early 1880s as a result of the
British Government's failure to extensively reform the 'landlordism' that so
plagued Irish agrarian life. Buller had undertaken intelligence work with the
local Kerry police in 1886 and trained them to hunt down and arrest the
Moonlighters, rather than simply acting as security guards for the property
and persons of the landlord class.[701] As a result of Buller's work, a number
of arrests had been made and the incidence of cattle-maiming, threats and
assaults was considerably reduced. Buller, now somewhat isolated in his

---

[701] Geoffrey Powell, *Buller: A Scapegoat? A life of General Sir Redvers Buller VC* (Leo Cooper,
London, 1994), pp 83–5.

elevated position in Dublin Castle, wanted Warren to find out what he could about the continued existence of secret bands of Moonlighters.

During Warren's visit to Kerry it quickly became widely known that the London Metropolitan Police Commissioner was staying at the Killarney Hotel. With such a high profile, it seemed most unlikely that he would be able to find out any information about the goings-on of a local secret society; but after he had been in Killarney for a few days he received a mysterious message. He was invited to take a boat across the lake to meet someone who wanted to talk to him about the detection of the murderers of Professor Palmer in 1882.[702]

Warren was warned against accepting this most unlikely of invitations, but, recalling that he had risked his life in far more dangerous circumstances on that very Palmer Search-Expedition, he decided that 'Arab laws of hospitality to strangers would hold good in Ireland'.[703] He accepted the invitation and was rowed unaccompanied across the lake. There he was taken to a barn above the lake where a gathering of about two dozen men questioned him about the methods he had used to unravel the mystery of the murder of Professor Palmer. In particular, they wanted to know whether the same methods might succeed in Ireland. It seems they may have been concerned that Warren's presence in Killarney was to impart his particular methods to the local police. Employing his protective principle of hospitality, Warren agreed to answer their questions, but pointed out that as he was a stranger in their country 'they must first carry out the ancient customs of Ireland' and share a meal with him. This went down well and a hasty meal was produced, accompanied by some local Irish whiskey.

With the atmosphere then convivial, Warren explained that his success in Sinai had depended to a large extent upon his knowledge of Bedouin 'customs and laws of hospitality'. This, his hosts responded, would not work in Ireland as ancient customs had so declined that they could not be relied upon either for evidence in court or for the protection of strangers, at which Warren showed his penchant for inventing knowledge of traditional customs and responded that he strongly disagreed, for

> … in that case they would not be bound to give me a safe escort back across the lake. I asserted that in my case they were bound by old tribal laws which they dare not break, for fear of the enmity of some Unknown Power. They did not deny this, and we parted in amity.[704]

[702] Williams, *The Life*, p 206.
[703] C. Warren, *The Significance of the Geography of Palestine* (lecture delivered to the Victoria Institute, March 1917), p 16.
[704] *Ibid.*, p 17.

It appeared that the Moonlighters were more interested in avoiding detection than in carrying out further atrocities. This was probably the conclusion that Warren reported to Sir Redvers Buller, who would have appreciated the former's audacity in extricating himself from a potentially dangerous situation.

And now, in January 1889, while Warren took temporary command of the Royal Engineers' Depot at Shorncliffe, near Folkestone on the south coast of Kent, Buller prompted Wolseley to give him an important new senior command that would be coming up in a few months' time. Any senior posting that Warren now received was likely to be that of a substantive Major-General; and it was not long in coming. *The Times* of 13 March reported that 'Colonel Sir Charles Warren, GCMG, KCB has been selected for the Command of Singapore and the Straits Settlements'. He was to depart as Acting Major-General, the full rank being confirmed after his arrival in Singapore. In the event, it was four years before his promotion to full Major-General was confirmed, in April 1893.

On Thursday 4 April 1889 Sir Charles, accompanied by Lady Fanny and their daughter Violet, took a cab to Liverpool Street station in the heart of the City; from there they would get a train to the new Royal Albert Dock (opened in 1880) for his embarkation on the P&O steamer *Bengal*. As they arrived at the station, the cabman, realising who his passenger was, remarked to the former Police Commissioner: 'I hope, Sir Charles, they will think more of you over there than they do here!' Warren relished the humour of the well-meant remark, and related the story with much amusement to the crowd of friends and former colleagues that had gathered on the platform to see him off.[705]

Fanny and Violet accompanied him as far as the docks, but no further. *The Times* reported they would 'at present remain in England',[706] which implies they would be joining him later, though they never did, probably because of the health dangers of Singapore's humid tropical climate.[707] Death from fever in those climes was not at all uncommon. Indeed, some years later, Warren was to lose his eldest son Frank to fever in Hong Kong. The Singapore posting was expected to last for two years;[708] and with two months' leave a year and the one-way journey taking at least a month, there was no prospect of his returning on home leave. As with nearly all his overseas postings, however,

[705] *The Times*, 5 April 1889, p 5.
[706] *Idem.*
[707] Williams, *The Life*, p 230.
[708] *St James's Gazette*, 22 March 1889, p 12.

341

Singapore and the Straits Settlements, c.1890.

duty called and he was away far longer than originally anticipated – in this case five years, by far his longest posting away from home.

The P&O liner *Bengal* took him via the Suez Canal as far as Calcutta (Kolkata) where he changed to the steamship *Sutlej* for the final leg of the journey to Singapore. As befitted his age and military rank, there was none of the tomfoolery that had characterised his first long sea voyage to South Africa. But he had plenty of time for reading up on Singapore and the Straits Settlements and for reflecting on the task ahead.

By the late 1880s the Straits Settlements had been a Crown colony for twenty years, having previously been a dependency of the East India Company's Bengal Presidency. It was named from the Malacca Straits which separated the Malay Peninsula from Dutch-controlled Sumatra to the west. The colony included the whole of the Malay Peninsula, from the island of Penang, at the northern entrance to the straits, to Singapore, the capital, in the south. Singapore had been founded by Sir Stamford Raffles in 1819, as a 'free port' on the trade route between India and China. Besides the main colonial settlements of Penang, Malacca (Melaka) and Singapore, the mainland consisted of numerous sultanates which, during the course of the 19th century were brought under varying degrees of colonial control.[709]

With the increasing use of steam-powered shipping, Singapore became an important refuelling station on the India-China shipping route through the Malacca Straits, and a large coaling depot was established on Brani Island, off 'New Harbour' (Keppel Harbour), a couple of miles to the west of the Singapore River. With rival European powers operating in the region and the French colonisation of Vietnam and Cambodia (*Union indochinoise*) in 1887, the protection of Singapore's coaling station became a major issue for the Imperial Government. Furthermore, a large tin smelting works for processing the mineral mined in the sultanates of the mainland was established on Brani Island in 1888.

That year the British took the decision to strengthen the garrison at Singapore, which hitherto had come under the authority of the British military commander of Hong Kong. The scale of the plans the War Office had in mind required an independent military command, and the military control of Singapore and the Straits Settlements was separated from Hong

[709] Walter Makepeace, Dr Gilbert Brooke and Roland Braddell (eds.), *One Hundred Years of Singapore*, Volume I (Murray, London, 1921; HardPress reprint edition, Miami, FL), pp 5–68.

Kong in February 1889. The man chosen to take up the post of the Colony's first General Officer Commanding (GOC) of Her Majesty's Forces in the Straits Settlements was Sir Charles Warren.

* * *

Warren arrived in Singapore on Monday 6 May 1889 to be greeted by a large crowd on Johnston's Pier. A guard of honour from the 58th Regiment was on parade with band and colours. A correspondent from the *Straits Advocate* was surprised to discover that 'the [49-year-old] hero of the day [was] a man in the prime of life, not the venerable old warrior whom many [had] expected to see'.[710] He was indeed in the prime of life and the energetic way he set about reorganising the military on Singapore and the Straits Settlements was to come as a surprise to many.

Initially, the appointment of a General Officer Commanding had been viewed as a welcome recognition of the rising status of the Colony and an elaborate welcome was laid on for the new arrival. The guns from Fort Canning, on Government Hill overlooking the port and town, boomed out a salute while the General shook hands with officials. And as he boarded the Governor's carriage to be driven to Government House, the band struck up 'that stirring old air, "A soldier and a man"'.[711] It would not be long before critics began sharpening their pens in the local press as their cosy colonial world appeared to be subsumed to imperial strategic interests.

Government House, built in the late-1860s in the grounds of a former nutmeg plantation on the northern edge of the then town of Singapore, was a palatial residence by any standards. In the opinion of former Governor Sir Frederick Weld (1880–87), 'it would be hard to find a more perfect picture of repose in a richer landscape'.[712]

Governor Sir Cecil Clementi Smith who greeted the new GOC on the steps of Government House was the same age as Warren and, like Warren, was a forceful character; but there the similarities ended. Although he held the double title of Governor and Commander-in-Chief, Clementi Smith had no personal military experience. His entire career had been spent in the colonial service in the Far East, commencing as a colonial cadet in Hong Kong where

---

[710] *Straits Advocate*, 11 May 1889.

[711] *Idem.*

[712] https://en.wikipedia.org/wiki/Istana_(Singapore), accessed 22 November 2016. Known as Istana (Malay for 'palace'), it is today the official residence of the President of Singapore, and houses the office of the Prime Minister.

344

he became 'an accomplished scholar of Chinese culture'.[713] From 1878 he had served in Singapore for six years as Colonial Secretary for the Straits Settlements, before taking over as Acting-Governor for a year. Two years as Lieutenant-Governor of Ceylon (Sri Lanka) followed before he returned to Singapore as full Governor in 1887. In the short period before Warren's arrival he managed to virtually eradicate the Chinese secret societies that had for years plagued the streets and businesses of Singapore and for this he was highly praised by both European colonists and the ordinary Chinese population.[714] Now in command of the colony to which he had devoted so much of his career, Clementi Smith was ill-prepared to share any of his authority with an incoming military man, no matter how distinguished. So far as he was concerned, this was *his* colony and *he* was Commander-in-Chief.

Warren had a similar perception of his own role. *He* was the General Officer Commanding all of the troops in the colony. Like the Governor, he carried the prefix 'His Excellency', and as far as he was concerned they were of equal rank, with power simply divided between them along military and civilian lines.

Conflict was inevitable, as became obvious on the first day when it appeared that no special provision had been made for suitable housing for the General, a neglect made all the more apparent by the palatial nature of the Governor's own residence. Clementi Smith appears to have assumed that Warren would be accommodated in the officers' quarters of the Army camp. Warren, however, was acutely aware of the status of his position. Bunking down with the men on field manoeuvres was one thing; but in the colonial capital of Singapore he expected to be accommodated more appropriately, in a house that he could treat as both an office and a residence in which he could receive visitors.

Initially Warren had to put up with sharing the officers' accommodation; but after a while he was rescued by the new Chief Justice, Sir Edward Loughlin O'Malley, who had just arrived from Hong Kong. O'Malley inherited the official residence of the Chief Justice and, being a widower, he offered to share it with Warren until such time as the latter got a suitable house of his own. According to Watkin Williams, 'Their bachelor *ménage* worked extremely well, and was the beginning of a life-long friendship between the two men – in spite of the fact that Warren had a Chinese cook and O'Malley an Indian, and

---

[713] http://eresources.nlb.gov.sg/infopedia/articles/SIP_69_2005-01-22.html, accessed 22 November 2016.
[714] *Idem.*

these two shared between them the duty of satisfying their masters' tastes!'[715] In due course Warren got his own residence, 'Balmoral', a large, two-storey, colonial-style house on a quiet residential road on the northern outskirts of the town.[716] The main living quarters – drawing room, library and study – were upstairs so as to benefit from any breeze that might be blowing. The status of the house may have been enhanced by its being named after Queen Victoria's favourite residence in Scotland.

* * *

By the time of Warren's arrival in Singapore the military strength of the force under his command had been increased to about 1500 officers and men, the largest contingent being an infantry battalion of just over 1000 men. There was a detachment of Royal Engineers and the local Singapore Volunteer Artillery made up most of the artillery component. A number of forts had been built over the previous two decades, but there had been little effort to co-ordinate their capabilities and, although they were armed with rifled guns, these were not the most up-to-date weapons. To Warren's eyes the most notable weakness of Singapore's military set-up was that there was no defence scheme or mobilisation plan. He was presented with a mass of soldiers and some forts. It was his task to convert these into a garrison and a fortress fit to defend the strategically important colony from any seaborne enemy attack.

The latest large, smokeless, breech-loading guns were on order and while he waited for these to arrive, Warren inspected his territory. There were two barracks, the main one at Tanglin on the northern outskirts of the town built in 1861, and the original one within Fort Canning overlooking the esplanade, the site of the original Governor's residence. He visited the gun emplacements and forts, the most significant ones being on the two islands that separated New Harbour from the open sea, Brani Island (now part of a huge container port) and Blakang Mati (now an exclusive island resort, renamed Sentosa – 'peace and tranquillity').

When he was not engaged in regular trips of military inspection in Penang, Malacca and Perak (Kuala Lumpur district), Warren reorganised the battalion. He did away with the two daily sessions of traditional drill that had hitherto been the main focus of the battalion's activity and in their place he devised a variety of field exercises, undertaken on a company basis. He drew up a

---

[715] Williams, *The Life*, p 231.
[716] Cyril Baxendale, *Personalities of Old Malaya* (Pinang Gazette Press, 1930), pp 16–17.

set of *Mobilisation Regulations* and developed a detailed plan for the rapid mobilisation of the troops in the event of war.

With no specific plan in place, full mobilisation could have taken days, perhaps even weeks. Warren was determined to get it down to just a few hours. And so that the Singapore Volunteer Artillery (SVA) could man the guns for an extended period in the event of mobilisation, he ordered the building of a small barracks at each of the gun emplacements. He drew up plans for strengthening the gun emplacements, and organised regular rifle practice for the troops and revolver practice for the officers.

At the beginning of July, realising he needed to extend the Military Rifle Range, Warren applied to the Colonial Engineer, Major (later Colonel Sir) Henry Edward McCallum RE for his opinion as to the safety of the ground beyond the planned new Rifle Range. He also sought McCallum's advice on the construction of a new barracks on some vacant government-owned land. McCallum had been Colonial Engineer at Singapore since 1884. It was he who had been responsible for the maintenance of the fortifications and military buildings before the arrival of the GOC, and Warren considered he was asking McCallum's opinion on a purely military matter, as a Royal Engineer. But it was here that he first came into conflict with Governor Sir Cecil Clementi Smith.

On the surface and socially, Governor Smith and GOC Warren appeared to be getting on well. At The Queen's Birthday Ball at Government House on 28 May, three weeks after Warren's arrival, the Governor had given Warren the honour of opening the ball, the General taking to the floor with Mrs Talbot, the wife of one of the colonial officials.[717] But beneath the surface, the two men eyed each other warily. Clementi Smith interpreted Warren's direct approach to his Colonial Engineer as an encroachment on the Governor's authority. And thus began an acrimonious correspondence that poisoned relations between them as they battled it out for the right to define the margins of their respective authorities.[718]

Warren acted all innocent – he had merely been asking a military man his military opinion, and since he was in charge of all things military, he insisted he was perfectly within his rights to do so without conducting his enquiries through official civilian channels. He stuck to this line so fervently that one suspects he was well aware of the potential conflict of authority at issue, for

---

[717] *Straits Times Weekly*, 29 May 1889, p 2.
[718] See *UKNA*, CO 273/61 for their extensive exchange of correspondence.

Colonial Engineer McCallum, although by training and rank a military man, was seconded to the civilian authority in Singapore. But in his customary manner, when Warren had convinced himself that he was right, he refused to compromise.

The Governor did not help matters by trying to force upon Warren a colonial protocol by which the GOC should not correspond directly with the Governor. Correspondence between them should be conducted through their respective Chiefs of Staff: Warren's Deputy Assistant Adjutant General (DAAG) and Smith's Colonial Secretary. Warren had had no time for civil servant procrastination in London and he was certainly not going to allow it to interfere with his efficient reorganisation and running of the military in Singapore.

The conflict was leaked to the local press and, the Governor being a popular and widely respected man, Warren was painted in some quarters as a regular Tartar who could do no right.[719] Warren himself ignored the press criticism and blithely let it all wash over him, believing that he would be vindicated in the end – which he was, although that took some years. *The Straits Times* and the *Daily Advertiser*, however, generally sprang to Warren's defence, the *Advertiser* referring to some of the local press as 'flatterers of the Governor' who hoped to win favour by publishing 'some sadly pitiful rubbish, abusive of Sir Charles'.[720]

The Governor referred the dispute to the Colonial Office in London in the hope that Secretary of State Lord Knutsford could get the War Office to put pressure on Warren. But Sir Redvers Buller, who had succeeded Lord Wolseley as Adjutant-General at the War Office in 1890, preferred to leave it to Warren to settle the matter locally.[721]

As conflict over the boundaries of authority extended over a couple of years, Warren became a stickler for military regulations. The heir to the Russian throne, Czarevitch Nicholas Alexandrovitch, visited Singapore in February 1891, and Warren, seeing the Governor's *aide-de-camp* in full dress uniform on the jetty, sent him back to Government House to change into a more suitable undress uniform. The *aide-de-camp* was an officer on loan to the Governor and Warren considered he had no business wearing full dress

---

[719] *The Straits Independent* and a publication called *Broad Arrow* were Warren's principal critics.

[720] *Daily Advertiser*, 2 April 1894, reminiscing on the record of Sir Charles Warren.

[721] *Straits Times*, 16 December 1889. For Buller as Adjutant-General, see G. Powell, *Buller: A Scapegoat? A Life of General Sir Redvers Buller VC* (Leo Cooper, London, 1984), pp 101–11.

uniform without permission from the General Officer Commanding. The Governor took Warren's order as a personal slight and protested to London.[722]

In due course Warren received a private letter from Buller gently chiding him: 'We are inundated with long correspondence regarding squabbles between you and your Governor'. Buller acknowledged that Warren had 'not a very comfortable berth', but added, 'I am bound to say that you seem to make a good many of the pricks for yourself':

> All I want to say [he pleaded], is for heaven's sake leave us alone, do not write and send everything here. If you have to fight the Governor, fight him, though I pray you fight as little as possible, surely the sun is hot enough in Singapore.

He ended by reassuring Warren that the War Office would back him whatever complaint the Governor sent home; but could he not approach the Governor on a personal and informal basis and attempt to smooth things over?[723]

Whether Warren took Buller's advice and tried to smooth things over on a personal level is not revealed. Possibly not, because there appears to have been even less communication between the Governor and the GOC.

In the new year of 1892 a rebellion broke out in Pahang Province against the presence and environmental destruction of a British tin mining company. A group of local Malays seized the tin mining stores and attempted to drive the British out of the region. *The Times* in London reported that the Governor considered it a minor affair that could be handled by the police. It also noted that the General Officer Commanding, Sir Charles Warren, had not been consulted.[724] A few weeks later reports reached Singapore that the small British force of Sikh police in Pahang was in retreat. They had fortified themselves in three sites and were asking for more ammunition.[725]

At this point Warren, who had still not been officially informed or consulted by the Governor, decided to act of his own initiative. According to the *Singapore Free Press*, a regular critic of Warren, he held 'a sort of council of war without the Governor's knowledge and created no little excitement by ordering supplies to be put on board one of H. M. Ships, and making arrangements for a campaign'.[726] The Governor considered Warren was

[722] *Daily Advertiser*, 29 May 1891; *Straits Times Weekly*, 3 June and 7 June 1891; and *Straits Times*, 24 January 1927, p 8.
[723] Buller to Warren, War Office, 22 April 1891. Quoted in Williams, *The Life*, p 235.
[724] *The Times*, 5 January 1892, p 3.
[725] *Straits Times Weekly*, 27 January 1892, p 45.
[726] *Singapore Free Press and Mercantile Advertiser*, 22 March 1892.

creating 'unnecessary alarm' and complained to London. The *Singapore Free Press* thought Warren's 'extraordinary behaviour [was] ridiculous'. In the opinion of the paper 'the only time the Colony appears to be at peace is when Sir Charles is not there'.[727] On this occasion the Sikh police re-established control in Pahang and the 'campaign' as such does not appear to have left port.

Warren realised that for the relatively small European population to feel secure in a widespread colony like Singapore and the Straits Settlements, it was advisable that every European male should be proficient in the use of a rifle. He recommended the establishment of regular rifle practice so that if need be in an emergency they could form a citizen army for the defence of the colony. This proposal was roundly condemned in the usual quarters, the *Straits Independent* referring to it as 'one of Sir Charles Warren's pet hobbies, the formation of a Volunteer Corps, no matter how or when, or at whose expense'.[728]

* * *

This sort of thing was grist to the mill of popular journalism, but there was a far more serious conflict being played out simultaneously in Singapore between the interests of the Colonial Office and the War Office. Indeed, it may have been partly responsible for the popular press's instinctive hostility to the person of General Warren.

The dispute was over what was known as the 'Military Contribution'. In the years before Warren's arrival the Colony had agreed to pay a fixed sum out of its own finances towards the cost of its military defence. But that was in the heyday of the opium trade when the military contribution accounted for just 6.7 per cent of the colony's income. Since then the value of the opium trade and tin exports had declined and the military 'fixed sum' now amounted to some 27 per cent. With the expanded military expenditure that accompanied Warren's arrival, the War Office expected to be able to increase the Colony's military contribution. But the unofficial appointees on the Legislative Council argued that the increase in military expenditure was part of an imperial strategic defence initiative and as such should not be borne by the colony.[729]

[727] *Idem.*
[728] Quoted in the *Straits Times Weekly*, 22 December 1891, p 2.
[729] *British House of Commons Papers*, A288 (1894), *Report of the Committee on Colonial Military Contribution. Section 9. Straits Settlements, No 2*, pp 1–26. See also, W. Makepeace, 'The Military Contribution', in Makepeace, Brooke and Braddell, *One Hundred Years*, Volume I, pp 399–402.

Warren, who was a co-opted member of both the Executive and the Legislative Council, was regarded as the local representative of the War Office and much of the criticism in Council and in the popular press was directed at him. While blithely ignoring the scurrilous attacks of the popular press, Warren recommended in Council that the Colony agree to a fixed percentage of its annual income, but, as the suggestion came from the perceived representative of the War Office, his eminently sensible suggestion was brushed aside. In the end, after a lengthy Parliamentary Committee of Inquiry a sliding scale of annual payment was accepted. A few years later, after Warren's departure, his suggestion of a percentage contribution was agreed upon.[730]

Warren had no time for the petty squabbles of colonial politics. He had seen enough of it in his years as Acting-Administrator of Griqualand West. As a result he seldom attended Singapore's Council meetings and when he did he usually dozed off. Walter Makepeace, a reporter for the *Singapore Free Press*, always enjoyed watching the General Officer Commanding, for though he was not the only one to snatch 40 winks during the interminable debates, 'Sir Charles Warren without disguise closed his eyes to think deeply upon the plans he was making for the conversion of Singapore into a fortress'.[731]

And the creation of a fortress was indeed Sir Charles Warren's great achievement in Singapore. It is difficult to picture it in the modern city of Singapore, especially with the amount of reclaimed land that has so altered the foreshore, but in the late-19th century the main town stretched for two miles east of the Singapore River, with the Chinese and Malay quarters stretching one mile to the west. In both cases the urban centre stretched only one mile inland. The large number of small hills that characterised the countryside beyond were ideal for gun emplacements. Fort Canning was merely the largest. For instance, a gun was mounted on a small hill near the Mosque, between New Harbour and the Singapore River. There were two on Brani Island: Fort Silinsing and Fort Teregeh; and three on Blakang Mali: Forts Connaught, Serapong and Siloso. Warren devised a method of communicating between the forts, from one side of Singapore to the other.

He trained his men in the art of rapid mobilisation. At just one hour's notice, steam launches could be ready at Johnston's Pier to transport the gun crews to the island forts and when he was not up-country inspecting the troops in Penang, Malacca or the Sultanates, the GOC was liable to spring a

[730] *Idem.* See also, Williams, *The Life*, pp 228–30.
[731] Makepeace, Brooke and Braddell, *One Hundred Years*, Volume I, p 156.

surprise predawn mobilisation practice on the troops in Singapore. He got it down to a fine art, with complete mobilisation in under three hours and he was proud to show off the garrison's capability.[732]

In February 1893 Admiral Sir Edmund Fremantle arrived in Singapore aboard the *Imperieuse*, accompanied by a small fleet of warships. He stayed in the colony for about a week as a guest of the Governor and he paid an official visit to the GOC at Fort Canning. A few days later a story emerged in the press that the Admiral had dined with General Warren and in the customary friendly rivalry between Army and Navy, the conversation got round to the defence capabilities of Singapore. The Admiral had not been impressed by what he had seen in Hong Kong and, assuming the same conditions applied in Singapore, he told the General he could 'knock the place into smithereens' (or words to that effect) before a soldier could have a look in. 'Come and see tomorrow morning,' replied the general.[733] The two men parted late that evening and a few hours later at 2 am Warren sounded the mobilisation alarm at Fort Canning and half an hour later at Tanglin Barracks. At dawn the Admiral and the Governor came down to inspect the Forts, and to the astonishment of the Admiral 'they found them fully manned with all branches of the Service, and the heavy guns laid on the Imperieuse and the other men-of-war'.[734]

By this time Warren had won over even his most vociferous critics. His work on transforming Singapore as a military garrison and fortress was more or less complete and it remained for him to maintain practice, discipline and morale. Consequently, there appears to have been less tension between GOC and Governor through 1893.

Warren kept morale high by encouraging his troops to engage in sports. He himself learned to play and appreciate golf and he presented a Warren Challenge Shield for a Golfing Competition. He also presented Challenge Shields for competitions in association football, rifle shooting and, the most popular for general entertainment, the Warren Challenge Shield for Tug of War. This latter was open to all branches of the service, including Volunteers. In 1893 it was held in Fort Canning and was won by the 2nd Battalion the Lincolnshire Regiment over the holders, a team from the Singapore Volunteer Artillery.[735]

---

[732] *Straits Times Weekly*, 31 March 1891, p 2.
[733] *Straits Times*, 18 February 1893.
[734] *Idem.*
[735] *Straits Times Weekly*, 14 June 1893, p 12.

In August 1891 Warren had been installed as Masonic Grand Master for the Eastern Archipelago,[736] and he appears to have regularly attended and officiated at various Masonic gatherings in Singapore as well as in the other Straits Settlements whenever he was visiting them on official duty. He appreciated that it was an effective way of binding together the military personnel with civilian colonists, to the benefit of both. Raffles and many prominent men in the history of Singapore had been Freemasons, and Warren was building on a well-established tradition.[737]

At the end of 1893 Sir Cecil Clementi Smith retired as Governor and he was replaced on 1 February 1894 by Sir Charles Mitchell, KCMG.[738] Mitchell had both military and civilian experience. Four years older than Warren, he had begun his professional career in the Royal Marines in 1852 and had risen to the rank of Lieutenant-Colonel before joining the colonial service in 1878. He served as Governor of Fiji and Lieutenant-Governor of Natal and Zululand before coming to Singapore. He was also a Freemason and he and Warren found they had a lot in common. His arrival in Singapore, however, was a bit late in terms of co-operation between the military and civilian powers in the colony. Warren was due to retire at the end of March.

In his last two months as GOC Warren was much in demand by the various societies and associations of Singapore. He was President of the Straits Branch of the Royal Asiatic Society and, in an attempt to stimulate the intellectual temper of the Colony beyond the purely commercial, he had been instrumental in setting up the Straits Philosophical Society, described by one member as 'a green oasis in a desert of commercialism'.[739]

In the final week of March he delivered a lecture to the Singapore Debating Society in which he explained the military task that he had been set and how he had achieved it, giving due praise to the Singapore Volunteer Artillery and impressing on his audience the importance of developing a citizen army of riflemen. He delivered a long-promised lecture in the Artillery Drill Hall on Palestine and Jerusalem, in aid of the St Nicholas Society.[740] And on 29 March the Masonic fraternity presented their departing District Grand Master with a portrait of himself in full Masonic regalia, together with an illuminated

[736] Colin Macdonald, *WARREN! The Bond of Brotherhood* (C. N. Macdonald, Singapore, 2007), pp 215–29.
[737] *Ibid.*, pp 128–42.
[738] *Singapore Free Press & Mercantile Advertiser*, 1 February 1894, p 2.
[739] Quoted from Revd George Reith in Williams, *The Life*, pp 237–38.
[740] *Straits Times*, 21 March 1894, p 2.

address which recorded the extent to which he had expanded and strengthened the Craft within the district. A copy of the portrait was hung in a place of honour in Freemasons' Hall in Singapore.[741] This was followed by a dinner at the Singapore Club. Governor Sir Charles Mitchell was present and Warren pressed him to allow his name to go forward to the Grand Lodge in England to become the next District Grand Master of the Eastern Archipelago. Mitchell was persuaded and was duly installed the following year.[742]

On the day of Warren's departure, 2 April, the popular press that had lambasted him so mercilessly over his first three years offered not a word of criticism. Their silence spoke volumes and left the way open for *The Straits Times* to sum up the feelings of many:

> [Sir Charles Warren] leaves a fortress that is one of the strongest in Asia, and he leaves a garrison whose readiness and perfection of mobilization cannot be surpassed.
>
> … in his time, Sir Charles has been the best abused man in the Colony, while at his departure he is as universally esteemed as any man could be. It is but a couple of years ago that he was a subject of persistent slander at the hands of persons who now sing his praises and lament his departure. That conquest of enmity Sir Charles had achieved by means at once simple and wise. When he was the subject of detraction, he paid no attention but proceeded quietly about the affairs he had in hand. When the persons who had attacked him repented of their methods, he ignored that he had been attacked and dealt with the advances of his unfriends as if he had not known that these had been unfriendly. …
>
> Sir Charles Warren leaves this Colony amidst a universal chorus of friendly greeting. To have achieved such a conquest of public opinion, amidst so small a community, is a great result … [The Straits Community] lose not only a soldier and a scholar, but also a most excellent example of a kindly and simple-hearted gentleman.[743]

A large crowd gathered at Johnston's Pier to see off their GOC and as the steamship *Surat* sailed away from Singapore, Sir Charles Warren must have been tempted to linger on deck and look back at the city, port and colony to which he had contributed so much over the past five years. From offshore he would have been able to see a number of the hilltop gun emplacements that he had built or strengthened, all facing out to sea to deter any would-be

---

[741] Williams, *The Life*, p 239.
[742] *Straits Times*, 29 March 1894; and 28 May 1895.
[743] *Straits Times*, 2 April 1894, p 2.

seaborne invader. As was appropriate to his era – the height of European imperialism – the sort of potential invader that Warren had in mind was some rival European power. In that respect the defences of Singapore that Warren designed were highly effective.

As Warren had planned, Singapore was a veritable fortress that could have seen off any seaborne invasion. Singapore's defences were updated during the Great War and after. But, ironically, when invasion did come, it was overland by bicycle and Warren's guns were facing in the wrong direction. Singapore, believed by the British military establishment to be impregnable, fell to the Japanese in February 1942, just short of 50 years after Warren's departure from the colony.

CHAPTER 20

Chatham and South Africa

Having travelled east from Singapore and completed a circumnavigation of the globe, a rare feat in those days, Warren arrived back in England to an uncertain future in the summer of 1894. Although now a substantive Major-General, he was unemployed and on half pay for nine months until on 1 May 1895 he was appointed General Officer Commanding the Troops in the Thames District.[744] He moved at once with Lady Fanny and his two daughters from their house in Belgravia to Government House in Chatham, the town so familiar to the family from their younger years.

Williams records that in Chatham they were 'well known and had many friends'. But Sir Charles's pleasure at the prospects of 'a congenial life' with his family in the familiar surroundings of Chatham was 'overshadowed by his grave anxiety for Lady Warren, who was at that time in a very delicate state of health'. While it is not clear what ailment afflicted her, doctors gave her only a few months to live. Fortunately, the crisis passed and she recovered, although her convalescence was long and for the three years they were in Chatham she was unable to play the sort of role that might have been expected of the hostess of Government House.[745] Under the circumstances, Sir Charles would have been particularly pleased to have his two daughters at home, for besides looking after their mother, their eldest daughter Violet, aged 29, probably assisted by Charlotte, aged 26, took on the responsibility of hostess of Government House.

The eldest son Frank, aged 23, was a Lieutenant in the Royal Artillery, stationed in Mauritius, while Richard, aged nineteen, was studying medicine at the University of Cambridge. Little is known of Sir Charles's only surviving sibling, his brother Billie, or what happened to him after the two brothers had been united on the Bechuanaland Expedition, aside from the fact that he received a Royal Humane Society award for bravery in 1892 for helping to rescue a five-year-old boy from drowning in the River Thames,[746] and the fact

---

[744] *London Gazette*, No 26622, 7 May 1895, p 2631.
[745] Williams, *The Life*, p 242.
[746] *London Metropolitan Archive*, LMA/4517/B/01/01/018.

Violet Warren and Charlotte Warren.
WARREN FAMILY COLLECTION

that Sir Charles provided his younger brother with some financial support in the form of a Post Office annuity.[747]

* * *

Not long after he had taken up his new position at Chatham in May 1895, Warren was appointed to command one of the two divisions that would take part in that summer's New Forest Manoeuvres. Warren was to command the Southern Division of 20,000 men and play the role of an invading enemy that had landed in Southampton and Weymouth. His opponent, commanding the Northern Division of similar strength, was Major-General Sir William Butler, GOC the Troops in South-East District.

Warren gathered his forces at Aldershot on 21 August and marched them south via Winchester to take up his 'landing positions' before proceeding with his 'invasion' northwards through the New Forest towards Salisbury. Butler's Northern Division took up a strong defensive position at Godshill, due east from Southampton and south of Salisbury. If he was to reach Salisbury without

---

[747] Billie was still alive in 1926 when Sir Charles drew up his final Will and Testament, for in it he made provision for an increase in the annuity of his brother William Warren.

exposing his left flank, Warren needed to dislodge Butler from Godshill, which he was unable to do. The conclusion of the judges was that Warren had not made sufficient use of his artillery. The two forces manoeuvred back and forth over the coming days with no further great conclusions drawn about either force.[748]

Brigade-Major (later Lt-General Sir) Thomas D'Oyly Snow, who was based at Aldershot at the time, later recalled an amusing story about Warren at the end of that summer's manoeuvres. Apparently, on the march south to Southampton a number of Warren's troops had dropped out, complaining about the weight of the kit they had to carry. So on the march home Warren, determined to test the validity of his squaddies' complaint, borrowed the full uniform, boots and kit of a private soldier and proceeded to march for some seven miles towards Aldershot at the head of his troops.

According to D'Oyly Snow, 'Somewhere *en route* H.R.H. the Duke of Connaught [GOC Aldershot District] took up a position to see the troops pass. He was rather surprised and horrified to see the G.O.C. [Warren] marching at the head of the Division, attired as a private in the line!' But Warren had made his point in a manner that would have won him respect from the rank and file, if not from their senior commanders. According to Private Buckley, whose uniform and boots had been borrowed for the demonstration, when he got his boots back he found that the General had treated the inside with Vaseline, which made them 'comfortable for more marching'.[749]

Warren maintained a close interest in the quality of the Army's marching boots. In this regard, while in command at Chatham, among the number of young officers with whom he developed good relationships was Lieutenant (later Brigadier-General Sir) Osborne Mance RE who was a pioneer in the making of 'skiagraphs' (X-ray photographs).

> Warren took keenly to this subject because he wished, by taking skiagraphs of good and bad feet in various types of boot, to improve the comfort of soldiers' footwear and increase their marching powers. Warren first had his own foot skiagraphed by Mance, and this was one of the first occasions on which an X-ray photograph of the bones of the feet was taken through the wearer's boot.[750]

[748] *The Times*, 22 August p 8, 27 August p 8, and 31 August 1895, p 10.
[749] Both reminiscences quoted in Williams, *The Life*, pp 243–4. Sir Thomas D'Oyly Snow, who later served with distinction in the First World War, was the great-grandfather of the TV historian Dan Snow.
[750] Williams, *The Life*, p 245.

Readers of a certain age may recall the widespread use of X-ray machines for viewing one's shoe-clad feet in shoe shops in the 1950s.

Warren's field of responsibility as GOC Thames District was the wider Thames Estuary, from which stemmed the defence of London; and Sir Redvers Buller, Adjutant-General at the War Office, depended upon him to plan the total mobilisation of the Thames and Medway defences, on the same model that he had established in the Straits Settlements.

There was much to reorganise and Warren was frequently on inspection of the Thames District, ordering mobilisation practices and generally making sure that his plans were properly implemented. On one of these inspections an incident occurred that was reported as far away as Singapore. Warren was going by carriage to inspect some Royal Engineers at Gravesend, accompanied by his *aide-de-camp* Lieutenant H. G. Sargent, his Chief Staff Officer Colonel Goldsmith, and Colonel Fellowes Commanding the Royal Engineers. Their horse took fright at the sound of gunfire, overturned the carriage and pitched Warren and the two colonels into a ditch filled with stagnant water. The youngest of the party, Lieutenant Sargent, had managed to jump free; but Warren found himself wedged under the carriage. In due course all three senior officers were safely extricated, with nothing more than a few bruises, though with their 'faces blackened and their uniforms spoiled'. Warren, never too concerned about his personal dignity, 'laughed heartily at the pitiable sight each presented'.[751] He had a loud, barking laugh that could explode out of him with great velocity at the faintest hint of the ridiculous and the two colonels felt compelled to take it in the same spirit.

Warren was promoted to Lieutenant-General on 1 October 1897[752] and completed his allotted three years' service in command of the Thames District in the summer of 1898. At the age of 58 he was physically fit, mentally alert and in no way ready for retirement. There was one potential job going, the Aldershot Command vacated by the Duke of Connaught, but this went to Sir Redvers Buller who had just been promoted to full General.

Warren could not be sure of getting another substantive appointment and he bought a house, 10 Wellington Crescent, in the seaside town of Ramsgate, near the north-eastern tip of Kent. The house was on the seafront close to the harbour and the family moved into what was to become their home for the next fifteen years. The house was fifteen minutes' brisk walk from Ramsgate station

[751] *Straits Observer*, 23 July 1897, p 6.
[752] *London Gazette*, No 26928, 11 January 1898, p 166.

A cryptic postcard sent by Charlotte to her father, then visiting Rome, February 1898. It illustrates the Warren family's love of humour and codes. Some clues for deciphering the code: M + eye = My; Sir Charles was known by his daughters as 'Pip'; the sixth picture is the kind of tree grown in a graveyard; the tortoise refers to an unidentified member of the family.

FROM JOHN PELHAM WARREN

with its good rail services to Dover, Canterbury, Chatham and London, and Warren was able to keep in touch with colleagues and international events.

In the light of his own participation in the New Forest Manoeuvres of 1895, Warren would have been particularly interested in the Salisbury Manoeuvres that took place in the first week of September 1898. The Duke of Connaught commanded the Northern 'Red' Army while Sir Redvers Buller commanded the Southern 'Blue' Army. They 'fought it out' over the Wiltshire and Dorset Downs between Salisbury and Shaftesbury, just south of the modern A30

*Charles Warren drawing his daughter Charlotte, aboard a
French train, drawn by Charlotte, May 1888.*
WARREN FAMILY COLLECTION

road, across the rolling countryside that provides the site for the modern
Chalke Valley History Festival.

The Manoeuvre was considered a success in that it exposed a number of
tactical and administrative weaknesses. In the opinion of the two commanders,
Connaught and Buller, there was a shortage of water and excessive marching
between camps. Lord Wolseley agreed that time spent on marching could have
been better spent on tactical operations, but pointed out that long marches
and shortages of water were no greater than in real warfare.[753]

Allowing for these problems, Buller failed to display much skill in the
handling of his troops. Despite several attempts, he failed to dislodge the
opposing Army from a well-defended position.[754] Wolseley's report implied
that a frontal attack ordered by Buller had lacked the necessary artillery support
and was launched with insufficient and weary troops. Indeed, according to

[753] For the full Confidential Print on the Salisbury Manoeuvres, see *UKNA*, WO 279/4. For
a summary of their findings, see 'The Official Report on the Salisbury Manoeuvres in 1898'
in *Royal United Services Journal*, Volume 43, No 253 (March 1899), pp 293–304.
[754] *The Times*, 3 September p 10 and 6 September p 8.

one source, Buller was heard to admit, 'I have been making a fool of myself all day'.[755] In the judgement of his biographer, 'more than ten years at an office desk had sapped the powers of a fifty-eight-year-old man rather too fond of good living'. He rode to hounds and was still physically fit, but his mental agility may have been somewhat impaired by, among other things, his regular consumption of champagne, and he 'lacked experience of commanding large formations in the field, either in war or in training'.[756]

The same could be said of Warren, though he, just two months younger than Buller, was both mentally and physically fit for his age. Warren's largest command in the field had been the 4000 men of the Bechuanaland Expedition that had never had to fire a shot in anger. In the New Forest Manoeuvres of three years previously, he, too, had failed to dislodge the Northern Army on his first attempt, although on his second attempt he had forced them to withdraw. Warren's actual fighting experience so far had been small fare, in the Eastern Cape and in Griqualand West in the 1870s. Buller's had been greater and more varied and the award of the Victoria Cross for rescuing several of his men during a hasty retreat in the Anglo-Zulu War of 1879 had added greatly to his reputation for fearlessness in action. It had been fifteen years, however, since he had seen any action and most of his recent experience had been in administration at Army headquarters.

Both generals were about to be severely tested in a real-life war in South Africa.

* * *

During his three years as GOC at Chatham, and now living in Ramsgate, Warren maintained a close interest in the affairs of South Africa.

Much had changed since he had last been there in 1885. The fortunes of the Transvaal had been transformed by the discovery in 1886 of a huge reef of gold ore at Witwatersrand ('white water's ridge') 60 kilometres south of the capital, Pretoria. Mining capitalists and speculators from the Cape Colony, Natal and further afield rushed to the site, and within months the city of Johannesburg sprang up in what had previously been open veldt.

The Transvaal Boers and their Government led by President Paul Kruger had little direct involvement in the mining activities, but they benefitted hugely from taxing the mining companies and exploiting monopolies for the

[755] Quoted in G. Powell, *Buller: A Scapegoat? A Life of General Sir Redvers Buller VC* (Leo Cooper, London, 1994), p 114.
[756] *Idem.*

provisioning of the city and the mines, especially with their control over the supply of dynamite. The largely English-speaking white mining community were regarded as *uitlanders* ('outsiders'). As such they were denied the vote and had no say in the government of the Republic that they were largely funding through taxation. The Boers, however, jealously guarded their hard-won independence from British overrule and feared that to allow the *uitlanders* the vote would effectively hand control of their Republic to Britain.

Gold underpinned the world's international trading currencies and by the 1890s the Witwatersrand had become the world's greatest single source of gold. Who controlled the Transvaal was thus of huge strategic interest to the British Empire, still the world's leading industrial power, though facing growing competition from Germany and the United States. Britain regarded the Transvaal as within her 'sphere of influence' in Southern Africa, although that was being challenged by the Germans who were building close links with Kruger's Government and providing the Transvaal with the most up-to-date weapons of war.

At this point Warren's former protagonist Cecil Rhodes stepped into the breach. His Consolidated Gold Fields, founded in 1887, was among the larger gold-mining companies in Johannesburg; and in 1889 his De Beers Company established a diamond-mining monopoly in Kimberley. The latter provided Rhodes with the capital to further his territorial ambitions, and in 1890–93 his British South Africa Company established the colony of 'Rhodesia' north of the Transvaal – today's Republic of Zimbabwe.

In the meantime Rhodes had become Prime Minister of the Cape, in alliance with the Afrikaner Bond, the grouping of Afrikaners in the Cape Parliament. Rhodes was thus at the height of his powers in 1895 when he decided to intervene in the *uitlander* dispute and overthrow Kruger's Government.

He smuggled rifles into Johannesburg where his brother Frank was to organise an uprising. At the same time his close friend and Rhodesian Administrator Leander Starr Jameson assembled a force of 400 Rhodesian police and 200 volunteers in the south-eastern corner of the Bechuanaland Protectorate, close to the Transvaal border. The moment the uprising began in Johannesburg, Jameson was to cross the border and ride to their aid. In the event Rhodes's plot was a fiasco. The *uitlanders* failed to rise, but Jameson crossed the border anyway and rode towards Johannesburg. His small force was surrounded as they approached Johannesburg, and those that were not killed were arrested and put on trial.

The British Government, having secretly approved the plot, was happy for

Jameson and Rhodes to carry the can. The 'Jameson Raid' marked the end of Rhodes's political career. He lost the support of the Cape Afrikaners and was forced to resign the Premiership. The most important consequence of the Jameson Raid was that it destroyed whatever trust may have existed between Boer and Briton and made war in South Africa almost inevitable. Kruger's Government stepped up its orders of French and German artillery and rifles; and the Orange Free State formed a defensive alliance with the Transvaal.

* * *

Meanwhile in England the affairs of South Africa were a regular news item and a widely expressed opinion was that the Boers needed to be taught a lesson. Warren was much in demand for his opinion on South African military matters, especially in relationship to the Boers, and in October 1897 his advice was sought by the Colonial Defence Committee.

Warren was one of the few of his peers who did not underestimate the Boers' military potential. He stressed the importance of having in South Africa 'an adequate force of volunteers, mounted, who should always be with the infantry on the line of march in the presence of an enemy who is mounted'. As we shall see, his view of the role of mounted infantry was to lead to some controversy when he was directing operations on the field of battle in January 1900. Finally, in what Williams called 'a grimly prophetic remark', Warren wrote that he considered it 'hazardous' to maintain three Batteries of Royal Artillery at Ladysmith [in northern Natal] 'with no infantry to cover them in the event of a sudden raid'.[757]

British jingoism reached new heights in 1898. In Sudan, Gordon was avenged by General Kitchener with huge slaughter at the Battle of Omdurman, just outside Khartoum, after which French claims to the Upper Nile were brushed aside. British sabre-rattling in South Africa, however, had only aided the re-election of President Kruger for a fourth term, postponing any possibility of a change of government in the Transvaal by constitutional means. A last-ditch attempt to avert a South African war was made the following year when Kruger met British High Commissioner Sir Alfred Milner at Bloemfontein from 31 May to 5 June 1899. But neither was willing to compromise enough and as the meeting broke up, both sides prepared for war. Sir Redvers Buller, who was then GOC at Aldershot, was informed that in the event of war, he would become Commander-in-Chief in South Africa.

[757] Williams, *The Life*, pp 245–6.

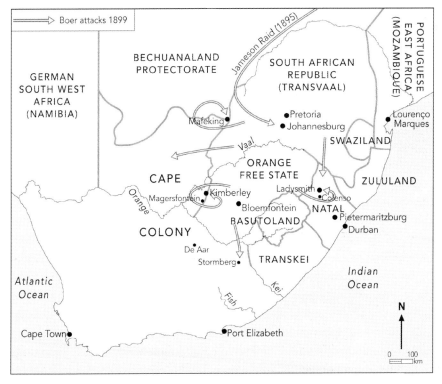

The South African War, October 1899.

At the time the British had not much more than 8000 troops in South Africa, half of whom were stationed at Ladysmith in northern Natal. In September 1899 10,000 troops were despatched from India to South Africa, and full British mobilisation was ordered on 7 October. This left Kruger with no choice. On 9 October he delivered an ultimatum to the British Resident in Pretoria: 'start withdrawing your troops from our borders by 5 pm on Wednesday 11 October or a state of war will exist between us'. The British rejected the ultimatum and in the early hours of 12 October Boer forces crossed into both Natal and the Cape Colony.

Between the Transvaal and the Orange Free State, the Boers could bring about 35,000 men into the field. Thus at the start of the war they had a clear numerical advantage, and the Boer leadership realised that to win any conflict with the British Empire they must strike first and strike hard and fast, before Buller's army landed from overseas. If they could gain some quick victories, as they had in the previous war of 1881, the British might again be persuaded to leave the Boers alone and guarantee their continued independence.

Thus although the Boers attacked first, putting the British on the defensive, the Boer strategy was essentially a defensive one. Their primary aim was to defend their republics.[758] The British attitude, however, strongly urged by High Commissioner Milner, was that the Boer Republics must cease to exist as independent entities. They must be conquered and incorporated into a wholly 'British' South Africa.

By 16 October the Boers had cut off and laid siege to Kimberley and Mafeking (today's Mahikeng) in the Northern Cape. On the other side of the country where 20,000 Free State and Transvaal Boers had crossed into Natal, Lieutenant-General Sir George White had 9500 men stationed at Ladysmith and 5000 under Symons 65 kilometres further north at Dundee. Within a fortnight Symons was dead, Dundee had been evacuated and the surviving troops driven back to Ladysmith.

By the time Buller landed at Cape Town on 31 October, White's Field Force that was supposed to defend the colony of Natal was confined to Ladysmith. The siege was about to begin. With troopships arriving daily in Cape Town's Table Bay, Buller decided he must divide his force, sending the greater part to Durban to relieve the 12,000 infantry and cavalry locked up in Ladysmith, while Lieutenant-General Lord Methuen took the 1st Infantry Division to the relief of Kimberley.

* * *

Meanwhile, back in Ramsgate, Warren was chafing at the bit. He was available and anxious to play his part. At his rank, he would have expected to command a Division, a force of about 11,000 men; but Buller's Divisional Commanders and his Chief of Staff were all appointed without a word in his direction. Warren got the feeling he was being passed over, and he thought he recognised why: 'Everybody concerned with South Africa knew that I had independent views on how to fight the Boer'.[759] And neither Wolseley nor Buller agreed with those views. Warren recognised the potential strength of a national Boer army made up of local commandos of mounted infantry, each man an experienced

[758] T. Pakenham, *The Boer War* (Weidenfeld and Nicolson, 1979; Futura Edition, London, 1982), pp 168–70, referencing J.H. Breytenbach, *Die Geskiedenis van die Tweede Vryheidsoorlog in Suid-Afrika, 1899–1902*, 4 vols (Staatsdrukker, Pretoria, 1969–77), vol I, pp 153–5
[759] From Warren's unpublished account of his service in the South African War, compiled some years later from his contemporaneous diaries and letters, and quoted in Williams, *The Life*, p 250.

hunter, familiar with the type of terrain and a crack shot. The Boer generals would have the advantage of adaptability and speed of manoeuvre. To counter this in 1885 Warren had insisted that a large part of his Bechuanaland Field Force should be made up of volunteer regiments of mounted infantry, most of them locally recruited in South Africa. And it was not for nothing that Warren on his various postings had promoted the concept of a volunteer citizen reserve army, with every man trained to shoot a rifle.

The bulk of the British Army, however, was made up of infantry battalions, and the war experience of most of Britain's field generals in 1899 had been against relatively ill-armed 'native' armies that the British had been able to confront with vastly superior weaponry. The Battle of Omdurman, 2 September 1898, was the most recent of the kind, in which British artillery, machine guns and rigid ranks of riflemen had mown down 11,000 Sudanese for the loss of only 48 British and Egyptians killed. The British Army establishment were aware that the Boers had been arming themselves with German artillery and rifles, but they mistakenly viewed the informality of the Boers' citizen army as a sign of weakness and disorganisation, and assumed they would be no match for highly disciplined British infantry battalions.

Through mid-October Warren read in the English newspapers of the infestation of Kimberley and Mafeking and that General White was failing to defeat the Boers in northern Natal. By 26 October he could contain himself no longer and he wrote to Lord Wolseley offering his services.

Warren was too independent-minded to have ever been part of the 'Wolseley ring' of preferred officers. And having defied Wolseley over standing for parliament in 1885, and more recently having been responsible for friction between War Office and Colonial Office during his Singapore Command, Warren was never likely to be an early choice for the South African campaign. Wolseley responded to Warren's letter claiming that he understood Warren to have been ill and not fit for active work, which may well have been a cover for the true reason – Lord Wolseley and his military establishment did not favour Warren.

Warren took Wolseley's excuse at face value and replied that his 'energies and powers of endurance were not in any way impaired … [He] could do a hard day's work in the saddle as well as most young men in South Africa; [he] could walk 35 miles against many of the best, and could cycle out to golf, play all day and cycle home again without the least fatigue'.[760]

---

[760] *Idem.*

Warren's reply gained him an audience with Wolseley on 2 November. According to Warren, the meeting did not last long and most of the time Wolseley 'dwelt on the desirability of outflanking the Boers'. Warren felt that Wolseley's strategy was more appropriate to 'a European foe'; but he kept his views to himself. 'He did not,' Warren reflected 'tell me how a cavalry man, with only one horse, who did not know the country, could outflank a Boer with two or three horses, who *did* know the country'.[761] Wolseley was 'exceedingly kind', but did not give any hint that there might be a role for Warren.

It was becoming increasingly clear, however, that Britain would need far larger forces in South Africa if she was to overcome the Boers, and five days later Warren was informed that he was on standby to command a Fifth Division. Preparations began immediately, and on 11 November Buller requested the Division be despatched as soon as possible.[762]

Logistical preparations were completed by Wednesday 22 November and Warren was able to spend Thursday 23rd quietly at home with his family. It was to be a gruelling nine months before he had another such day. On Friday 24th he left by train for Southampton via London. War fever was high and the people of Kent were proud to know that 'their General' was going out to South Africa to restore British pride. Large crowds gathered to wave him off at Ramsgate and at the stations of Broadstairs, Margate and Westgate. 'It was most affecting', he recorded in his diary:

> There were gathered the families of many soldiers and Police who had served with me at different times, and I had known nothing about their being in the neighbourhood. One old lady at Broadstairs came and hugged me, and whispered in my ear that her son had been with me in Bechuanaland.[763]

Warren spent a night in London and joined his Divisional Staff at Waterloo station the next morning where 'a great crowd' came to see them off, including some Metropolitan Police officers from Scotland Yard. It was assumed by all, including Warren, that he was bound for his old stomping ground, the Northern Cape, and someone had chalked on their carriages 'To Mafeking'. The exploits of Colonel Robert Baden-Powell in the defence of that town had already made the name 'Mafeking' synonymous with British pluck in the face

---

[761] *Idem.*
[762] HCPP (1903), Cd. 1791, *Minutes of Evidence taken before the Royal Commission on the War in South Africa*, Vol II, Appendix J, p 620.
[763] Quoted in Williams, *The Life*, p 253.

of adversity. Warren and his party embarked on the mail ship *Norham Castle* and steamed down the Solent that afternoon to the sound of cheering crowds, confident that 'General Warren' would help bring victory and glory to British troops in South Africa.[764]

* * *

Once the ship had got through the rough waters of the Bay of Biscay and was heading south to the warmer climes off West Africa, Warren engaged his Divisional Staff and other officers in daily 'war games' that lasted for the duration of the voyage. Warren practised his war games on the assumption he would be going initially to his old stomping ground, the Northern Cape, territory that he knew better than any other senior officer in the British Army.

The *Norham Castle* docked in Cape Town on Wednesday 13 December, halfway through what was to become known as 'Black Week'. The first thing that struck Warren and those familiar with the city was the sullen silence that greeted them as they came ashore. There had been no telegraph aboard ship, and for two and a half weeks Warren and his men had received no news of any kind about the progress of the war. The silence boded ill, and nobody wanted to be the first to tell them the news.

After paying his respects to Governor and High Commissioner Sir Alfred Milner, Warren was briefed by Chief of Staff Colonel Arthur Wynne and his old Bechuanaland friend Lieutenant-General Sir Frederick Forestier-Walker, who was GOC the Lines of Communication. Forestier-Walker began by handing Warren a telegram from Wolseley conveying the message that in the event of General Buller being killed or otherwise incapacitated, he was to take over as Commander-in-Chief of HM Forces in South Africa. A letter would follow. Warren was being handed what was known as a 'Dormant Commission'. Wynne and Forestier-Walker then briefed Warren on the news from the front, and it was mostly bad.

Methuen's attempt to cross the Modder on 28 November had been unexpectedly halted by intense Boer rifle fire from their hidden position below the lip of the river bank. It was in effect an ambush. The British suffered heavy losses and found the next day that the Boers had withdrawn to Magersfontein, a hilly position six miles north of the Modder River crossing. Methuen decided to rest his men and prepare for the next assault.

Then on Sunday 10 December General Gatacre's chaotic dawn attempt

[764] *Ibid.*, p 254.

to retake Stormberg Junction in the Eastern Cape turned into a rout. Gatacre considered himself lucky to manage a retreat with only 90 casualties, but he had inadvertently left behind nearly 700 men who were forced to surrender and were captured later in the day. It was a serious blow to British prestige, but worse was to come.

Methuen's artillery had spent 10 December pounding the hills of Magersfontein on the assumption that it was on the high ground that the Boers would make their stand. General J. H. ('Koos') de la Rey, however, was determined to repeat the success he had achieved at the Modder. Rather than taking up the traditional Boer position on the hilltops, he deeply entrenched his men in a defensive line *in front of* the hills, curving their trenches round towards the Modder to prevent their being outflanked, and in a manner that prefigured the European Western Front in The Great War, he strewed low-lying barbed wire across the approach to the trenches. Methuen marched his 13,000 troops up the line of rail overnight in anticipation of a heroic charge to take the hill position in the morning. But it was a new kind of warfare that Methuen's men charged into at dawn on 11 December.

Major-General Wauchope's Highland Brigade, 4000-strong, headed the charge and suffered unexpectedly heavy losses, tripped by barbed wire and cut down by a hidden enemy firing at ground level with smokeless rifles. By the end of the day the British had suffered 1000 losses to no more than about 250 for the Boers. Methuen was forced to acknowledge defeat and withdraw to Modder River, allowing the Boers to strengthen their position at Magersfontein.[765]

Over dinner at Government House the night of his arrival, 13 December, Warren argued the need to recruit 'five to ten thousand Colonial Mounted Troops', as the best way to match the Boers in local knowledge, experience and mobility. But his ideas received little attention.[766] The next morning Warren, eager to proceed at once to the relief of Kimberley, to the country that he knew so well, was pleased to read a telegram from Lord Lansdowne, the Secretary of State for War, confirming that Warren was to proceed immediately 'to assume command of the forces under Methuen'.[767] Warren had no desire to *supersede* Lord Methuen as such; but he felt that he could go up and offer his Division and his local experience in support of his old friend.

Late that Thursday evening, 14 December, Buller received Lansdowne's telegram telling him of the decision to send Warren and his Division up to

[765] Pakenham, *Boer War*, pp 193–206.
[766] Quoted in Williams, *The Life*, pp 155–6.
[767] Cd. 1791, Appendix J, p 623.

the Modder to supersede Methuen. The telegram added to Buller's conviction that his needs and authority were being ignored and overruled. Furthermore, he knew of Warren's Dormant Commission and felt therefore that Warren should be in Natal with him. Lansdowne's telegram had come at a critical moment, when Buller's confidence was in greatest need of boosting, for he was poised to launch, the very next morning, his first attempt to break the Boer line along the Tugela River at Colenso, some fifteen miles south of Ladysmith. He sent an immediate telegram to Wynne in Cape Town cancelling Lansdowne's order to Warren. He was, however, too tied up with his own affairs to provide Warren with any alternative orders, and Warren decided to stick to his official orders from Lansdowne.

* * *

'Good old Buller' was supposed to retrieve British honour, after the failures of Gatacre and Methuen. Instead, he added to them. His attack at Colenso on Friday 15 December was a disaster, completing the trio of what became known as 'Black Week'.

Just like those at Modder River and Magersfontein, Buller's troops advanced in close order against an ill-reconnoitred position in the belief that the Boers had withdrawn as a result of heavy artillery bombardment of the hills beyond the river. But they had not. They were hidden on the plain in front of the hills and below the lip of the riverbank. Once again the British surged forward into what was in effect a Boer ambush. Not only did a battalion of infantry lose its way, confused by a bend in the river; but the field artillery also got too far forward before the Boers sprang the trap. The artillery suffered so heavily in horses and men that the survivors were forced to hide in a gulley some distance from their guns while they awaited reinforcements and more ammunition.

Buller, seeing the guns exposed and unmanned, assumed they had been abandoned and anxious to avoid even heavier losses, he ordered a general withdrawal. Now the guns really were abandoned. In suicidal attempts to rescue them, two were retrieved; but ten guns were lost to the enemy, who boldly dragged them across the river that evening for use against the British in the months to come. By the end of the day the British had lost 143 killed and over 1000 wounded, to Boer losses of seven killed and about twenty wounded.[768]

---

[768] Lewis Childs, *Ladysmith* (Leo Cooper, London, 1998), p 60.

Buller was devastated by his humiliating defeat, added to which he blamed himself for the death of Lieutenant Freddy Roberts, the only son of Field Marshal Lord Roberts. Freddy Roberts had been mortally wounded in a heroic attempt to rescue the abandoned guns. In a fit of extreme anger and traumatic stress, and with his mind probably loosened by an excess of champagne, Buller sent off two messages that in retrospect were to undermine his heroic reputation and ultimately to destroy his career.

To Sir George White in Ladysmith he heliographed the news of his failure to break through the Boer lines and advised him to destroy his ciphers, fire off all his ammunition and make the best terms he could with the Boers. White, so shocked by the order to surrender, assumed it must be a Boer trick and wisely decided to ignore it. Buller's second message was an 'ill-conceived and ill-worded'[769] telegram to Lord Lansdowne:

> My failure today raises a serious question. I do not think I am strong enough to relieve White … My view is that I ought to let Ladysmith go, and occupy good positions for the defence of South Natal … I now feel that I cannot say I can relieve Ladysmith with my available force.[770]

This telegram reached a London that was already reeling from the triple shocks of 'Black Week', and within hours the Government had decided that Buller had lost his nerve and should be superseded as Commander-in-Chief, South Africa. Buller was not immediately informed of this decision; but the next day, Saturday 16 December, he was told:

> The abandonment of White's force and its consequent surrender is regarded by the Government as a national disaster of the greatest magnitude. We would urge you to devise another attempt to carry out its relief, not necessarily *via* Colenso, making use of the additional men now arriving if you think fit.[771]

Regarding Warren, the Government's position remained that he should take charge of the relief of Kimberley, and that Saturday evening Warren and his staff and a large part of his Division departed on the train to the north.

36 hours later, on Monday morning 18 December, they arrived at De Aar, the junction of the two lines north from Cape Town and Port Elizabeth. As Warren got down from the train to stretch his legs, a young officer from the

[769] Powell, *Buller*, pp 152–3.
[770] *Idem.*
[771] Cd. 1791, Appendix J, p 624.

Line of Communication thrust a telegram into his hand. It read: 'You will instruct General Warren to return at once'.

Warren was shocked and not a little annoyed by the peremptory manner of the counter-command: 'Not a word to me personally – I am a shuttle-cock to be ranged about up and down the line!' He blamed neither Buller nor Forestier-Walker for the disrespect displayed, but rather the '*Alice in Wonderland*' world of the 'Line of Communication' by whose mechanistic methods 'all [men] from General to Private lose [their] identity'.[772] With no further word as to what was happening or why, they reboarded the train for the return journey to Cape Town, during which Warren hid his true feelings and put on a 'very cheery' front for the benefit of his despondent staff.[773]

Arriving back in Cape Town on Wednesday 20 December, Warren learned that he and most of his Division were destined to join Buller in Natal. He also learned, as Buller had been informed on Monday, that, while Buller was to remain in command of the forces in Natal, Field Marshal Lord Roberts had been appointed to replace him as Commander-in-Chief South Africa, with General Lord Kitchener as his Chief of Staff. Roberts had been summoned from Dublin on Saturday 16 December, arriving in London on the Sunday to be informed of his son's death. It was a sombre Roberts who sailed from Southampton on 23 December, thinking of his lost son and hoping that no further disasters would occur while he was incommunicado aboard the *Dunnottar Castle*.[774]

Warren and his staff made hurried preparations for their departure from Cape Town, including buying up all available maps of Natal. They embarked the following day, 21 December, aboard the *Mohawk* bound for Durban. For the four days of the journey, Warren put his staff through intensive war games in which, making what use they could of the maps, they practised every possible route for the Relief of Ladysmith. The maps were not up to much. They were nowhere near the quality or reliability of Warren's hastily surveyed reconnaissance maps of Palestine. But it was all they had to go on.

Warren was convinced that the disasters British forces had suffered in the early months of the war were 'due to want of precautions and contempt for the enemy'.[775] He had fought alongside Boers in 1878 and led an expedition

---

[772] Williams, *The Life*, p 259.
[773] *Idem.*, quoting from the diary of Lt. Colonel George Hamilton Sim, Commanding the Royal Engineers on Warren's Staff.
[774] Pakenham, *Boer War*, p 244.
[775] Letter from Warren to his grandson, Watkin Williams, written in July 1925, copy forwarded to the author by the late Revd Christopher Warren in 2013.

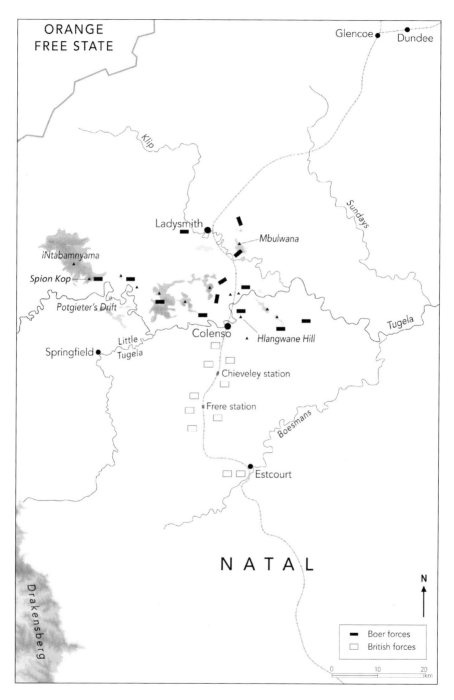

Colenso and Ladysmith, December 1899.

against them in 1885. He understood their strengths, especially their mobility and their familiarity with the type of terrain and climate and their experience gained in the hunting field: '... they could see 2 or 3 miles and shoot up to 2000 yards. It was like fighting an army of GAMEKEEPERS'. This was quite apart from their being advised by expert German officers. The only advantage the British had was 'GRIT AND STAYING POWER, PERTINACITY AND ORGANISATION'.[776] All of this he impressed upon his staff officers.

From what little they had garnered from the Natal front, it was clear that the Boers had established the Tugela as their defensive line south of Ladysmith. The river meandered from west to east through a broad valley that was overlooked from the north by a range of steep hills. The Boers had destroyed the railway bridge at Colenso; but in dry winter weather the river was normally easily fordable via several 'drifts' (fords) as well as a couple of rope-pulled ferries. During the heavy summer rains that were imminent, however, the Tugela would become a deep and swiftly flowing torrent that would require specially built pontoon bridges for the crossing of infantry, artillery and heavy supply wagons. Wherever they crossed, it was clear they would be under fire, probably from the hills beyond.

It was also clear from the maps that just after passing Colenso, which was on the south bank of the river and still occupied by the Boers, the Tugela turned northwards for a couple of miles before returning to its easterly direction. Within this bend to the east of Colenso was the Hlangwane Hill complex. It was the only major position that the Boers occupied south of the river, and this, to Warren's artillery-trained eyes, was the key to an assault on the river crossing and the subsequent Relief of Ladysmith. Artillery placed on Hlangwane could clear the Boers from the complex of small hills to the immediate north of the river, and could also enfilade the entrenched river positions that the Boers had used to such deadly effect on 15 December. Indeed, Hlangwane had been partially occupied by the British during the Battle of Colenso, but they needed more support than Buller could spare at a critical moment in the battle and they were withdrawn.

With the outline of a plan in his head, Warren and his staff disembarked at Durban on Christmas Day 1899.

---

[776] *Idem.* His emphasis.

CHAPTER 21

The Approach to Spion Kop

Lt-General Sir Charles Warren was about to embark on the most difficult and controversial challenge of his career. General Sir Redvers Buller, still GOC the troops in Natal, was to give him command of the force that was intended to clear the way for an advance to the Relief of Ladysmith. But Buller's instructions were a poisoned chalice which Warren, against his better judgement, had no option but to accept. What transpired has been described as 'the biggest and most controversial British disaster of the Anglo-Boer War',[777] namely the Battle of Spion Kop (Spioenkop).[778]

* * *

Within three hours of Warren's arrival at Durban on Christmas Day 1899, he and his staff were on the train to Pietermaritzburg, the administrative capital of Natal. At Government House he learned that Buller had been badly shaken by his reverse at Colenso, that he was saying his men were dispirited, and that since the battle two weeks previously the men had had no contact with the enemy. Apparently, Buller's idea of restoring the men's spirits was to allow them 'athletic sports and Christmas carnivals'.

Warren was shocked. What was needed, he told his audience in Government House, was 'constant *contact with the Boer*: habit makes second nature … No one seemed to realise,' he confided later to his diary, 'that *our first objective was to beat and demoralize the Boer and to show him that the British soldier was the better man*'.[779] According to Warren, the governor and his dinner companions

---

[777] Ron Lock, *Hill of Squandered Valour: The Battle for Spion Kop, 1900* (Casemate, Newbury & Philadelphia, 2011), p 94.

[778] This, the largest in the line of hills dominating the north bank of the Tugela River upstream from Colenso, was named Spion Kop (*Spioenkop* in Afrikaans) – 'Spy Hill' – from the Afrikaans tradition that it was from its summit that the Voortrekkers crossing the Drakensberg in 1837 caught their first glimpse of Natal, the primary goal of many of those who had trekked north from the Cape Colony in 1835–37.

[779] Williams, *The Life*, p 265, quoting from Warren's diary for 26 December 1899. The emphasis was Warren's own.

376

made it clear they expected him to 'go forward to restore confidence'.[780]

The next day, Warren took the train to Estcourt, 100 km up the line towards the battlefront. Leaving his staff to arrange a camp to receive the Fifth Division with all its guns and equipment, he travelled the remaining 20 km to Buller's headquarters at Frere to report his arrival. It was late at night and he found Buller in a particularly morose mood with no sign of the friendly relations they had shared in the past, and Warren decided it was not worth having any discussion that night.

The next morning Buller told Warren he had no intention of making any further move until the arrival of Field Marshal Lord Roberts and his Sixth Division, in two weeks' time. Warren urged the need for more immediate action that would give the men direct contact with the enemy and raise their morale far better than athletic sports and carnivals. He proposed a prompt attack on the Hlangwane Hills, the Boers' only position south of the Tugela and close to the township of Colenso. This, in Warren's opinion, was where the Boers were most vulnerable. Capture of Hlangwane would enable the British to mount their powerful naval guns and enfilade the Boers' entrenched positions across the river which had been the key to their successful defence of Colenso on 15 December.

Indeed, the Boer commander, General Louis Botha, had recognised the vulnerability of this position. His greatest fear before the battle on 15 December had been the British seizure of Hlangwane, and he had sent 800 men to hold it.[781]

But Hlangwane was a sore point with Buller who had abandoned a foothold on the hills during the fiasco of Colenso. He turned angrily on Warren:

'What do you know about it?'

To which Warren could only reply, 'General knowledge, and war games'.[782]

With a snort of derision Buller cast aside a scheme that ultimately, after more disasters, was to prove the key to the Relief of Ladysmith.

Buller then revealed a plan he had in fact considered before he changed his mind and made his disastrous direct attack on Colenso, namely to outflank the Colenso Boers by crossing the Tugela some 25 km upstream at Potgieter's Drift.

Warren was acutely aware that his Fifth Division was made up largely of green troops, with no experience of direct warfare. He knew the Boers had

---

[780] *Idem.*

[781] Hubert Du Cane (trs., German Official Account), *The War in South Africa*, Vol II (John Murray, London, 1906), p 34. Hereafter cited as *German Account*.

[782] Williams, *The Life*, p 264.

an advantage in the wide open spaces of South Africa. They had the hunting experience of judging long distances of 1000 metres or more. And they had the powerful German Mauser smokeless rifles that were accurate at those sorts of distances. By contrast, the British soldier straight out from home had 'no knowledge of distances beyond the barrack square, the cricket field or the end of the street'. He confided to his diary later that day, 'I want to attack Hlangwane because there our men could get practice and be trained in fighting with the Boer more equally, and *I know that the Boers dislike Bush fighting*'.[783]

Disappointed, Warren returned to Estcourt where over the following week he organised his troops as they arrived from the coast and conducted them in manoeuvres, training them in particular in taking cover. The accuracy of modern infantry rifles and artillery over long distances had given *cover* a new importance. They made obsolete the heroic charge across open ground, something that Buller had failed to appreciate during the military manoeuvres over the Wiltshire Downs in 1898. And his tactics at Colenso revealed he had still not learned that lesson.[784]

Warren had not given up on his preferred plan of attack and after discussing it with Major-General Neville Lyttelton of the Fourth Brigade, the two of them went up to see Buller and urge upon him the wisdom of taking Hlangwane before any move towards Potgieter's Drift. They argued that it was not only a good position, but also it would give Warren's green troops the practice they so sorely needed.[785] But Buller would not be moved. They were destined for Potgieter's.

Meanwhile, the Boers attempted to end the siege before Warren's additional forces were ready for action. On Saturday 6 January they made a valiant attempt to capture Ladysmith's outer defences. It was a close-fought battle, the closest the Boers were to come to breaking into the town, but General White's forces held them off.

The next day, Warren's artillery arrived at Estcourt and he was ready to move; but by the time orders from Buller reached him a day later the rains had started in earnest with an all-night torrential storm, turning the gullies that lay in their path into a seething mass of mud.

Colonel Lord Dundonald's Mounted Brigade, a composite force of 1500 Hussars, Dragoons and Mounted Infantry with a battery of field artillery,

[783] *Idem*. His emphasis.
[784] D. M. Leeson, 'Playing at War: The British Military Manoeuvres on 1898', *War in History*, 2008, 15, pp 432–61: http://wih.sagepub.com (Accessed 5 December 2018).
[785] Williams, *The Life*, pp 268–9.

was sent on ahead to Spearman's Farm in the hills above Potgieter's Drift. He covered the 43 kilometres via Frere in just two days. In dry conditions Warren's Fifth Division and those of Buller's troops that he was not leaving opposite Colenso might not have taken much longer. In the event, it took them five days.

No additional roads or bridges had been prepared and once on the move, the single column of 22,000 men and 600 wagons, most of them drawn by teams of between eight and sixteen oxen, stretched for more than 20 kilometres. Streams and gullies were so full of fast-flowing water and mud that wagons stuck fast, blocking the road for those behind. Steam-driven traction engines were called up to haul overloaded wagons and heavy artillery out of the mud. And still the rain fell.

Warren, who until this point was a relatively unknown figure to most of his men, got down into the mud to physically help hauling on ropes, directing operations and improvising bridges across steep-sided gullies. His later critics were to point to this as evidence that he was a man who did not understand the role of a commanding officer; but Warren was not prepared to fit the image of a distant figure mounted on a horse while his men floundered in the mud. He was pleased to note that by the journey's end his men knew exactly who he was and that he was not above a bit of hard, physical graft. On the evening of the third day they reached Springfield Farm (today's Winterton) on the east bank of the Little Tugela River, a tributary two-thirds of the way to their destination.

On 12 January, Buller went on to Spearman's with Lyttelton's Brigade to support Dundonald who had so far met no opposition although Boers could be seen building *schanze* (stone defences) on the mountain ranges opposite. At Spearman's Buller took up an observation position on Mount Alice, a small, steep hill behind the farmhouse. From there he had a clear view of Potgieter's Drift and the hills north of the Tugela, from Vaal Krantz and the Brakfontein ridge to Spion Kop. Potgieter's Drift lay at the southern end of a loop in the river. There were some small hills within the loop, just beyond the drift, and in the distance, guarding the exit from the loop, lay the Brakfontein ridge where it was believed the Boers had taken up a strong position. It was clearly going to be difficult if not impossible to advance a whole division through the Potgieter loop under rifle and artillery fire from the entrenched hills beyond.

On Saturday 13 January, while Warren was negotiating the crossing of the Little Tugela, Buller came down to Springfield to talk tactics. At this point Buller must have spoken of the dangers inherent in crossing a whole division at Potgieter's Drift. According to Warren's later account of this meeting, he suggested to Buller that they cross the Tugela lower downstream and from there attack Doornkop, a hill about eight kilometres east of the Potgieter loop and due north of the confluence of the Little Tugela with the main Tugela River.[786] No record of the details of this discussion has survived, but it is clear that powerful naval guns mounted on Doornkop would have been able to enfilade the Boer entrenchments on Brakfontein and clear the way for a division to mount the main assault across Potgieter's Drift. But Buller rejected the idea and so far as Warren knew at this stage, the plan was still to cross at Potgieter's.[787]

On Sunday 14 January, in a spell of hot dry weather,[788] Warren brought the remaining infantry, artillery and wagons of equipment, up to Spearman's, all non-essential baggage having been left at Springfield, and he ordered camp to be set up on an area of flat land to the rear of Mount Alice.

The following morning, 15 January, the two generals met to discuss tactics and Buller announced that it was too dangerous to make the Potgieter crossing without clearing the Boer artillery positions in the Brakfontein hills and on Spion Kop, the largest of the hills opposing them. This was something that Warren had been aware of when he suggested taking Doornkop, but Buller now presented his alternative. Warren was to take three of the five brigades of infantry available and make a crossing at Trichardt's Drift some 20 kilometres further upstream to the west.

Unbeknown to Warren, Buller had already reconnoitred Trichardt's Drift and had even telegraphed Lansdowne to the effect that he would be sending Warren to lead the main crossing of the Tugela west of Trichardt's Drift. The plan, which Buller admitted was 'undoubtedly risky', was to turn the Boer lines out of the mountains opposite Potgieter's. He told Lansdowne that Warren had agreed to the plan. Warren was later to claim he was not told of Buller's intentions until the morning of 15 January.[789] It was an early sign of impending problems of communication between the two generals.

As soon as he heard of Buller's new plan, Warren set off to reconnoitre as far as Trichardt's Drift. He returned that afternoon to inform Buller that the crossing could be made but it would involve hard fighting for the position was dominated by further hills to the west of Spion Kop in which the Boers were

[786] UKNA, WO/880, Warren to Roberts, Cape Town, 6 August 1900, pp 1–2.
[787] HCPP, Cd. 1791, *Royal Commission on the War in South Africa*, II, Appendix M, Statement by Sir Charles Warren, p 644.
[788] No more rain was to fall for the duration of the campaign on the Upper Tugela.
[789] Cd. 1791, *Royal Commission*, II, pp 627 and 644; Williams, *The Life*, p 280.

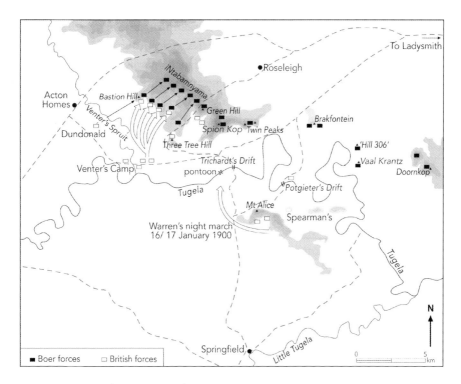

To Ladysmith

•Roseleigh

iNtabamnyama

Acton
Homes •

Bastion Hill

Venter's Spruit

Green Hill

Brakfontein

Dundonald

Spion Kop Twin Peaks

'Hill 306'

Three Tree Hill

Vaal Krantz

Venter's Camp

Trichardt's Drift
pontoon

Doornkop

Tugela

Potgieter's Drift

Mt Alice

Spearman's

Warren's night march
16/ 17 January 1900

Tugela

N

Springfield•

Little Tugela

■ Boer forces   □ British forces

0   5
km

The Upper Tugela Campaign, 17–22 January 1900.

already beginning to entrench themselves.[790]

As soon as the long march from Estcourt via Frere to Spearman's Farm had begun, it had been clear to the Boers that the British were going to try and outflank them on the Upper Tugela.[791] Hitherto the Boers had kept a small force, possibly as few as 400 burghers of the Carolina Commando in the hills around Spion Kop under General Schalk Burger. But as the British column struggled westwards through the mud, these men were joined by reinforcements from the Colenso front, and together with their African servants, they set about entrenching their positions in the hills overlooking the north bank of the river.

By 15 January the Boers had 2000 men firmly entrenched across Vaal Krantz, Brakfontein and Spion Kop. Over the next few days more burghers

[790] Cd. 1791, p 644.
[791] Owen Coetzer, *The Anglo-Boer War: The Road to Infamy*, 1899–1900 (Arms & Armour, London, 1996), p 159.

were drawn from the Colenso front and from the encirclement of Ladysmith[792] so that by the time the British began their crossing at Trichardt's Drift on 17 January, the Boers had 5000 men facing them, not only from Brakfontein to Spion Kop, but also busy extending their entrenchments across the iNtabamnyama plateau ('Rangeworthy Heights') to the west of Spion Kop.[793]

On the afternoon of Monday 15 January, after Warren had returned from his reconnoitre of Trichardt's Drift, he received secret instructions from Buller. He was being given command of three-fifths of the force on the Upper Tugela while Buller remained at Spearman's Farm with two brigades under Lyttelton and the long-range naval guns. With no further reconnaissance or discussion of the topography across the river, Warren was to take 12,000 infantry, 36 pieces of field artillery together with three and a half days' supplies and Dundonald's Mounted Brigade and make a crossing at or near Trichardt's Drift while Lyttelton made a demonstration at Potgieter's to draw Boer attention away from Warren's crossing.

Failing to appreciate the manoeuvrability of the enemy, Buller seems to have believed that there were still only 400 Boers west of Spion Kop and that it would be easy for Warren to overrun them on the iNtabamnyama Hills.[794] The exact wording of Buller's secret instructions was crucial to an understanding of what happened in the days that followed. There was little detail in the instructions, leaving Warren considerable latitude:

> You will of course act as circumstances require, but my idea is that you should continue refusing your right and throwing your left forward till you gain the open plain north of Spion Kop.[795]

Warren had little further time to discuss tactics with Buller for he had to plan and issue orders for the westwards march, but he was clear in his own mind as to Buller's intent:

> … in other words, sweeping our left around and forward, with our right as a pivot, until the line became north south.[796]

---

[792] Deneys Reitz, *Commando: A Boer Journal of the Boer War* (1st edition 1929, this edition, CruGuru, 2009), p 43.
[793] *German Account*, Vol II, p 55.
[794] Frederick Maurice, *History of the War in South Africa 1899–1902* (Hurst and Blackett, London, 1902), Volume II, App. 8 (H).9, pp 347–48 and 625. Hereafter cited as Maurice, *Official History*.
[795] HCPP (1902), Cd. 968, *South Africa. The Spion Kop Despatches*, pp 13–14, hereafter cited as *Spion Kop Despatches*.
[796] Williams, *The Life*, p 282.

Royal Engineers constructing one of the two pontoons
across the Tugela near Trichardt's Drift, 17 January 1900.
MCGREGOR MUSEUM, KIMBERLEY, SOUTH AFRICA

Once the Boer flank had been turned in this fashion, Buller would be able to launch Lyttelton's two brigades across Potgieter's Drift. It is clear from Buller's orders to Warren that he considered his own assault to be the main attack, for he kept all the big guns and ordered Warren to return the pontoons to him once the Tugela had been crossed.[797] The two forces would then unite and together take the direct road to Ladysmith.

During the course of that Monday afternoon, Warren despatched platoons of Royal Engineers to start making pontoons for the river crossing and to clear a road from Spearman's to Trichardt's Drift, flattening out troublesome gullies along the route.

At 4 am on Tuesday 16 January, the pontoons moved off, on a circuitous route out of sight of the Boers. Warren realised that speed and secrecy were of the essence and by that afternoon he had assembled his wagons of equipment in six parallel columns so there would be no clogging up of a long, single column as had happened on the march from Estcourt. Leaving the tents

[797] Maurice, *Official Account*, II, p 625.

383

Infantry crossing the Tugela pontoon 17 January 1900.
MCGREGOR MUSEUM, KIMBERLEY, SOUTH AFRICA

assembled at Spearman's under a skeleton guard to give the impression to the Boers across the river that the camp was still occupied, the artillery left at 6 pm and the infantry and wagons at sunset (about 7.30 pm).

According to the official history published immediately after the war 'the passage of Sir Charles Warren's transport was painfully slow'.[798] While that may have been the case for the passage from Estcourt to Spearman's, it was a serious misjudgement for the overnight march to Trichardt's Drift.

The bulk of Warren's force had covered the 20 kilometres to Trichardt's Drift by the early hours of the morning, and by dawn on the 17th the engineers had erected a pontoon across the Tugela. The infantry began crossing first thing in the morning, and by the afternoon Woodgate's and Hart's brigades and one battery of artillery were assembled on the north bank. Buller was present during the day and instructed Woodgate as to the disposition of his battalion once he was across. Dundonald's mounted brigade crossed independently slightly downstream. And while all this was happening, Lyttelton demonstrated across Potgieter's Drift and occupied the small hills on the north bank.[799]

[798] *Ibid.*, p 358.
[799] *Ibid.*, p 354.

During the course of the morning a second pontoon was erected slightly further upstream to assist the passage of the wagons and artillery and in the afternoon the wagons began the business of crossing the river. On Buller's recommendation the oxen were swum across while the wagons were hauled by mules and men. The passage of equipment continued all night and was completed at dusk the next day. According to Warren's estimate, what should have taken between two and a half and three and a half days was completed in 37 hours, with Warren, who claimed one hour's sleep in 60, present throughout.[800] It is interesting to note that the withdrawal of troops back across the Tugela that took place ten days later, and for which Buller claimed full credit, took ten hours longer.[801]

On Thursday 18 January, leaving General Clery[802] to hold his right opposite Spion Kop, Warren ordered two brigades to make a flank march to the west as far as Venter's Spruit, a tributary of the Tugela about seven kilometres upstream from Trichardt's Drift. He was to make this his base camp on the north bank, and as the wagons completed their crossing that day, they were moved up to the Venter's Spruit camp.

Venter's Spruit flowed from the north-west, more or less parallel to the iNtabamnyama Hills, and Warren ordered Dundonald to leave a picket of 400 Royal Dragoons to protect the wagons and thousands of oxen at base camp, and to take the rest of his brigade to reconnoitre the country to the north-west along the line of the Venter's Spruit. Warren anticipated stretching the left of his infantry line in this direction in preparation for an assault on the hills.

Dundonald established a camp halfway along the west bank of the stream and in the afternoon sent Warren a report with sketches of the approaches to the iNtabamnyama range. It is clear from this despatch that Dundonald accepted Warren's interpretation of Buller's plan that he would mount his flanking assault on the iNtabamnyama Hills, and he advised him to approach along the west bank of Venter's Spruit. To advance along the east bank would leave his column too exposed to rifle fire from the enemy-occupied iNtabamnyama foothills.[803]

Meanwhile, Dundonald had sent two exploratory squadrons under Major Graham to investigate further along the north-west track as far as Acton Homes. Here they met the main Boer supply road that ran behind the iNtabamnyama Hills and linked the Orange Free State to Ladysmith. On

---

[800] Williams, *The Life*, pp 286–7.
[801] See below, p 413.
[802] Lieutenant-General C. F. Clery was divisional commander of the Second Division.
[803] Maurice, *Official History*, II, Appendix 9 (c), p 61.

reaching Acton Homes they surprised a troop of Boers who were riding out from behind the hills. About twenty Boers were killed and fifteen captured, the rest being scattered. British casualties numbered only three.[804] Graham's men secured their position and sent to Dundonald for reinforcements. The first Warren knew about it was a message that evening from Dundonald that read:

> My advanced squadrons are engaged with the enemy. I am supporting them. Can you let me have the Royals?[805]

This was a reference to the Royal Dragoons left guarding Warren's wagons, guns and oxen. It was unclear to Warren just how engaged with the enemy Dundonald was. He was loath to lose his mounted picket, but he let him have three squadrons of the Royals, leaving himself with only about 100 cavalry to guard his camp. A later despatch from Dundonald, received by Warren at 9 pm, gave a little more detail of the action that day, but contained a phrase that worried Warren:

> … am holding position and kopjes [small hills] commanding the west of your line; details later.[806]

But Warren had no line yet beyond his base camp. This left Dundonald out on a limb, with no indication yet as to how strong the enemy was either at Acton Homes, or between there and Warren's base camp. Warren responded:

> The position you have occupied seems to be too far to the northwest, but of this I cannot be certain.

He told Dundonald he would be advancing along Venter's Spruit the following day in preparation for the assault on the iNtabamnyama, but he felt vulnerable with so few mounted men to guard his camp:

> What number of mounted men can you send me, as I have practically none?[807]

Meanwhile, on his right General Clery had been coming under rifle fire as he advanced towards the foothills close to the south-west corner of Spion Kop, and Warren was pleased to note that 'the men are getting into splendid practice at taking cover'.[808]

[804] Maurice, *Official History*, II, pp 360–361.
[805] Maurice, *Official History*, II, Appendix 9 (c), p 632.
[806] *Idem.*
[807] *Idem.*
[808] Williams, *The Life*, p 292, quoting from Warren's diary.

At dawn the next morning (Friday 19 January), Warren received a note from Dundonald urging that there was a clear road to Ladysmith via Acton Homes. Dundonald was clearly excited by the ease of his initial clash with the enemy and perhaps was unaware that intelligence reports from as far back as 10 January were reporting that there was a strong encampment of Boers at Acton Homes from whence the commandos encamped behind Spion Kop drew their supplies, and that this position was daily being strengthened.[809] But even if this were not the case and the road via Acton Homes had indeed been clear, there was no way Warren was simply going to follow Dundonald to Acton Homes.

The track along Venter's Spruit that Dundonald had recommended was narrow and Warren would have to advance his infantry and wagons of equipment in single column while dangerously exposed to enemy rifle and artillery fire from iNtabamnyama. In any case, it was far too long a route and would leave the Boers still entrenched on the iNtabamnyama plateau. He worried that Dundonald was acting independently and had become detached from the main force. The current object of the campaign so far as Warren was concerned was to defeat the Boers, not simply evade them and ride into Ladysmith. At 7 am he instructed Dundonald:

> Our objective is not Ladysmith. Our objective is to effect a junction with Sir Redvers Buller's force and then to receive orders from him. … I require your men to act as part of my force.[810]

During the course of that day the last of the supply wagons assembled at the Venter's Spruit camp, while the infantry brigades began their advance towards the foothills to the west of Spion Kop. Buller was present during the course of the day and reported that Warren had 'attacked and gained a considerable advantage on that day'.[811] But most contemporary observers, including Buller in retrospect, were later to comment that Warren was far too slow at advancing and engaging the enemy.[812]

Warren, however, only felt secure to launch a serious attack upon the

---

[809] *UKNA*, WO 32/880, Warren to Roberts, 6 August 1900. I am grateful to Gilbert Torlage for a copy of this letter, also housed in the South African National Archives, FK 1862.

[810] Maurice, *Official History*, II, Appendix 9 (c), p 632.

[811] *Spion Kop Despatches*, p 15.

[812] L. S. Amery, *The Times History of the War 1899–1900* (London, 1902), Vol.III, p 221; Bennet Burleigh, *The Natal Campaign* (Chapman & Hall, London, 1900), p 306; and Winston Churchill, *London to Ladysmith via Pretoria* (Longman Green, London, 1900), p 297.

enemy once his base camp was firmly established and securely guarded. He was not worried about the enemy becoming entrenched while he was getting his men assembled. They were entrenched already by 17 January. He was not going to rush his troops into action over ground which had not been properly reconnoitred, for which he had totally inadequate maps, and where he had little idea exactly where the enemy or their artillery were positioned.

Furthermore, his troops were mostly inexperienced at coming under fire and needed more practice at taking cover and receiving and returning fire. They needed, in his unfortunate phrase, 'to be blooded'.[813] And that meant moving forward slowly but surely against the enemy. With three days' experience of advancing and taking cover, the troops would gain confidence, and Warren had no doubt that the British Tommy was the better soldier and would overcome the Boers once the serious hill fighting began.

By Saturday 20 January Warren's rehearsals were more or less complete and he launched an attack on all fronts. In the centre he gained control of the foothills immediately to the west of Spion Kop, including Three Tree Hill which was to become his advance headquarters and on which a battery of artillery was mounted. And to his left he gained control of the southern slopes of the eastern half of the iNtabamnyama plateau. The following day these advances were continued further west, drawing in Dundonald's mounted troops as General Hildyard launched a successful assault on Bastion Hill, a promontory near the western end of the plateau. This was as far west as Warren was prepared to go. Meanwhile, his infantry gained control all along the southern lip of the plateau.

Thus far the British infantry had gained in both experience and confidence for they had been advancing from cover to cover, engaging the Boers at their own game, and proving just as accurate with the rifle.[814]

But there they stuck, on the southern edge of the plateau, for the Boers had withdrawn across an expanse of flat, open land to the slightly higher northern crest where they were firmly entrenched. It was proving impossible for the British to advance across the flat land that separated the two forces without unacceptably high casualties. There were, in effect, two entrenched lines separated by a 'no man's land', the feature of modern warfare that was to characterise the Western Front in The Great War a decade and a half later.

---

[813] A phrase from English fox-hunting practice whereby a novice hunter was initiated by being smeared with the blood of his first kill.
[814] Burleigh, *Natal Campaign*, p 320.

On Sunday 21 January Buller warned Warren that intelligence reports indicated the Boers had sent 2000 men to strengthen their position near Acton Homes, so more troops and artillery were despatched to support General Hildyard at Bastion Hill, and the day's action was focussed on Warren's left. That evening Buller reported to the War Office that fighting had continued all day on Warren's left and, despite the difficulty of fighting uphill, Buller observed, 'I think we are making substantial progress'.[815] But he was soon to change his mind when he realised that any real progress to the left that day was barely discernible while Warren's troops lay strung out all along the southern edge of the iNtabamnyama plateau, making no progress at all.

By close of day on 21 January it was clear that Buller's plan for clearing the Boers from their positions in the hills overlooking the Upper Tugela had reached stalemate. Warren was confident that howitzers, that he now called for, would clear the Boers from their entrenched position after several days of bombardment.[816] But Buller did not share Warren's confidence in the ability to shift the Boers. He feared he was once more staring failure in the face and he looked for a scapegoat in his subordinate commander, to whom he had delegated responsibility for the action.

Since the 19th Buller had been fed the idea by Dundonald that Warren had missed his chance of pushing his infantry rapidly up to Acton Homes and thus reaching the clear road to Ladysmith, which a squadron of his mounted men had reached on the 18th. Then it had been relatively lightly guarded by the Boers, though the latter were hourly strengthening their position in that direction. From about the 21st Buller began to reinterpret his original secret orders to Warren and claim that a rapid advance to Acton Homes, not the iNtabamnyama Hills, was what he had intended all along, but Warren had been too slow, hesitant and unimaginative to act on it. At the time Buller said nothing to Warren of his misgivings, though he went over from his strategic position on Mount Alice to converse with Warren daily and to make suggestions such as moving his artillery or strengthening his left.

Warren was faced with an impossible situation as his large force of infantry tried, in difficult terrain, to grapple with a highly mobile, if smaller force of Boers who were able to use the terrain to their maximum advantage.

Warren could see that the only way a large force of infantry and artillery

---

[815] Quoted in Williams, *The Life*, p 299.
[816] Warren to his grandson, Watkin Williams, July 1925, from a private letter communicated to the author by the late Revd Christopher Warren.

could win in the South African conditions was to pound the enemy into near submission through a massive artillery barrage and then overwhelm them with the sheer strength in numbers of an extended line of infantry. It was what Warren had recommended doing at Hlangwane and it was now what he had tried to do in the hills of the Upper Tugela. The problem was his artillery batteries could not see the enemy who were well entrenched, with their own artillery concealed on the reverse slopes of a wide expanse of hills. Warren's artillery was confined to the relatively narrow expanse of low ground and foothills such as Three Tree Hill and had to direct their fire upwards at, they knew not what. That was why, rather late in the day, he had called for howitzers.

Meanwhile, the topography of the iNtabamnyama Hills had granted the Boers a superb natural defensive position against the British infantry, and their superior mobility enabled them to strengthen any point that was threatened. Their expert marksmanship, with some of the best rifles in the world, and just enough of the right kind of artillery were a bonus. All they needed was the right leadership to bring it all together and they got this in General Louis Botha, the victor of Colenso, who was appointed on 19 January, on the direct orders of President Paul Kruger, to command the Boer defence of the Upper Tugela.

CHAPTER 22

The Battle of Spion Kop

On the morning of Monday 22 January Buller came over to discuss the situation with Warren. In exasperation at the lack of progress he put pressure on his second-in-command to find a way through or face the humiliation of withdrawing across the Tugela. Warren had already dismissed the Acton Homes road as too narrow and hazardous for a long line of infantry and wagons, while several days of fighting on the iNtabamnyama had shown that the British could not sweep over the hills as Warren, and Buller, had originally hoped.

That only left the Fairview road. It was barely worthy of the name 'road', but it was the main wagon track north from Trichardt's Drift that ran just to the west of Three Tree Hill, through the eastern edge of the iNtabamnyama Hills and on to Rosalie Farm behind Spion Kop. And yet the result of that meeting between the two generals was that Warren should take Spion Kop, that prominent bastion that the British had so far avoided.

Almost every account of the battle that was to come has portrayed the decision to take Spion Kop as suddenly being presented by Warren, more or less because he could not think of anything else to do. And Buller, if he is included in the decision at all, is portrayed as somewhat reluctantly agreeing, 'Of course you must take Spion Kop'.[817] Warren's account of the rationale behind this decision is contained in his letter to Field Marshal Lord Roberts written some six months later, and yet very few historians appear to have consulted this source.[818] Only Gilbert Torlage has made use of its evidence in his short account of the battle produced for the 'Battles of the Anglo-Boer War Series'.[819]

---

[817] This line was even followed by Williams, *The Life*, p 300.
[818] UKNA, WO 32/880, Warren to Roberts, Cape Town, 6 August 1900. I am grateful to Gilbert Torlage for forwarding me copies of this correspondence, acquired from the South African National Archives (Ref. FK 1862). I am also grateful to Gilbert Torlage for giving me a copy of his draft typescript paper provisionally entitled, 'A War Within a War. The conflict between Generals Sir Redvers Buller and Sir Charles Warren'.
[819] Gilbert Torlage, *The Battle of Spioenkop, 23–24 January 1900* (30° South Publishers, Pinetown, 2014), pp 12–13.

As Warren points out in his letter to Roberts, Buller's account implies that

…when I had ascertained that an advance by Acton Homes Road was impossible, the attack on Spion Kop was necessitated.

But he goes on to state:

This certainly was never my view of the situation. I looked upon both the roads by Acton Homes and Fairview Farm as impossible for wagons. The former on account of its length and the strength of the enemy's position, the latter on account of the commanding position of Spion Kop. I therefore proposed to send back the wagons and proceed [along the Fairview road] without them, after having driven back the enemy.

He then maintains:

It was Sir R. Buller who first proposed attacking Spion Kop. On 22nd Jan when discussing the subject of an advance I again told him that … we could not take our wagons. He said I *must* take them. I protested that it was impossible to take the wagons without first taking Spion Kop. He replied, 'of course you must take Spion Kop'.[820]

Warren maintains that Buller left him with two options: a frontal attack on the iNtabamnyama plateau, which he had already tried and now regarded as 'too hazardous', and an attack on Spion Kop, which he believed was 'not necessary' if they took the Fairview road without wagons; but that at least the latter was 'practicable'.[821] But with Buller insisting on his taking the wagons, the decision was made to capture Spion Kop.

Warren proposed leading the assault himself, but Buller, perhaps remembering the death of Major-General Sir George Colley on Majuba Hill in 1881, pointed out that War Office regulations would not allow it. He himself as Commander-in-Chief of the Natal Force was not allowed in the front line, which was why he had delegated the trans-Tugela force to Warren; following the same principle, Warren must remain below, in overall command of all the troops on the north bank. Command of the Spion Kop assault thus fell to Major-General Talbot Coke. It was proposed that Coke should leave that night, but he requested a delay of 24 hours so that he could reconnoitre the position.

---

[820] WO 32/880, Warren to Roberts, 6 August 1900, p 8.
[821] *Idem.*

This was accepted as a reasonable request, although in the event neither he nor Warren did any more reconnoitring the next day than go to the base of Spion Kop to determine the best way up. They could see nothing of the summit from below, though from Buller's command post on Mount Alice, it appeared to be a slightly curved plateau. With the southern face almost sheer cliff, the best way up was to follow a spur that extended from the mountain's south-west corner. During the course of the day Buller, who later tried to distance himself from the entire Spion Kop operation, pointed out that Coke was somewhat lame from a previous broken leg, and he recommended Major-General Woodgate of the Lancashire Brigade to replace Coke.

The assaulting force was thus made up of the 2nd Lancashire Fusiliers and six companies of the Royal Lancashire Regiment, accompanied by Colonel Thorneycroft with 200 of his Mounted Infantry (dismounted) and half a company of sappers (the troops of the Royal Engineers). Buller added his own staff officer, Colonel à Court Repington, to accompany Woodgate and to report to him on the progress of the assault. No further preparations seem to have been made that day, other than issuing instructions to the officers in charge of the assault force.

The most conspicuous thing missing on the summit once the battle was underway was well-entrenched artillery. It appears that Warren dare not send his engineers to construct a pathway up the spur during the hours of daylight on the 23rd for fear the Boers would realise what he was planning, but he did request from Buller a Mountain Battery that could be sent up and entrenched once Spion Kop had been taken. It turned out that the only Mountain Battery available was back at Springfield on the Little Tugela and it did not leave Springfield until 11.00 am on the 24th. In the event it covered the distance remarkably quickly and it reached Trichardt's Drift that evening, but by that time the battle had been raging for twelve hours and it was already too late to be effective.[822] Warren was to lay the blame on Buller for the late arrival of the guns, claiming that he 'did not send them in time to arrive at the foot of Spionkop [*sic*] before sunset'.[823] But exactly when Warren sent for the guns remains unclear, and as they did not leave Springfield for a full 48 hours after the decision to take Spion Kop, a large part of the blame for their late arrival must remain with him.

* * *

---

[822] *Spion Kop Despatches*, p 46.
[823] WO 32/880, Warren to Roberts, 6 August 1900, pp 17–18.

During the late-afternoon that Tuesday 23 January the chosen force assembled out of sight of the enemy in a small ravine south of Three Tree Hill. The advance to the spur began about 7.30 pm. It was over very rough ground and it took three hours to reach the base of the spur. Thorneycroft and his men scouted ahead and led the way up. With pauses for the line to close up, they reached a small plateau at the top of the spur just after 3 am and found that a thick mist had come down to cover the whole of the top of the mountain. They closed up, fixed bayonets, formed a series of lines and at 3.30 am they advanced on the summit. On being challenged by a Boer picket, they flung themselves to the ground. After the Boers discharged their rifles, they got up and charged with a wild shout.[824]

The summit of Spion Kop had been a regular target of Buller's heavy naval guns on Mount Alice and little more than 100 burghers of the Carolina Commando had been left to guard it during the night. The British rush caught them completely by surprise. One burgher was killed in the bayonet charge and the rest hurried towards the north-east where their camp was on the slopes below. A triumphal British shout told Warren and those below on the south side that the summit had been taken. At the same time word rapidly spread among the commandos that the British had seized Spion Kop.

General Botha realised that a firm British position on Spion Kop, especially if backed by well-protected artillery, would be able to clear the Boers from what had hitherto been secure defensive positions and put at risk his whole defence of the Upper Tugela. As Deneys Reitz of the Pretoria Commando observed:

> … if the hill went the entire Tugela line would go with it, and we could hardly bring ourselves to believe the news.[825]

Thus, while the British sappers, with a totally inadequate supply of picks and spades (many having been dropped during the climb), hacked away at the rocky surface on the summit in a vain attempt to dig a defensive trench on an east-west line across what appeared in the dark and mist to be the peak of the mountain, General Botha was repositioning his artillery in an arc focussed on Spion Kop, and with his guns on the reverse slopes of hills they were invisible to the British artillery batteries. At the same time he ordered General Schalk Burger to retake the mountain at all costs. At first light below the mist other

---

[824] 'Account of the ascent of Spion Kop' by Lt.-Colonel Alex Thorneycroft. I am grateful to Gilbert Torlage for providing me with a copy of this typescript account.
[825] Reitz, *Commando*, p 47.

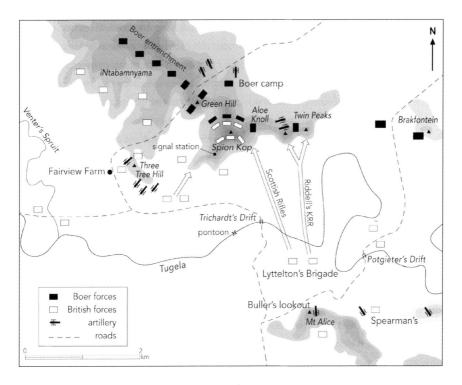

Spion Kop, 23–24 January 1900.

commandos were ordered to support the Carolinas and to take positions in the hills both east and west of Spion Kop.

By 7 am the sappers had managed to clear a shallow ditch barely half a metre deep across their trenching line and raise some rocks and stones into a low breastwork along its northern front. Hundreds of sandbags had been destined for the top, but in the dark of the ascent they had inadvertently been left at the bottom. Unable to do more under the circumstances, most of the sappers went back to attend to the widening of the path up the spur.

Until 7.30 that morning, Wednesday 24 January, the British were protected by the thick mist that still shrouded the mountain, and Woodgate could not assess the strength or weakness of his position. Content he had achieved his task of occupying the summit, and unable to heliograph because of the mist, he sent a written message to Warren at 7.15 am by the hand of Colonel à Court Repington.

It was 9.15 am by the time Warren received this message at Three Tree Hill. It assured him that the assault force had taken advantage of the mist and the capture of the summit had gone well. As Woodgate had reported two hours earlier:

> We have entrenched a position, and are, I hope, secure; but fog is too thick to see …[826]

The satisfactory occupation of the summit was confirmed verbally by Colonel à Court who had jubilantly told the journalist Bennet Burleigh that the summit could be held 'till Doomsday against all comers'.[827] Neither à Court nor Woodgate indicated the inadequacy of the entrenchment, or the lack of sandbags on the summit; nor did anybody else, and throughout the day of the battle Warren was under the misplaced impression that the troops on the summit were well entrenched.

By the time Warren received Woodgate's message, the occupying troops had been under heavy Boer rifle and artillery fire for an hour and a half, and Woodgate himself had been mortally wounded.

As the mist had begun to lift from about 7.30 am it had become clear that the British makeshift entrenchment was too far back. The northern crest of the summit where they should have been was 150 metres ahead of them and the Lancashires quickly pushed forward to occupy it, though they had not time to entrench and relied on the makeshift shelter of individual rocks. By this time the Carolina Commando was pushing up to the same crest from the north-east. And through the morning the Boer position was reinforced all along the northern crest while commandos in the hills to east and west focussed their rifle fire on enfilading the British central trench.

Once the mist was fully cleared the 1700 British troops packed into the acre that was the summit of Spion Kop began to feel the full effects of the Boers' heavy Krupp guns as well as the dreaded Maxim-Nordenfelt rapid-firing light artillery. The latter, fed by belts each containing 25 one-pound explosive shells, were known to the British who suffered under them as 'Pom-Poms', from the sound of their rapid fire. There was one such gun positioned to the west and another a kilometre to the east, on a pair of hills known as Twin Peaks. At this point Woodgate received a shrapnel bullet in the head as he walked around the summit organising its defence and command fell to Colonel Crofton of the Royal Lancashires as the next most senior officer on the summit.

As Warren read Woodgate's somewhat reassuring message, he could

---

[826] Quoted in Williams, *The Life*, p 306.
[827] Bennet Burleigh, *The Natal Campaign* (Chapman & Hall, London, 1900), p 331.

The Boers' Pretoria Commando encamped behind Spion Kop.
MCGREGOR MUSEUM, KIMBERLEY, SOUTH AFRICA

hear the sound of battle on the summit and, confident he had the western side covered by his artillery, he ordered General Coke, who was with the Connaught Rangers near the base of Spion Kop, to send reinforcements to the south-eastern slopes to tackle the Boers on that flank. The main Boer position there was on a small hill, known as Aloe Knoll, connected to the eastern edge of Spion Kop by a shallow saddle, and it was in this direction that Coke sent the Imperial Light Infantry and the Middlesex Regiment. It was to take them several hours to make their way across the southern face of Spion Kop.

* * *

By the time Colonel Crofton realised he was in command on the summit, the situation had deteriorated considerably. Woodgate's death had revealed how difficult it was to move around under such incessant fire, and it took Crofton a while to organise a message to Warren. He appeared not to have a signals pad with him and he gave a verbal message to a signals officer:

General Woodgate dead. Reinforcements urgently required.[828]

[828] Maurice, *Official History*, App. 10 (A), p 639. In fact Woodgate survived, in delirium, for a further two months.

397

Had Crofton sent a written message, he might have given some information on the true position on the summit, such as the inadequate entrenchment, and in particular where the worst of the rifle and artillery fire was coming from. The heliograph point on the western side of the spur, in direct line with Warren's command post at Three Tree Hill, was destroyed by shrapnel early in the battle and a new signal point had to be established on the eastern side of the ridge. This took it out of Warren's line of sight and so messages had to be sent to Buller's post on Mount Alice above Spearman's Farm. From there messages were first seen by Buller and then telegraphed to Warren.

By the time Crofton's signals officer had reached the signaller, Crofton's original verbal message had increased in urgency. In the excitement of battle the signaller ratcheted it up even further so that the message Warren received at 9.50 am was:

Reinforce at once or all is lost. General dead.[829]

Having already sent two battalions from Coke's brigade to the eastern slopes, Warren now made a direct appeal to Lyttelton at Potgieter's Drift to assist in turning the Boer's eastern flank. His message to Lyttelton was not sent via Buller, as it should have been, as Lyttelton was under Buller's command and this was to cause problems later in the day.

Warren may have been alarmed at the defeatist tone of Crofton's message, but he was still reassured by à Court's verbal report that the troops were well entrenched on Spion Kop, and he had little sense of the true state of emergency on the summit. He rode over to General Coke at the foot of the spur and ordered him, despite his lameness, to take command on Spion Kop. As Coke prepared to make the ascent, Warren's last words to him were:

You must hold on to the last. No surrender.[830]

Despite these words, the lack of urgency was palpable and it was 11.10 am before Coke started his ascent along with the Dorset Regiment.

Buller, with his telescope on Mount Alice trained on the summit, could see the battle better than anybody. Several attempts had been made to rush the northern crest, which was actually beyond Buller's view, and those that reached some rock for shelter found themselves barely a rifle's length from the enemy.[831] Several of these rushes were beaten back to the central trench,

---

[829] Quoted in Williams, *The Life*, p 308.
[830] *Spion Kop Despatches*, Appendix M.
[831] *German Account*, II, p 90.

and this was observed by Buller. He recognised the agile bulk of Colonel Thorneycroft fearlessly ranging around, urging the troops not to give way under what was clearly devastating fire. Even so, it was 11.45 am when Buller telegraphed Warren:

> Unless you put some really good hard fighting man in command on the top you will lose the hill. I suggest Thorneycroft.[832]

It was difficult to know what Crofton had been doing in terms of command on the summit, beyond sending for reinforcements, and Warren, knowing that Buller had a better view of the battle and had seen the few heliographs from Spion Kop before himself, took the suggestion as an order. He immediately telegraphed a message to be heliographed to Crofton from Mount Alice:

> With the approval of the Commander-in-Chief, I place Lt.-Colonel Thorneycroft in command of the summit, with the local rank of Brigadier-General.[833]

The messenger on the summit was killed before he could deliver this message, and it was a while before Thorneycroft's orderly managed to crawl close enough towards his colonel to shout:

> Sir Charles Warren has heliographed that you are to take command. You are a General.[834]

In a private letter to his brother after the battle Thorneycroft acknowledged that a heliograph from Warren had put him in command, although he did not realise he had been given the rank of Brigadier-General: 'but it made no difference as I continued to command'.[835]

Meanwhile, Coke was still climbing the spur and out of communication with Warren. By the time he reached the small plateau by the signal station just below the summit, it was 12.50 pm. Much criticism has been levelled at Warren for the apparent confusion as to who was in command of Spion Kop. So far as Warren was concerned the position was clear: Major-General Coke was in overall command of the operation on Spion Kop, but, on the urging of General Buller, he had placed Colonel Thorneycroft 'in command on the summit', knowing that Coke would reasonably base himself in a secure

---

[832] *Idem.*
[833] *Spion Kop Despatches*, p 25.
[834] Quoted from Williams, *The Life*, p 310.
[835] Thorneycroft to his brother Jim, Spearman's Camp, 30 January 1900. I am grateful to Gilbert Terlage for providing me with a typed copy of this letter.

position just behind the front line of fighting.[836]

As a commander, however, Coke was far from active. Despite not having ventured onto the summit itself, he felt free to heliograph Warren that the men on top were holding out well under heavy shellfire. The summit, he said, was overcrowded with men and he was thus holding back the reinforcements, the Dorsets, that had accompanied him. With lack of urgency, he ended on a complacent note:

> … the troops engaged know that help is near at hand. Ammunition is being pushed up.[837]

The latter was partly due to Warren who was heavily engaged in supervising the mule trains of ammunition and water and the improvement of the track up the spur in preparation for the guns that he expected to send up that evening.

One of the persistent complaints of Colonel Thorneycroft and the men on the front line who had gone up the night before was that they had no water apart from the little they had carried up on their persons in the original assault.[838] Warren and others who had not been on the summit protested that plenty of water had been sent up in large biscuit tins strapped to mules. But none of these ever reached the exhausted men under fire on the summit. Much was spilled on the way up and that which got as far as the dressing stations near the top of the spur was commandeered for the wounded. With wounded and unwounded men slipping away and making their way down the mountain in the afternoon, few were prepared to risk the acre of death to carry water to those still on the front line.[839]

Part of the problem lay in Warren's lack of staff officers, for Buller had refused to spare him the full range of staff officers that should have accompanied such a large command.[840] As a result there were few available officers to whom he could delegate and who could keep him informed of the true and ever-changing state of affairs on the summit.

---

[836] Warren's position on the command on Spion Kop is made clear in his subsequent letter to Field-Marshal Roberts, dated 6 August, section 18, p 23, in UKNA, WO 32/880.

[837] *HCPP*, Cd. 1791, *Royal Commission on the War in South Africa*, II, Q. 20210, p 443.

[838] Torlage, *Spioenkop*, pp 40–42, quoting a personal letter from Lt.-Colonel Thorneycroft to his brother, 3 February 1900, in which he complained that none of the water sent up reached those on the summit.

[839] Lock, *Squandered Valour*, pp 221–2, quoting from a range of sources.

[840] WO 32/880, Warren to Roberts, 6 August 1900, p 2.

Thus with his primary focus on the logistics of Spion Kop, Warren lacked a view of the wider picture and he failed to make any attempt to utilise the thousands of troops strung out along the southern crest of the iNtabamnyama plateau. Their lack of activity had enabled General Botha to withdraw the Krupp gun from Acton Homes as well as large numbers of men from iNtabamnyama to focus on Spion Kop. A strong push by Hildyard at this point might well have broken through on the west and turned the whole course of the battle. But Warren issued no such orders; and neither did Buller make any of his 'suggestions' in that direction, despite his later complaint of Warren's failure on his left.

Throughout the morning the Lancashires who had been up all night bravely held the line along the northern crest of Spion Kop, although by late-morning some had simply had enough and 187 spontaneously surrendered and were captured by the Boers. Any further surrender had been ended by a furious Thorneycroft.

Warren's artillery on Three Tree Hill pounded away all day, but the gunners had no idea where Botha's guns were positioned, even if they could reach them on their reverse slopes and they remained, in Thorneycroft's words, 'absolutely unmolested'.[841] Neither could Buller see them from Mount Alice. His long naval guns probed but failed to find them.

By midday the British front line on the summit had been beaten back to the central trench. This offered a little relief for the Carolina and Pretoria commandos who had suffered high casualties on their side of the crest, with many fighting men lying among their dead and wounded comrades, short of water and running low on ammunition. But from east and west of Spion Kop the Boer onslaught was relentless from rifle and artillery. Indeed, enfilading fire from Aloe Knoll and from Twin Peaks had been so accurate that many of those killed in the eastern part of the British trench died from a bullet in the right temple.

From his position on the ground Warren could not see Aloe Knoll and he may not even have been aware of its existence. Buller, who had a good view from Mount Alice, should have been more liberal with his 'suggestions' at this point. Perhaps by the afternoon he could see disaster unfolding and preferred to keep his thoughts to himself.

Meanwhile, at 2.30 pm on the summit itself Colonel Thorneycroft finally got a chance to send a written message to Warren, giving him the clearest

---

[841] Thorneycroft to his brother Jim, 30 January 1900.

Spion Kop as viewed from Buller's position on Mount Alice. The small spike on top marks the memorial pillar and the position of the British central 'trench' on the summit.

KEVIN SHILLINGTON

view yet of the true situation on the summit. He appealed for artillery fire to be brought to bear on the enemy gun positions to east and west. In a private letter to his brother after the battle, he wrote that the unmolested Boer artillery *'literally swept the hill'*.[842] Casualties were high, he informed Warren: more men were needed to replace these and to relieve those of the original assault force who had been in action since early morning. There was also a desperate need for water. He concluded with the words:

> If you wish to make a certainty of hill for night, you must send more infantry and attack enemy's guns.[843]

In retrospect one can discern here that Thorneycroft was already considering the possibility of having to withdraw at nightfall.

The officer who carried Thorneycroft's despatch down to the signal station

[842] *Ibid.,* his emphasis.
[843] *Spion Kop Despatches,* p 27.

70 metres below the summit showed it to General Coke who was established there with his staff. Coke, confident that he was in overall command on Spion Kop, added his own message to Thorneycroft's, indicating that he had already sent forward reinforcements and, despite not having visited the summit himself, added the unhelpfully positive note:

We appear to be holding our own.[844]

The tone of Coke's postscript negated much of the urgency of Thorneycroft's original. Warren's response was merely to hurry up the supply of water, provisions and sandbags.[845]

* * *

In the opinion of Ron Lock, 'The only creative move, throughout the battle, made by a British general' was that by Major-General Lyttelton.[846]

From his position at Potgieter's, Lyttelton could see with his telescope the dangers on the eastern front and was prepared to use his initiative. In response to Warren's 10 am request for support, he had sent the Scottish Rifles to mount the south-eastern edge of Spion Kop, where later in the day they helped the Middlesex and Imperial Light Infantry repel a Boer advance from Aloe Knoll. But in addition and entirely of his own initiative, Lyttelton ordered the King's Royal Rifles (KRR) under Lt.-Colonel Robert Buchanan Riddell to cross the Tugela upstream from Potgieter's and attack the Boer artillery point on Twin Peaks from where one Krupp and one Pom-Pom had been causing havoc on the summit since early morning.[847] This, Lyttelton judged, would bring greater relief to the troops on Spion Kop than sending more infantry to what was already an overcrowded summit.

It took Riddell's KRR several hours to wade across the Tugela and make their way across very uneven ground towards the Twin Peaks. They approached the base of the pair of hills at about 2 pm, and Riddell divided his force into two wings for the assault up the steep face of the Twin Peaks. The very steepness of the climb acted in the British favour for the defending Boers had to lean over the crest and expose themselves against the clear sky, providing easy targets for British rifle fire. It was a repeat scenario of the Battle of Majuba Hill (27 February 1881) which had given the Boers victory in the first Anglo-

---

[844] *Idem.*
[845] Williams, *The Life*, p 311; and *German Account*, II, p 95.
[846] Lock, *Squandered Valour*, p 180.
[847] *Spion Kop Despatches*, p 41.

The view from the eastern summit of Spion Kop today, with Aloe Knoll nearest and the Boer artillery point of Twin Peaks beyond.
KEVIN SHILLINGTON

Boer War, only this time it was the British who had the advantage.[848] It was a slow climb, but with the well-rehearsed co-ordination of the two wings of the KRR and a fierce fight near the top, the Boers were put to flight, taking their guns with them. In the later-expressed opinion of Lt.-Colonel Thorneycroft, if the Twin Peaks had been part of the original plan of assault on Spion Kop and had been taken in the night or early morning, guns mounted there could have enfiladed the Boer gun emplacements and made the whole Spion Kop strategy viable.[849]

Having captured and fortified his position, Riddell's main opponent now was his generals' loss of nerve. Since about 3 pm, while under fire and scrambling up the hill, Riddell had been bombarded with heliographed messages from Buller, via Lyttelton, ordering him to retire.

[848] Lock, *Squandered Valour*, p 190.
[849] Torlage, *Spioenkop*, p 41.

Lyttelton, who approved Riddell's action, was under pressure from the Commander-in-Chief, and Buller was furious to see troops under his command advance towards danger without his authority. The fact that he was also Colonel-Commandant of the KRR may have added to his anxiety.[850] But it must have been more than personal pique. He feared to see them out there on their own, unsupported. An alternative would have been to give Lyttelton the authority to provide that support and to have sent some guns across to position on the hills; but it is possible he already saw defeat in the larger spectacle of the battle for Spion Kop and he wanted to distance himself from any direct part in the disaster.

Riddell, however, was made of sterner stuff. He put the first message in his pocket and continued the climb. Confident he was succeeding in taking the hill, Riddell treated further messages in a similar manner. In the end Lyttelton sent a despatch rider who caught up with Riddell close to the Twin Peaks summit. The KRR were ordered to retire to the Tugela at dusk. Riddell still resisted the order, making an evasive reply, and when he finally put the Boers to flight shortly after 5.30 pm he signalled triumphantly:

We are on top of the hill. Unless I get order to retire I shall stay here.

Lyttelton signalled back:

Retire when dark.[851]

Before he could decide how to respond to this latest order, Riddell was killed by a rifle bullet in the head as he peered over the northern crest of the hill to view the Boers' retreat. The order to retire was duly obeyed.[852]

Unaware of Buller's order to retire the KRR, Warren signalled Lyttelton at about this time:

The assistance you are giving most valuable. ... Balloon would be invaluable to me.[853]

It is extraordinary that Buller had retained the balloon detachment that would have been invaluable to Warren in his 'almost blind' position on the low hills below Spion Kop. It is true the balloons were said not to work that well because of the height of the Upper Tugela above sea level; but General White

[850] Lock, *Squandered Valour*, p 195.
[851] *Ibid.*, p 194, quoting from *Spion Kop Despatches*.
[852] *Idem.*
[853] Maurice, *Official History*, II, Appendix 10 (H), p 641.

used one with some success in Ladysmith.[854] Indeed, in the light of Warren's extensive interest in ballooning, it is equally extraordinary that he himself had not requested the balloon detachment as soon as he knew he was required to assault the unreconnoitred range of hills north of the Tugela. Perhaps he had verbally asked Buller and, as with his request for the naval guns, Buller had refused it. As it was, without the visual evidence that could have been provided by a balloon throughout the course of that fateful day, Warren had little evidence of the true needs and shortcomings of the defence of Spion Kop other than that of his own eyes, which was of very little, if any, substance.

* * *

In the late-afternoon Coke for the first time made his way across to the south-eastern edge of the summit where he found Colonel A. W. Hill whose Scottish Rifles, sent by Lyttelton, had recently driven back a Boer incursion from Aloe Knoll. Hill may have been unaware that Thorneycroft, junior to him in rank, had been given command on the summit, but he acknowledged the seniority and therefore the command of General Coke on the overall position of Spion Kop. Nevertheless, through his personal experience and direct observation, Hill was better informed than Coke about the true nature of fighting conditions on and around the summit. Neither officer tried to get close to the central fighting trench, but after consulting with Hill, Coke sent Warren a thoroughly revised assessment of the situation.

For the first time he described the true severity of conditions on the summit, 'with many dead and wounded … still in the trenches' and shellfire 'very severe', and he raised the spectre of failure:

> If I hold on to the position all night is there any guarantee that our artillery can silence the enemy's guns? … The men will not stand another complete day's shelling. … The situation is extremely critical.

Recalling Warren's parting words to him – ' No surrender' – Coke asked for orders, suggesting his own option:

> If you wish me to withdraw, cover retirement from Connaught's Hill.[855]

---

[854] W. A. Tilney, (ed.), *Colonel Standfast: The Memoirs of W. A. Tilney, 1868–1947. A Soldier's Life in India, England, The Boer War and Ireland* (Edited by Nini Murray-Philipson, Michael Russell, Norwich, 1901), pp 60, 62, 67, 69. Tilney was one of the officers commanding the Balloon Detachment in Ladysmith.

[855] Williams, *The Life*, p 316, quoting from evidence to the Royal Commission, Vol. II, p 443.

The heliograph on Spion Kop had long been out of service and messages from the top had to be carried down by hand. It was therefore after dark at 8.00 pm by the time Warren received this message. He had already ordered the Royal Engineers' Commander, Lt.-Colonel G. H. Sim, to go up with 200 sappers and to draw a further 1200 men from Coke's reserves to prepare emplacements on the summit for two naval guns and the Mountain Battery. But it was all to prove too late.

At about this time an agitated lieutenant was seen to approach Warren who was pacing up and down deep in thought. After hearing some of what the man said, concerning conditions on the summit, about which Warren had just been informed by Coke, Warren called out angrily to his staff officer Captain Cecil B. Levita:

Who is this man? Take him away. Put him under arrest.

Levita replied:

This is Mr Winston Churchill, Sir, Member of Parliament and newspaper correspondent.[856]

Churchill, who had come out to South Africa to cover the war as a well-paid correspondent for *The Morning Post*, had gained recent fame as an escaped prisoner of war, having been captured by the Boers in Natal early on in the war. After his escape from Pretoria Gaol he made his way to Portuguese East Africa (Mozambique) and arrived by ship in Durban to a hero's welcome on 23 December, two days before the arrival of Warren and the Fifth Division. He made his way quickly to Pietermaritzburg, where he dined at Government House, before hurrying on to Frere to meet with Buller, a great admirer of Churchill's. Without hesitation, Buller had given Churchill an unofficial commission as a Lieutenant in the South African Light Horse, a locally raised mounted infantry regiment.

This left Churchill free to do pretty much as he pleased: to be embedded with the military – he had taken part in the clash with the Boers at Acton Homes on 18 January – and to act as a front-line journalist when it suited him. And now, on 24 January, he wanted to know what was going on on top of Spion Kop, which seemed to be the only point on the Upper Tugela where there was any fighting that day.

[856] Williams, *The Life*, pp 314–5, quoting from an original account by Cecil Levita, who was at the time Warren's Deputy Assistant Adjutant General (DAAG). Churchill only became an MP in 1901.

At about 4.00 pm Churchill had ridden over to the base of the Spion Kop spur where he dismounted and climbed almost to the summit. On the way up he met 'streams of wounded' coming down. He had seen the horrors of battle in India and Sudan, but the mutilated state of many of those British soldiers he saw on the slopes of Spion Kop really shocked him. Without reaching the full summit, he hastened back down in the fading light to report what he had seen to General Warren.

According to Churchill's own account, Warren listened to him with great patience and attention.[857] Pakenham, allowing himself to be swayed by Churchill's self-promotion, grossly exaggerated his role and influence, referring to this young lieutenant and newspaper correspondent as 'instinctively taking over the role of general'.[858] Under the circumstances, Levita's account of Warren's spurning of Churchill is the more plausible, though Levita had learned not to take seriously Warren's order to put him under arrest. He had a better use for Churchill.

As officer responsible for Warren's messages, Levita was anxious to be sure of getting a message through to Thorneycroft as they had heard nothing from him since the somewhat contradictory Thorneycroft-Coke message sent at 2.30 pm. Levita called Churchill over and asked if he would be willing to take a message up to be handed direct to Thorneycroft, informing him of the reinforcements, water and guns that were on the way up and asking for his full assessment of the situation on the summit.[859]

While Churchill began his second climb Thorneycroft made his decision. At 8.15, having received no word from General Warren, he called together as many of the surviving senior officers as he could find on the summit (which did not include Coke who was below the summit). He explained to them his decision to retire. Hill was among the small number who protested, but Thorneycroft insisted that he had been placed in command on the summit and the decision had been made. In his view there was no possibility of holding out another day without the 'Boer artillery being silenced or partially silenced'.[860] To be fair to Thorneycroft, he knew nothing at that stage of the guns and reinforcements that were on their way up and, in any case, 'they

---

[857] Winston Churchill, *London to Ladysmith via Pretoria* (Longman Green, London, 1900), p 308.
[858] Pakenham, *Boer War*, pp 303–4.
[859] Williams, *The Life*, p 315.
[860] Thorneycroft to his brother Jim, 30 January 1900.

could only share his difficulties, not remove them'.[861] Indeed, Thorneycroft believed that 'any Artillery which might have been dragged up there would have been put out of action by the close rifle fire of the Boers as well as by the long range Boer guns, [at] 9000 yds'.[862] Rumours of impending withdrawal had been circulating since dark and by the time Thorneycroft issued the final orders for evacuation a little before 10.00 pm, many of the troops had already begun their descent.

Churchill, still on the way up, found them straggling down, mingled remnants of former regiments making the hazardous downward journey in the dark, although he reported finding many individuals still willing to fight.[863] On the summit,

> Sitting on the ground surrounded by the remnants of the regiment he had raised. … Thorneycroft was in a state of shock, of complete physical and moral breakdown.[864]

Churchill's message about Sim and the guns on their way up meant nothing to him. His decision had been made. According to Churchill he explained:

> Better six good battalions safely down the hill than a bloody mop-up in the morning.[865]

Thorneycroft led the rearguard down the hill, leaving the British dead and seriously wounded on the summit.[866]

Unbeknown to the British at the time, the Boers had also spontaneously withdrawn from their position on Spion Kop where they had suffered just as heavily in proportion to their numbers and where they had been unnerved by the British seizure of the strategic position of the Twin Peaks. A few remained on the northern slopes, but most made their way down to their horses and wagons in preparation for departure.

At 11.30 pm Coke's Staff Officer, Captain H. G. C. Phillips, was woken from his position 70 metres below the summit by the sound of men in full retreat. Coke himself had two hours earlier been summoned down to confer with Warren. Thorneycroft and the remnants of the Lancashires had

[861] Maurice, *Official History*, II, p 397.
[862] Thorneycroft to his brother Jim, 30 January 1900.
[863] Churchill, *London to Ladysmith*, pp 309–11.
[864] Pakenham, *Boer War*, p 304.
[865] Churchill, *London to Ladysmith*, pp 311–12.
[866] Pakenham, *Boer War*, p 305.

already passed by and Phillips halted the downhill flow of men from the Dorsets, Middlesex, Imperial Light Infantry and Scottish Rifles. He issued a memorandum in the name of General Coke to the effect that they had no authority to retire, but the officers commanding the men insisted they were following the orders of Lieutenant-Colonel Thorneycroft and they continued down the hill. Phillips could not signal a warning to General Warren as the signalling oil had been spilled.[867]

Two-thirds of the way down the spur, Thorneycroft met Sim and the mountain guns on their way up. He informed them that Spion Kop had been evacuated and Sim, unsupported by men at the top, had no option but to turn his party back.

Meanwhile, Warren, content that the guns and sappers he had despatched would secure the summit in the morning, retired to his wagon to catch a few hours' sleep. It was Churchill who woke him at 2.00 am to inform him that Thorneycroft was there to see him. Coke arrived at about the same time.[868] According to Thorneycroft, when Warren heard his first-hand account of conditions on the summit and the reasoning behind his decision to withdraw:

> … he said that as I was on the spot I only could judge and that he was satisfied I had done everything that was possible.[869]

Despite these reassuring words to Thorneycroft, Warren saw all his plans in disarray. His instinct was to reoccupy Spion Kop, but he knew he needed to consult with his Commander-in-Chief first as it had been at his instigation that Thorneycroft had been placed in command. He sent a despatch rider to Buller to inform him of the abandonment and to request that he come over to consult.

Meanwhile, Captain Levita learned from 'native intelligence' and from patrols he had sent out that the Boers had also abandoned Spion Kop.[870] According to Levita's recollection, he told Buller this news as soon as he arrived at Warren's headquarters at dawn. But Buller was adamant – there would be no reoccupation of Spion Kop. And having himself ordered the

[867] 'Defender' *Sir Charles Warren and Spion Kop* (Smith, Elder & Co, London, 1902), pp 153–54.
[868] Churchill, *My Early Life* (Macmillan, London, 1941), pp 328–29; 'Defender', Spion Kop, p 155.
[869] Thorneycroft to his brother Jim, 30 January 1900.
[870] See Williams, *The Life*, pp 324–25, for Levita's unpublished account.

earlier withdrawal of the KRR from their defiantly won position on the Twin Peaks, he was probably right – any attempt to reoccupy at this late stage would be futile. Claiming he now had 'the Key to Ladysmith' – a phrase he never satisfactorily explained – Buller retook direct control of the whole force and ordered a withdrawal across the Tugela.

By this time the Boers realised the British had abandoned their hard-fought position. General Botha successfully rallied the demoralised commandos and by daybreak they had retaken control of Spion Kop. But the burghers were too exhausted and shocked by the ferocity of the previous day's battle to interfere with the British retirement across the Tugela.

Botha agreed to a short truce for the removal of wounded and burial of the dead on both sides. While Mohandas Gandhi and his group of 800 Indian volunteers – the Natal Volunteer Medical Corps – stretchered the remaining wounded down the hill, it took the British three days to bury their 243 dead

BELOW LEFT *Gandhi's Indian volunteers collect the wounded on the morning after the battle.* BELOW RIGHT *The central trench on the summit formed a mass grave for most of those British killed on Spion Kop.* FROM THE DISPLAY ON THE SUMMIT OF SPION KOP

The mass grave on the summit of Spion Kop today.
KEVIN SHILLINGTON

on the summit.[871] Most were buried in the mass grave of the eastern half of the central trench where they lay, covered by stones and they remain there to this day. A few officers were given individual graves, but most of the remainder were buried in smaller multiple graves on the summit.

It was one of the heaviest British one day's losses of the entire war. The total British loss in that one week of fighting from 17 to 24 January was more than 412 killed or died of wounds, and a further 1034 wounded. In addition, 285 men and two officers were reported missing, most of them captured by the Boers. The Lancashire regiments that formed the original Spion Kop assault group suffered the heaviest casualties: the 2nd Battalion of the Lancashire Fusiliers lost 40 per cent of their strength, and the 2nd Battalion Royal Lancashire Regiment 21 per cent.[872] The loss of Spion Kop was felt deeply back home in Lancashire, and after the war a huge, new open stadium built at Liverpool Football Club's Anfield ground was named 'The Kop' in memory of the many brave Liverpool and Lancashire men who died that day on Spion Kop.

* * *

[871] It has never been absolutely clear whether Gandhi himself was actually on the summit of Spion Kop, but as it was very much his group of volunteers, it is usually assumed that he was.
[872] For the detailed casualty list, see Maurice, *Official History*, II, Appendix 2, p 597.

According to Churchill, it was Buller who organised the recrossing of the Tugela:

> [He] gripped the whole business in his strong hands, and so shook it into shape that we crossed the river in safety, comfort and good order, with a most remarkable mechanical precision …[873]

In fact it was Warren who was left to organise the withdrawal of troops, guns and wagons across the river, beginning soon after dawn on Thursday 25 January. Buller went on to praise the efficient passage of the river – it took 47 hours to complete, as already noted, ten hours longer than Warren's original crossing – commenting that 'it reflected great credit on the Staff of all degrees'.[874] Although the wording of the despatch could be said to have included Warren, there is no mention of the fact that it was he who had direct control of this second crossing of the river.[875] Buller had clearly made up his mind: Warren was to carry the can for the failure of his strategy for outflanking the Boers on the Upper Tugela.

At midday on Thursday 25 January, while Warren was organising the recrossing of Trichardt's Drift, Buller was at Spearman's Farm from where he sent the following despatch to the War Office:

> Warren's garrison, I am sorry to say, I find this morning had in the night abandoned Spion Kop.

The War Office, equally eager for a scapegoat for the failures in South Africa, released the telegram for publication by the London papers over the following days.[876]

It was the beginning of the denigration of Warren as a field commander, a denigration that would destroy his reputation for thoroughness and efficiency. His name hereafter, at least in military matters, would be linked with the loss of Spion Kop.

On 30 January Buller followed up his initial telegram with two detailed despatches to the War Office reporting his view of what went wrong in his latest failed attempt to relieve Ladysmith. According to Buller the reasons for this failure lay at the feet of his second-in-command, Charles Warren.[877] Buller

---

[873] Churchill, *London to Ladysmith*, p 340.
[874] *Spion Kop Despatches*, p 6.
[875] Williams, *The Life*, p 324.
[876] *Ibid.*, p 325.
[877] *Spion Kop Despatches*, pp 19–24.

reinterpreted his original plan as being to follow Dundonald up the Acton Homes road and thus circumvent the Boers in the hills overlooking the Tugela. But this plan had been undermined by the actions, or rather inaction, of Warren who had wasted the element of surprise achieved when crossing the river on 17 January by focussing on his 'baggage train' for two days and then doing nothing for several days before deciding to attack Spion Kop. He even claimed that as early as 19 January he had wanted to take over direct command himself, but had felt this would undermine Warren in the eyes of his officers and men.

Buller's despatches were later shown to be full of inaccuracies in matters of detail and especially his assertion that he had had nothing to do with the campaign north of the Tugela. And this, despite being Commander-in-Chief, having a good view of the action from his 'commanding' position on Mount Alice, visiting Warren daily except on the day of the Spion Kop Battle, approving his advances on the iNtabamnyama and offering numerous 'suggestions' – effectively orders – as to the position of Warren's brigades, or the recommendation of Thorneycroft to take command on the summit of Spion Kop. To Warren's detriment and in violation of Army protocol, Buller failed to show him the content of his reports on what he claimed was solely Warren's campaign. Warren thus had no chance to correct Buller's inaccuracies of detail or to respond to the personal criticisms levelled against him.

On 17 April 1900 one of Buller's despatches was published in *The London Gazette* at the orders of a British Government that was under public and political pressure to explain the failure to relieve Ladysmith. Buller's second despatch of 30 January, marked 'not necessarily for publication', was published two years later on the eve of the sitting of the Royal Commission on the War in South Africa. That was the first that Warren knew of it and he saw the damning conclusion of Buller's assessment of his capabilities:

> We had lost our chance by Sir C. Warren's slowness. He seems to me a man who can do well what he can do himself, but who cannot command, as he can use neither his Staff nor subordinates. I can never employ him again on an independent command.[878]

In fact, as we shall see in the following chapter, Buller was to employ Warren again, in command of much of the final Relief of Ladysmith. But the publication of this second despatch was to prove the final nail in the coffin of Warren's military reputation.

---

[878] *Spion Kop Despatches*, p 17; and quoted in full in Coetzer, *The Road to Infamy*, p 140.

CHAPTER 23

The Relief of Ladysmith and Other Battles

By 29 January 1900 Warren's troops were back at Spearman's Farm in the tented camp which they had left standing nearly two weeks previously. That day Buller came over to address the men. He extolled their courage and told them their sacrifices and the work they had done between 17 and 24 January had given him 'the Key to Ladysmith'.[879] The men were cheered by his words and it was clear they had lost no faith in him as their commander.

In fact, Buller already had a plan for his own attempt on the Boer position on the Upper Tugela. The hill he had chosen for his spearhead to break through the Boers lines was Vaal Krantz. This steep, rugged hill was immediately to the east of the loop in the river that contained Potgieter's Drift, and required the troops to cross further downstream before making their advance north on Vaal Krantz (see Map, p 381).

After a few days' rest, Buller called his generals together on Saturday 3 February to explain his plan. Warren was to oversee Wynne's Brigade that would make a demonstration from Potgieter's towards Brakfontein, the ridge that formed the northern end of the arc of hills opposite Potgieter's Drift. Lyttelton's Brigade was to lead the assault on Vaal Krantz itself, with Hildyard's and Hart's Brigades in support.

Action began at dawn on Monday 5 February with Wynne's demonstration towards Brakfontein while Lyttelton made a pontoon crossing of the Tugela and advanced towards Vaal Krantz. They fought their way up the steep, rocky terrain of Vaal Krantz and managed to occupy it by the early afternoon, by which point, the Boers having withdrawn, the hill was subjected to heavy artillery fire from hills to the north and east. Nevertheless, with the initial goal achieved, Warren ordered the end of Wynne's demonstration which had been under heavy fire from Brakfontein. The brigade retired under good order and with small loss that afternoon and established themselves in the hills near Potgieter's Drift.

---

[879] Williams, *The Life*, p 328.

415

By dawn on the second day the British were entrenched on Vaal Krantz but unable to establish an artillery placement on top as planned. The hill was too steep and too rocky to haul up the guns and the nearly 4000 men crowded onto the hill remained where they were under constant shell and rifle fire. The situation was similar to Spion Kop, except that in this case the men were well entrenched among the profusion of rocks and did not suffer heavy casualties. But by the end of the day Buller had been stalemated: his spearhead on Vaal Krantz was ineffectual, but neither could the Boers eject the British from their position.

Wednesday 7 February was Warren's 60th birthday. His work regarding Wynne's demonstration being completed, he had no particular duties that day. He had, however, heard Buller lamenting that no one had poked their head above the defences on the front line of Vaal Krantz to see what the terrain was like ahead of the British position. Feeling in need of a little relaxation, spiced with the thrill of personal danger, Warren volunteered to do just that. As he was not the commander of this operation, Buller agreed to let him go, with the jocular warning, 'Be sure you don't get yourself killed!'[880]

Taking two officers with him, Warren rode across the plain to the pontoon river crossing where they left their horses. Shellfire was heavy on the north bank, and initially Warren had to seek shelter in a narrow ravine packed with men. He literally climbed over the sheltering men. 'When we began to ascend it was more exciting,' he wrote in a letter home to Fanny, 'as the shells were coming both ways all about us, and we made dashes from cover to cover'.[881]

Taking advantage of the *schanze* the Boers before them had built and the British had expanded, Warren finally made it to the top and crawled across to the front firing line:

> Then by lifting up my head fitfully, as the least movement caused a patter of bullets, I looked out and reconnoitred the country, and made little sketches and notes about the ground, which I took back to Sir Redvers Buller.[882]

Warren's reconnaissance revealed there was no alternative commanding position as Boer artillery commanded 'Hill 360' to the north of Vaal Krantz and Doorn Kop to the east. Clearly any advance from Vaal Krantz would incur heavy loss of life, though he did note that there was a determined 'do or

---

[880] Williams, *The Life*, p 338, quoting Warren from a letter home to his wife.
[881] *Idem.*
[882] *Ibid.*, p 339.

die' mood among the men who had lost so many of their comrades and could not accept that their sacrifice had been in vain.[883]

Late that afternoon Buller summoned a council of war and asked his generals: 'Attack or retire?' Most argued for retire. When asked for his opinion, Warren advised 'attack'. He was convinced the men were ready for it, unless, he added, there was a better line of attack. Buller, who must have known what Warren was getting at, asked if he knew of a better line, to which Warren inevitably replied, 'By Hlangwane'.[884] It was almost with a sigh of relief that the generals reached unanimous agreement on Hlangwane. They would return to the Colenso battlefront and take the assault to the hills on the south side of the Tugela that Warren had recommended when he first arrived on the scene six weeks previously.

* * *

That evening Buller left Spearman's Camp for Springfield *en route* for Chieveley, the original position from which he had attacked Colenso. And despite having written just eight days previously that he would never employ Warren in an independent command again, for three days he left Warren in command of the retirement of the forces back across the Tugela, still under fire, the packing up of Spearman's Camp and the transfer of all forces to Chieveley. Despite the men's disappointment at yet another retirement, they never lost their faith in General Buller. The most their frustration extended to was gentle mocking of their Commander-in-Chief as 'Sir Reverse Buller' and 'The Ferryman of the Tugela'.

Buller back at Chieveley was in something approaching despair: all three of his attempts at relieving Ladysmith had left him with many casualties and nothing concrete achieved. He was in fact back where he started, before his disastrous attack on Colenso. Wherever he turned the enemy was already there in force. The one lesson he had learned from the Upper Tugela was that he could not compete with the Boers' mobility. Lacking the nerve or the strategy to pursue another attempt on his own, he felt he needed reinforcements from Roberts, or at least the latter's rapid advance on the Free State capital Bloemfontein so as to draw off Boers from Ladysmith.

In a series of telegrams to Roberts expressing his doubts about being able to relieve Ladysmith, Buller ended with the offer:

---

[883] *Ibid.*, p 340.
[884] *Idem.*, for Warren's unpublished account of this meeting.

> … if it is thought anyone else can do better, I would far rather be sacrificed than run the risk of losing Ladysmith.[885]

That could only mean handing over to his second-in-command. Williams points out that such an offer showed Buller's remarkable sense of duty in admitting that perhaps the man he had so comprehensively condemned on 30 January might be the man to replace him, if that would lead to the Relief of Ladysmith.[886] Roberts, who had not yet seen Buller's 30 January despatch, replied:

> I should like to have the views of your second in command on this question [of being unable to relieve Ladysmith], which is one of such vital importance to our position in South Africa, that it is very necessary I should know whether Sir Charles Warren shares your views.[887]

By this time Warren and the whole Natal Field Force were back at Chieveley. Buller summoned Warren to a private conference and showed him the recent telegraphic correspondence with Roberts.

This was Warren's opportunity to do some plain speaking. He argued that it was most important to keep the men in constant contact with the enemy: no more 'stab and retire'. Buller seems to have agreed to work according to Warren's strategy, starting with an attack on the Hlangwane Hill complex and proceeding from there on a daily basis. Warren would meet with Buller daily; they would discuss progress and the lessons of the last 24 hours' action; and then largely following Warren's strategy of constant artillery and infantry pressure, Buller would issue orders for the next day's action. Together they devised a response to Roberts' request which Warren telegraphed to Roberts indicating that he and Buller were in agreement on this strategy.[888]

It was thus Buller who led the Natal Field Force for the successful Relief of Ladysmith, and historians have generally given him all the credit for finally getting it right. But it was Warren's daily strategy that he followed. Warren had always favoured close-quarter fighting with the Boers as he knew it robbed them of their advantage on the open veldt. In the assault on the Hlangwane Hill complex Warren was at last able to put his theory to the test.

---

[885] Cd. 1791, *Royal Commission*, II, Appendix J, pp 628–29 for this telegraphic correspondence.
[886] Williams, *The Life*, pp 344–49.
[887] Cd. 1791, pp 628–29.
[888] *Ibid.*, pp 629–630.

They made their first move on 14 February, taking the southernmost, Hussar Hill, to little opposition. But they were then subjected to heavy shellfire from the Boer-held Hlangwane, and in the very hot weather Buller hesitated to move for two whole days. On 16 February Warren, to amuse the troops and keep up morale, ordered his orderly to heat up some water and fill his canvas bath for he was going to take a bath in the full sight and range of the enemy. As luck would have it, Buller chose this moment to send for him. Warren politely asked his Commander-in-Chief to come to him as he was currently having a bath. The men were thoroughly amused to see Warren in his bath towel surrounded by Buller and his staff on horseback.[889] Warren may also have been trying to impress upon Buller, who himself had immense personal courage, that the men were secure here, and there would be no need to retire.

There was indeed plenty of cover around Hussar Hill and the shelling, though intense and noisy, did not cause too much damage. Buller may have got the point, for on Saturday 17 February the British were on the move again. Dundonald's Mounted Brigade with a couple of light guns took the lead in advancing the right and wheeling the whole line of infantry on Hussar Hill as a pivot. They took the Boers by surprise and captured Cingolo, Monte Cristo and Green Hill later that day. The Boers, eager not to get trapped on the south side of the river, withdrew hurriedly, leaving much of their equipment. Buller declined to follow in hot pursuit. By Monday 19th the British were in a position to advance and finally take Hlangwane itself, a task completed the following day. Warren then instructed that a road be built from Hussar Hill to Hlangwane so that the big naval guns could be brought up and mounted on Hlangwane, the position he had imagined since his war games aboard ship to Durban.

Until now the general mood among the Boers was that the British, defeated at Colenso and on the Upper Tugela, would surely sue for peace, as they had done in 1881. But the British capture of Hlangwane on 20 February, combined with the news that Kimberley had been relieved on the 15th, changed all that. In the words of Deneys Reitz, Hlangwane Hill was 'a commanding position that was considered the key to the Tugela line',[890] and for the first time in the war on the Natal front the Boers began to smell the air of defeat.

Buller wanted to head due north from Hlangwane and attack Pieter's Hill that dominated the north bank of the Tugela after its sharp bend eastwards,

[889] Williams, *The Life*, p 354.
[890] Reitz, *Commando* (2009 edition), p 52.

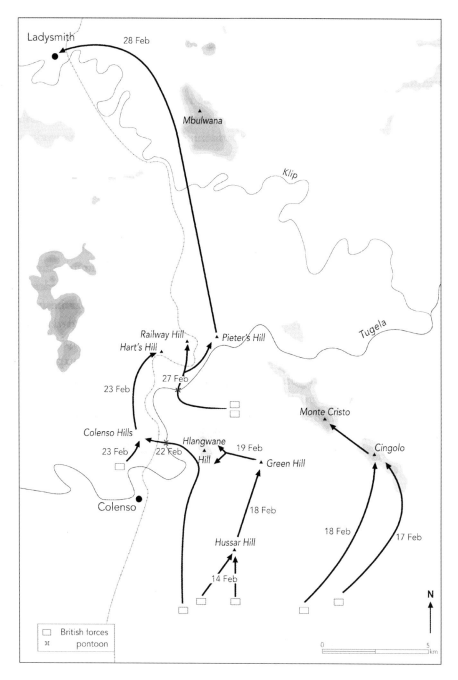

The Relief of Ladysmith, 14–28 February 1900.

but he was persuaded that was too dangerous a place to make the river crossing. Instead, he handed command to Warren to pursue his preferred route.

On Wednesday 21 February Warren ordered the Royal Engineers to throw a pontoon across the Tugela to the west of Hlangwane, downstream from Colenso. That afternoon Warren crossed the pontoon with Coke's Brigade and his artillery, with Wynne's Brigade crossing that night, and Hart's Brigade on the 23rd. There followed five days of intense close-quarter fighting to and fro, but ultimately with the British relentlessly pushing forward, hill by hill, both sides suffering significant casualties.

On Monday 26 February the pontoon was moved up to the great bend in the river near Colenso Falls for the ease of transport of guns and supplies as the troops advanced. Buller had command of the big guns and reserve troops on the south bank, while Warren was given command of the mobile troops on the north bank for the final stage of the assault on 27 February.[891]

The main target that day was Pieter's Hill which Warren had considered too dangerous to attack from the south. Now that he was on the north bank Warren ordered General Barton with three battalions of Dublin Fusiliers to lead the attack on Pieter's Hill while Colonel (later Lt-General Sir) Frederick W. Kitchener[892] with the Lancashires and Colonel C. H. B. Norcott with a mix of regiments were to clear the other hills onto which some Boers were still clinging. Before the attack was launched Buller received a telegram from Roberts announcing the surrender of General Cronjé at Paardeberg in the western Orange Free State. He passed the news on to the troops who were already fired up, for it was Majuba Day and the British attacks were pushed home to shouts of 'Avenge Majuba'. The Boers, too, had heard the news of Cronjé's surrender and their resolve began to falter. The main British attack was launched in the afternoon and by sunset all the hills on the north bank were in British hands. That evening Buller sent an enthusiastic message to Warren which began with the words, 'I congratulate you on the day'.[893]

Most of 28 February was taken up in securing the hills and bringing up the big guns to mount on Pieter's Hill and another that was renamed Kitchener's Hill after the man who had led the assault on it the previous day. The Boers could now be seen in full retreat from their encirclement of Ladysmith, but Buller refused to order an assault on the chaotic mass of retreating men and wagons. In his evidence to the Royal Commission he stated his first priority

---

[891] Williams, *The Life*, pp 363–5.
[892] Younger brother of Lord Kitchener of Khartoum who was Roberts' Chief-of-Staff.
[893] Williams, *The Life*, p 366.

as the urgent re-provisioning of the besieged at Ladysmith.[894] But Buller also had a deep respect for the Boers as fighting men. He had led them in battle in the Zulu War in 1879 and he was acutely aware that they had restrained from attacking his retreat from Spion Kop.

In the afternoon of that last day of February, Warren sent Dundonald's Mounted Brigade to scout Mbulwana Hill to the east of Ladysmith. Dundonald found it only lightly guarded by a few Boers, and leaving the bulk of his brigade to camp near Mbulwana, he and a small corps of mounted men, including Winston Churchill, galloped across the plain, eager to be the first into Ladysmith. They were welcomed by General White, and stared at in disbelief by a visibly starving populace. White provided his welcome visitors that evening with a meagre dinner – of horseflesh.

Meanwhile, Warren, not having heard from Dundonald, advanced in force towards Mbulwana only to find it deserted, and he and the troops bivouacked by Dundonald's camp for the night. The following day, Thursday 1 March 1900, Buller and Warren marched into Ladysmith with a small mounted troop to formally relieve the town while the infantry and guns remained camped outside. The population, military and civilian, was urgently in need of re-provisioning, something that Buller had long planned, and on 2 March 'a long convoy of seventy-three wagons laden with food and medical comforts slowly made its way into Ladysmith'.[895]

A triumphal march into the town was arranged for the following day. A number of officers felt that under the circumstances such a display was inappropriate. W. A. Tilney of the Ladysmith Balloon Department remarked:

> Instead of pursuing the routed enemy, every man available was called upon for a ceremonial parade of welcome for Sir Redvers's army. It was a pathetic sight to see the skeleton men who had been defending Ladysmith standing in the streets on a sort of ceremonial parade.[896]

Warren, obliged to take part in the ceremony, was deeply embarrassed by the sight of

> … the march of 20,000 healthy men triumphant and victorious, through the ranks of the weary and emaciated garrison, who were expected to cheer us and who actually tried to do so – it was an ordeal for me and many another.[897]

[894] Cd. 1791, p 182.
[895] Maurice, *Official History*, II, p 530.
[896] Tilney, *Colonel Steadfast*, p 70.
[897] Williams, *The Life*, p 368, quoting from Warren's unpublished papers.

Colonel Sim had no doubt it was 'one of the most mournful pageants that could have been devised by idiotic Generals'.[898]

* * *

In Buller's details of commendation for the whole Natal campaign, which covers six pages of *The Spion Kop Despatches*, he describes with praise the services of senior officers and others who had served under Warren, but Lt-General Sir C. Warren himself received merely a mention of name and rank, alongside several other Major-Generals that were not in Buller's favour.[899] Clearly, having committed himself to a condemnatory judgement of Warren on 30 January, Buller could not bring himself to reverse that judgement now, no matter how much he owed to Warren for the final Relief of Ladysmith.

During the final stage in the campaign and the days that followed, Warren became increasingly aware that certain officers were briefing against him for the Spion Kop disaster. And by the time he finally left Natal at the end of April, Warren realised he was being made the scapegoat for the failure of the iNtabamnyama and Spion Kop campaign. In a letter to his son-in-law a couple of months later he jokingly referred to himself as 'the Scapegoat-in-Chief of the Army in South Africa'.[900]

So far as Warren was concerned, when he left Natal he and Buller were on the best of terms and he would not hear a criticism of his Commander-in-Chief. Although in due course he was to respond to what he felt were inaccuracies in Buller's account of the iNtabamnyama and Spion Kop campaign, Warren never openly attempted to shift the blame either to his subordinates or to General Buller. The responsibility for Spion Kop weighed heavily upon him for the rest of his life, more for the 'squandered valour'[901] of those who died that day than for its effect on his reputation.

There were errors made by Warren, and things he could have done differently that might have helped the name 'Spion Kop' to go down in the annals of the war as a great British victory. The fundamental problem was that his heart was never in it. Nevertheless, things he could and should have done included better reconnaissance of Spion Kop before ordering the climb, for which the Balloon Detachment would have been useful; the ordering of the Mountain Battery on 22 January, the moment he decided to take Spion

[898] *Idem.*, quoting from a personal letter from Sim.
[899] Cd. 458, pp 40–46; and Williams, *The Life*, p 369.
[900] Williams, *The Life*, p 393.
[901] The phrase borrowed from Ron Lock's account of the battle: *Hill of Squandered Valour*.

Kop, so that it would have been ready to follow the troops up the mountain on the night of 23 January; the ordering of a telegraph line to be laid up the mountain which would not have been difficult for a platoon of sappers; and finally the ordering of an assault on the Boers' iNtabamnyama positions while the fight for Spion Kop was taking place. His failure to order the latter probably stemmed from the fact that he had already, by 22 January, decided any further attack on iNtabamnyama was 'too hazardous'. Although Warren's failure to take any of these initiatives must rest firmly with him, none of them formed any part of Buller's critique. And it was the latter to which contemporary commentators and subsequent historians have paid most attention.

On 4 March Warren went on a pilgrimage from Ladysmith to Spion Kop, accompanied by his staff and Major-General Coke. They left their horses at the base of the famous spur and climbed up the roughly hewn track that the sappers had scraped clear. Tackling it at their leisure, they found it a relatively easy climb.

The four-sided memorial erected on the summit for the officers, NCOs and men of the Lancashire regiments who died on Spion Kop on 24 January 1900.
KEVIN SHILLINGTON

Contemplating the terrain in the silence of the graveyard on the summit, it was easy for Warren and Coke to persuade themselves that Spion Kop ought not to have been abandoned.[902] But neither of them, not even Coke, had been subjected to the full horror of exposure to twelve hours of incessant shrapnel and enfilading rifle fire with inadequate entrenchment, no water on the front line and no sign of British artillery support.

* * *

On return from his one-day's pilgrimage Warren received orders to proceed with his division to the Cape. There followed a farcical two months of inactivity on the Natal front, during which Warren and his Fifth Division were first sent down to Durban to embark for the Cape, then ordered back to Pietermaritzburg, Ladysmith and finally to Elandslaagte, further up the line of rail from Ladysmith. The cause of the confusion and inactivity was a dispute between General Buller and Field-Marshal Roberts as to who needed Warren's division the most.

The priority of Field-Marshal Roberts on the western front had been to relieve Kimberley and to advance into the Orange Free State to defeat General Cronjé. Aside from Mafeking, still under siege until 17 May, this left most of the remaining towns of Griqualand West and the former British Bechuanaland[903] in the hands of resident Boers who had taken up arms on the outbreak of war and were now considered to be 'in rebellion'. High Commissioner and Governor of the Cape Colony, Sir Alfred Milner, requested the appointment of a senior officer with experience of the region to take control of the situation and re-establish British civil administration there.

Warren fitted the bill perfectly. He knew the ground, the farms and many of the Boer and British settlers, 'loyalists' and 'rebels' alike. Roberts, aware of the tension between Warren and Buller, approved the move though left the Fifth Division with Buller's Natal Field Force. Warren, reluctant to depart from the officers and men of his division, had no option but to accept the appointment on the understanding that it was considered a promotion and he was duly appointed Military Governor of the Cape Colony north of the Orange River. Accompanied only by his two *aides-de-camp*, Major R. R. Kelly and Lieutenant I. V. Paton, with their grooms and horses, Warren took the train to Durban where he boarded the SS *Pavonia* bound for Cape Town.

[902] Williams, *The Life*, p 373.
[903] The Crown Colony of British Bechuanaland had been absorbed into the Cape Colony in 1895.

They arrived in Cape Town on 30 April 1900 to see the edited contents of Buller's despatch of 30 January – published in *The London Gazette* on 17 April – all over the Cape newspapers. It was the first Warren had seen of this report and it confirmed the rumours he had heard, but hitherto dismissed, that he was being made the scapegoat for the military failures in Natal.

Warren was devastated. Not only had his Commander-in-Chief failed to follow Army protocol and shown him a copy of this highly critical report before forwarding it so that he could give his version of events, but also so far as he could see it was based upon a series of blatant inaccuracies. However, he was unable to respond immediately, especially as he no longer had access to the original relevant reports and telegrams. Besides, he had just two days in Cape Town during which he was fully engaged in recruiting the volunteer regiments who were to serve under him in Griqualand West. But it must have been in a very angry and frustrated state that Warren travelled north on the train on 3 May[904] in the full knowledge that he must put the matter of his personal reputation to one side until after he had completed his current mission.

Crossing the Orange River on 4 May, Warren travelled 20 kilometres into Griqualand West before establishing his first camp at Belmont, the farm of British colonist Mr Wayland whom he had befriended in the 1870s. Here his force of 2000 men assembled over the next ten days. They were mostly South African volunteers, the sort of small fighting force that Warren favoured. It consisted of seven companies of The Duke of Edinburgh's Own Volunteer Rifles (DEOVR) under Colonel W. A. Spence; two companies of volunteers from north-west England under the flag of the Imperial Yeomanry; four companies of Paget's Horse; one company of Munster Mounted Infantry; 30 former members of Warren's Diamond Fields Horse, now serving as 'Warren's Scouts'; 30 Cape Police; two guns from the Royal Cape Artillery; and a battery of four guns from the Royal Canadian Artillery under Colonel Sam Hughes.

By 15 May his supply wagons had still not arrived, but, aware of the criticism levelled at him for the attention he gave to his wagons in Natal, Warren decided he could wait no longer. He ordered an advance towards the Boer-occupied town of Douglas on the south bank of the Vaal River, a little above its confluence with the Orange. Leaving a small rearguard at Belmont, he divided his force. Colonel Spence and Lieutenant Paton were to make a demonstration towards Douglas from the south, while Warren accompanied

---

[904] *The Times*, Friday 4 May 1900, p 5.

the main force under Colonel Hughes on a circuitous route to the right so as to attack Douglas from the east. The ruse caught the Boers by surprise and, assisted by two of the Canadian guns, the attacking force managed to clear the rebels from the town.

Over the next few days, Warren re-established British civil administration in Douglas while sending out skirmishing parties across the Vaal River, north towards Campbell and north-west towards Griquatown. It not only gave him the opportunity to estimate the strength of the rebels in those directions; it also gave the relatively inexperienced troops under his command experience at getting up close to the enemy and coming under fire. The main rebel rallying point seemed to be around Campbell and on Saturday 26 May, without waiting any longer for his supply wagons, Warren advanced his main force in that direction. He established a forward camp at Faber's Put Farm, halfway between Douglas and Campbell.

It seemed a well-chosen spot from which to launch an attack on Campbell. As Warren noted, 'there was plenty of water, and [the farm was in] a hollow surrounded by hills where horses could be kept more or less secure from musketry at long ranges'.[905] There were two farmhouses, an old one in the central clearing, and a newer one on a slight ridge to the north where Warren established his headquarters. There was an acre of irrigated garden to the east of the old farmhouse. The troops were bivouacked at various points around the site while Warren established four pickets on the surrounding ridges, but considering the proximity of the enemy, this was hardly sufficient. There were considerable gaps between the pickets and no arrangement appears to have been made for patrols between them.[906] One can only wonder that Warren may have been distracted by his personal concerns, and a photograph taken of him at about this time shows considerable stress in his appearance.

Warren sent out daily skirmishing parties to feel the strength and disposition of the rebels. The latter tended to withdraw on contact. Warren himself led out a party of about 100 men towards Campbell on Monday 28 May, and from the top of a small hill he was able to observe the Boers 'buzzing excitedly about' near the town.[907]

On the evening of Tuesday 29 May the long-awaited supply wagons arrived with their escort of Paget's Horse and in the excitement of their arrival, the

---

[905] Cd. 457 from Warren's official report, quoted in Williams, *The Life*, p 383.

[906] L. S. Amery, *Times History of the War in South Africa* (Times, London, 1900–1909), Vol. IV, p 232.

[907] Williams, *The Life*, p 384, quoting from the unpublished diary of Lt Paton.

pickets may have been distracted and not thoroughly supported. That night a group of 600 Boers advanced from Campbell in preparation for a three-pronged dawn attack. They knew from their own observation that Warren's position was poorly guarded and they believed that the largely volunteer force would put up little fight.[908] Two of the prongs took up positions just outside the British line of pickets in the hills to north and south, while a select group of 56 men, all familiar with the layout of the farm, crawled through the eastern picket line into the garden where they were little more than 200 metres from the corralled horses and many of the bivouacked British troops.

At 5.30 am on 30 May Warren, always an early riser, was stoking up the fire when in the predawn light one of the Yeomanry on the southern picket spotted an intruder and the firing started. With many of the British troops still only half-dressed, the whole camp sprang instantly into action. Warren was everywhere: riding fully exposed from one position to another as he directed the defence. Once the Boers were driven back from the northern hills by Maxim machine gun and artillery, Warren was able to turn his full attention to the intruders in the garden where most damage was being done. Here the British suffered their heaviest casualties, with Warren's two ADCs wounded, Colonel Spence killed, and many of the horses panicked into flight. Warren ordered the garden to be raked by a Maxim gun for ten minutes and this was followed by a bayonet charge. The surviving Boers fled, leaving behind thirteen dead and two mortally wounded. It was only an hour since the fighting started, and with the garden now cleared, the majority of the British troops could be directed to strengthen the pickets on the southern ridge. By 7.30 the fighting was over.[909]

It was a close-run thing – British casualties were 23 killed and 32 wounded, although the Boers suffered proportionately higher losses, leaving behind 38 killed and 32 seriously wounded. Warren had hoped to pursue the fleeing rebels, but he had lost too many horses to be able to do so. Had Warren's inexperienced men failed to hold firm and repel the surprise attack, his reputation would have been finished. No amount of subsequent evidence in his support could have saved him.

After being resupplied and reinforced, Warren began his advance from Faber's Put, entering Campbell unopposed on 3 June, and by 8 June he had

---

[908] Amery, *Times History*, IV, p 232.
[909] Cd. 457, pp 129–132 for official reports on Faber's Put. For other reports, see: Maurice, *Official History*, III, pp 19–22; Amery, *Times History*, IV, pp 232–36; and Williams, *The Life*, pp 383–89.

Warren in Griqualand West, after the Relief of Ladysmith, June 1900.
MCGREGOR MUSEUM, KIMBERLEY, SOUTH AFRICA

The South African War medal awarded to Warren after the war, with
clasps for Relief of Ladysmith, Tugela Heights and Cape Colony.
FROM A PRIVATE COLLECTION

occupied Griquatown. The rebel resolve appears to have suffered following their surprise defeat at Faber's Put, especially considering the high casualty rate among the élite group that had infiltrated the garden, many of whom were known to be among the best shots in Griqualand West. With Colonel Hughes and the Canadians leading most of the advances, Warren accepted rebel surrenders in one town after another and entered Kuruman on 24 June.

Through July Warren posted small infantry garrisons at all the main towns and left 300 mounted men to patrol the whole district. The remainder of the troops under his command were despatched to other war fronts and, leaving the region firmly under British control, Warren proceeded south to Cape Town in preparation for his return home.

* * *

He arrived in Cape Town at the beginning of August and over the next few days assembled what 'fragments of documents as are now available' with which to refute Buller's allegations. Mostly at this stage he had to rely upon his personal diary and his memory of events. He wrote to Field-Marshal Roberts in the calmest of terms, pointing out that Buller's published despatches were

> … founded apparently upon misconceptions as to what actually took place and I have to request that I may be permitted to supplement my report of 27th January with such additional information and explanation as will show several points under a very different aspect.
>
> … [In the meantime] I will give as briefly as I can the several points at least 20 in number on which my action has not been accurately represented, trusting that thereafter I may be permitted to vindicate my actions in greater detail when documents can be produced.[910]

Warren's 'several points' extended over 26 closely written foolscap pages in handwriting much neater than his regular notes and letters. This indicated an expectation that his letter would be copied for wide circulation and hopefully published, as had been Buller's ill-founded despatch of 30 January.

The main focus of Warren's early points in this letter was on the meaning and intent of Buller's original orders, which Warren had been accused of not carrying out. This, he argued, was clearly intended to be an assault on the iNtabamnyama ('Rangeworthy') hills, in order to wheel round on a pivot of Spion Kop. It was never originally intended to be encirclement via the Acton Homes road. A further point that particularly raised Warren's ire was Buller's attempt to distance himself from the action under Warren's command and his claim that Warren did nothing for the three days from 19 to 21 January. Buller, Warren complained, came over to speak with him virtually every day, apart from the day of the Spion Kop battle itself. They daily exchanged a large number of telegrams, and Buller sent laudatory telegrams to London on Warren's progress, at least up until 22 January.

On receipt of Warren's letter, so critical of his former Commander-in-Chief, Sir Redvers Buller, Roberts correctly sent a copy to Buller for his comment.

Buller was furious. He was encamped with the former Natal Field Force in the Eastern Transvaal and did not have available copies of the relevant telegrams and despatches, but this did not prevent him from laying into Warren in no uncertain terms. Warren, he asserted in his reply to Roberts, had 'allowed his imagination to overcome his recollection'.[911] He denied that Warren had ever expressed an opinion on military matters that disagreed with

[910] UKNA, WO 20/880, Warren to Roberts, Cape Town, 6 August 1900.
[911] WO 32/880, Buller to Roberts, Camp Crocodile River, Transvaal, 4 September 1990, p 2.

Buller's view as to how Ladysmith should be relieved:

> Whatever ideas of military policy Sir Charles Warren may have had, he kept them locked in his own mind, and ... he never at any time made any suggestion of any sort to me.[912]

Buller was confident that, once he had access to the full documentation, he would be able to show 'how much Sir Charles Warren has permitted his imagination to colour his statements'. And to get his message home, he repeated his allegations of Warren's 'incapacity for command ... [and] not only incapable but thoroughly disloyal'. He finished with the worst accusation of all, alleging that Warren had

> ... accepted the mission [across the Tugela] with the deliberate intention of disobeying his orders ... [913]

Roberts knew there had been tension between his two generals, but he had never believed it was as bad as this. In forwarding the two letters to the War Office, Roberts reported:

> I do not think that anything would be gained by instituting an enquiry into the circumstances connected with the capture and abandonment of Spionkop, especially in view of the remarkable divergence between the statements of the two officers primarily concerned with regard to such an important question as the plan of operations.[914]

As a further precaution, he forbade Warren from responding publicly in any way, in speech or in print, to Buller's allegations. To have done so, argued Roberts, might have endangered British morale at home and in South Africa where the war was not yet over. He would get his chance to respond in due course, after the war.[915] As a result of this lack of public response from Warren, Buller's reports went on to form the basis for most historical accounts of the Relief of Ladysmith.[916]

[912] *Ibid.*, pp 2–3.
[913] *Ibid.*, pp 7–8.
[914] WO 32/880, Roberts to War Office, Pretoria, 28 September 1900.
[915] Williams, *The Life*, pp 394–95.
[916] Apart from Williams, *The Life*, two other attempts have been made to put Warren's point of view. One, an anonymous contemporary publication, thought to have been written at the behest of Warren himself – 'Defender', *Sir Charles Warren and Spion Kop* (1902); the other by Owen Coetzer, *The Anglo-Boer War: The Road to Infamy, 1899–1900* (Arms and Armour, London, 1996).

Despite the vindication of Warren by the Royal Commission after the war, it has been difficult to shake off the denigration of his name at the hands of his Commander-in-Chief, especially among non-specialists on the war. For instance, as late as 1997 Warren's name was linked with Spion Kop in a book relating the world's greatest *Military Blunders*, in which Warren is described as 'arguably the most incompetent British commander of the whole of the Second Boer War of 1899–1902'[917] – a theme taken up by at least one of the many books on the Jack the Ripper story.[918]

[917] Saul David, *Military Blunders* (Constable & Robinson, London), p 35.
[918] Bruce Robinson, *They All Love Jack: Busting the Ripper* (Fourth Estate, London, 2015), p 61.

CHAPTER 24

Vindication and Retirement

There was no hero's welcome to greet Warren on his return to England in September 1900. He was slighted by the establishment and denied the audience with The Queen that was the norm for returning generals from imperial wars. By contrast, Buller received a hero's welcome from the moment he landed at Southampton in November and was received at Windsor Castle by the ailing Queen, for whom Buller had long been a favourite. But Buller's heroic days were numbered.

Although always popular with the regular troops and the general public, especially in the West Country where his family owned vast estates, Sir Redvers Buller VC had enemies within the political establishment and the

Despite his loss of political and media support, Sir Redvers Buller retained huge popularity and support in his own South Devon, where this equestrian statue was erected in his honour in the city of Exeter.
KEVIN SHILLINGTON

press. A particularly strong critic was Leo Amery, journalist and general editor of the *Times History of the War in South Africa*.[919] News of Buller's surrender telegram to General Sir George White in Ladysmith, sent after the disaster of Colenso, had been circulating freely in *The Times* and elsewhere long before the publication of the *Spion Kop Despatches*.

Previously protected by his friendship with The Queen, Buller failed to win the support of King Edward VII after the death of Queen Victoria in January 1901. His critics were sharpening their knives, and 'In the end Buller's patience snapped'.[920] On 11 October 1901 he made an angry and impromptu speech confirming the wording of the surrender telegram and attempting to defend it. Such a speech was against all military protocol and it gave the military and political establishment the opportunity to sack him. On 22 October Buller was dismissed from his former Aldershot Command and put on half pay.[921]

The dismissal established Buller as the principal scapegoat and necessary sacrifice demanded by Government and the press for the failures of the war in South Africa. This shift of blame eased the passage for the restoration of Warren's reputation once the Royal Commission began hearing evidence a little over a year later.

In the meantime the war in South Africa had still to be won. In December 1900, with the republican capitals Bloemfontein and Pretoria in British hands and Kruger having fled into exile in Europe, Roberts had told an eager crowd in Durban that the war was effectively at an end. In fact it had already entered a new protracted guerrilla stage, during which tens of thousands of Boer women and children, and Africans living on Boer farms, were incarcerated in segregated, overcrowded 'concentration camps'. The appalling conditions in which they lived, with inadequate food and high mortality rates, were exposed by the compassionate English campaigner and pacifist Emily Hobhouse, who visited the camps in early 1901. Her campaign led initially to British denial, and then to some slight improvements. She became a hero to the women of the camps, but she was denigrated back home in England, for disloyalty to the British empire.[922]

[919] Published in 6 volumes between 1900 and 1909.
[920] Geoffrey Powell, *Buller: A Scapegoat? A Life of General Sir Redvers Buller VC* (Leo Cooper, London, 1994) p 197.
[921] *Ibid.*, p 199.
[922] Elsabé Brits, *Rebel English Woman: The Remarkable Life of Emily Hobhouse* (first published in South Africa in 2016, this edition, Robinson, London, 2019).

Meanwhile, Warren was still not permitted to answer his critics until after the war finally ended in May 1902. Others, however, were prepared to speak up for him. A friend of his, identified by Owen Coetzer as D. Lambton, wrote an anonymous defence of Warren's command of the Upper Tugela under the pseudonym 'Defender'.[923] It was prefaced by an account of Warren's early life and career up to the outbreak of war and as such is assumed to have been with the close co-operation, if not the direction, of Charles Warren himself. It was published in 1902 at about the same time as the formal end of the war and the publication of the full *Spion Kop Despatches*.[924]

South Africa was never far from Warren's mind in those first two years after his return to England. Unable to write on the war itself, he decided to gather together his journals and letters from an earlier time in South Africa and publish them as a personal contemporaneous account of his life *On the Veldt in the Seventies*. Published in 1902,[925] when South Africa was still very much in the news, it appears to have sold well and it may have helped place him in a positive frame of mind for the challenge of the Royal Commission that was to come.

With the signing of the Peace of Vereeniging in Pretoria on 31 May 1902, the way was finally clear for the sitting of the Royal Commission on the War in South Africa. Chaired by Lord Elgin, former Viceroy of India, the Commission began its work in October 1902, although it did not begin hearing the evidence of witnesses until February 1903. Generally the commissioners dealt with two or three witnesses a day, although Sir Redvers Buller was in the witness box for two full days, 17 and 18 February.

Warren was due to give evidence on Thursday 19 February. Late the previous evening he had received from the Secretary of the Commission, Bernard Holland, a copy of a statement submitted by Buller outlining his account of the campaign on the Upper Tugela and the final Relief of Ladysmith.[926] It was highly critical of Warren who was shocked to read that Buller had not changed in any way the stance he had taken in his damning report of 30 January 1900, sent five days after the withdrawal from Spion Kop.

---

[923] Owen Coetzer, *The Anglo-Boer War: The Road to Infamy, 1899–1900* (Arms and Armour, London, 1996), p 154; 'Defender', *Sir Charles Warren and Spion Kop. A Vindication* (Smith & Elder, London, 1902).
[924] Cd. 968.
[925] Published by Isbister & Co, London.
[926] Cd. 1791, *Royal Commission*, II, p 178.

Hitherto Warren had consoled himself that Buller's despatch of 30 January, with all its inaccuracies, had been written without a full knowledge of the facts. Now that no longer applied, all the facts and despatches were available to him and yet it appeared to Warren that Buller put the salvaging of his own reputation before an accurate presentation of events. Warren attended the Commission at St Stephen's House on the Victoria Embankment on 19 February 1903 determined to put the record straight.[927]

When asked by the Chairman if he had received a copy of Buller's statement, he said he had, but with 'scarcely more time than to look through it'.[928] With the Commission's permission he read out the reply to the Secretary that he had written that morning:

> I have read over [Sir Redvers Buller's] statement; it appears to me to be very incorrect and very misleading, and I ask that I may have facilities and opportunities of refuting it.[929]

In the meantime, all he had had time to refer to in this brief letter was a handful of salient points arising from Buller's statement. For instance, he felt the reference to *baggage*, on which Buller said he wasted so much time passing over Trichardt's Drift, was very misleading for it implied the carrying of non-essentials that had in fact been left behind at Springfield. What the wagons actually contained was essential military equipment: 'artillery and ammunition, machine guns and ammunition, great coats and cooking utensils'. Furthermore, Buller had been present throughout that first day of the crossing and could see what the wagons contained. Warren went on to request that Sir Redvers Buller be asked to state definitely what his orders on 15 January 1900 were intended to convey, for Warren was confident he had carried out his instructions 'so far as they were then understood'. In conclusion, Warren wrote, his operations for the Relief of Ladysmith would have succeeded if Buller had not 'interfered constantly … and finally withdrawn the force in the hour of success'.[930]

Fairly damning stuff and the Commission had no option but to agree to Warren's request that he have access to all the telegrams relating to Spion

---

[927] St Stephen's House, named after a former chapel on the site, lay between New Scotland Yard (opened in 1890, two years after Warren's time as Police Commissioner) and Westminster Bridge. It has since been demolished to make way for Portcullis House, a block of parliamentary offices and meeting rooms.

[928] Cd. 1791, *Royal Commission*, II, p 223, Q 15656.

[929] Cd. 1791, pp 223–24.

[930] *Idem.*

Kop and to all the staff reports of the Fifth Division, from the time he took command of the Tugela crossing on 15 January 1900, up to the final Relief of Ladysmith on 28 February. The Chairman accepted that Warren would respond in detail to Buller's allegations in writing at a later date.

The Commission was thus obliged to confine its questions that morning to Warren's views on the general organisation of the Army in South Africa and the lessons that might be learned for the future. Warren had plenty to say on the matter, spread over fourteen pages of evidence. Among other things it gave him the opportunity to promote his idea of a citizen force along the model of the Boer commandos. This would, he believed, in the case of the Cape Colony have led to the early discovery of 'suspected burghers' before they broke out in rebellion. It would also, he argued, have formed a considerable field force at a moment's notice, with the result that it would only have needed the augmentation of 90,000 imperial troops to defeat the republics, instead of the 250,000 that were eventually required.[931]

Another point he raised was the frequent outbreak of typhoid among the troops in South Africa. He felt this was eminently avoidable if there had been proper regard for sanitation. He went into considerable detail on the matter and in conclusion told the Commission:

> … The whole sanitary service requires recasting. It ought to be automatic, so that on starting a camp or bivouac anywhere things should go straight. … The only safe expedient is to establish a rule that whenever a case of typhoid fever occurs the medical officer and Royal Engineer officer will be liable to be tried by court-martial unless they can show that they have adopted all precautions. This will force the general staff to attend to the matter.[932]

Warren submitted his full statement on the Buller allegations on 18 April 1903, three years to the day since Buller's 30 January report was published in the British newspapers.

In sticking to his original critique of Warren's capability, Buller had stirred up a considerable opponent. In typical Warren fashion his written statement answered, one by one, all the critical points laid against him and what he considered to be every inaccuracy in Buller's notorious 30 January despatch. There were 38 numbered points in all, spread over ten printed pages of Commission evidence, starting with Buller's original orders and plan of attack

---

[931] Cd. 1791, pp 224–5, Q 15660.
[932] *Ibid.*, p 231, Q 15813.

and ending with his statement that he could never employ Warren again in an independent command.[933]

It was a devastating chronology of events, which should have destroyed Buller's allegations and restored Warren's battered reputation. But although it was published as an appendix to the Commission's volume of evidence, it seems to have received little attention from historians of the Natal campaign. It was not until the publication in 1996 of Owen Coetzer's book, based largely upon the evidence of that Royal Commission volume, that Warren's statement received the attention it deserved.[934] Until then most historians had relied on Buller's reports as published in the *Spion Kop Despatches*. Indeed, most of the contemporary memoirs of those who played a part in the Natal campaign reflected the distortions of Buller's published reports.

Nevertheless, the British military establishment accepted that the evidence presented to the Royal Commission vindicated Warren and on 24 February 1904 he was promoted to full General. This was followed in 1905, the year of his official retirement, by his appointment as Colonel Commandant of the Royal Engineers, the highest accolade he could have wished for when he had entered the service as an ensign in 1857.

Warren's South African experience, however, left him deeply disillusioned by the lack of support he felt he should have received from his fellow Freemasons: Wolseley, Roberts and Buller. Indeed, it has been noted among Freemasons that Warren never again attended a Freemasonry meeting of the Quatuor Coronati Lodge that he had helped to found. Nor did he take part in 'any other Masonic activities'.[935]

* * *

Not long after he had returned from South Africa Warren sought the advice of General Sir Alexander Montgomery Moore as to what he should do about Buller's criticisms. Montgomery Moore had taken over the Aldershot Command when Buller had been sent to South Africa in 1899, and he told Warren that so far as his military reputation was concerned, he must simply 'grin and bear it' for it was totally contrary to military etiquette for a subordinate officer to challenge the remarks of his Commander-in-Chief, no

---

[933] Cd. 1791, Appendix M, pp 644–54.
[934] Coetzer, *The Road to Infamy* (1996).
[935] Bro. A. C. F. Jackson, 'Sir Charles Warren, G.C.M.G., K.C.B. Founding Master of Quatuor Coronati Lodge, No 2076', *Transactions of the Quatuor Coronati Lodge*, 11 September 1986, p 178.

matter how hostile those remarks.[936]

In that case, Warren asked, what should he do? Montgomery Moore said, 'Wait 20 years, and then do what you like', to which Warren responded, 'I shall not probably live so long; what can I do *now*?' Montgomery Moore then gave Warren the most useful advice he could have received at that moment in his life:

> There is only one thing you can do. Begin all over again in some other line, and show the world that you are not the idiot Buller makes you out to be. Show that you can lead men, and that you have superior ability.[937]

With this sound advice Warren resolved on two things. The first was 'to make order out of the confused chaos of weights and measures', something that he had been toying with for some considerable years; and the second was to make some sort of contribution to the education of boys, on the basis that 'boys are more difficult to govern than men'.

Warren had been working on the history of weights and measures before being posted to South Africa in 1899 and he happily returned to it. He had been drawn to the subject, both by his own surveys and measurements of ancient buildings in Palestine and by the work of William Flinders Petrie. Petrie, thirteen years younger than Warren, was a home-educated and self-taught surveyor and genius of archaeology who had made the first mathematical survey of the ancient British monument of Stonehenge in 1872 at the age of nineteen, and gone on to be the first to do likewise on the Egyptian pyramids of Giza in the early 1880s.[938]

Like Petrie, Warren was fascinated by the geometrical precision of the Great Pyramid, and this got him thinking about the origins of human systems of measurement in the ancient world, on which the whole discipline of mathematics was ultimately founded. He was particularly interested in the ancient measurement, the cubit, and how it originated from measurements of parts of the human body – the hand, the forearm, the span from fingertip to fingertip, and the foot. His research followed how these evolved into precise

---

[936] Williams, *The Life*, pp 400–401, quoting from a letter Warren wrote to Sir Bartle Frere (junior) in October 1924.

[937] *Ibid.*, p 401.

[938] William M. Flinders Petrie, *Seventy Years in Archaeology* (Holt & Co. London, 1932), p 10; Palestine Exploration Fund, 'Sir William M. Flinders Petrie, 1853-1942' (www.pef.org. uk/profiles/sir-william-flinders-petrie-1853–1942: accessed 11 December 2019). His *The Pyramids and Temples of Giza* was first published in 1883.

geometrical measurements, which were essential for any substantial building work and for surveying.

He undertook this work through 1901 and 1902 in between many other calls upon his time, for he was much in demand for public engagements. These ranged from presentation of war medals and the opening of memorials for those who had died in the South African war, to talks on various subjects for organisations such as the Palestine Exploration Fund, the London Missionary Society and the St John Ambulance Brigade of which he was elected Life President.[939]

To his satisfaction, he found that despite the denigration from certain military and political circles at this time, wherever he went he was popularly received by the general public and those who knew of his life's various works. In June 1901, for instance, the *Canterbury Journal* reported that he addressed a large gathering at St Augustine's College Missionary Society on the subject of missionary societies and the dangers of their competing against each other in the field.[940] On that occasion the Dean of Canterbury Cathedral, Dr F. W. Farrar, who had put up publicity posters around the city, met Warren at the station. Students from the college were also there to welcome their honoured guest. They removed the horses from the Dean's carriage and pulled it themselves through the large, cheering crowds that had gathered between the station and the college.

Warren completed his study of *The Ancient Cubit and our Weights and Measures* in December 1902.[941] Among those he thanked in his preface was his eldest son Captain Frank Warren, RA, for 'assisting me to render many of the intricate arithmetical calculations clearer than they would otherwise have been'.[942] Nevertheless, in spite of Frank's and his father's best efforts, the book reviewer of *The Spectator* found the mathematics a little too intricate and specialist for his taste.[943]

Frank had been home on leave from Mauritius before his transfer to Hong Kong. He had read through most of the proofs of his father's book and offered valuable advice. The time spent together working on *The Ancient Cubit* would have meant a lot to both of them. Hitherto the relationship between father and son had of necessity been somewhat distant, what with Sir Charles's frequent

[939] Williams, *The Life*, p 399.
[940] *The Canterbury Journal, Kentish Times and Farmer's Gazette*, Saturday, 22 June 1901, p 5.
[941] Published by the Palestine Exploration Fund in January 1903.
[942] *Ancient Cubit*, p iii.
[943] *The Spectator*, 24 January 1903, p 24.

absences abroad during Frank's formative years from the late-1870s through to the mid-1890s. And no sooner had his father returned from the Singapore Command than Frank was posted to Mauritius. Sadly, 1901–02 was the last time they were to spend together for Captain Frank Warren, 18th Company, Royal Garrison Artillery, never returned from Hong Kong. He died there of enteric (typhoid) fever on 12 February 1907.[944]

With the publication of *The Ancient Cubit* Warren had to a large extent fulfilled his first resolution following the advice of General Montgomery Moore. The book added to his reputation as a mathematician and established him as an expert in this particular field. He followed it up in 1913 with the publication of *The Early Weights and Measures of Mankind*.[945]

* * *

His second resolution, namely the education of boys, was not so easily fulfilled. He remained unsure how to set about it, until the opportunity presented itself 'unexpectedly on the threshold of his own home' in the summer of 1904.[946]

His younger daughter Charlotte had been teaching the infants' class at the Sunday school of their local St George's Anglican church in Ramsgate. But there was a vacancy for someone to take over the senior class. Their previous superintendent had been unable to cope with the unruly behaviour of the boys, which was affecting the smaller children in Charlotte's care. Indeed, they had become 'openly rebellious' and were refusing to go to church on Sunday mornings. The vicar approached Warren and appealed to him to take over the senior class and indeed the overall superintendence of the Sunday school. It was just the challenge Warren needed.

Before attending his first session with the boys he inspected the meeting room and found the acoustics from the teacher's raised wooden dais to be very poor. Clearly the teacher could not be heard. He moved the lectern to a corner where he believed the acoustics to be much better. Then, as he recalled years later, that first Sunday morning 'my rabble tumbled into the room, making vigorous noises so that my voice could not be heard'.[947] Warren responded unexpectedly with his own 'strange and vigorous animal cries' which silenced the class for a moment – just long enough for him to speak.

He held up a pin and told them he would not proceed until they could all

[944] *Straits Times*, 22 February 1907.
[945] Published by the Palestine Exploration Fund, London.
[946] Williams, *The Life*, p 401.
[947] *Ibid.*, p 402

hear it drop. That got their attention and there was complete silence as they all strained to hear the pin drop. He explained that he would start each class in this manner, and 'after the pin dropped they would have thirty seconds in which to pray for their parents in silence, and their parents would be asked to pray for them at the same time'.[948] He then read the school prayer and announced that 'in future boys would not be *permitted* to go to church unless their conduct showed that they were fit to do so'. At once, he recalled, 'all the boys wanted to go to church and there was no more trouble of revolt: they were my friends'.[949]

Subsequently, he became concerned about the Christian education of the most senior boys who dropped out of class at the age of fourteen when they left school. He consulted among educationists and found they all 'looked upon boys from 14 to 18 as terrors outside the path of civilized beings'. But it seemed to Warren 'most unreasonable to turn boys loose out of your Sunday school for four whole years and then move heaven and earth to get them back again when they are young men of 18 years'.[950]

Warren's desire to start a Bible class for those who left the senior Sunday school led to his founding a local branch of the Church Lads' Brigade (CLB), and this in turn was to lead in due course to his work with the Boy Scouts movement. The CLB was an Anglican-based organisation that provided boys with Bible classes and moral education, combined with plenty of physical activity. At his own expense Warren organised a meeting place with swimming pool attached, and besides swimming he trained the boys in competitive athletics and rifle shooting.

Warren was far from alone in his concern about the moral and physical fitness of the youth of England. Indeed the recent war in South Africa had shown a distinct lack of physical fitness among many of the raw recruits. Church Lads' Brigades were simply one among many efforts to provide useful focus and occupation for the youth, especially male youth, after the age of elementary education. No organisation, however, was to become so effective and so widespread as Baden-Powell's Boy Scouts movement.

Colonel Robert Baden-Powell, the hero of the siege of Mafeking, had long been interested in the business of scouting in the military and believed in the importance of producing an intelligent, thinking soldier rather than a

[948] *Idem.*, quoting from an address Warren gave to the Scoutmasters and members of the Dover Boy Scouts' Association in January 1921.
[949] *Idem.*
[950] *Ibid.*, pp 402–03.

blindly obedient one. His *Aids to Scouting for NCOs and Men*,[951] published just as the Boers encircled Mafeking in 1899, contained instructions on the skills of observation, sketching and writing of reports, all spiced up with his own drawings and anecdotes picked up from his experiences in India and South Africa. On his return from South Africa after the war, Baden-Powell applied the same scouting principles to the basic concept of Lads' Brigades and produced *Scouting for Boys*, published in 1908, and that year he founded his first Boy Scouts Troop.[952]

Warren was immediately impressed by Baden-Powell's scouting ideas and was among the first to take up the challenge. In May 1908 he set up the 1st Ramsgate ('Sir Charles Warren's Own') Boy Scout Troop, starting with just eighteen boys, so as not to poach any away from other organisations. Warren played a full and active part in all these activities and thoroughly enjoyed himself – reliving an idealistic image of his own boyhood. In the memory of his grandson, who was himself a child in these years, Sir Charles 'was as active at seventy as many a man of little more than half his age'.[953]

* * *

In 1913 an important change occurred in the personal life of the Warren family. In January of that year, Lady Fanny Warren's brother, Revd George P. Haydon, died and their 98-year-old mother, Fanny Bethell Haydon, who had been living with George in the tiny Kent village of Westbere, came to live with the Warrens in Ramsgate. A few months later Sir Charles bought 'The Oaks', his late brother-in-law's house in Westbere, and that summer he and Lady Fanny moved there with her frail and elderly mother. Violet, who had until then lived with her parents, remained in Ramsgate, while Charlotte, who had married Revd Watkin Williams in 1905, lived nearby in Thanet.

Lady Fanny's mother was to die the following year, just short of her 100th birthday, and was laid to rest next to the grave of her son in the cemetery of the Westbere village church. Deciding that 'The Oaks' with its extensive garden bordering onto the small village cemetery was where they wanted to end their days, Sir Charles bought the two adjoining cemetery plots for himself and Lady Fanny.

[951] Published by Gale and Polden, Aldershott, 1899.
[952] Quoted in Tim Jeal, *Baden-Powell: Founder of the Boy Scouts* (first published 1989; this edition Yale University Press, New Haven and London, 2001), pp 361–62.
[953] Williams, *The Life*, p 406. Watkin Williams was born in 1906, the son of Warren's younger daughter Charlotte who had married Revd Watkin Wynne Williams in 1905.

'The Oaks', home of Sir Charles and Lady Warren (d. 1919), 1913–24.
KEVIN SHILLINGTON

'The Oaks' was a large, late-Victorian house set in seven and a half acres of garden and adjoining field, and one of the first things Warren did on moving into Westbere was to found a small Scout group. This in due course became part of the 2nd Canterbury Scout Troop. In his grandson's words:

> Westbere soon became a Mecca for scouts from Canterbury and Ramsgate, and parties of them cycled over to camp in the grounds almost every weekend through the summer months.[954]

On the outbreak of the Great War in 1914 the patrolling of the Westbere stretch of the Canterbury-Ramsgate road was allotted to the 2nd Canterbury Troop and the field at 'The Oaks' became their permanent camping ground from where they patrolled in rotation under the eye of General Warren who was enrolled as a Special Constable.

Lady Fanny was not able to appreciate the full benefits of living at 'The Oaks'. Her health had been poorly for some time, and during the short time she lived in Westbere, she suffered from severe sciatica, which paralysed her

[954] *Idem.*

445

legs and made movement always painful and almost impossible. By the new year of 1919 it was clear that Fanny's health was going steadily downhill. In a moving letter that he wrote in March 1919 he described the time he spent with her during these, her final months:

> She is so brave and patient and unselfish – such a wonderful example. … Generally after reading the psalms in the morning we hold hands, and squeeze each other's hands for 40 or 50 minutes until her dinner comes. She shuts her eyes most of the time but I do not think she is asleep. It is very sorrowful but I do not think I have ever felt so happy as I have done during the last months whilst holding her hand on these occasions.[955]

She died at 'The Oaks' on 24 May 1919 at the age of 79. Sir Charles wrote, 'All sign of suffering gone, her face is lovely'.[956] She was buried next to her brother and mother in the small Westbere churchyard at the bottom of the garden.

Now on his own at 'The Oaks', Sir Charles continued to be very active in Westbere and was appointed District Commissioner of the Canterbury and Whitstable Boy Scouts' Associations. He held the post for the next four years, during which time he became a well-known figure in the scouting circles of East Kent. He kept in close contact with his old schools, Bridgnorth, Wem and Cheltenham, and had 'the honour of becoming President of the old boys' associations of each of his three schools in turn'.[957]

* * *

In about 1920 Warren turned his attention back to something that had been niggling him for the past twenty years, namely the South African War. So far as Buller's allegations were concerned, he had been following General Montgomery Moore's advice and 'grinning and bearing it' for the past twenty years, but now he finally felt free to write his own full account of the war. He assembled his papers and set to work. On 28 February 1921 he wrote to his grandson John Gunn Warren,[958] then at Charterhouse, an élite private boarding school in Surrey:

> I am busy writing up about the Boer War. I have got on very well with it. It's now so long ago that I can tackle it without feeling any resentment about unjust treatment.

[955] Quoted in Williams, *The Life*, p 410.
[956] *Idem.*
[957] Williams, *The Life,* p 428.
[958] The younger son of the late Captain Frank Warren RA.

Clearly there had been some level of resentment simmering in his mind over all those intervening years and at last it could be expiated. Buller had been dead for thirteen years and Warren finally felt free to express his true feelings:

> There is no doubt that Buller was quite off his head, and I had to deal with a madman.[959]

Over the next four years he pulled all his South African papers together and completed his account of the war. He had finally got the whole issue off his chest, although he seems not to have pursued its publication. Perhaps he felt that after the horrors of the Great War of 1914–18, people in Britain did not want to hear about an older and somehow less significant war. Besides, he may have been thinking of contemporary South Africa, where the two former Boer republics and the two British colonies had been peacefully amalgamated into the Union of South Africa in 1910. The latter was a delicate union between the interests of the British empire and those of Afrikaner nationalists, and Warren may have decided that the early 1920s, when he might have published his book, was not the time to stir up old memories and antagonisms of the war between Boer and Briton.

* * *

In the new year of 1924 Warren was approaching his 84th birthday and with his suffering bouts of flu and bronchitis each winter, it was becoming increasingly clear that he was going to have to give up living on his own at 'The Oaks'. That February the house was sold and he moved with his books and papers to an apartment in the seaside town of Weston-super-Mare in West Somerset, where his son Richard, a medical doctor, had recently moved with his wife and three young children.

Despite suffering from influenza most winters now, he remained determined to live life to the full. He enjoyed long walks and expended a lot of energy reorganising the Weston Boy Scouts, which had recently been in the doldrums. In the summer of 1926 he obtained a sloping piece of unused land for their use, on the outskirts of the town. He named it 'Spion Kop', and no doubt explained to them the significance of the name. That September he organised a great bonfire party on 'Spion Kop' to officially inaugurate the

---

[959] I am grateful to John Gunn Warren's son John Pelham Warren and his brother Charles for sending me a copy of this letter. The original is housed in the McGregor Museum Kimberley, South Africa, from whom I also got a copy.

The medals of Sir Charles Warren as laid on the coffin in the parish church, Weston-super-Mare, 25 January 1927. The medals on the bar at the top are (L TO R) *for military service in South Africa 1877–78, Egypt 1882 and South Africa 1899–1900, Commemorative Medal for Queen Victoria's Diamond Jubilee of 1897, the Metropolitan Police Medal for the Golden Jubilee of 1887, and the Order of the Medjidié 1882. The Star on the left within the gold chain is that of the Order of St Michael and St George, as is the seven-figured star attached to the gold chain. The star on the right within the gold chain is for the Order of the Bath. The separate medals below the chain are* (L TO R) *St Michael and St George, The Bath, The Medjidié, and St Michael and St George.*

FROM A PRIVATE COLLECTION

ground.[960] It was the last public event he was to organise.

That winter he contracted influenza, as he had done most winters in recent years; but this time in January it was complicated by the onset of pneumonia. His son Dr Richard Warren summoned the family to his bedside.

He was comforted over the following week by his daughter Charlotte reading to him his own father's favourite Psalm, the 91st:

> … I will say of the Lord, He is my refuge and my fortress: my God; in Him will I trust.

And she would sing to him his favourite hymn:

> Teach me to live, that I may dread
> The grave as little as my bed;
> Teach me to die, that so I may
> Rise glorious at the awful day.

Charlotte's husband Revd Williams, prayed with him and read to him from his favourite book, the Bible. Comforted by his strong spiritual faith, Charles Warren passed away peacefully on the evening of Friday 21 January 1927. He was just two weeks short of his 87th birthday.

Early on Tuesday morning, 25 January, a memorial service was held in Weston parish church. The coffin was draped in the Union Flag on top of which was laid the green and white Stellaland Banner which Warren had presented to Queen Victoria in 1885. It had since been returned to him. And on top of the flags was placed his general's cocked hat, his medals and his police sword. The Weston Boy Scouts provided a guard of honour. The 91st Psalm was sung, as were his two favourite hymns, 'Glory to Thee, My God, This Night' and 'The King of Love My Shepherd Is'.

The coffin was then conveyed by road to Canterbury where it was to lie in state in the great Cathedral.[961] The nave was filled for the funeral service on the morning of Thursday 27 January 1927, with King George V represented by Sir Alexander Godley, GOC, Southern Command. The War Office, the School of Military Engineering, the Royal Engineers, the Commissioner of the Metropolitan Police, St John Ambulance, the Palestine Exploration Fund, the Boy Scouts Association, various Masonic lodges and many more organisations with which Sir Charles Warren had been associated through his long life were

---

[960] *Ibid.*, p 436.
[961] Williams, *The Life*, p 438.

all represented. 200 troops of the Royal East Kent Regiment – 'The Buffs' – attended the service, while 200 more lined the street outside. And, as they had the previous evening, the Scouts of Canterbury District provided a guard of honour. Once more the 91st Psalm was sung and after the first part of the service, conducted by the Dean of the Cathedral, the coffin was carried the length of the nave by four officers from the School of Military Engineering to the anthem of Parry's setting of Tennyson's 'Sunset and Evening Star'.[962]

Outside, the coffin was placed on a gun carriage, with the flags and his cocked hat, as before, though not this time, the medals. The funeral procession was preceded by its escort of 200 Buffs who pulled the gun carriage at a slow march through the streets of eastern Canterbury. A further 200 troops lined the streets to honour the old soldier and to hold back the huge crowds who had come to pay their respects. Sir Charles Warren had been well known in the city since his time living at Westbere and all the activities he was engaged in to raise the moral standing of East Kent's youth. His grandson Watkin Williams, who was among the chief mourners, observed a few old soldiers wearing their Africa medals doff their hats as the procession passed. As he recollected that funeral procession:

> … The January wind blew cold across the marshes, and the feathers of the cocked hat on the coffin fluttered in the breeze. The three mile march was long, but outside the city the procession had broken into quick time, and the measured tread of the soldiers' feet was like a solemn rhythm of applause as the warrior neared his final resting place.[963]

Crossing the railway line at Sturry, the procession made its way up Westbere Hill. As they reached the narrow turning on the right that led down into Westbere village, the pace returned to a slow march and the Band of the Royal Buffs played Beethoven's 'Funeral March'.

The grave had already been dug, next to that of Lady Fanny Warren, in the churchyard at the foot of the garden of their beloved home, 'The Oaks'. His son-in-law, Revd Watkin Williams (senior), conducted the remainder of the funeral service, and as the coffin was lowered into the grave the firing party fired the last salute and the Scouts' Bugle Band played the Last Post.[964]

* * *

[962] *The Times*, 28 January 1927.
[963] *Ibid.*, p 439.
[964] *Ibid.*, p 440.

The grave of Sir Charles (R) *and Lady Fanny Warren* (L) *in the graveyard at the bottom of the garden of 'The Oaks', facing All Saints church, Westbere.*
KEVIN SHILLINGTON

The Times obituary led the way in establishing Warren's archaeological work in Palestine as his most significant achievement,[965] and the Royal Geographical Society called his work in Jerusalem 'an important chapter in the history of archaeology'.[966]

His moniker 'Jerusalem Warren', however, must not be allowed to overshadow his other remarkable career achievements, in Gibraltar and South Africa, even Sinai, and the seldom appreciated Bechuanaland Expedition. It was only when he took on the Commissionership of the Metropolitan Police that his star began to falter. Even there, he achieved much in bringing discipline and reform to a rapidly growing police force, though he is only remembered for 'Bloody Sunday' and the failure to catch 'Jack the Ripper'.

[965] *The Times*, 24 January 1927, 'Charles Warren: Soldier and Archaeologist'.
[966] 'OBITUARY: General Sir Charles Warren, G.C.M.G, K.C.B., F.R.S.', *The Geographical Journal*, Volume 69, No 4 (April 1927), pp 382–83.

Whatever his faults, Charles Warren was an honourable man, who shouldered much – though never all – of the blame for the loss of Spion Kop and was deeply affected by the unnecessary loss of life under his command. After the South African War he found solace and enjoyment in the education of the young in body and spirit through the Boy Scout movement. It was, no doubt, the youthful stimulation this gave him, combined with his great sense of humour – always high in his list of social graces – and his deep religious faith that kept him so active until the final month of his life.

Charles Warren was a man of his time – an avowed imperialist of the Victorian era – a rightly controversial concept in the present century. As a soldier of the empire, he was always willing to 'do his duty' and volunteer to defend the interests of the empire as he saw it. But he was also conscious of the empire's deep responsibility to treat its subject peoples with honour and respect. From today's perspective, this can be seen as a contradiction in terms; but there were many conflicting forces in the world of the Victorian empire, not all of them bad, as clearly shown through the life of this extraordinary Royal Engineer.

Acknowledgements

During the long years of research for this book, I have been grateful to Neil Parsons and Fiona Barbour in particular who have always believed in the project from the beginning, and by feeding me with snippets of Warren-related information, references or potential contacts, have helped to keep the Warren project alive.

I am indebted to the Palestine Exploration Fund for awarding me a grant that enabled me to travel to Jerusalem to meet with current archaeologists and walk in the footsteps, so to speak, of Charles Warren, one of the Fund's original grantees. And I am grateful to Felicity Cobbing, Chief Executive and Curator of the Palestine Exploration Fund, for her constant support and guidance through the subject of Jerusalem archaeology, which was initially for me an unknown entity, and for her permission to use illustrations from the Fund's extensive archive.

Like all researchers of history and biography, I am indebted to the staff of archives and libraries whose untiring support and assistance make the business of research not only possible, but also so enjoyable. My thanks to all those staff of the various institutions listed in the bibliography.

My thanks in particular to Shirley James of the Africana Library in Kimberley, Danielle Sellers of the Royal Engineers Library and Archive, Mark Bunt of Hove Library, Sebastian Puncher of the RMA Sandhurst Archive, Weng Kee Leong of the National Archives of Singapore, Jean-Michel de Tarragon of the École Biblique Photo-library in Jerusalem, Wendy Cawthorne of the Geological Society Library and Archive, Christine Leighton Archivist of Cheltenham College, Jane Peeler of Bridgnorth Endowed School, Heather Needham of Hampshire Archives, Liz Trevethick of Falconer Museum, Forres, Scotland, Paul Evans of the Royal Artillery Library, Robert Hart and Sunet Swanepoel of the McGregor Museum, Kimberley, Robert in particular for permission to use images from the McGregor Museum's extensive photographic archive, Gideon Avni of the Israel Antiquities Authority, and the archaeologist Shlomit Weksler-Bdolah, who set all aside and spent half a day showing me round Warren's 'Underground Jerusalem'.

Charles Warren was one of the prominent Freemasons of his day, and wherever my research took me, I found the local Freemasons welcoming and happy to share with me whatever local evidence relative to Charles Warren that they may have had available. I am thinking in particular of Brother Keith Sheriff of the Gibraltar Masonic Institute, Brother Colin Macdonald and the Masons of the Masonic Hall in Singapore, and likewise, the Masons of the Masonic Temple in Kimberley. I am grateful to Brother Yasha Beresiner of the Quatuor Coronati Lodge and the staff of the library of Freemason's Hall in London, where I was able to spend many fruitful hours researching into all things Masonic in relation to Brother Charles Warren.

Others whom I met and/or corresponded with and who helped in various ways through the long years of research, for which I am very grateful, include: Val Daniel, Philip Howse, Philip Everitt, Ken Gillings, Gilbert Torlage, Chris and Grietjie van Schalkwyk, Vida Allen, Robert Morris, Shimon Gibson, Gabriel Barkay, Eilat Mazar, David Gurevich, David Jacobson, Leon Zeldis, Hisham Khatib, Amara Thornton and Ivona Lloyd-Jones. Furthermore, my thanks are due to cartographer Janet Alexander who made sense of my amateur sketches and drew the maps for the book.

I am particularly grateful to Jane Ferentzi-Sheppard who introduced me to the complexities of ancestor, or in my case, descendant research. It was through her help that I was able to track down Richard Inge Wigram whose late wife Angela had been a granddaughter of Sir Charles Warren's younger son, Dr Richard Warren, of Weston-super-Mare. My thanks to Richard Wigram who sent me a copy of the Warren family tree and put me in touch with a great-grandson of Sir Charles, the Revd Christopher Pelham Warren (since deceased) and his now widow, Isabella. Christopher and Isabella gave me free access to their collection of family photographs and the 'Warren Family Scrapbook' drawn up by Sir Charles's daughter Charlotte during his time as Metropolitan Police Commissioner. The latter consists of a large collection of published cartoons, most of them mocking Sir Charles, which would clearly have amused them both. Since then, I have fortunately been in touch with another great-grandson of Sir Charles and grandson of Captain Frank Warren, RA, John Pelham Warren and his wife Ruth, and through them in indirect contact with John's brother Charles and Virginia and Alicia Warren. They have all been very helpful in sharing with me Warren-related anecdotes and illustrations.

Finally, for being with me through this project from before the beginning, my wife Pip, thank you for everything.

Kevin Shillington

Bibliography

ARCHIVES AND LIBRARIES

Africana Library, Kimberley
British Library and British Newspaper Library
Gibraltar Archives
Gibraltar Public Library
Library and Museum of Freemasonry, London
London Metropolitan Archives, LMA/4517/B/01/01/018
Metropolitan Police Heritage Centre, File D769, Trafalgar Square 1887
National Archives of Singapore
National Army Museum
Palestine Exploration Fund Archive and Library
Royal Engineers Library and Archive
Senate House Library
United Kingdom National Archives (UKNA, formerly PRO) – Colonial
   Office (CO 273/61; CO 879/24); Home Office (HO 45/9635, 9678,
   9681, 9781, 9964; HO 144/198; HO 144/221; HO 247/12; HO
   347/12); War Office (WO 32/880; WO 33/45; WO 45/293; WO
   279/4); Metropolitan Police (MEPO 5/306, 7/49)
University of Witwatersrand Archives, Mackenzie Papers, A75
Wiltshire and Swindon Record Office (Lord Methuen Papers)

OFFICIAL PUBLICATIONS

List of the Royal Military College Sandhurst: Corrected to 1 May 1855 (Parker
   and Co, London, 1855)
Hart's Annual Army List, 1856–1904
Hymns Ancient and Modern (edition of 1889, reset, William Clowes and
   Sons, London, 1924)
Report from the Select Committee on Sandhurst Royal Military College,
   submitted to the House of Commons, 18 June 1855
Report on the Land Question in Griqualand West by Lt. Col. Warren (Colonial
   Office, London, 1880). Copy held Kimberley Africana Library

The War in Egypt, with Illustrations by Richard Simpkin and based on reports in The Times (Routledge, London, 1883)

HCPP (House of Commons Parliamentary Papers) (1878/79), Cd. 2220 & Cd. 2252, *Further Correspondence re. the Affairs of South Africa*

HCPP (1883), Cd. 3635, *Summary of Events in Bechuanaland by Colonel Warren*

HCPP (1902), Cd. 968, *South Africa. The Spion Kop Despatches*

HCPP (1903), Cd. 1791, *Minutes of Evidence taken before the Royal Commission on the War in South Africa,* Vol II

NEWSPAPERS AND PERIODICALS

Ars Quatuor Coronatorum (AQC)
The Canterbury Journal, Kentish Times and Farmers' Gazette
Daily Advertiser (Singapore)
The Daily Telegraph
Gibraltar Chronicle
Illustrated London News
Lloyd's Weekly Newspaper
The Pall Mall Gazette
PEF Quarterly Statement (PEFQS) – now *PEQ*
Punch
Royal Engineers Journal
Singapore Free Press and Mercantile Advertiser
Straits Advocate
Straits Independent
Straits Observer
Straits Times
Straits Times Weekly
The Cape Argus
The Cape Times
The Geographical Journal
The London Gazette
The Spectator
The Times
United Service Magazine

CONTEMPORARY BOOKS, PAMPHLETS AND ARTICLES

'An Experienced Officer', *Complete Guide to the Junior and Senior Departments of the Royal Military College, Sandhurst. With a reply to the aspersions on the cadets, contained in the 'Quarterly Review'* (March 1846, September 1848) (C. H. Law, London, 1849)

Aikin, Dr., *Select Works of the British Poets with biographical and critical prefaces* (first published, Longman Hurst, London, 1820)

Amery, Leopold S., *The Times History of the War 1899–1900* (London, 1902), Vol. III

Anderson, Robert, *The Lighter Side of My Official Life* (Hodder & Stoughton, London and New York, 1910)

Anon, *The War in Egypt, with Illustrations by Richard Simpkin and based on reports in The Times* (Routledge, London, 1883)

Atkins, John Black, *The Relief of Ladysmith* (Methuen Colonial Library, Hardpress Reprint, Miami, FL, 1900)

Baden-Powell, Robert, *Aids to Scouting for NCOs and Men* (Gale and Polden, Aldershot, 1899)

Baden-Powell, Robert, *Scouting for Boys* (1st edition, 1908, with numerous reprints)

Bartlett, W. H., *Gleanings on The Overland Route* (Nelson and Sons, London, 1868)

Baxendale, Cyril, *Personalities of Old Malaya* (Pinang Gazette Press, 1930)

Benson, A.C. and Viscount Esher (eds.), *The Letters of Queen Victoria, 1837–61*, Vol. II (John Murray, London, 1908)

Besant, Walter, *The Life and Achievements of Edward Henry Palmer* (John Murray, London, 1883)

Blunt, Wilfrid Scawen, *Secret History of the English Occupation of Egypt, Being a Personal Narrative of Events* (A. Knopf, New York, 1922)

Buckley, Arabella B. (Mrs Fisher), *Eyes and No Eyes, with numerous illustrations* (Cassell, London, n.d.)

Burleigh, Bennet, *The Natal Campaign* (Chapman & Hall, London, 1900)

Childers, Lt. Colonel Spencer, RE, *The Life and Correspondence of The Rt. Hon. Hugh C. E. Childers* (Murray, London, 1901)

Churchill, Winston, *London to Ladysmith via Pretoria* (Longman Green, London, 1900)

Clarke, A. R., *Account of the Observations and Calculations of the Principal Triangulation of Great Britain and Ireland* (Eyre & Spottiswoode, London, 1858)

Clarkson, C. T. and J. Hall Richardson, *Police!* (Leadenhall Press, London, 1889)

Conan Doyle, Sir Arthur, *The Great Boer War* (1st World Library, Fairfield, IA, 1902/2004)

'Defender', *Sir Charles Warren and Spion Kop. A Vindication* (Smith & Elder, London, 1902)

Du Cane, Hubert (trs., German Official Account), *The War in South Africa*, Vol II (John Murray, London, 1906)

Fergusson, James, *Notes on the Site of the Holy Sepulchre in Jerusalem* (John Murray, London, 1861)

Fergusson, James, *The Holy Sepulchre and the Temple at Jerusalem* (John Murray, London, 1865)

Fergusson, James, *The Temple of the Jews and the other buildings in the Haram area at Jerusalem* (John Murray, London, 1878)

Ford, Richard, *The Handbook for Travellers in SPAIN*, 8th edition, Part II (Murray, London, 1892)

Frome, E. C., *Outline of the method of conducting a Trigonometrical Survey, for the formation of Geographical and Topographical Maps and Plans* (Lockwood and Co, London, 1840)

Gould, Robert Freke, *A Concise History of Freemasonry* (Gale & Polden, London, 1904)

Graves, Charles L., *The Life and Letters of Sir George Grove, CB* (Macmillan, London, 1903)

Guggisberg, F. G., *The Shop: The Story of the Royal Military Academy* (Cassell, London, 1900)

Haynes, Alfred E., *Man-hunting in the Desert: Being a Narrative of the Palmer Search-Expedition* (Horace Cox, London, 1894)

Hull, Edward, *Mount Seir, Sinai And Western Palestine, Being A Narrative Of A Scientific Expedition* (Bentley and Son, London, 1885)

Johnston, J. F. W., *The Chemistry of Modern Life,* 2 Volumes (D. Appleton & Co, New York, 1853–54)

Lyell, Charles, *Principles of Geology: Being an attempt to explain the former changes of the earth's surface, by reference to causes now in operation*, 3 vols (John Murray, London, 1830–33)

Mackenzie, John, 'England and South Africa', *The Nineteenth Century*, XIII, (April 1883), pp 700–28

Mackenzie, John, *Austral Africa: Ruling it or Losing it*, Volume II (Sampson Low, London, 1887)

Maurice, Frederick, *History of the War in South Africa 1899–1902* (Hurst and Blackett, London, 1902), 'The Official History', Volume II

Morris, Robert, LL.D., *Freemasonry in the Holy Land: or, Handmarks of Hiram's Builders* (Masonic Publishing Company, New York, 1872)

Morris, William, *Alfred Linnell, killed in Trafalgar Square, November 20 1887* (R. Lambert, London, 1887)

Murchison, Charles (ed.), *Palæontological Memoirs and Notes of the late Hugh Falconer*, Vol II, 'On the Fossil Contents of the Genista Cave, Gibraltar' (Robert Hardwicke, London, 1868)

Noakes, George, *A Historical Account of the Services of the 34th and 55th Regiments* (Thurnam & Sons, Carlisle, 1875)

Palmer, Edward H., *The Desert of the Exodus: Journeys on Foot in the Wilderness of the Forty Years' Wanderings* (Harper, New York, 1872)

Petrie, William M. Flinders, *Inductive Metrology: Or the Recovery of Ancient Measures from the Monuments* (first edition 1877, with numerous paperback reprints)

Robinson, Edward, *Biblical Researches in Palestine* (2nd edition, John Murray, London, 1856)

Robinson, Edward, *Biblical Researches in Palestine and Adjacent Countries* (John Murray, London, 1841)

Smith, William (ed.), *A Dictionary of the Bible*, 3 vols (John Murray, London, 1863)

Tilney, W. A. (ed.), *Colonel Standfast: The Memoirs of W. A. Tilney, 1868–1947. A Soldier's Life in India, England, The Boer War and Ireland* (Edited by Nini Murray-Philipson, Michael Russell, Norwich, 1901)

Tristram, Henry Baker, *The Land of Israel: A Journal of Travels in Palestine* (SPKA, London, 1856)

Twain, Mark, *The Innocents Abroad or The new Pilgrim's Progress* (Signet Classics, New York, 1869/2007)

Ward, Colonel B. R., RE, *The School of Military Engineering, 1812–1909* (RE Institute, Chatham, 1909)

Warren, Charles, 'Notes on the Caves of Gibraltar', *Quarterly Journal of the Geological Society*, Vol 21, (1865), p 371

Warren, C. and Wilson, C., *The Recovery of Jerusalem: A Narrative of Exploration and Discovery in the City and the Holy Land* (New York, Appleton & Company, 1871)

Warren, Charles, *The Land of Promise: or Turkey's Guarantee* (George Bell & Sons, London, 1875)

Warren, C, *Underground Jerusalem: An Account of some of the Principal Difficulties Encountered in its Exploration and the Results Obtained* (London: Richard Bentley & Son, 1876)

Warren, Charles, *The Temple or The Tomb. Giving further evidence in favour of the authenticity of the present site of the Holy Sepulchre, and pointing out some of the principal misconceptions contained in Fergusson's 'Holy Sepulchre' and 'The Temple of the Jews.'* (Richard Bentley and Son, London, 1880)

Warren, Lt.-Colonel Charles, CMG, RE, 'Notes on Colonel Wilson's Paper on the Masonry of the Haram Wall', *PEF Quarterly*, April 1880, pp 161–166

Warren, Col. Charles, 'Limits of error in the latitudes and longitudes of places obtainable in a reconnaissance,' *RE Journal*, 2 August 1880, p 83

Warren, Charles, 'A Journey from Kimberley to Delagoa Bay', *Royal Engineers Journal*, 2 May 1881, p 82

Warren, Captain Charles, RE, *Plans, Elevations, Sections, &c. showing the results of the Excavation of Jerusalem, 1867–70, executed for the Committee of the Palestine Exploration Fund* (PEF, London, 1881), known as the 'Warren Atlas'

Warren, Col. Sir Charles, KCMG, RE and Capt. Claude Reignier Conder, RE, *The Survey of Western Palestine: Jerusalem* (PEF, London, 1884)

Warren, Sir Charles, *Report of the Proceedings of the Bechuanaland Field Force* (War Office, London, 1885)

Warren, Charles, 'The Police of the Metropolis', *Murray's Magazine*, Vol IV, No. XXIII, November 1888, pp 577–9

Warren, Sir Charles, 'Cecil Rhodes' Early Days in South Africa', *The Contemporary Review*, 1 January 1902, pp 649–52

Warren, Sir Charles, *On the Veldt in the Seventies* (Isbister & Company, London, 1902)

Warren, Sir Charles, *The Ancient Cubit and our Weights and Measures* (Palestine Exploration Fund, London, 1903)

Warren, Sir Charles, *The Early Weights and Measures of Mankind* (PEF, London, 1913)

Watson, C. M., *Fifty Years' Work in the Holy Land* (PEF, London, 1915)

Watson, C. M., *The Life of Major-General Sir Charles William Wilson, RE* (John Murray, London, 1909)

Watson, Colonel C. M., 'Military Ballooning in the British Army', *Royal Engineers Institute Occasional Papers*, Volume XXVIII, 1902

Williams, Revd. George, *The Holy City, or Historical and Topographical Notices of JERUSALEM* (John Murray, London, 1845, 2nd edition 1849)

Williams, Sir Ralph, KCMG, *How I Became a Governor* (John Murray, London, 1913)

Wilson, Colonel C. W., RE, CB, 'The Masonry of the Haram Wall', *PEF Quarterly*, January 1880, pp 9–60

Woodford, A., 'The Quatuor Coronati', *AQC*, Vol I (1887), pp 59–60

SELECT SECONDARY SOURCES

Agar-Hamilton, J. A. I., *The Road to the North* (Longman Green, London, 1937)

Armstrong, Karen, *Jerusalem: One City, Three Faiths* (Ballantine Books, New York, 1979)

Ascoli, David, *The Queen's Peace: The Origins and Development of the Metropolitan Police, 1829–1979* (Hamilton, London, 1979)

Begg, Paul and John Bennett, *The Complete and Essential Jack the Ripper* (Penguin Books, London, 2013)

Begg, Paul, *Jack the Ripper: The Definitive History* (Pearson Education, Harlow, 2004)

Benady, S. G. and T. J. Finlayson, 'Models of the Rock', *Gibraltar Heritage Journal*, Vol 2 (2nd edition, 1994)

Ben-Arieh, Y., *Jerusalem in the 19th Century: Emergence of the New City* (St. Martin's Press, New York, 1986)

Blackbeard, S. I., 'Blaming Brabant: Another look at the so-called military 'disobedience' of Captain, later Major-General Sir Edward Brabant, KCB, CMG', *Military History Journal*, Vol. 14, No. 6 (December 2009)

Bradford, Ernle, *Gibraltar: The History of a Fortress* (Grenada, London, 1971)

Brits, Elsabé, *Rebel English Woman: The Remarkable Life of Emily Hobhouse* (first published, South Africa, 2016; this edition, Robinson, London, 2019)

Broke-Smith, P. W. L., *The History of Early British Aeronautics* (Academic Reprint,1968)

Browne, Douglas G., *The Rise of Scotland Yard: A History of the Metropolitan Police* (Harrap, London, 1956)

Campbell, Christy, *Fenian Fire: The British Government Plot to Assassinate Queen Victoria* (HarperCollins, London, 2002)

Childs, Lewis, *LADYSMITH: Colenso/Spion Kop/Hlangwane/Tugela* (Leo Cooper, London, 1998)

Coetzer, Owen, *The Anglo-Boer War: The Road to Infamy, 1899–1900* (Arms & Armour, London, 1996)

Cole, J. R. I., *Colonialism and Revolution in the Middle East: Social and Cultural Origins of Egypt's 'Urabi Movement* (Princeton University Press, New Jersey, 1993)

Cope, R. L. (1986), 'Carnarvon's South African confederation policy', *History in Africa*, 13, (1986), pp 11–34

Creighton, Sean, 'From Revolution to New Unionism: The Impact of 'Bloody Sunday' on the Development of John Burns' Politics', in Keith Flett (ed.) *A History of Riots* (Cambridge Scholars Publishing, Newcastle, 2015), pp 11–37

Delius, Peter, *The Land Belongs To Us* (Ravan Press, Johannesburg, 1983)

Drinkwater, G. C. and T. R. B. Sanders (1929), *The University Boat Race: Official Centenary History* (Cassell, London)

Dyer, Colin, *The history of the first 100 years of the Quatuor Coronati Lodge No. 2076* (Garden City Press, 1986)

Eliav, Mordechai, *Britain and the Holy Land, 1838–1914: Selected Documents from the British Consulate in Jerusalem* (Magnes Press, Hebrew University, Jerusalem, 1997)

Etherington, N. A., 'Labour supply and the genesis of South African Confederation in the 1870s', *The Journal of African History*, 20, (1979), pp 235–53

Evans, Stewart P. and Donald Rumbelow, *Jack the Ripper: Scotland Yard Investigates* (Sutton Publishing, Stroud, 2006)

Fa, Darren & Clive Finlayson, *The Fortifications of Gibraltar 1068–1945* (Osprey, Oxford, 2006)

Fido, Martin and Keith Skinner, *The Official Encyclopedia of Scotland Yard* (Virgin Books, London, 1999)

Flett, Keith (ed.), *A History of Riots* (Cambridge Scholars Publishing, Newcastle, 2015)

Flint, John, *Cecil Rhodes* (Hutchinson, London, 1976)

Gibson, Shimon and David M. Jacobson, *Below the Temple Mount in Jerusalem: A sourcebook on the cisterns, subterranean chambers and conduits of the* Haram al-Sharif (Archaeopress, BAR International Series 637, Oxford, 1996)

Gibson, Shimon, Yoni Shapira and Rupert L. Chapman III, T*ourists,*

Travellers and Hotels in Nineteenth-Century Jerusalem (Maney Publishing for the Palestine Exploration Fund, Leeds, 2013)

Goodfellow, C. F., *Great Britain & South African Confederation, (1870–1881)* (Oxford University Press, Cape Town, 1966)

Hadland, Tony, *Glimpses of a Victorian Hero: Captain William Gill, Explorer and Spy* (Hadland Books, Farringdon, 2013)

Harland-Jacobs, Jessica L., *Builders of Empire: Freemasons and British Imperialism, 1717–1927* (University of North Carolina Press, Chapel Hill, 2013)

Haythornthwaite, Philip J., *The Colonial Wars Source Book* (Arms and Armour Press, London, 1995)

Hill, Tony, *Guns and Gunners at Shoeburyness: The Experimental Establishment and Garrison* (Baron Books, Buckingham, 1999)

Hills, G., *Rock of Contention: A History of Gibraltar* (Robert Hale, London, 1974)

Hogg, Ian V., *Coast Defences of England and Wales 1856–1956* (David & Charles, London, 1974)

Holmberg, Åke, *African Tribes and European Agencies: Colonialism and Humanitarianism in British South and East Africa 1870–1895* (Akademiförlaget, Stockholm, 1966)

Jacobson, David M., 'Charles Warren: An Appraisal of his Contribution to the Archaeology of Jerusalem', *Strata: Bulletin of the Anglo-Israel Archaeological Society*, Volume 27, (2009), pp 31–60

Jakubowski, Maxim and Nathan Braund (eds.), *The Mammoth Book of Jack the Ripper* (Robinson, London, 1999)

Jeal, Tim, *Baden-Powell: Founder of the Boy Scouts* (first published 1989, paperback edition Yale University Press, New Haven and London, 2001)

Jones, Maureen (ed.), *Bridgnorth Grammar & Endowed Schools: Five hundred years of change, 1503–2003* (BGS 500th Anniversary Group, Bridgnorth, 2003)

Kelly, Saul, *Captain Gill's Walking Stick: The True Story of the Sinai Murders* (I.B.Tauris, London, 2019)

Kendall, Peter, *The Royal Engineers at Chatham 1750–2012* (English Heritage, 2012)

Keneally, Thomas, *The Great Shame: A Story of the Irish in the Old World and the New* (Chatto & Windus, London, 1998)

Kenyon, Kathleen M., *Digging Up Jerusalem* (Ernest Benn, London & Tonbridge, 1974)

Knight, Stephen, *Jack the Ripper: The Final Solution* (HarperCollins, London, 1994)

Knight, Stephen, *Jack the Ripper: The Final Solution. New Revised Edition* (Chancellor Press, London, 2000)

Leeson, D. M. 'Playing at War: The British Military Manoeuvres of 1898', *War in History*, 15, (2008), pp 432–61

Lock, Ron, *Hill of Squandered Valour: The Battle for Spion Kop, 1900* (Casemate, Newbury & Philadelphia, 2011)

Macdonald, Colin, *WARREN! The Bond of Brotherhood* (C. N. Macdonald, Singapore, 2007)

Mace, Rodney, *Trafalgar Square: Emblem of Empire* (Lawrence & Wishart, London, 2005)

Makepeace, Walter, Dr Gilbert Brooke and Roland Braddell (eds.), *One Hundred Years of Singapore,* Volume I (Murray, London, 1921; HardPress reprint edition, Miami, FL)

Marks, Shula, 'Khoisan resistance to the Dutch in the seventeenth and 18th centuries', *The Journal of African History*, XIII, (1972), pp 55–80

Mason, J. F. A., 'Thomas Rowley: Energy and Pre-eminence 1821–1850', in Maureen Jones, ed, *Bridgnorth Grammar & Endowed Schools: Five hundred years of change, 1503–2003* (BGS 500th Anniversary Group, Bridgnorth, 2003)

Mazar, Eilat, *The Walls of the Temple Mount* (Shoham Academic Research and Publication, Jerusalem, 2011)

Montefiore, Simon Sebag, *Jerusalem: The Biography* (Phoenix, London, 2012)

Mostert, Noël, *Frontiers: The Epic of South Africa's Creation and the Tragedy of the Xhosa People* (Jonathan Cape, Cape Town, 1993)

Newsinger, John, *The Blood Never Dried: A People's History of the British Empire* (Bookmarks Publications, London, 2nd edn, 2013)

Norris, John, *Artillery: A History* (The History Press, Stroud, 2011)

Onn A., Weksler-Bdolah S. and Bar-Nathan R., 'Jerusalem, The Old City, Wilson's Arch and the Great Causeway', HAESI121, (2011). http://www.hadashotesi.org.il/Report_Detail_Eng.aspx?id=1738&mag_id=118

Pakenham, Thomas, *The Boer War* (Weidenfeld & Nicolson, 1979; Futura Edition, London, 1982)

Pakenham, Thomas, *The Scramble for Africa* (Weidenfeld & Nicolson, London, 1991)

Parsons, Neil, *King Khama: Emperor Joe and the Great White Queen*

(University of Chicago Press, Chicago and London, 1998)

Peers, Chris, *The African Wars: Warriors and Soldiers of the Colonial Campaigns* (Pen & Sword Military, Barnsley, 2010)

Petrie, William M. Flinders, *Seventy Years in Archaeology* (Holt & Co, London, 1932)

Petrow, Stefan, *Policing Morals: The Metropolitan Police and the Home Office 1870–1914* (Clarendon, Oxford, 1994)

Poulter, Bruce, *The Reverend George Philip Haydon and his Daffodils* (Village Preservation Society, Westbere, 2011)

Powell, Geoffrey, *Buller: A Scapegoat? A Life of General Sir Redvers Buller VC* (Leo Cooper, London, 1994)

Raw, Louise, *Striking a Light: The Bryant and May Matchwomen and their Place in History* (Bloomsbury, London, 2011)

Reitz, Deneys, *Commando. A Boer Journal of the Boer War* (1st edition 1929, this edition, CruGuru, 2009)

Roberts, Andrew, *Salisbury: Victorian Titan (*Weidenfeld & Nicolson, London, 1999)

Robinson, Bruce, *They All Love Jack: Busting the Ripper* (Fourth Estate, London, 2015)

Robinson, Jane, *Mary Seacole: The Charismatic Black Nurse Who Became a Heroine of the Crimea* (Robinson, London, 2006)

Rose, Edward and John Diemer, 'British Pioneers of the Geology of Gibraltar, Part 2: Cave Archaeology and Geological Survey of the Rock, 1863 to 1878', *Earth Sciences History*, Vol. 33, No. 1, (2014), pp. 26–58

Rotberg, Robert I., *The Founder: Cecil Rhodes and the Pursuit of Power* (Oxford University Press, Oxford and New York, 1988, 2nd edition 2002)

Royle, Trevor, *Crimea: The Great Crimean War 1854–1856* (Little, Brown & Co, London, 1999)

Rubenhold, Hallie, *The Five: The Untold Lives of the Women Killed by Jack the Ripper* (Doubleday, London, 2019)

Sheriff, Keith, *The Rough Ashlar: The History of English Freemasonry in Gibraltar 1727–2002* (private pub., n.d.)

Shillington, Kevin, *An African Adventure: A Brief Life of Cecil Rhodes* (Rhodes Memorial Museum and Commonwealth Centre, Bishop's Stortford, 1992)

Shillington, Kevin, *Luka Jantjie: Resistance Hero of the South African Frontier* (Aldridge Press, London, 2011)

Shillington, Kevin, *The Colonisation of the Southern Tswana 1870–1900* (Ravan Press, Johannesburg, 1985)

Silberman, Neil A., *Digging for God & Country: Exploration, Archeology, and the Secret Struggle for the Holy Land, 1799–1917* (Alfred Knopf, New York, 1982)

Sunderland, David, *These Chivalrous Brothers: The Mysterious Disappearance of the 1882 Palmer Sinai Expedition* (Chronos Books, Winchester, 2016)

Torlage, Gilbert, *The Battle of Spioenkop, 23–24 January 1900* (30° South Publishers, Pinetown, 2014)

Trow, M. J., *Jack the Ripper: Quest for a Killer* (Wharncliffe True Crime, Barnsley, 2009)

Weksler-Bdolah, S., 'The Foundation of Aelia Capitolina in Light of New Excavations along the Eastern Cardo', *Israel Exploration Journal*, Volume 64, No. 1, (2014), 38–62

Williams, Basil, *Cecil Rhodes* (Holt & Co, New York, 1921)

Williams, Watkin W., T*he Life of General Sir Charles Warren* (Blackwell, Oxford, 1941)

WEBSITES CONSULTED

(with dates accessed in footnotes)

http://eresources.nlb.gov.sg/infopedia/articles/SIP_69_2005-01-22.html

http://samilitaryhistory.org/vol056pg.html

http://www.army.mod.uk/documents/general/history_of_rmas.pdf

http://www.casebook.org/police_officials/po-monro.html

http://www.cheltenhamcollege.org/history-and-archives

http://www.ghgraham.org/charleswarren1840.html

http://www.gilbertandsullivanarchive.org/pirates/web-op

http://www.hmswarrior.org/history

http://www.jack-the-ripper.org/swanson.htm

http://www.nam.ac.uk/research/famous-units/30th-cambridgeshire-regiment-foot

http://www.newworldencyclopedia.org/entry/Mesha_Stele

http://www.oum.ox.ac.uk/learning/pdfs/debate.pdf

http://www.pef.org.uk/profiles/sir-william-flinders-petrie-1853-1942

http://www.phrases.org.uk/meanings/73300.html

http://www.royalengineers.ca/RMA.html

https://en.wikipedia.org/wiki/Istana_(Singapore)

https://en.wikipedia.org/wiki/Johannes_Brand

Index

Italicised page numbers indicate references within captions.